THE CHANGING ENGLISH

Bringing together experts from historical linguistics and psychology, this volume addresses core factors and processes in language change, exploring the potential (and limitations) of such an interdisciplinary approach. Easily accessible chapters by psycholinguists present cutting-edge research on frequency, salience, chunking, priming, analogy, ambiguity and acquisition, and develop models of how these may be involved in language change. Each chapter is complemented with one or more case studies in the history of English in which the psycholinguistic factor in question may be argued to have played a decisive role. Thus, for the first time, a single volume provides a platform for an integrated exchange between psycholinguistics and historical linguistics on the question of how language changes over time.

MARIANNE HUNDT is Professor of English Linguistics at the University of Zürich. Her research interests include grammatical variation and change in World Englishes. She is the author of *English Mediopassive Constructions* (2007), co-author of *Change in Contemporary English: A Grammatical Study* (2009) and co-editor of *English World-Wide*.

SANDRA MOLLIN is Senior Lecturer in English Linguistics at the University of Heidelberg. Her research focuses on phraseology, varieties of English, and the combination of corpus linguistic and psycholinguistic methodology. She is the author of *The (Ir)Reversibility of English Binomials* (2014) and *Euro-English – Assessing Variety Status* (2006).

SIMONE E. PFENNINGER is Assistant Professor at the University of Salzburg. Her principal research areas are multilingualism, psycholinguistics and individual differences in SLA, especially in regard to quantitative approaches and statistical methods and techniques for language application in education. She is the co-editor of the Second Language Acquisition book series for Multilingual Matters.

STUDIES IN ENGLISH LANGUAGE

General editor
Merja Kytö (Uppsala University)

Editorial Board
Bas Aarts (University College London),
John Algeo (University of Georgia),
Susan Fitzmaurice (University of Sheffield),
Christian Mair (University of Freiburg),
Charles F. Meyer (University of Massachusetts)

The aim of this series is to provide a framework for original studies of English, both present-day and past. All books are based securely on empirical research, and represent theoretical and descriptive contributions to our knowledge of national and international varieties of English, both written and spoken. The series covers a broad range of topics and approaches, including syntax, phonology, grammar, vocabulary, discourse, pragmatics and sociolinguistics, and is aimed at an international readership.

Already published in this series:

THE CHANGING ENGLISH LANGUAGE

Psycholinguistic Perspectives

EDITED BY

MARIANNE HUNDT

University of Zürich

SANDRA MOLLIN

University of Heidelberg

SIMONE E. PFENNINGER

University of Salzburg

CAMBRIDGE
UNIVERSITY PRESS

CAMBRIDGE
UNIVERSITY PRESS

University Printing House, Cambridge CB2 8BS, United Kingdom

One Liberty Plaza, 20th Floor, New York, NY 10006, USA

477 Williamstown Road, Port Melbourne, VIC 3207, Australia

314-321, 3rd Floor, Plot 3, Splendor Forum, Jasola District Centre, New Delhi - 110025, India

79 Anson Road, #06-04/06, Singapore 079906

Cambridge University Press is part of the University of Cambridge.

It furthers the University's mission by disseminating knowledge in the pursuit of
education, learning and research at the highest international levels of excellence.

www.cambridge.org
Information on this title: www.cambridge.org/9781107451728
DOI: 10.1017/9781316091746

First published 2017
First paperback edition 2020

A catalogue record for this publication is available from the British Library

ISBN 978-1-107-08686-9 Hardback
ISBN 978-1-107-45172-8 Paperback

Contents

vii

Figures

Tables

Contributors

HARALD BAAYEN, Department of Linguistics, University of Tübingen and Department of Linguistics, University of Alberta

HEIKE BEHRENS, German Department and English Department, University of Basel

JOAN L. BYBEE, Department of Linguistics, University of New Mexico

DAVID DENISON, Department of Linguistics and English Language, University of Manchester

HENDRIK DE SMET, Faculty of Arts, University of Leuven

NICK C. ELLIS, Department of Psychology, University of Michigan

CLAUDIA FELSER, Potsdam Research Institute for Multilingualism, University of Potsdam

OLGA FISCHER, Department of Linguistics, University of Amsterdam

SUSANNE GAHL, Department of Linguistics, University of California Berkeley

SIMON GARROD, Institute of Neuroscience and Psychology, University of Glasgow

MARTIN HILPERT, Department of English Language and Literature, University of Neuchâtel

MARIANNE HUNDT, Department of English, University of Zürich

ELENA V. M. LIEVEN, ESRC International Centre for Language and Communicative Development at the Universities of Manchester, Liverpool and Lancaster

MARÍA JOSÉ LÓPEZ-COUSO, Department of English and German, University of Santiago de Compostela

CHRISTIAN MAIR, English Department, University of Freiburg

CAROL LYNN MODER, English Department, Oklahoma State University

SANDRA MOLLIN, English Department, University of Heidelberg

SIMONE E. PFENNINGER, Department of English and American Studies, University of Salzburg

MARTIN J. PICKERING, Psychology Department, University of Edinburgh

MICHAEL RAMSCAR, Department of Linguistics, University of Tübingen

FABIAN TOMASCHEK, Department of Linguistics, University of Tübingen

ELIZABETH C. TRAUGOTT, Department of English and Department of Linguistics, Stanford University

Acknowledgments

Many people have been involved in the preparation of this volume. First of all, we would like to thank the contributors for the work they produced. We would also like to express our heartfelt thanks to all the colleagues who kindly made the time to review the chapters in this volume and provide valuable feedback (in alphabetical order): Inbal Arnon, Laurie Bauer, Anne Curzan, Ewa Dąbrowska, Cheryl Frenck-Mestre, Dedre Gentner, Stefan Thomas Gries, Anette Rosenbach, David Singleton (three chapters), Benedikt Szmrecsanyi, Freek Van de Velde and Ans van Kemenade.

Most of the chapters in this volume were presented and discussed at an invitational workshop held during the third ISLE conference in Zürich in August 2014. We would like to thank the University of Zürich, the Zürcher Universitätsverein (ZUNIV) and the Zürich Centre for Linguistics (ZüKL) for the generous funding that made the organisation of the workshop possible. As always, it has been a joy to work with Helen Barton (Cambridge University Press) and the series editor, Merja Kytö. We are grateful for their enthusiastic support, encouragement and flexibility as well as the valuable input they provided at various stages of the project. Georgina Wood and Sophie Willimann, the editorial assistants at the Zürich English department, did a great job in helping to prepare the manuscript and the index. Thanks also go to Jim Coats, Julie Hrischeva and Karthik Orukaimani for safely seeing the book through the production process.

Data Sources

Dictionaries

DARE *Dictionary of American Regional English*. 1985–2012. Edited by Frederic Gomes Cassidy and Joan Houston Hall. 5 vols. Cambridge, MA: Belknap Press.

MED *Middle English Dictionary*. http://quod.lib.umich.edu/m/med/

OED *The Oxford English Dictionary*. 1989. Edited by John A. Simpson and Edmund S. C. Weiner. Oxford: Clarendon Press.

OED Online *The Oxford English Dictionary Online*. www.oed.com

WNT *Woordenboek der Nederlandsche Taal*. http://gtb.inl.nl/

Corpora and Databases

BNC *British National Corpus*. 1994. BNC Consortium. www.natcorp .ox.ac.uk

CED *A Corpus of English Dialogues 1560–1760*. 2006. Compiled by Merja Kytö and Jonathan Culpeper. www.engelska.uu.se/Research/ English_Language/Research_Areas/Electronic_Resource_Projects/ A_Corpus_of_English_Dialogues/

CELEX *The CELEX Lexical Database Release 2*. 1995. Created by R. Harald Baayen, Richard Piepenbrock and Hedderik van Rijn. Nijmegen: Centre for Lexical Information, Max Planck Institute for Psycholinguistics.

CHK *Corpus Historische Kranten*. http://kbkranten.politicalmashup.nl

CL (CLMETEV) *Corpus of Late Modern English Texts, Extended Version (CLMETEV)*. 2006. Compiled by Hendrik De Smet. Department of Linguistics, University of Leuven. https://perswww.kuleuven.be/ ~u0044428/

CLMET 3.0 *Corpus of Late Modern English Texts, version 3.0.* Compiled by Hendrik De Smet, Hans-Jürgen Diller and Jukka Tyrkkö. https:// perswww.kuleuven.be/~u0044428/clmet3_0.htm

COCA *Corpus of Contemporary American English: 450 Million Words, 1990–Present.* 2008. Created by Mark Davies. http://corpus.byu.edu/ coca/

COHA *Corpus of Historical American English: 400 Million Words, 1810–2009.* 2010. Created by Mark Davies. http://corpus.byu.edu/coha/

DOEC *Dictionary of Old English Corpus.* 2009. Compiled by Antonette diPaolo Healey, Joan Holland, Ian McDougall and David McDougall, with Xin Xiang. http://doe.utoronto.ca/pages/index .html

ECCO *Eighteenth-Century Collections Online.* http://quod.lib.umich .edu/e/ecco/

EEBO *Early English Books Online.* http://eebo.chadwyck.com/home, http://quod.lib.umich.edu/e/eebogroup/

EEBOCorp1.0 *Early English Books Online Corpus (Version 1.0).*

HC *The Helsinki Corpus of English Texts.* 1991. Department of Modern Languages, University of Helsinki. Compiled by Matti Rissanen, Merja Kytö, Leena Kahlas-Tarkka, Matti Kilpiö, Saara Nevanlinna, Irma Taavitsainen, Terttu Nevalainen and Helena Raumolin-Brunberg.

IMEPC *Innsbruck Middle English Prose Corpus.* 1992–1997. Manfred Markus. www.uibk.ac.at/anglistik/projects/icamet/

IMEPCS *Innsbruck Middle English Prose Corpus Sampler.* www.uibk.ac .at/anglistik/projects/icamet/

L18 C PROSE *A Corpus of Late 18c Prose.* 2003. Created by David Denison. http://personalpages.manchester.ac.uk/staff/david.deni son/late18c

LCSAE *Longman Corpus of Spoken American English.* Edinburgh Gate, Harlow, Essex: Addison Wesley Longman. www.pearsonlongman .com/dictionaries/corpus/spoken-american.html

LION *Literature Online.* http://literature.proquest.com/

ME Corpus (CMEPV) *Corpus of Middle English Prose and Verse (CMEPV).* 2006. The Humanities Text Initiative, University of Michigan. http://quod.lib.umich.edu/c/cme/

OBC *Old Bailey Corpus.* 2012. Compiled by Magnus Huber, Magnus Nissel, Patrick Maiwald and Bianca Widlitzki. www1.uni-giessen.de/ oldbaileycorpus/

PPCMBE *Penn Parsed Corpus of Modern British English.* 2010. Compiled by Anthony Kroch, Beatrice Santorini and Ariel Diertani. www.ling.upenn.edu/hist-corpora/PPCMBE2-RELEASE -1/index.html [second release 2016]

TIME *TIME Magazine Corpus: 100 Million Words, 1920s–2000s.* 2007. Created by Mark Davies. http://corpus.byu.edu/time/

TNC *Twente Nieuws Corpus.* 2007. http://hmi.ewi.utwente.nl/TwNC

WebCorp *WebCorp Live.* 1999–2015. Developed and maintained by the Research and Development Unit for English Studies, School of English, Birmingham City University. www.webcorp.org.uk/live/

WebCorp LSE *WebCorp Linguist's Search Engine.* 1999–2013. Developed and maintained by the Research and Development Unit for English Studies, School of English, Birmingham City University. http://wse1.webcorp.org.uk

CHAPTER I

Introduction: Language History Meets Psychology

Marianne Hundt, Sandra Mollin and Simone E. Pfenninger

1.1 Introduction

The present volume, *The Changing English Language: Psycholinguistic Perspectives*, focuses on language change, using the history of the English language to illustrate mechanisms of change. However, it is more than just another volume on language change: it brings together two subdisciplines – psycholinguistics and historical linguistics – in discussing those mechanisms of grammatical and lexical change that are cognitive in nature. In each section of the book, a psycholinguistic and a historical linguistic chapter – each on the same cognitive process or factor – are juxtaposed, thereby fostering interaction between two disciplines that have had surprisingly little connection so far.

We were prompted to provide this platform for a dialogue across the two subdisciplines because of what we perceived to be a serious gap in the understanding of processes of linguistic change. Language change as it proceeds from generation to generation through daily interaction of speakers may be shaped by language-internal, social and psycholinguistic factors. While the first two factors have been thoroughly researched in historical linguistics and sociolinguistics, the third has not been as systematically addressed as one might have expected. Even though recourse is made quite frequently to psycholinguistic explanations of change in historical linguistics, systematic, psychologically based discussions are still lacking. More important still, historical linguistics has not previously benefitted from direct expert input from scholars familiar with fundamental cognitive processes that are likely, or commonly taken, to shape pathways of change.

1.2 Previous Work

Obviously, historical studies in the past have considered individual psycholinguistic factors of language change – typically with a focus on the role of language acquisition; examples would be Baron (1977), Lightfoot (1991, 1999, 2010), Johnson (2001), Diessel (2012) or Stanford (2014). Early forerunners of this perspective include Schleicher (1861),[1] Paul (1880), Saussure (1916, 1983)[2] and Meillet (1951). Hermann Paul, in his *Principien* (1880: 32), also points out that the process of language acquisition leads to a slightly different version of the 'same' language in every individual, implying that this might be one reason for change. When we turn to the other psycholinguistic processes treated in this volume, we realise that their history of being considered as factors in language change is often much shorter and that some have not previously received the attention that they deserve. For example, the idea that priming may influence language change was introduced by Jäger and Rosenbach as recently as 2008 (discussed by several responses in *Theoretical Linguistics* 34:2). *Salience* is not a widely used or well-defined concept in historical or synchronic linguistics, either. With regard to dialect convergence and divergence, Hinskens, Auer and Kerswill (2005) argue that salience is determined by an extremely complex set of linguistic and non-linguistic factors. They express concern that it may be impossible to determine whether a given level of salience, once established, leads to the adoption or non-adoption of a feature (see also Kerswill and Williams 2002). Discussing physiological, cognitive and sociolinguistic factors that contribute to salience, Auer (2014) cautions that the psychological notion of salience should be kept strictly apart from its causes and effects (on language change or language accommodation). He concludes that salience based on social stereotyping is the best predictor of change and accommodation, but needs to be supported by the right evaluation of the salient feature in order to have an effect.

Thus, while the individual concepts discussed in this volume have been investigated individually as factors in language change for longer or shorter times in the past (for extensive discussions, see the individual historical linguistic chapters in the volume), what is lacking thus far is a more systematic discussion of cognitive factors that drive language change. Even recent handbooks of (English) historical linguistics do not include systematic discussions of psycholinguistic factors, with the exception of the sketch by Aitchison in Joseph and Janda (eds., 2003) and a chapter by Bybee and Beckner that appeared as recently as 2014. Discussions of language change by psycholinguists are also quite rare (but see Baayen 1993; Beckner and Bybee 2009; Clark 1982; Ellis 2002). Smith (2012), who discusses paradigm shifts in the history of English historical linguistics and mentions new trends, only draws attention to the importance of sociolinguistic and socio-pragmatic approaches to variation and change in recent years. Systematic cross-fertilisation with psycholinguistic research is not mentioned as a future avenue of research. Processing strategies that emerged from experimental psycholinguistic studies into relative clauses are mapped back onto historical (Middle and Old English) data in a recent study by Bergs and Pentrel (2015) in a section that is – rather tellingly – labeled 'Emerging Paradigms: New Methods, New Evidence'.

We argue that the time is ripe for a paradigm shift in (English) historical linguistics, and aim to fill the gap with this volume, providing a systematic treatment of core cognitive factors in language change from two perspectives – the historical linguistic as well as the psycholinguistic. We pair the historical perspective with psycholinguistics proper to discuss psycholinguistic factors, rather than pairing it with a more general cognitive linguistic perspective which may or may not be experimental or even empirical, since psycholinguistic research is better suited to inform scholars of language change on how the processes considered actually proceed cognitively. In this respect, the present volume differs markedly from previous publications that held a more general cognitive perspective inspired by cognitive grammar, e.g. the volume on *Historical Cognitive Linguistics*, edited by Winters et al. (2010).

1.3   Aim and Scope of the Volume

In light of the surprisingly weak connection between psycholinguistic research and studies on language change, this volume addresses core issues of language change in English from historical-linguistic and psycholinguistic perspectives, bringing experts from the two disciplines together in order to explore the potential (and limitations) of an interdisciplinary approach to language change. Historical linguistics profits from this exchange in that concepts such as 'salience', which at times have been used uncritically and often without clear definition in previous research, gain a sound psychological basis. Psycholinguistics, in turn, is encouraged not only to take synchronic structures into account, but to develop models which help explain diachronic change as well.

In order to foster interaction between the authors contributing to this volume, we held a workshop at the third triennial conference of the International Society for the Linguistics of English (ISLE) in Zürich in August 2014. Almost all contributions to this volume were first presented there, with subsequent cooperation between the psycho- and historical linguist(s) working in tandem on the set of core psychological factors relevant to language change. Accordingly, the seven parts of this volume are each made up of two paired chapters. In the first chapter of each part, a psycholinguist provides the state of the art in psycholinguistic research on a core concept and develops a model of how it may be involved in language change. This serves as a backdrop for the subsequent chapter, in which an English historical linguist presents case studies in the history of the English language in which the psycholinguistic concept in question may be argued to have played a decisive role. As a result, the contributions focus on clearly defined cognitive mechanisms of language change and showcase their role in language change.

More generally, the contributions also point out the potential – as well as the limitations – of combining such disparate disciplines. In particular, questions of dissimilar research foci, evidence and methodologies arise at several points. All the same, the following dictum clearly does not apply to the present volume:

> Linguists and psychologists talk about different things . . . Grammarians are more interested in what could be said than in what people actually say, which irritates psychologists, and psychologists insist on supplementing intuition with objective evidence, which irritates linguists. (Miller 1990: 321)

With the use of authentic data, as routinely practiced by historical linguists and exemplarily so by those represented in this volume, working within a usage-based account toward language and linguistic change, both disciplines are soundly empirical, drawing not on intuition but on systematically collected data.

Nevertheless, there appear to remain important differences in scope between the disciplines, foremost among these being the fundamental difference that psycholinguistics focuses on the cognitive processes at the individual level, while historical linguistics considers the language as used by a larger community of speakers. However, this volume argues that this difference may be overcome – or that it is, in fact, only a fundamental difference on a superficial level. After all, the factors and processes investigated here are cognitive in nature, i.e. they arise in the individual and individual acts of *parole*, but since they may result in innovations which a speech community may adopt, they hold the potential to impact the language system as a whole over time. Furthermore, it is not true that psycholinguists are not interested in the language system – psychologists study individuals, but with the aim of modeling more general cognitive processes beyond the individual. Likewise, historical linguists cannot be reduced to an interest in the language system – after all, they study individual acts of *parole* produced by individual speakers at particular points in time in order to get at the underlying abstract system. The contributions in the volume illustrate that the individual–collective divide can be bridged, and indeed needs to be bridged in order for us to fully understand the mechanisms of language change.

The difference between psycholinguistics and historical linguistics, then, seems mainly to be methodological. The historical dimension does not allow for experimentation on subjects to probe into online language processing, but necessarily relies on authentic language output as data – which is not generally regarded a primary data source by psycholinguists, who prefer closely controlled experimentation. However, if we take for granted that cognitive processes were the same for speakers in past periods as for those today (see Winters 2010) and accept that authentic output is the only feasible data source to model change over time, then we can combine historical linguistic data and psycholinguistic research findings fruitfully.

1.4 Cognitive Factors and Processes in Psycholinguistics and Language Change: An Overview

The psycholinguistic concepts/processes covered in the seven parts of this volume, each presented by two chapters, are *frequency, salience, chunking, priming, analogy, ambiguity* (and *vagueness*) and *language acquisition*. Socio-psycholinguistic concepts (such as variation and transmission) are not included, since these are covered in recent sociolinguistic research (Preston 2004, Gries 2013, Loudermilk 2013) or handbooks on language history (e.g. Nevala 2016). Rather, we focus here on core cognitive processes and phenomena, some of which have a long tradition of discussion as mechanisms of language change (especially acquisition), while others (such as chunking) are only now emerging in the discussion of historical linguistic work. The psycholinguists contributing their point of view to the discussion typically do so from the point of view of their specialisation in the field (e.g. second language learning research or the study of first language acquisition).

Frequency

The book opens with two chapters that tackle the complex – occasionally called 'vexed' (Gass and Mackey, 2002) – topic of frequency effects in language learning, language use, language processing and language change.

The main focus of Chapter 2 by Harald Baayen and his co-authors is on the micro-level of changes over the lifetime of speakers and their potential consequences for macro-changes over generations of speakers. Although a broad range of studies on the social and geographical distribution of linguistic variants have documented widespread variation within nations and speech communities, little systematic attention has thus far been directed to the changes in an individual speaker's grammar and increase in collocational knowledge across time as the inevitable consequence of an on-going process of learning.

Baayen et al.'s psycholinguistic perspective on frequency effects deals with discrimination learning (see Rescorla and Wagner 1972; Rescorla 1988; Ramscar et al. 2010; Baayen et al. 2011) on the one hand and information theory (see Shannon 1949) on the other. One of the main lessons for historical linguists and corpus linguists to be learned in this chapter is that simple frequency counts are not precise enough, as they do not take into account the effects of co-learning and the costs that accrue with the accumulation of knowledge. In order to be able to fully understand the dynamics of lifelong learning, Baayen et al. suggest the use of measures that reflect the consequences of the accumulation of knowledge under the constraints of discrimination learning. In other words, discrimination learning might provide us with quantitative measures that are more informative than straightforward counts of frequency of occurrence.

Understanding language change over an individual's lifetime also requires that we take changes in culture and society into account. The complexity of our societies has grown exponentially in modern times, with a concomitant exponential growth in the numbers of names for novel technical and cultural objects and processes (see Meibauer et al. 2004; Scherer 2005). As a consequence, we know more words than ever before. The downside of the story is that this accumulation of knowledge comes at a cost: Baayen et al. discuss how the changing onomasiological demands of increasingly complex modern societies give rise to continuously increasing name- and word-finding difficulties – and consequently an increase in the use of pronouns. Not only does the use of pronouns increase over a person's lifespan – which is in line with the 'Ecclesiastes Principle' that they introduce – but the use of pronouns also increases in the whole speech community.

The main goal of Martin Hilpert's companion chapter is to explore how what we know about frequency effects from psycholinguistic work can be fruitfully transferred to the study of historical language change on the basis of diachronic corpora. In particular, he focuses on different frequency measurements in a historical corpus and what they may reveal about the knowledge of language that speakers in earlier historical periods would have had. In an overview of different aspects of frequency and the ways these can be measured in corpora, he discusses what is known about their cognitive correlates, what corpus linguistic methods are used to measure them, and finally, how such measurements can be usefully applied to the cognitive study of language change. In particular, he reviews findings from current diachronic corpus studies that analyse not only text frequencies but, crucially, also the frequencies of contextualised constructional variants. In doing so, Hilpert accounts for the fact that individual speakers typically diverge with respect to their experience with linguistic variants, just as Baayen et al. point out. Hilpert suggests that if diachronic corpus studies aim to model changes in speakers' linguistic knowledge, as much as possible of this variation has to be taken into account. Specifically, using the example of the alternation between *mine* / *thine* and their successors *my* / *thy*, he argues that frequencies of contextualised constructional variants can be used to make inferences about the linguistic knowledge of speakers who lived in the past.

To summarise the main points of Chapters 2 and 3, the common theme that unites current psycholinguistic research on frequency and historical, corpus linguistic approaches to frequency is the assumption that language use shapes the individual speaker's knowledge of language and is at the same time an expression of that knowledge. To the extent that diachronic corpus linguists aim at investigating cognitive aspects of use in earlier generations of speakers, they have to build on psycholinguists' assessments of how frequency of use and the mental representation of linguistic units are related. What Baayen et al. have to say about the role of frequency for the individual speaker in synchrony thus has direct repercussions for the study of diachronic corpora, that is, aggregate data of many speakers over time.

Salience

The goal of Part II is to put forward particular ways of operationalizing salience in psycholinguistics and historical linguistics. Salience is a psycho-perceptual effect which correlates with a number of psycho-perceptual properties. The central roles of salience and attention in learning have been emphasised repeatedly, and psycholinguists have long studied how humans and animals learn to allocate attention across potentially informative cues. Recent years have also seen an upsurge of interest in the notion of salience in historical linguistics. What is the role of perceptual salience in different types of language change? How does the salience of linguistic items influence their trajectory in situations of language contact?

The three different aspects of salience considered by Nick C. Ellis in the psycholinguistic discussion of the phenomenon – psychophysical salience, salience of associations and predictability/surprisal – are essential factors in any instance of associative learning. Ellis first reviews the psychology of these factors as a foundation for consideration of their role in language change. He then shows how the low physical salience of grammatical functors, its effects amplified in second language learners with no learned expectations of how the L2 operates, affects language learning and language change. The chapter outlines an emergentist perspective on the limited end-state typical of adult second language learners, involving dynamic cycles of language use, language change, language perception and language learning in the ways members of language communities interact. Specifically, it focuses upon the psycholinguistic processes by which frequent usage affects the salience of linguistic forms:

- *Usage leads to change* High-frequency use of grammatical functors causes their phonological erosion and homonymy.
- *Change affects perception* Phonologically reduced cues are hard to perceive.
- *Perception affects learning* Low-salience cues are difficult to learn, as are homonymous/polysemous constructions because of the low contingency of their form-function association.
- *Learning affects usage* Where language is predominantly learned naturalistically by adults without any form-focus, a typical result is a 'Basic Variety' of interlanguage, low in grammatical complexity but communicatively effective.
- *Usage leads to change* Because of this, maximum-contact languages simplify and lose grammatical intricacies.

In the companion Chapter 5, Elizabeth C. Traugott considers these various aspects of salience in play in more typical situations of primarily native-speaker language use. Drawing on Degand and Simon (2005) and Wagner et al. (2010), among others, Traugott takes salience to be a factor separate from prominence, with which it is often identified. This is in contrast to Ellis's association of novelty with surprise and high salience. However, not all highly salient expressions are prominent, e.g. topics that are highly salient in the discourse are often marked by pronouns or zero (Ariel 1990). Likewise, not all prominent expressions are salient, e.g. contrastive stress is prominent and may be used to introduce new, non-salient referents.

Therefore, low salience may be an important enabling factor in morpho-syntactic change.

Traugott also regards salience as a multidimensional property of language use that may differ in strength for speaker and hearer. While salience is relevant to situations and all domains of language use, her focus is on ways to refine hitherto rather vague notions of pragmatic salience in a usage-based cognitive view of language change (e.g. the association of generalised invited inferencing with salience proposed in Traugott 2012: 554).

In historical work, salience can only be inferred, given that we cannot run experiments on centuries-old language users or find empirical evidence for the activation of supposedly salient factors. Traugott's main question is: To what extent can various aspects of pragmatic salience be considered to be enabling factors in morphosyntactic change? She moves on to discuss ramifications of this perspective on change for Boye and Harder's (2012) hypothesis that lexical expressions have a potential for being discourse prominent, and that they grammaticalise through loss of this potential. This connects back to Ellis (2013: 371), who argues that grammatical elements are low in salience and therefore hard to learn.

Chunking

The two chapters on chunking in Part III highlight important differences between the search for explanation by psychologists versus that by historical linguists. Nick C. Ellis starts out in Chapter 6 by describing the learning theory and psycholinguistic evidence of chunking. To this end, he focuses on the three major experiential factors that affect cognition and determine chunking: frequency, recency and context. Ellis explains how learning symbolic chunks and their arrangement in language involves learning associations across and within modalities, and how frequency of experience affects both. Also, the more any word or formula is repeated in phonological working memory, the more its regularities and chunks are abstracted, and the more accurately and readily these can be called to working memory, either for accurate pronunciation as articulatory output or as labels for association with other representations (see also Chapter 3). It is from these potential associations with other representations that further interesting properties of language emerge, such as grammaticalisation as the process of automatisation of frequently occurring sequences of linguistic elements, or the productivity of phonological, morphological and syntactic patterns as a function of type rather than token frequency. All of these are described in the corresponding historical linguistic Chapter 7 by Bybee and Moder.

In his discussion of how language processing also reflects recency effects, Ellis agrees with Hilpert (Chapter 3) and Pickering and Garrod (Chapter 8) that priming is an essential part of conversation partners aligning and co-constructing meanings: we pick up the way our conversation partners say things and we associate these symbols, these speakers and their contexts. Priming sums to life-span practice effects and the frequency effects discussed above. Finally, implicit learning underlies contextual learning effects whereby a stimulus and its interpretation becomes associated with a context, and we become more likely to perceive it in that context. The context can involve particular speakers, cultures, dialects, or places, and all can have influence in relation to language usage – and, because of usage-based learning, language understanding.

Through a detailed analysis of the pathway of development of the phrase *beg the question*, Joan L. Bybee and Carol Moder investigate the factors frequency, recency and context – and thus chunking – as they affect language change. The model of language change that they adopt assumes that change occurs during language use, as experience with linguistic elements and situations activates and updates the network of connected exemplars (Bybee 2010). Repetition of sequences of elements leads to conventionalisation and then to entrenchment with a growing loss of analysability. In an approach that builds on notions developed in construction grammar (Goldberg 2006; Croft 2001), they consider these processes to apply at multiple levels of form-meaning mapping, ranging from phonological units to multiword constructions. The internal components of conventionalised chunks maintain connections of varying strengths with related items in the larger network. A key determinant of the associations within the network is the discourse context in which the unit is used. A common trajectory of change is the weakening of the connections that determine the compositionality and analysability of the chunk. The factors related to this weakening include relative frequency and changes in the context of use. Although research on language change has highlighted loss of analysability and compositionality, we also find multiple instances, such as *beg the question*, in which items can maintain their analysability.

The psycholinguist and the historical linguists thus come to the following agreement: chunking is a basic, domain-general associative learning process which can occur in and between all representational systems. It not only builds the representations, but also organises their relative availability and fluency according to need and thus optimises efficiency. As such, the consequences of chunking, notably changes in compositionality, can lead to grammatical change – although we have to be careful when trying to determine the causal direction of the relation between chunking and efficient communication, as Bybee and Moder rightly point out. While the psycholinguistic chapter by Ellis takes a more goal-oriented perspective on chunking and language change, focusing on the end result of the change as the motivation for the change (efficient communication as a result of chunking), Bybee and Moder shed light on the importance of understanding the mechanisms that actually create these correlations, i.e. the mechanisms that occur during language use for the purpose of communication.

Priming

Priming is the term used to refer to the well-established phenomenon that speakers are more likely to repeat structures or meanings that they have recently encountered (or used themselves) rather than new ones. Psycholinguistics explains this by pointing out that activation of these structures in the mind endures for a short while, so that it is easier to access the same or similar structures again than to access new ones. In Chapter 8, Martin J. Pickering and Simon Garrod begin Part IV by reviewing the concept of priming in psycholinguistic research, drawing together the findings from many different experiments to suggest that priming is highly likely to effect language change. They focus on cross-speaker priming rather than within-speaker priming in order to explain how changes may be passed from one speaker to the next. In doing so, they emphasise the role of interactive conversations, introducing alignment as the process by which speakers converge on similar expressions or schemes of description in order to communicate successfully. In addition, Pickering and Garrod provide evidence from studies on structural priming that show how priming may have long-term effects, and that adults may even be primed to use ungrammatical structures. A central mechanism by which priming is translated into language change is, in Pickering and Garrod's view, routinisation, by which repeated structures or expressions become routine due to their usefulness in interaction. The authors emphasise how strongly experimental and corpus evidence converge on the insight that priming is a substantial factor in language use and argue that it is likely to be a substantial factor in language change, too.

Christian Mair, in the companion Chapter 9, responds that it seems 'a long shot' to see priming, a laboratory-established phenomenon pertaining to an individual's language processing in the range of milliseconds, as a factor in the language change of communities over decades and centuries. Nevertheless, he is cautiously optimistic that priming, via alignment and routinisation, may provide one explanation of the linkage of individual language use and communal language change. The case study he presents focuses on an instance of ongoing language change: the establishment of the contracted form *wanna* for *want to*. Mair is able to show on the basis of the COCA corpus that the use of *wanna* is facilitated by a previous use or encounter of *wanna* itself (i.e. persistence), but also by a previous occurrence of the already established, but analogously formed, *gonna* – and even by contracted negation particles. Mair thus raises the possibility for future research to conduct priming studies on ongoing changes, closing the gap between the research foci of historical linguistics and psycholinguistics.

Analogy

In Part V, Heike Behrens takes as her starting point for Chapter 10 the role that analogy – a general cognitive processing mechanism – plays in language acquisition. Analogy is defined as a structure mapping process that relies on either perceptual similarity or more abstract relations between a source and a target (Gentner 1983). In language processing and change, analogy comes into play when novel structures (exemplars) need to be mapped onto a category. Categories are seen as emergent and malleable, i.e. dynamic entities. This property is important both for language acquisition, where categories need to grow out of a process of abstraction and pattern recognition, and language change, where categories have to allow for extension. Behrens uses examples from acquisition data for German morphology (plurals) and English syntax (argument structure) to illustrate how certain kinds of errors show that, in addition to type and token frequency, similarities between an exemplar and the target category as well as more abstract pattern mapping play a role in the development of a child's grammar. Just like Lieven (Chapter 14), Behrens stresses the parallels that can be observed between the processes observed in error data and psycholinguistic experiments and the processes involved in language change, pointing in particular to the tendency to regularise in both children and change. But she also draws attention to the differences between the two areas, juxtaposing acquisition and grammaticalisation by pointing out that children do not have to acquire lexical meanings of items first, before learning those that are also used with a grammatical function. Moreover, Behrens (like Lieven) stresses the different outcomes that analogical reasoning has in both children acquiring a language and language change: while analogical overextensions in language acquisition do not result in language change, analogical processes in grammaticalisation do result in a change of the system. Crucially, analogical pattern mapping in acquisition and change does not only depend on frequencies of various types (type and string frequency), but also on recency and salience, as Behrens points out. Category extension is more likely to spread throughout a community if the link between source and target is a salient one, for instance, and the pattern occurs with some frequency.

In Chapter 11, Hendrik De Smet and Olga Fischer use the grammaticalisation of semi-modal *have to* and the degree modifier *as good as* as case studies to discuss analogy as a factor in historical change. They point out that, while most grammaticalisation research focuses on the diachronic developments, in order to be able to fully understand the role that analogy plays one has to consider the synchronic situation, in particular those constructions that are likely to have served as the source for analogical mapping. For *have to*, they identify the development of adjacency, a changeover from *that* to *to*-infinitival complement clauses and inanimate subjects in existential *have*-constructions as structural analogical processes that are important for the grammaticalisation of the semi-modal. Additional support to the development of semi-modal *have to* comes from analogy with constructions like *have (object) (for) to do* as well as *have need to V* and related constructions with *need* (especially the loss of impersonal constructions). The support construction that emerges as an important factor in the development of the degree modifier *as good as* is *all but*: De Smet and Fischer detail the similarities in the development of the two constructions, arguing that the extension of one of them to a particular context lent support to similar developments in the other grammaticalising construction; divergent developments between the two constructions are attributed to the availability or absence of further supporting constructions (e.g. the extension of *as good as* – but not of *all but* – to *do*-support contexts). In other words, De Smet and Fischer apply the notion of 'supporting constructions' from psycholinguistic studies on language acquisition (e.g. Abbot-Smith and Behrens 2006) to the *synchronic* study of how analogy plays a role in the historical development of two English constructions.

Ambiguity

Ambiguity (Part VI) is a pervasive feature of human language, but is it also a driving force of language change? Claudia Felser, in Chapter 12, the psycholinguistic contribution on ambiguity, highlights the ubiquity of ambiguity at all language levels, even though they are not typically noticed by comprehenders. She then focuses on syntactic ambiguities, which have long been a central research focus in psycholinguistics. Typically here, garden path sentences are constructed which trigger the misanalysis of an ambiguous item, so that comprehenders need to backtrack in order to correct their interpretation. Felser reviews both serial and interactive models of language processing and how they explain misanalysis as well as reanalysis (serial models assume a syntax-privileged interpretation of language processing, and interactive models an influence of several language level cues on sentence analysis). Most relevant for the implications for language change, however, is her focus on 'good-enough processing' – the fact that comprehenders frequently retain an incorrect interpretation even when its incorrectness has become apparent. In addition, interpretations may remain shallow, or underspecified, without hindering a 'good-enough' processing of the input. In linguistic terms, ambiguity is not always clearly resolved, and vagueness (underspecification) does not need to be, or cannot be, resolved. Felser concludes with a section comparing online misanalysis to diachronic neoanalysis (the term *reanalysis* is reserved for online corrections of misanalysis), with the most important difference being that misanalysis plays out within the constraints of grammar, whereas neoanalysis extends the range of what is grammatical. Two case studies are provided in which Felser explains cases of historical neoanalysis as the possible result of online misanalysis, namely noun-to-adjective conversion, and constituent boundary shift, as in the development of the *be going to*-future (both of which are taken up in the companion chapter by Denison).

David Denison in Chapter 13 concentrates on ambiguity and vagueness in language change, arguing that vagueness – underspecification – may be more central in this respect than true ambiguity, in which there is a correct and an incorrect interpretation. Denison brings together examples from a wide variety of linguistic areas in which vagueness and/or ambiguity play a role: semantic change, word class change and the development of prefabs, as well as syntactic neoanalysis (termed *reanalysis*, as is traditional in historical linguistics). For semantic change, Denison covers examples where an existing underspecification opens up the possibility of a new sense of a word – with the old one co-existing with it, at least temporarily, as in the semantic shift of *holiday* from 'religious festival' to 'work-free period'. In word class change, Denison concentrates on the step-wise development from noun to adjective, as in *fun* or *rubbish*, noting that the change is not completed in only one step. Prefabs, as in *sort of* or *piece of work*, are interesting in the context of ambiguity because their idiomatic and literal meanings exist side by side, making them ambiguous. Finally, structural changes, as in the development of a phrasal verb out of a prepositional one (e.g. *run over*), also may derive from vague contexts. Denison concludes that while ambiguity is often the result of change (as also pointed out by Felser), vagueness is the enabler. Vagueness offers the possibility for new readings, with conservative readings remaining in use for some time.

Acquisition

In Part VII the psycholinguistic contribution on acquisition (LA), Elena V. M. Lieven starts off with the well-known controversy between the Universal Grammar (UG) and the Usage-based (UB) account of how children acquire their first language. The focus in her Chapter 14 is on the question on how errors can be explained and whether or not they play a role in language change. Errors are seen as more important from a UG perspective, since change in this approach needs to occur before the parameters are set (i.e. during the critical period for LA). In a UB account, errors are not required to explain language variability and change, since innovation and change can also occur later in a person's lifetime. Lieven uses numerous examples from LA research (not exclusively on the acquisition of English) to illustrate how language can be shown to emerge from usage, with general cognitive processes at work, such as the development of prototypes, but also factors like frequency, salience or processing speed. Alongside naturalistic data, LA research typically uses experimentation (e.g. priming experiments) to investigate the underlying psycholinguistic processes. It is thus able to gauge the effect that, for instance, input frequencies may have on the likelihood of errors in child speech.

The crucial question for a historical linguist interested in change is how children finally achieve acquisition of the target language, i.e. how they move beyond the overgeneralisations that are often the source of errors in child language. Research from psycholinguistics (e.g. Blything, Ambridge and Lieven 2014) shows that both frequency and semantics play a role in helping children to arrive at the target grammar. The crucial facts for the present volume are that, while child language shows various types of errors early on in the acquisition process, most of these are overcome very early (i.e. before children start school), and that child LA is therefore highly unlikely to be the locus of innovation. If acquisition plays a role in historical change, as Lieven points out, it is more likely second language acquisition in language contact situations that will give rise to novel constructions. She concludes that the parallels between child LA and change are limited to the general, underlying processes and factors at work.

In the corresponding historical linguistic chapter (Chapter 15), María José López-Couso provides a critical review of the recapitulationist view of language change, i.e. the idea (borrowed from biology and adopted in developmental psychology) that the evolutionary steps in phylogeny are repeated in ontogeny. She provides numerous examples from previous research into language acquisition and historical change (including languages other than English) to substantiate the claim that developments in child language learning and grammaticalisation show surprising parallels, quoting research that questions whether these similarities might be only superficial (e.g. Slobin 2002).

The case study she presents in more detail also shows striking parallels between the grammaticalisation of the *going to* future time expression in the history of English and stages in L1 acquisition. However, as López-Couso convincingly argues, the parallels in early L1 acquisition have to be attributed to different underlying processes, while similar processes (notably frequency) can be taken to account for parallel developments in the later stages of language acquisition/change. A central question in diachronic linguistics has been the agency of children in language change, running through a lot of generative research (e.g. Lightfoot 1991, 2006). Questioning the validity of the innateness and critical age hypothesis, López-Couso falls on the side of usage-based accounts of language change.

1.5   Concluding Remarks

This volume treats seven different cognitive factors and processes and their role in language change – frequency, salience, chunking, priming, analogy, ambiguity and acquisition. All except the last (acquisition) are found by the authors of both the respective psycholinguistic and historical linguistic chapters to play important roles in language change, as is evidenced by case studies of changes in the more-or-less distant history of the English language. However, while the different factors are treated separately in the separate parts of the volume, all chapters show that they are, in fact, highly interdependent. For example, priming contributes to chunking, ambiguity facilitates analogical reasoning, and various types of frequency (type, token, string frequency) as well as salience, for instance, play roles in analogical pattern mapping and category extension, both in language acquisition and in language change. None of the factors thus drives language change by itself, so future studies of specific changes will need to consider their interplay.

All in all, we hope to achieve a fostering of connections between psycholinguistic and historical linguistic research with this volume. The contributions show that differences in scope and methodology can be bridged, achieving a sense in psychologists that their findings have wider applications and implications, and providing models for historical linguists on how cognitive factors in language change can be included in their analyses.

Notes

1. Note that Schleicher himself does not explicitly make the connection between developmental stages in the acquisition of individual sounds and historical sound change, nor does he draw any conclusions from the observation that children overgeneralise morphological endings by analogy to forms that are not part of the input. However, considering that his observations were published in a journal that focused on language change, we can assume that he intended them to be read in that context. Nonetheless, it is interesting that Schleicher does not postulate that changes result directly from analogical overextension of morphological endings to novel contexts or that developmental stages in the acquisition of a phoneme system mirror those in the history of a language.

2. The mention of language acquisition as a locus of language change is automatically followed by a critical comment in de Saussure (1916, 1983: 148): 'Ces constations méritent toute attention, mais laissent le problème intact; en effet, on ne voit pas pourquoi une génération convient de retenir tells inexactitudes à l'exclusion de tells autres, toutes étant également naturelles; . . . (Observations of this nature cannot be ignored: but they leave the problem unsolved. For it is difficult to see why one generation settles for preserving certain inaccuracies and not others, since all of them are just as natural)'.

PART I

Frequency

CHAPTER 2

The Ecclesiastes Principle in Language Change

Harald Baayen, Fabian Tomaschek, Susanne Gahl
and Michael Ramscar

2.1 Introduction

The history of mankind is characterized by constant change. One aspect of this change is the rise, spread and demise in time and space of civilizations and religions. Another, perhaps more systematic aspect of this constant change is that technological innovations and (thanks to these innovations) the amount of information available to agents in human societies have been increasing exponentially.

Societal changes lead to changes in language. Meibauer et al. (2004) and Scherer (2005) observed in a diachronic corpus of German newspapers that the use of multilexemic words increased over time in response to increasing onomasiological needs for new technologies and a growing body of knowledge. Figure 2.1 illustrates for American English that over the last 200 years, the number of different words in use increased steadily. Counts were obtained by sampling, from the COHA corpus, from each of the four registers distinguished in this corpus (news, fiction, non-fiction and magazines), 1.5 million words, and counting the number of different types. The numbers in Figure 2.1 were obtained by averaging the counts for 100 random samples taken for a given genre and decade. (For the first decade, the number of tokens was below 1.5 million. Therefore, for the first decade of the nineteenth century, Figure 2.1 plots the total number of types in the corpus for the different genres, as available for that first decade.) For each of the four registers, we observe a steady increase in the number of different words. (A regression model indicated that from 1860 onward, the rate of increase was greater for magazines and news than for non-fiction and fiction, and the rates of increase for magazines and news were similar, as were the rates for non-fiction and fiction.)

One area where a growth is particularly visible is English personal names (Ramscar et al. 2013c). Names, whether for people, natural species, artifacts or products, are part of the lexicon and co-determine the structure of the

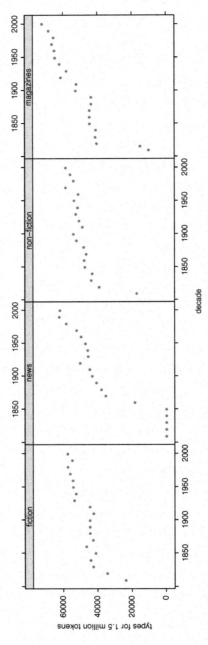

Figure 2.1 Number of different word types in 1.5 million tokens randomly sampled from the successive decades of American English in the COHA corpus, averaged across 100 samples.

language. This is clearly documented for morphological structure, as pointed out (for compounding) by Scherer (2005) and (for derivation) by Lüdeling and Evert (2005). The accumulation of names has consequences that go beyond simply having a larger list of lexical items. For sound structure, the changing vocabulary comes with changes in lexical similarity and neighborhood density, which in turn has consequences for lexical processing (Gahl et al. 2012). Above the word level, the influx of new verbs such as *to ping* (in the sense of testing the availability of a computer on a network, which goes back to 1983) changes the quantitative structure of collostructural sets. Importantly, like common nouns, proper nouns have collocational structure: compare the names of three English Renaissance composers, Thomas Knyght, Anthony Holborne and John Johnson, with the names of three species of trees, Ponderosa Pine, Narrowleaf Cottonwood and Rocky Mountain Juniper. Investigation of how different languages structure collocations for person reference shows that these follow specific conventions. Thus, the name grammar of pre-industrial England was more similar to the name grammar of modern Korean than to the present-day name grammar of English (Ramscar et al. 2013c), which is changing rapidly. This can be seen in Figure 2.2, which presents US Social Security registration data on personal names. The horizontal axis represents the time period from 1880 to 2010. The vertical axis presents the entropy of the distribution of personal names for males and females separately. The entropy measure quantifies the amount of uncertainty about a male or female name. Entropies are larger when there are more different names, and when these names have more similar probabilities. Thus, a greater entropy indicates, informally, that it is more difficult to guess a name and that it will take more time to retrieve a name from memory.

Figure 2.2 shows a sharp rise in name entropy that may have had its onset around the end of the Second World War. By the beginning of the eighties, there was a greater variety of names in use than ever before (female names especially), and by 2010, the entropy of names had skyrocketed. This means that, for an individual speaker born around the end of the Second World War, name vocabulary will have increased exponentially across her lifetime.

The goal of this study is to present an overview of some of our findings on the consequences for grammar and lexical processing of the need for language to accommodate the ever-growing onomasiological needs of modern societies. Our main focus will be at the micro-level of changes over the lifetime of speakers and their processing consequences, but where possible

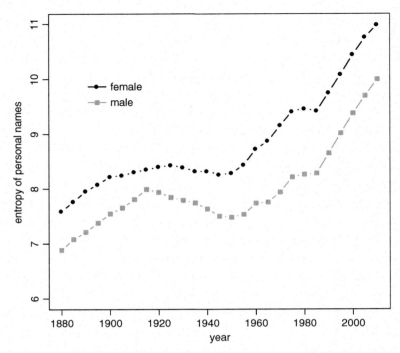

Figure 2.2 The increase in entropy of US given names, 1880–2010.

we will link our findings about aging and language to macro-changes over generations of speakers.

2.2 Language Change over the Lifetime

As speakers proceed through life, they not only meet more and more people with different names, but also encounter more street names, place names, brand names and specialized vocabulary for domains in which they acquire expert knowledge. That older adults know more words is apparent from lexical decision studies. An analysis of the accuracy data in the English Lexicon Project (Balota et al. 2007) for monosyllabic monomorphemic words shows that the accuracy that older adults exhibit when deciding whether a letter sequence presented to them is a word of their language is greater than the accuracy displayed by younger adults. Figure 2.3 presents the difference curve for the accuracy of old versus young respondents. Across the full range of frequencies, older adults are more accurate, except for the

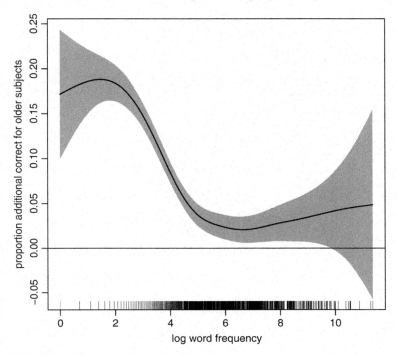

Figure 2.3 Difference in the proportion of additional correct lexical decisions that older adults make, compared to young adults, in the English Lexicon Project.

highest-frequency words, where estimates are uncertain due to the sparsity of data (the rug in Figure 2.3 thins out at the right-hand side of the horizontal axis). For words with a log frequency lower than 5 in the British National Corpus, we see a dramatic increase in performance for older versus younger subjects. A recent crowd-sourcing study (Keuleers et al. 2015) comfirmed the same pattern for a wide range of ages. Accuracy increases systematically over the lifetime, reaching a correctness score of about 75 percent by the age of 60. These results fit well with an analysis of the Switchboard corpus (Meylan and Gahl 2014), which revealed that, as compared to younger speakers, older speakers exhibit greater vocabulary richness, and share fewer common words with their interlocutors in conversation.

What these studies show is that over our lifetime, we slowly but steadily increase our mastery of the vocabulary. This mastery, however, is not restricted to knowledge of more words; it extends to collocational knowledge and to articulatory fluency.

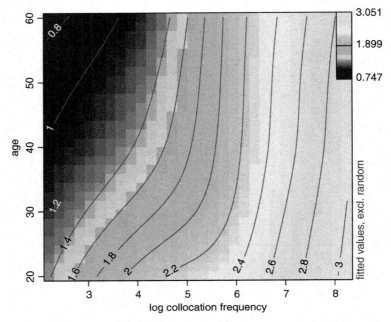

Figure 2.4 Correctness scores in the paired associate learning task as a function of log collocation frequency and age. Deeper shades of blue indicate lower correctness scores; warmer shades of yellow indicate higher scores.

The increase in collocational knowledge becomes apparent when we examine results obtained with the paired associate learning task (PAL) (Ramscar et al. 2014, 2013b). In this task, subjects are first presented with pairs of words, some of which are associated to some extent (such as *baby* and *cries*), and some of which are arbitrary pairs (*obey* and *inch*). Subsequently, subjects are presented with the first word (*baby* or *obey*) and are asked to say out loud the second word (*cries* or *inch*). Unsurprisingly, subjects make more errors for hard pairs such as *obey* and *inch* than for easy pairs such as *baby* and *cries*.

What is at first blush surprising is that performance on this task decreases with age. In the psychological literature, the task has established itself as a diagnostic for cognitive decline over the lifetime. However, this body of work has never paid attention to the linguistic properties of the stimuli used. It turns out that collocation frequency (estimated here using counts of Google hits for the word pairs) is a strong predictor of performance. Figure 2.4 presents the regression surface for PAL performance with log collocation frequency and age as predictors, using data reported in des Rosiers and Ivison (1986), fitted with a generalized additive mixed model (Wood 2006; Baayen 2014). Darker shades toward blue indicate lower scores, indicating less-accurate performance. More yellow and reddish shades indicate more accurate performance. The contour lines connect points for which performance is identical. For a fixed value on the vertical axis, the contour lines represent the effect of collocation frequency. Across all ages, performance improves with frequency. When we fix collocation frequency, we find a strongly downward-sloping surface for low values, but hardly any effect for the highest frequencies. To see which age exhibits the strongest effect of collocation frequency, we count contour lines from left to right. For age 20, we count 9 contour lines. For age 60, we count 11 contour lines. This indicates that the oldest subjects are most sensitive to collocation frequency, whereas the youngest subjects are the least sensitive. This finding is consistent with the fact that older subjects have had more experience with the language and have, as a consequence, become more sensitive to lexical co-occurrence probabilities. In other words, with age, our knowledge of the language increases. However, it is also remarkable that the older subjects perform worse for the lower co-occurrence frequencies than the younger subjects. We will return to this issue below, where it will become clear that this is an inevitable consequence of learning.

The reasons vocabulary increases across the lifespan are obvious. With age comes experience, and the more experiences of the world we learn to discriminate and encode in the language signal when communicating about these experiences, the more complex the code must become. To see this, consider a simple situation in which there are four experiences that constitute the universe of what we communicate about. In this case, four two-bit codes (10, 01, 00, 11) suffice to discriminate between these four experiences. When there are 10,000 experiences, we need binary codes with 14 bits to distinguish between all of them. Similarly, when onomasiological needs increase, a language will need to find ways to properly differentiate between what we seek to communicate. Of course, one could resort to phrasal circumlocution, but this is likely to be a wasteful solution, energy-wise (cf. Zipf's law of abbreviation: Zipf 1949). Languages such as Chinese and Vietnamese started out with lexicons in which monosyllabic words were the norm (see, e.g., Arcodia, 2007). Given severe phonotactic constraints on what constitutes a usable monosyllabic word, the number of possible forms is soon exhausted. The code can allow for homonymic ambiguity thanks to contextually driven ambiguity resolution. But even this has its limits, and the majority of words in Chinese and Vietnamese are now bisyllabic compounds.

Instead of, or complementary to, resorting to compounding (or other less-productive word-formation processes), it is possible to implement discrimination by modulating the fine phonetic detail of articulation. 'Subphonemic' onomasiological discrimination is well established for so-called suprasegmentals such as tone (familiar from Chinese or Vietnamese), stress (familiar from English) and acoustic duration (such as the three durational contrasts in Estonian). However, other more subtle subphonemic contrasts have recently come to light for English and related Germanic languages such as Dutch. Gahl (2008) reported systematic differences in acoustic duration for English homophones such as *time* and *thyme*, Kemps et al. (2005a, 2005b) observed systematic differences in acoustic durations between stems in isolation and stems in inflected or derived words, and Plag et al. (2014) found systematic differences in acoustic duration for the English suffix -*s* that co-varied with its morphological function.

The subtlety of these findings underlines how daunting the task of mastering the motor control required for articulation is. Here, as for any other motor skill, be it playing tennis or playing the violin, improvement comes with practice. We can see the effects of practice over the lifetime by investigating the fine details of articulatory trajectories for words of different frequencies. The more frequent a word is, the more opportunities a speaker has had to practice her motor system on the articulation of that word, and the more likely it is that we can observe discriminative differentiation as a function of experience. Thus, by studying words of different frequency with respect to how articulatory gestures are executed, we can gain insight into changes that are likely to take place within a given word as a speaker becomes more practiced in uttering that word.

There are several ways in which the trajectories of articulators can be measured. Of a wide range of techniques, the simplest and most widely used are ultrasound (Gick 2002) and electromagnetic articulography, EMA (Schönle et al. 1987). Tomaschek et al. (2014) used EMA to study how articulation covaries with frequency. They glued small metallic sensors to a subject's tongue and lips, and placed the subject in an electromagnetic field generated by an EMA system. While speaking, the movements of the sensors give rise to changes in this field, which are registered and used to calculate time series of X, Y and Z coordinates for each of the sensors. When time-locked with the acoustic signal, the part of the time series that corresponds to an event of interest, such as the articulation of a vowel, can be identified, and then subjected to statistical analysis.

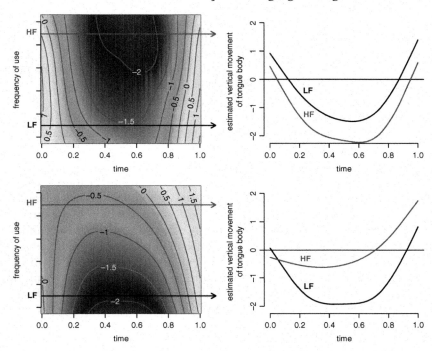

Figure 2.5 Vertical displacement of the tongue body sensor during the articulation of German /aː/ as a function of frequency of use and (normalized) time. Darker colors indicate lower positions of the tongue body sensor.

Figure 2.5 presents the trajectories of the tongue body sensor during the articulation of the vowel /aː/ in German verbs and nouns which varied in their frequency of use. Horizontal axes represent time (normalized between 0 and 1). In the left panels, the vertical axis represents log-transformed frequency of use. In the right panels, the vertical axis represents vertical displacement of the same sensor. The left panels show regression surfaces estimated with the help of generalized additive mixed models. The contour lines connect points defined by time and frequency for which the vertical displacement of the tongue body sensor is estimated to be the same. The color coding indicates the direction of the displacement: darker colors indicate further down; lighter colors, further up. The curves presented in the right-hand panels highlight two specific trajectories, one for a specific lower-frequency and one for a specific higher frequency.

The upper panels show that the tongue body sensor moves further down when producing the vowel /aː/ when the word has a higher frequency of occurrence. In other words, for higher-frequency words in which the next syllable realizes the third person plural ending (an apical /n/), a higher frequency affords a more precise and distinctive articulation of this low vowel. The lower panels show the pattern in reverse, when a /t/ realizes the second person plural inflection. The more frequent this inflectional variant is, the earlier the tongue starts preparing for the articulation of the (laminal) /t/.[1]

An influential hypothesis first advanced by Aylett and Turk (2004) holds that higher-frequency (and, from the perspective of information theory, less-informative) words would be articulated with more centralized vowels and shorter durations (Aylett and Turk 2006) in order to keep the rate at which information is transmitted relatively constant (smooth) in a channel with limited transmission capacity. However, we do not replicate these findings in the articulatory domain. When an apical inflection follows, speakers learn over time to realize a more distinctive *a*. When a laminal inflection follows, we see more coarticulation with the upcoming suffix as frequency increases. In other words, what experience makes possible is for a person to speak in such a way that the fine phonetic detail of how a segment is realized becomes discriminative between higher- and lower-frequency words (see Kuperman et al. 2007 and Ferrer-i Cancho et al. 2013 for further empirical and also mathematical problems with the smooth-signal redundancy hypothesis).

An increase in subphonemic discrimination is also visible in real time in the realization of English vowels over the lifetime. Figure 2.6 presents the changes in the first and second formants of English monophthongs as spoken by 11 speakers in the Up corpus. This corpus, which is described in Gahl et al. (2014), is based on five films from the film series known as the 'Up' series of documentary by director Michael Apted. These films follow a set of individuals at seven-year intervals over a period of 42 years. The most recent material included in the corpus shows the participants at age 49. The corpus is based on utterances of at least 20 seconds of uninterrupted speech. It comprises 250 utterances for each of the eleven documentary participants, for a total of 21,328 word tokens representing 2,463 unique word types. The changes in the formants graphed in Figure 2.6 are those predicted by a linear, mixed-effects model that includes speaker and word as random-effect factors. Darker shades of gray indicate realizations later in life. What Figure 2.6 shows is that, on the whole, the vowel space expands with age when we control for speaker and lexical variability.

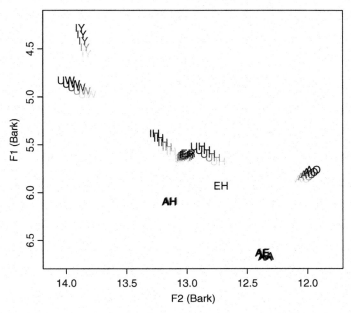

Figure 2.6 Expansion of the vowel space with age. The Up (Michael Apted) corpus.
Darker shades of gray represent later points in time.

This pattern of change is interesting in the light of the idea that changes in the speech of older adults are adaptive. Biological and physiological changes occur throughout the lifetime. Hearing loss, as well as changes such as atrophy of the vocal folds and calcification of the laryngeal cartilages may give rise to adaptive strategies that, in all, are remarkably successful (Hooper and Cralidis 2009). The speakers at the latest point in time available in our sample, however, were in their forties, and it is therefore unlikely that the changes that we observe here are due to adaptation to hearing loss.[2] Rather, it is much more likely that this pattern reveals a genuine continuity of language development and change in healthy aging, such that, over time, speakers become ever more proficient in producing increasingly discriminative speech signals.

What these examples show is that obtaining full mastery of the language as used in complex modern societies is a process that extends over the lifetime. As we grow older, we master more words, we become less prone to learn nonsense, our vowel space expands, and we articulate segments with greater skill. There is an interesting parallel in the culture of knowledge acquisition and knowledge extension. Jones (2005) reported that the greatest achievements in science are no longer the preserve of the young. Using data on Nobel Prize winners and great inventors, he observed that by the end of the twentieth century, great inventions were made 8 years later in the inventor's lifetime, on average, than at the beginning of the century. Econometric modeling suggests that this is not an effect just of an aging population, but also an effect due to productivity starting later in life – the accumulation of knowledge across generations forces innovators to seek more education over time. Although the acquisition of the skill of speaking is not one marked by great landmark achievements, it seems likely that, compared to, for instance, Early Modern English, the lexis of present-day English is more complex and requires more time to master.

2.3   The Ecclesiastes Principle in Language Change

In the third century BC, the philosopher and wisdom teacher Qohelet wrote

> For in much wisdom is much grief: and he that increaseth knowledge increaseth sorrow. (Ecclesiastes 1:18, translation King James Version)

This characterization of the human condition applies straightforwardly to human learning. The accumulation of knowledge does not come for free. We refer to this as the Ecclesiastes Principle.

We noted above that name entropy has been increasing rapidly over the last 60 years (see Figure 2.2). This finding sheds new light on the well-known difficulties we often experience with remembering people's names. As we age, and continue to sample from an ever-increasing vocabulary of names, this problem is exacerbated. Several aspects of this phenomenon are worth considering.

First, by the Ecclesiastes Principle, it is unavoidable that as we know more names, finding a specific name becomes more difficult. Looking up a name in a small telephone directory takes less time than looking up a name in a large directory. Thus, as we go through life and get to know more people, the entropy of the names we know increases, and as a consequence, greater processing times are inevitable.

Second, the name finding problem is exacerbated by the way naming practices in English have developed over the second half of the twentieth century. Before the industrial revolution, *John, Thomas* and *William* were the most popular names for boys, accounting for some 50 percent of all different names in use (Galbi 2002). For girls, *Mary, Elizabeth* and *Anne* represented the top ranks in the name distribution. Further differentiation between the different Williams and Annes is achieved with discriminators for occupation (Smith), ancestry (Johnson) or place of origin (London). Ramscar et al. (2013c) point out that this results in a system that is very efficient for retrieving names.

Consider, by way of example, a situation in which 900 people need to be distinguished, and assume, for simplicity, that all names are equiprobable. If each individual has a unique name, name uncertainty (gauged by Shannon's entropy) is maximal, and equal to $\log_2(900) = 9.8$. If we have 30 first names and 30 family names, which also allows us to discriminate between 900 people, the entropy of retrieving the first name is halved, $\log_2(30) = 4.9$, and the same holds for the entropy of retrieving the family name. Since the industrial revolution, English has been trending toward the latter situation. As a consequence, the name finding problem has been increasing. In light of the census data shown in Figure 2.2, a 70-year-old in 2010 is faced with a much higher variety in names compared to when this same person was a 20-year-old in 1960. Ramscar et al. (2014) report simulation studies suggesting that the joint consequence of encountering more names, and more diverse names, over a period of 50 years results in a processing delay of no less than some 150 ms. This example illustrates that, independently of the Ecclesiastes Principle, societal changes can modulate language change in a way that is dysfunctional for its speakers. Ramscar et al. (2013c) note that naming systems need not be dysfunctional in this way, and mention Korean as an example of a language with an efficient name grammar.

The Ecclesiastes Principle has more subtle, but no less far-reaching, consequences when we consider the details of lexical learning. Above, we examined the performance on the paired associate learning task as a function of collocation frequency and age. We observed that older speakers reveal greater sensitivity to collocation frequency, which fits with our hypothesis that language proficiency increases as experience accumulates over the lifetime. What we have not yet discussed is why it is that older speakers perform less well than younger speakers on the pairs with lower collocation frequencies.

To see why this happens, we consider a highly simplified example of collocational learning in which a Rescorla–Wagner network (Rescorla 1988; Ramscar et al. 2010; Baayen et al. 2011; Baayen and Ramscar 2015) is required to learn six word pairs, as shown in Table 2.1. (Below, we provide further details on this computational model.) During the first

Table 2.1 *Data for the learning simulation with six collocations*

	Cues	Outcomes	Frequency	Training phase
1	baby	window	10	A
2	obey	inch	10	A
3	baby	cries	80	B
4	baby	sleeps	40	B
5	obey	teacher	60	B
6	obey	command	60	B

training phase, we present the model with 10 examples each of the pairs *baby – window* and *obey – inch*. The model is instructed to learn to predict the second word, given the first word. Following this training phase, the model is presented with further word pairs in which *baby* and *obey* are the first words. The word pair *baby – cries* has a frequency of 80, *baby – sleeps* has a frequency of 40 and the two pairs with *obey* have a frequency of 60 each. Thus, the total number of occurrences of *baby* as first word is equal to that of *obey* as first word. The order in which pairs were presented was chosen at random. Each presentation of a word pair constitutes a learning event at which the model is given the first word as input cue, and is asked to predict the second word as the output outcome. If the prediction was correct, the weight on the connection from the first to the second word is strengthened; otherwise, it is weakened.

Figure 2.7 illustrates how the weights on the connections from the first to the second words develop during the second training phase, from learning event to learning event. The solid and dashed lines show the development of the weights for the four frequent pairs. The pair *baby – cries* occurs twice as frequently as the pair *baby – sleeps*, which explains why the curve for the first pair is located above that of the second pair. The two blue curves represent pairs with identical frequencies midway between those of *baby – cries* and *baby – sleeps*. Unsurprisingly, we find them in between the two red curves. The dotted lines represent the two pairs that were presented only 10 times during the initial training phase, after which they were never presented again. These pairs show the weakest weights. Thus, after about a hundred trials and continuing up to the end of learning, the model reflects the collocation frequency effect that we observed for the paired associate learning task. The model also captures the effect of age. After 100 trials, the model represents a young

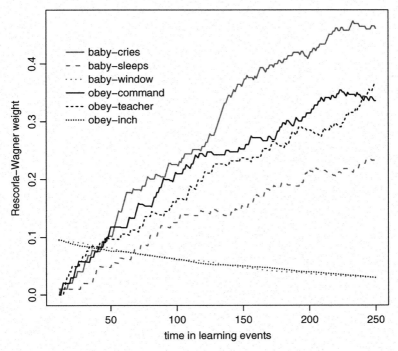

Figure 2.7 Development in a Rescorla–Wagner network of the weights from the first word to the second word for the six word pairs in Table 2.1.

adult. After 250 trials, the model reflects more advanced learning. For the young adult, the effect of collocation frequency, although already present, is not as differentiated yet to the extent that becomes apparent with further learning.

What is important is that the weights on the connections from *obey* to *inch* and from *baby* to *window* decrease as the other pairs are learned (see also Ramscar et al. 2013b). This is a straightforward consequence of discrimination learning. Every time the word *obey* occurs in a learning event, the model considers all possible outcomes and adjusts weights upward if the outcome is present (which will happen for *obey – command* and *obey – teacher*), but adjusts them downward when the outcome is not present (*obey – inch*). In other words, the model learns that it can expect *command* or *teacher*, given *obey*, and it also learns that it doesn't make sense to expect *inch*. Because both *obey – inch* and *baby – window* are downgraded the same number of times, as both first words occur in the same

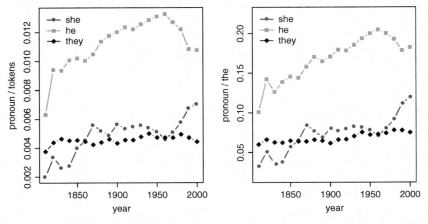

Figure 2.8 Development of the use of third-person pronouns *he, she, they* in American English as gauged by the COHA corpus. *Left:* counts normed by tokens. *Right:* counts baselined against the frequency of *the*.

number of other collocations, their curves are the same, modulo how the random numbers turned out in the simulation.

Thus, the Ecclesiastes Principle manifests itself in the context of learning as a force prohibiting the learning of novel knowledge if and only if that novel knowledge does not make sense given prior experience.[3] We think this same force may serve to speed the demise of words that are in the process of becoming obsolete. It is not only that the contexts in which words such as *telegraph* or *walkman* were once used will become increasingly rare, but the lexical collocates that were once predictive of these words will increasingly lose this predictivity where they continue to be encountered in other contexts.

We discussed earlier how the changing onomasiological demands of increasingly complex modern societies give rise to continuously increasing name- and word-finding difficulties. One possible adaptation that offers a way to sidestep this problem is to revert to favoring pronouns instead of names. Two predictions follow. First, over time, the use of pronouns should increase in the speech community. Second, over the lifespan, the use of pronouns should increase likewise.

The first prediction is well supported by an inspection of the frequencies of use of the pronouns *he, she, they* in the samples in the COHA corpus over two centuries of American English. Figure 2.8 graphs their by-decade relative frequencies. The left panel shows the pronoun frequencies divided by the number of tokens in COHA for the respective decades. The right panel presents the pronoun counts, but now normed against the corresponding frequencies of the definite article *the*. The right-hand plot is more informative as it specifically compares pronominal definite reference with non-pronominal definite reference.[4] For each pronoun in the right-hand panel of Figure 2.8, we see an increase over time, which is small but well-supported overall for *they* (r = 0.89, t(18) = 8.27, p < 0.0001) and more pronounced for *she* (r = 0.867, t(18) = 7.39, p < 0.0001) and *he* (r = 0.884, t(18) = 8.04, p < 0.0001). In the second half of the twentieth century, we may be observing the generic use of *he* for both genders giving way to more gender-specific use for males, which allows frequency to accrue to *she*. The global pattern is one in which writers are increasingly favoring the use of anaphora instead of definite referring expressions. It seems likely that the more rapid increase in the use of *he* and *she* compared to *they* reflects the exponential increase in the number of different personal names as compared to the more modest increase in types in other parts of the vocabulary.

The Ecclesiastes Principle predicts that a similar trend should be visible across the lifespan of individual speakers. Interestingly, Hendriks et al. (2008) report that older adults use more pronouns than younger adults, exactly as expected. Their interpretation of this finding, however, is very different from ours. Hendriks et al. interpret their results as indicating that older speakers' cognitive capacities are in decline. By contrast, just as the increase in use of pronouns in American English is not a symptom that the language is somehow terminally ill, the increased use of pronouns in older speakers is a sensible adaptive strategy to manage the increased knowledge that is inevitably accrued in healthy aging. The view of aging as an inevitable process of cognitive decline is incompatible with the present findings, which consistently indicate that with age adults become more proficient speakers of their language. Surprisingly, the myth of cognitive decline (Ramscar et al. 2014) is propagated in the psychological literature in total ignorance of the Ecclesiastes Principle, reflecting a general attitude to the elderly that in the gerontological literature has been dubbed ageism (in parallel to racism and sexism, see Palmore and Manton 1973).[5]

2.4   Entrenchment and the Ecclesiastes Principle

Frequency of occurrence is widely used as a measure of entrenchment in memory (see Hilpert, this volume). However, simple frequency counts do not take into account the effects of co-learning and the costs that accrue with the accumulation of knowledge. Statistical measures as used in studies of lexicogrammatical attraction (Allan 1980; Stefanowitsch and Gries 2003; Ellis 2006a; Schmid and Küchenhoff 2013) take into consideration that words are used as part of a system (see also Ellis, this volume). However, the 2 × 2 contingency tables on which these measures are calculated require simplified binary contrasts that do not do full justice to the complexity of the language system. The same holds for behavioral profiles (see Gries and Divjak 2009; Hilpert, this volume), which call attention to the many paradigmatic relations in which a construction may participate, but that will tend not to consider such relations across a multiplicity of constructions. Furthermore, the burstiness of words and their non-uniform dispersion across documents potentially have consequences for entrenchment that go beyond what can be gauged with simple frequency counts.

This leaves the analyst with two options. One option is to complement frequency counts with a wide range of other measures, such as burstiness, dispersion, age of acquisition, conditional probabilities given preceding or following words and multiword probabilities (Bannard and Matthews 2008). Baayen (2011b) showed, using multiple regression, that when a wide range of variables correlated with word frequency is taken into account, there is very little variance left for word frequency to explain. Simple counts isolate units such as words from the system of which they are part. The more measures that probe the system are taken into account, the less useful bare frequency counts become.

Another option, which we pursue here, is to use measures that reflect the consequences of the accumulation of knowledge under the constraints of discrimination learning. Baayen (2011a) proposed to use the activation measure of the naïve discriminative reader model presented by Baayen et al. (2011), and discussed similarities and differences with other measures such as ΔP (Allan 1980) and distinctive collexeme strength (Gries and Stefanowitsch 2004). Recent developments in naïve discriminative learning theory (Milin et al. 2017; Baayen et al. 2016; Shaoul et al. under revision) offer a new measure that not only is highly predictive for lexical processing as gauged with the visual lexical decision task, but that we believe is also particularly promising as a measure of lexical entrenchment.

However, let us first address the question of why discrimination learning might provide us with quantitative measures that are more informative than straightforward counts of frequency of occurrence. To answer this question, consider a simple priming experiment in which pictures precede words that subjects have to read out loud. Marsolek (2008) showed that when a picture of a grand piano is the prime for the word *table*, subjects are slower compared to a control condition with a picture that does not share visual features (such as having a large horizontal flat surface, and having legs) with the word's denotatum (e.g. a picture of a bowl with oranges). Marsolek named this phenomenon anti-priming, and explains it with the principles of discriminative learning. Upon seeing a grand piano, the strength of the link between the feature of having a large flat surface is strengthened to the musical instrument, and at the same time associations to other objects, including tables, are weakened. Because oranges do not share many features with tables, they do not 'negatively prime' the target *table* to the same extent as does the grand piano. The consequences of this constant recalibration of the strengths of connections between features (henceforth 'cues') and outcome classes (tables, oranges, pianos) are profound (see Ramscar et al. 2010, 2013a, for detailed discussion). For corpus linguistics, the implication is that simple counts are not precise enough.

For example, the word *great* can be followed by many other words (*care, deal, story, about, for, if, on, used*, ...). Whenever *great* is followed by *story*, the link between *great* and *story* is strengthened, while the links between *great* and all other words that have been encountered following it are weakened. As a consequence, simply counting frequencies and co-occurrence frequencies will not do justice to the constantly on-going recalibration of the language system with respect to the words that could have appeared, but did not. Collostructional analysis and distinctive collexeme analysis (Stefanowitsch and Gries 2003; Gries and Stefanowitsch 2004) as well as the Delta-P measure (Allan 1980) advocated by Ellis (2006a) take aspects of this constant recalibration into account, but do so only for cross-tabulations of constructions and lexical items (e.g. double-object versus prepositional object constructions, and *give* versus all other verbs used with datives). The recalibration that takes place across all lexical items and across all potential constructions in which these lexical items participate is not taken into account (see also Baayen et al. 2016) for a critical discussion of frequency of occurrence as a predictor for language processing).

This is where discriminative learning becomes useful. It allows the researcher to bite the bullet and systematically work through all positive and negative adjustments of lexical associations, given a corpus. The simplest way of approaching the constant recalibration of the web of lexical relations is to study word-to-word predictivity. Of course, such a simple approach simplifies the intricacies of the language system substantially, but our current strategy is to see how far simple solutions can take us. Reassuringly, Shaoul et al. (under revision) show that this approach sets up a semantic vector space, and Baayen et al. (2016) show that measures obtained by corpus-based discrimination learning are excellent predictors of various experimental measures gauging lexical processing (see also Hendrix 2015 for the reading of compound words).

In what follows, we will not focus on providing further empirical justification of the discriminative stance, but instead will start exploring what a discrimination-based statistic may reveal about language change. Before proceeding, however, a brief introduction to the basics of discrimination learning will provide a better basis for understanding the measure with which we will probe our corpus data.

Naïve discrimination learning (NDL) is implemented with a simple network with two layers of nodes: an input layer with cue nodes and an output layer with outcome nodes. Each cue has a connection to every outcome. Each of these connections comes with a weight that specifies how well a given cue supports a given outcome. These weights are estimated by applying the learning equations of Rescorla and Wagner (1972). These learning equations specify how the weights should be adjusted for a given set of cues and outcomes present in a learning event. Weights on the connections from these cues to these outcomes are strengthened, while the weights to other outcomes that are not present in the learning event are weakened. The values of the weights thus change with each successive learning event. The more often an outcome is present in learning events, the stronger the weights on its incoming connections will be. However, because the Rescorla–Wagner equations also implement cue competition, the strengths of the weights are co-determined by the other cues in the learning events.

An important property of the NDL model is that it scales up to hundreds of millions of learning events extracted from large corpora. Furthermore, whenever corpora contain order information, be it the order of sentences in text or the ordering of subcorpora in historical time, the learning events presented to the model can be sequenced such that this order information is respected. In other words, given appropriate data, the model can be used to study learning over the lifetime as well as language change in historical time.

Let us explore the connection between discrimination learning and language change in historical time a little more closely by examining lexical entrenchment, which in standard approaches is typically gauged by means of frequency of occurrence. Within the framework of naïve discriminative learning, a measure developed by Milin et al. (2017) is of particular interest for assessing entrenchment. This study found the median absolute deviation (MAD) of the weights on the connections from the cues to a given outcome to be especially effective for predicting lexical decision latencies (see also Baayen et al., 2016, for replication and extension of these findings). This measure, referred to here as the NDL network prior, reflects how well an outcome is entrenched in the network. Words that are well entrenched have many strong connections. Thanks to these strong connections, they acquire a higher prior availability for lexical processing. The NDL network priors are correlated with frequency of occurrence, but unlike frequency, they incorporate the history of past learning and also take into account the kind of co-learning exemplified above in Figure 2.7. One can also regard the NDL network prior as an abstract statistic for the behavioral profile (see Hilpert, this volume), though not of a construction, but rather of a word.

In what follows, we explore the potential for understanding language change of the NDL network prior (as a measure of entrenchment) by means of a data set that we compiled from the COHA corpus by extracting the counts, across 20 decades in the nineteenth and twentieth centuries, for the top 100 three-word phrases returned when querying the COHA website for phrases of the form [a | the] [young | old] [*] and phrases of the form [a | the] [*] [boy | girl | man | woman].

This resulted in a total of 1,192 unique phrases. The upper left panel of Figure 2.9 plots the frequency of the words *old* and *young* in these phrases as a function of time. We see that the word *old* is more frequent than the word *young*. Furthermore, the word *young* reaches its peak use earlier, and shows a greater decline in use over time compared to the word *old*.

From the perspective of accumulation of knowledge, the binning of experience is unrealistic: learning does not start from zero with each new decade. The second top panel therefore plots the cumulated frequencies for 1800–2000. Instead of inverse U-shaped curves, we now see monotonically increasing curves with points of inflection.

The third top panel plots the NDL network prior. The learning events for the network were based on the individual phrases. For each phrase (e.g. *the young boy*), we constructed two learning events. For the first learning event, the cues were *the* and *young*, and the outcome was *boy*. For the second learning event, the cues were *the* and *boy*, and the outcome was *young*. In other words, the network was trained to predict one of the content words from the other two words in the phrase. We made use of the NDL2 package for R (Shaoul et al. 2014) to train the network on the 279,192 phrase tokens of the 1,192 phrase types in our data. The network was trained decade by decade. As we did not have information on the order in which phrases appeared within a given decade, the phrases within a given decade were presented for learning in a random order. In other

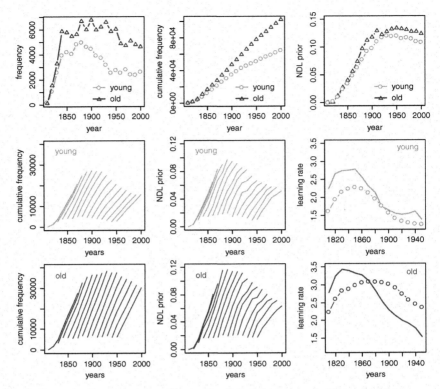

Figure 2.9 Changes in entrenchment for the words *young* and *old* over the lifetime, in American English in the period 1800–2000 (data from COHA).

words, the network was updated, phrase by phrase, respecting (to the extent possible) the order in which these phrases occurred over the last two centuries. For each of the 20 successive decades, we saved the current state of weights in the network. The upper right panel of Figure 2.9 presents the development of the NDL network priors for the words *young* and *old* across the last two centuries. After about 120 years, both curves reach their maximum, following which they show a small decrease.

Unfortunately, the curves shown in the upper center and right panels of Figure 2.9 are still highly unsatisfactory, as speakers don't live to be 200 years old. The network is accumulating too much experience, and the asymptotes we see reflect more the limit of what can be learned (see, e.g., Danks 2003) than what individual speakers could have learned over their lifetimes.

We therefore calculated the accumulation of experience for lifespans of 60 years, with the decades 1810, 1820, ..., 1950 as starting years. The second row of panels of Figure 2.9 plots the results for the word *young*, and the bottom row of panels shows the results for *old*. The first panels in these rows evaluate the accumulation of experience by cumulating frequency counts, whereas the second panels clarify the development of the NDL network priors. Unsurprisingly, the entrenchment of the words *young* and *old* increases over the lifetime, irrespective of whether entrenchment is estimated by cumulative frequency or by NDL network prior. Equally unsurprising is that more experience accumulates for *old* than for *young*. What is more interesting, however, is the fact that the slope of the lifetime curves decreases with each successive starting decade. The third panels for *young* and *old* plot the slopes obtained by fitting individual linear models to each individual lifetime curve. The solid lines represent the slopes for the learning curves based on NDL network priors, whereas the dotted lines represent the frequency-based learning curves. After an initial increase in slopes, indicating more rapid entrenchment, all four curves show a decrease.

Let us now consider the differences between the lifetime curves based on frequency and those derived from discrimination learning. First, note that the lifetime curves in the center panels reveal more wiggliness. This is because, unlike frequency, network priors are sensitive to differences in burstiness and dispersion, as well as to co-learning with the other words in the phrases in our data set. Second, the learning rates (i.e. the slopes of the lifetime curves) decrease much faster when the NDL network priors are used than when cumulated frequency counts are used. In other words, the discriminative learning model brings to the fore a learning problem that is less visible in a model using frequency of occurrence as a measure of entrenchment. Third, the decline in learning rate is greater for the more frequently used of the two words, i.e. for *old*.

These observations raise the question of what gives rise to this declining entrenchment. To address this question, consider Figure 2.10, which graphs lexical entropy as a function of decade. The left panel presents the changes in entropy for the word following the word *young* in the phrases in our sample. Entropy increased during the early years of the industrial revolution in the United States. Entropy peaks a second time after the end of the Second World War; strikingly, this is a time strongly associated with the onset of what has become known as the 'baby boom'. For the word *old*, the entropy of the following word reaches its maximum around the turn of the century. Although interesting by themselves, these changes do not help explain the

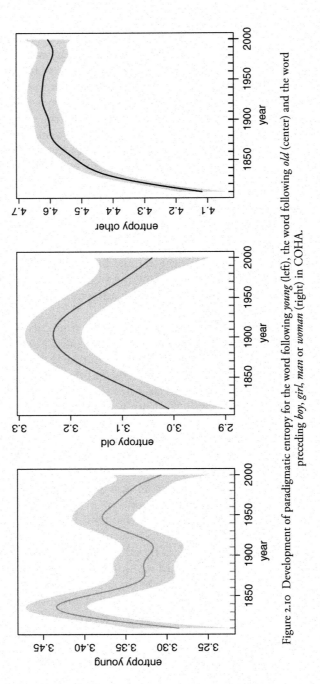

Figure 2.10 Development of paradigmatic entropy for the word following *young* (left), the word following *old* (center) and the word preceding *boy, girl, man* or *woman* (right) in COHA.

stronger declines in entrenchment predicted by the learning model, because the model learns to predict the adjectives from the third word and the article in the phrases. We therefore consider the entropy of the words preceding these third words (in the present exploratory case study, these third words are restricted to *boy, girl, man* and *woman*). The third panel of Figure 2.10 shows that during the nineteenth century, this entropy was undergoing a marked increase. This increase was severely attenuated during the early decades of the twentieth century, and peaked in the years of the great economic crisis.

The increase in entropy reflects that a wider variety of words came into use (plots graphing counts of words look similar to those in Figure 2.10, but fail to take differences in token frequency into account). As a consequence, it became increasingly difficult to correctly predict the use of the word *old* (or *young*) in phrases of the form [a | the] [*] [boy | girl | man | woman]. Every time that a word other than *old* (or *young*) was used, the weights on the connections from *boy* or *girl* or *man* or *woman* to *old* (or *young*) are downgraded, resulting in decreased entrenchment. This is again the Ecclesiastes Principle at work: the increase in prenominal lexical diversity comes at the cost of decreasing entrenchment of high-frequency words such as *young* and *old*. We think that the rise and fall in the frequency of use of these words, as documented in the upper left panel of Figure 2.9 is due to exactly this trade-off between the increasing demands on discriminating between – in the present example – events and other human agents in an increasingly more complex world, and the dynamics of discrimination learning.

This case study illustrates the possibilities offered by discrimination learning for research on language change. The present implementation of learning events is very simple, and based on selected examples of language use. A more in-depth analysis, which is beyond the scope of the present chapter, would profit from richer learning events (i.e. learning events with more words and their grammatical functions, such as number, tense, aspect, thematic role, etc.) and training on the full COHA.

2.5 Final Remarks

In this study, we have sketched a perspective on language change in which changes in language use over the course of healthy human aging share critical dynamics with changes in language as used in societies character-ized by a steady growth in the accumulation of knowledge. Our study focused on the consequences of the increase of knowledge for the domain of lexis. As onomasiological demands on a language increase, languages have to find ways to meet these demands. Creating new words is one option, as exemplified by the rise of compounding in Chinese and Vietnamese, which originally were isolating languages. Systematic changes in fine phonetic detail provide a complementary means for discrimination.

The accumulation of knowledge comes with undeniable costs. Older subjects are slower respondents in chronometric tasks (Ramscar et al. 2014), but this is the price for knowing more: older subjects stunningly outperform young subjects in terms of accuracy. Older subjects likewise reveal greater sensitivity to collocational patterns in the language. That they perform less well on matching word pairs that make no sense underlines the Ecclesiastes Principle, since once one learns that two words do not belong together, it follows that one must overcome this prior learning before one can learn to pair them. Accordingly, although it might seem that being less effective at learning nonsense is a cognitive deficit, further reflection indicates that learning to discard irrelevant associations is an evolutionary advantage (see Trimmer et al. 2012, for Rescorla–Wagner learning in evolutionary contexts).

There is one important dimension on which the parallel between society and the individual breaks down. The knowledge accumulated in our present-day society far surpasses what any individual can ever know. The Renaissance ideal of the Homo Universalis is farther away than ever. The corpora that are now becoming available are far larger than the experience any single user can gather over a lifetime. As a consequence, the knowledge we harvest from corpora reveals more about us as a social species than about the individual.

Especially in the domain of lexis, we are faced with the problem that although the highest-frequency words are common knowledge, as we move out into the low-frequency tail of Zipfian word frequency distributions, knowledge fractionates across individuals. Both classical factorial (Carroll and White 1973) and recent crowd-sourcing studies (Keuleers et al. 2015) highlight the specialized, and hence restricted, knowledge of individual language users. But perhaps knowledge specialization is the evolutionary answer to the limits on what an individual member of a community can achieve. From this perspective, the registers, genres and specialist vocabularies appear as just another variation of nature on intra-species variation and eusociality.

For historical corpora such as COHA, we have illustrated one way in which the fractionation problem can be addressed, at least in part, by zooming-in on fictive individual speakers representing (equally fictive) generations. By restricting generational lifespans to 60 years, with different decades at which generational learning is initiated, we were able to show how increasing paradigmatic lexical diversity comes, by the Ecclesiastes Principle, at the cost of a reduction in the entrenchment of high-frequency words.

More in general, we think it is worth reflecting on parallels between language change within the lifespan of an individual and language change in the course of the history of a given society. It is not the case that by the age of twenty-one, a language has been learned, to remain stationary and unaltered over the remaining lifetime. Over the lifetime, new words and expressions are constantly encountered as speakers read, watch TV, travel to new places with unfamiliar names for streets and buildings, meet new people and buy novel products. This accumulation of experience is unlikely to be uniform across the lexicon and the construction, and we anticipate that trade-offs at individual and aggregate levels, such as the adaptation toward pronouns under onomasiological overload, or the increase in the use of compounds (Scherer, 2005), are more widespread than we can currently imagine.

Notes

1. These findings are of particular interest in light of the scarcity of frequency effects in speech production for regular inflected words. The model of Levelt et al. (1999), for instance, explicitly rules out such frequency effects, and the evidence from both speech errors (Stemberger and MacWhinney, 1986) and behavioral paradigms (see, e.g., Bien et al. 2011; Tabak et al. 2010) is ambiguous.
2. According to Walling and Dickson (2012), approximately one out of three adults in the age range from 61 to 70 years suffers from hearing loss. This proportion increases to 80 percent for those older than 85.
3. In other words, as knowledge accumulates over the lifetime, it becomes increasingly difficult to learn nonsense in the form of word pairs that simply don't make any sense. For such pairs, connection strengths have been driven toward zero during learning, or may even have become negative. At the same time, as the number of words that a speaker knows increases, such a speaker will perform with greater accuracy in the lexical decision task, but due to the greater complexity of her lexicon, this speaker will necessarily respond more slowly. The crucial point here is that response speed and accuracy in paired associate learning should not be considered in isolation, but rather in the context of the language system as a whole.
4. By-decade corpus size and by-decade frequency of *the* are highly correlated (r = 0.987), but a regression analysis with a quadratic polynomial supports a slight leveling-off of the counts for *the* for the more recent decades.

5. Ageism is also apparent in the claim that vocabulary size decreases with age, starting around the age of 40 (Singh-Manoux et al. 2012), which, as we have demonstrated above, is incorrect. Increased use of pronouns has also been taken to provide evidence of loss of cognitive skills (Hendriks et al. 2008). Below, we offer a very different perspective on this finding. The longer response times of the elderly in chronometric tasks would at first blush also suggest deteriorating performance, paralleling the hardships of the failing body in old age, until it is realized that their accuracy is so much higher. It is worth noting that declines in cognitive faculties as a consequence of neurodegenerative disease is correlated with age of retirement (Dufouil et al., 2014): the earlier the age of retirement is, the earlier the onset of dementia, consistent with the hypotheses of 'use it or lose it.' Under normal conditions of cognitive and social stimulation, there is no reason to suppose that mental capacities decline with age.

CHAPTER 3

Frequencies in Diachronic Corpora and Knowledge of Language

Martin Hilpert

3.1 Introduction

This chapter addresses the topic of frequency measurements in historical corpus linguistics. Its aim is to investigate what such measurements may reveal about the knowledge of language that speakers in earlier historical periods would have had. While it is by no means unusual for corpus-based studies of language change to report frequency values, it is less often the case that studies of this kind draw an explicit connection between measurements of corpus frequencies, on the one hand, and speakers' knowledge of language, on the other. It is easy to see why one should indeed be cautious in this regard: historical corpora tend to be small, limited to writing and strongly restricted in the varieties and text types they represent, so that extrapolating from such a corpus to the linguistic knowledge of a speaker may seem too much of a stretch. Considering that even with synchronic corpora, which are larger and more balanced, it is not a trivial matter to pin down the exact cognitive correlates of frequency (Blumenthal-Dramé 2012; Schmid and Küchenhoff 2013), there is all the more reason to be mindful of the limitations that are inherent in such an approach. Nonetheless, this chapter will, with all due caution, try to work out whether we can infer something about cognitive matters by looking at frequency data from historical corpora. This will be done through an overview that discusses what different aspects of frequency there are and how these can be measured in corpora. Importantly, frequency is not a single, unified phenomenon that could be measured in only one way and that would have only one cognitive correlate. In linguistics, the term 'frequency' is arguably most strongly associated with the idea of text frequency, because of the many studies that testify to its effects: the text frequency with which a linguistic item occurs is an important determinant of how early and how easily that item is learned, how strongly it is mentally represented, and how quickly it can be retrieved from memory, amongst other things (Ellis 2002; Bybee 2010). Yet, it is clear that frequency effects do not only emerge from high text frequency, but also from high type frequency (Bybee and Thompson 1997; de Jong et al. 2000), high frequency of co-occurrence (Jurafsky et al. 2001; Gries et al. 2005) and high frequency in the recent linguistic context (Szmrecsanyi 2006). There is now a sizable literature on frequency effects that also discusses the roles of relative frequency, transitional probabilities and perplexity (see for example the contributions in Gries and Divjak 2012). It will be the goal of this chapter to explore how what is known about frequency effects from psycholinguistic work can be fruitfully trans-ferred to the study of historical language change on the basis of diachronic corpora. The starting observation for the discussion is that many different types of frequency relate to cognitive matters, so that we need an overview. Going through several different types of frequency, this chapter will review psycholinguistic findings concerning their respective cognitive correlates, and will explain how the retrieval of such frequencies from historical corpora may advance our understanding of language change as a cogni-tively grounded phenomenon.

The following sections of this chapter will address five different types of frequency. The first three of these, (1) text frequency, (2) relative frequency and (3) type frequency, represent well-recognized concepts, even beyond corpus linguistics. The fourth type, (4) burstiness (or dispersion), is less regularly discussed in corpus linguistic studies. The fifth type, too, is a type of frequency that is not too well established but is increasingly being used in current corpus-based research. For want of a better term, this type of frequency will be referred to as (5) behavioral profile frequency for the remainder of this chapter.

This is the general plan of the next sections of the chapter. All types of frequency will be presented individually. For each type, we will discuss what is known about its cognitive correlates, what corpus linguistic meth-ods are used to measure it and, finally, how such measurements can be usefully applied to the cognitive study of language change.

3.2 Text Frequency

In recent years, diachronic corpora have established themselves as a useful tool for studying language change in real time. The spectrum of historical resources reaches from corpora such as the Helsinki corpus (Kytö 1991) to online applications such as Google's Ngram Viewer (Michel et al. 2011). A very common analytical use for these resources is the tracking of

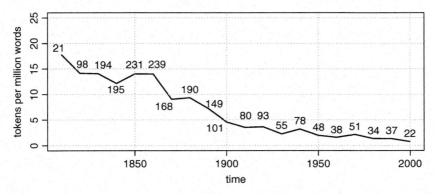

Figure 3.1 Text frequency decline of *for want of* in COHA.

normalized text frequency over time: given a linguistic unit, has this unit become more or less frequent? With a diachronic corpus such as the COHA, it takes a matter of seconds to investigate frequency developments such as, for example, the decline of the collocation *for want of*, which was used earlier in this chapter, in the set phrase *for want of a better term* (a literal paraphrase would be *because there is no better term*). Figure 3.1 illustrates the temporal dynamics of that change. The line shows normalized text frequencies. The raw token frequencies are shown as numbers above the line.

For many historical linguists, developments of this kind are actually interesting in themselves, regardless of any cognitive implications. If an item increases or decreases substantially in frequency, that signals a process of change in the language system, which can be investigated in complete detachment from its speakers and their cognition. However, since text frequency is associated with a range of cognitive correlates, even a simple measurement such as the one shown above has psychological repercussions. Based on what is known about the effects of text frequency in synchronic language use, it can be speculated that for speakers of English during the early nineteenth century, processing the string *for want of* was slightly different from what it is for present-day speakers.

Ellis (2002) presents a comprehensive overview of the effects that text frequency has on language processing. The list of affected domains that Ellis presents includes 'phonology, phonotactics, reading, spelling, lexis, morphosyntax, formulaic language, language comprehension, grammaticality, sentence production and syntax' (Ellis 2002: 143). The following discussion will concentrate on only three selected effects of text frequency:

chunking, entrenchment and conservation. The first of these concerns the mental representation of *for want of* as a unified whole, that is, a 'chunk'. The collocation *for want of* belongs to the set of formulaic word sequences that speakers learn and memorize as units. As a whole, the phrase conveys idiomatic, non-compositional meaning. Chunking is dependent on text frequency; that is, the more frequently a string of elements is processed together, the greater the likelihood that speakers do not decompose the string into its component parts but instead process it as a single unit (Bybee and Scheibman 1999; Bybee and Moder, this volume). A collocation such as *for want of a better term*, which occurs in present-day English with relatively high frequency, is thus quite likely to be processed holistically, as a single chunk. However, not all examples of *for want of* lend themselves equally well to this kind of holistic processing. The following examples, which are taken from the early decades of the COHA, offer an illustration.

(1)   a. Perhaps you suffer for want of good nursing.
      b. The others would not long be idle for want of employment.
      c. They can't get much education in the schools for want of knowing
         the language.

Compared to *for want of a better term*, these examples sound less familiar to present-day speakers of English. Since speakers hear phrases like *for want of knowing the language* relatively less often, they might be prompted to process them analytically, assigning separate meanings to *for, want, of,* and the elements that follow, before reaching a global interpretation. The COHA frequencies suggest that speakers of English during earlier times were more accustomed to hearing examples of this kind, and hence presumably had a greater disposition toward holistic processing. Conversely, collocations that have gained substantially in text frequency over the past two centuries, such as *get dressed, it's fun*, or *at the start*, are likely to be processed as chunks by today's speakers.

A second, closely related effect of text frequency is the strength with which a string such as *at the start* or *for want of* is represented in speakers' minds. This phenomenon is commonly discussed under the heading of entrenchment (Schmid 2010, to appear; Blumenthal-Dramé 2012). Highly entrenched items are processed more quickly and more accurately, and these effects can be explained as a direct consequence of a learning process that is fueled by repeated experience (Ellis 2002: 152, this volume). The data from the COHA indicate that speakers of nineteenth-century English were exposed to *for want of* at a higher rate, which again gives rise to the hypothesis that they would have processed the string with relatively greater efficacy.

A third consequence of high text frequency is what Bybee (2006: 715) has called the conserving effect of frequency. Note that the preposition *for* in *for want of* conveys the meaning of a cause, rather than a beneficiary (cf. Hundt and Leech 2012 on the decline of causal *for*). The noun *want* expresses the lack of something. Both of these word meanings are perceived as anachronistic by present-day speakers of English (see nineteenth-century examples such as *They breathed the easier for the news* or *Many was the time that want had come in at her door*). Whereas the words *for* and *want* by themselves only maintain very weak associations with these older meanings, the collocation *for want of* provides a niche in which those meanings are conserved, even in modern usage. Importantly, this kind of retention is an effect of high text frequency during earlier historical stages. If the text frequency of a complex linguistic unit leads to entrenchment, the characteristics of that unit may be preserved, even if structurally similar units are subject to change, and even if that unit itself becomes less frequent as time goes on. This phenomenon can be illustrated with idiomatic phrases that are relatively rare, but that nonetheless retain older syntactic patterns of English (examples from COHA):

(2)   a. Fret not, Phil, the world still is a safe place.
      b. Far be it from me to speak flippantly.
      c. Uneasy lies the head that wears a crown.

Whereas negative sentences in present-day English ordinarily require *do*-support (Huddleston and Pullum 2002: 93), phrases such as *Fret not* were frequent enough to be conserved as such. The phrase *far be it from me*, meaning 'Heaven forbid that I' includes a modally marked form of the present tense that can be found in a several other idiomatic phrases (*God save the Queen, So help me God*, etc.), but that is far more restricted, and much less frequent, than it was in earlier periods of English (Visser 1984: 795, §841). Similarly, the fronted use of an adjective with verb-second syntax that is seen in the third example is very much restricted in present-day English (cf. *?Happy came they home, ?Disappointed looked the players*).

In summary, text frequencies reflect how familiar speakers at a given historical stage would have been with a linguistic unit. More specifically, high text frequencies relate to the chunking of a complex unit, its strength of mental representation, and its potential to be conserved in the language system over longer periods of time. Corpora, needless to say, are partial and impoverished representations of language use, so that the text frequencies that are taken from corpora are only an approximation of the frequencies that actual speakers would have experienced.

3.3   Relative Frequency

Another type of measurement that is regularly found in historical corpus-based studies is the measurement of relative frequencies, that is, the frequency of one linguistic unit as compared to the frequency of another. Figure 3.2, which is based on data from the TIME Magazine corpus (*TIME*), offers an example. It shows the increasing market share of aspectual *keep V-ing* against the background of all other uses of the verb *keep* (Hilpert and Gries 2009). The y-axis represents 100 percent of all uses of *keep*, and over time, *keep V-ing* takes up an increasingly larger share. The line shows the relative frequency development; the raw token frequencies are shown in the numbers above the line.

Again, relative frequencies are routinely reported by researchers who do not mean to touch on cognitive matters. Changes in relative frequencies can be used to describe changes in a language system without making reference to psychological phenomena. However, measurements of relative frequencies typically have an underlying psychological assumption, namely that the two or more forms that are being compared form part of a single cognitive category in the minds of speakers. Hence, the display of the frequency development of *keep V-ing* in Figure 3.2 suggests that some relation between grammatical *keep V-ing* and other, lexical uses of *keep* is tacitly assumed. The fact that *keep V-ing* increases its market share would then indicate that in the overarching category that mentally represents the

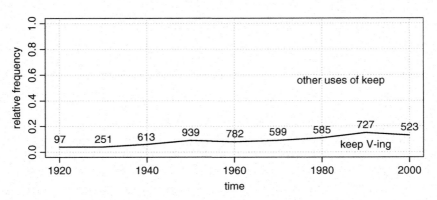

Figure 3.2 Relative frequency increase of *keep V-ing* in TIME.

Table 3.1 *Base and derivative frequencies*
of congruous *and* vulnerable *in the BNC*

	Congruous	Vulnerable
Base	6 (3.5%)	3,503 (60.5%)
Derivative with *in-*	166 (96.5%)	2,268 (39.5%)

verb *keep*, there has been some re-organization. Speakers today entertain somewhat stronger associative ties between *keep* and a verb in the *ing*-form than speakers used to do about a century ago.

In psycholinguistic work, effects of relative frequency have been demonstrated for example in the area of derivational morphology (Hay 2001). A cognitive process that is affected by relative frequency is the processing of words such as *incongruous* or *invulnerable*. Both of these words are composed of an adjectival stem and the negative prefix *in-*, but there is a crucial difference in the way speakers tend to process these words: While *incongruous* is processed holistically, as a simplex word, speakers tend to process *invulnerable* analytically, as a morphologically complex word. Hay presents evidence that naïve speakers, when asked to compare *incongruous* and *invulnerable*, judge the latter to be more complex, even though the morpheme count of the two words does not differ (Hay 2001: 1049). The explanation for these differing judgments lies in the relative frequencies of the respective bases and derivatives. Table 3.1 contrasts the base and derivative frequencies of *congruous* and *vulnerable* in the BNC. What can be seen is that the derivative *incongruous* has a very high relative frequency (shown in brackets) vis-à-vis its morphological base, meaning that speakers are much less likely to hear the word *congruous* on its own, rather than as a part of *incongruous*. The same is not true of *invulnerable*: The adjective *vulnerable* occurs more often on its own than as part of the derivative *invulnerable*.

The observation that the relative frequencies of words and their bases are implicated in the way that complex words are processed is immediately relevant for issues in language change. In particular, it concerns the development of non-compositional meanings, which can over time render complex words semantically opaque. A word such as *immediate*, despite its etymological origins as a complex word with a negative prefix (cf. *implausible*), is processed holistically. The same holds for *embellish* (cf. *empower*) or *tedious* (cf. *luxurious*). It is safe to say that present-day speakers of English do not connect these words to their respective bases *mediate, bellish* and *tedium*, which have made only fleeting appearances in the English lexicon. The likelihood of a derived word becoming opaque over time is related to the relative frequencies of the derivative and its base.

Hay (2001: 1057) gathers systematic support for this idea by analyzing dictionary entries for complex words with different relative frequency profiles. She measures semantic drift by checking whether a dictionary definition of a derivative, such as *dissatisfy*, contains the base word *satisfy*. In cases where the base does not appear (as for example in the entry of *encrust* in *Webster's Unabridged Dictionary*), semantic drift has applied. Hay's findings complement her experimental results, showing that complex forms that are more frequent than their bases are indeed more likely to undergo semantic drift.

Another aspect of relative frequency that makes it relevant for matters of both cognition and language change is its role in the probability of encountering a word in a given context, i.e. the conditional probability of a word. The probability of encountering a certain word in a text is dependent on the relative frequency of that word. For example, the determiner *the* accounts for a sizable share of the words in this book, so that readers are very likely to encounter and re-encounter it throughout the text. Importantly however, that likelihood is modulated by the immediate context, i.e. the neighboring elements of any given word in the text: after the words *This is an . . .*, the likelihood of *the* is close to zero, despite its high overall relative frequency. Conditional probabilities can be computed for words that follow a given element (*floor* in *hardwood floor*), words that precede a given element (*swivel* in *swivel chair*) and words that are surrounded by two given elements (*and* in *gin and tonic*). Jurafsky et al. (2001) show that high conditional probabilities predict effects of vowel reduction and shorter word duration in speech.

Reduction effects are thus not only a result of high text frequency (cf. Section 3.2). Even infrequent words may be reduced, as long as they are predictable enough. In environments where words are highly predictable, speakers subconsciously estimate that the risk of misunderstanding is low and therefore they permit themselves a less effortful pronunciation. Diachronically, this can lead to word coalescence and phonological erosion, as for example in *gonna, kinda* or *wouldya*.

To conclude this section, relative frequencies capture how often a linguistic unit appears, as compared to the appearance of a second linguistic unit. Relative frequencies are relevant to cognition insofar as the two linguistic units are assumed to stan in some sort of relation. In the first example that was discussed, both *keep V-ing* and other, lexical uses of *keep* can be thought of as belonging to an overarching category of the verb *keep*. The example of complex words (*incongruous*) and their bases (*congruous*) has shown that relative frequency reflects the strength of association between the two. If the relative frequency of the derivative is high, the strength of association is low: speakers are then likely to process the derivative holistically, that is, without recurrence to the base. This relation is quite central to studies of historical language change, as it pertains to the gradual emancipation of new words and constructions from their host structures. A complex word that is processed holistically and no longer with reference to its morphological base can take on new and different meanings. Hence, relative frequencies are important to studies of both lexicalization (Brinton and Traugott 2005) and grammaticalization (Hopper and Traugott 2003).

3.4 Type Frequency

The type frequency of a linguistic unit is measured as the number of different variants in which that unit appears in a given corpus. Type frequencies are commonly discussed as properties of derivational affixes. To illustrate, measuring the type frequency of the English nominalizing suffix *−ness* would require the researcher to search a corpus in order to retrieve all nouns ending in that suffix and to determine how many different nouns (*greatness, sweetness, softness,* etc.) there are. Similarly, it is possible to determine the type frequencies of particular syntactic patterns. An exhaustive retrieval of all ditransitive sentences (e.g. *John gave Mary the book, He sent me a postcard*) from a corpus will yield a type frequency count of all the different verbs (*give, send, promise,* etc.) that occur in the ditransitive construction.

Measurements of type frequencies are crucial for the study of productivity, that is, the statistical readiness with which speakers produce new variants of a linguistic unit (Mayerthaler 1981; van Marle 1985). Speakers regularly produce new formations with the suffix *−ness* (such as *over-the-top-ness*) or the ditransitive construction (*Please whatsapp me the photos asap!*), which is anecdotal evidence that these patterns are mentally represented as cognitive schemas that allow the addition of new types. In current corpus linguistic investigations of productivity, measures of type frequencies are typically complemented by counts of hapax legomena, i.e. forms that occur only once in the corpus that is used. Several hapax-based measures of productivity are described in Baayen (2005). The reason for examining hapax legomena is that highly productive schemas will lead speakers to produce neologisms, some of which will only be recorded once, even in a large corpus. A suffix or construction that exhibits a high ratio of hapaxes, relative to all tokens that are retrieved from the corpus, can thus be assumed to be highly productive.

Historically, the productivity of suffixes and constructions is subject to change. For instance, the suffix *–dom*, which has given rise to words such as *freedom* or *wisdom*, is no longer used by speakers of present-day English to coin new words. The historical dynamics of productivity in word formation processes have been analyzed, for instance, by Anshen and Aronoff (1999), who relied on the *Oxford English Dictionary* (OED) to determine how many new types of words ending in *–ment* and *–ity* entered the English lexicon between 1300 and the year 2000. Anshen and Aronoff show that the rates of newly incoming types differ for the two affixes, which is consistent with the observation that *–ity* retains its productivity in present-day English, whereas the same is not true for *–ment* (1999: 22).

While the OED is a highly valuable resource for the study of changes in productivity, it has to be acknowledged that its coverage is very uneven across time, which may of course distort the results, and which by extension makes any conclusions about speakers' mental representations very difficult (cf. Gardner 2014). The same problem affects many historical corpora, insofar as the amount of data and the composition of the data may differ from period to period. Several solutions have been proposed to alleviate these problems.

Gaeta and Ricca (2006) advocate the use of historical corpus samples that are matched in size. This solution is very practical, but it may force the researcher to ignore large proportions of the available data. Hilpert (2013: 133) suggests that one of Baayen's hapax-based measures of productivity, namely expanding productivity, could be used. This measure determines how many hapaxes with a particular affix there are in a given subperiod of a corpus, and compares that figure against the total number of hapax legomena in that subcorpus. What this captures is how much the affix under analysis contributes to overall vocabulary growth. Säily (2014: 239) argues that hapax-based measures of productivity do not yield reliable results in small corpora, and she therefore advocates a measure that relies on type frequency counts and permutation testing. Säily's approach is based on type accumulation curves that show the gradual increase of type frequency across the running words of a corpus. An illustration of this is offered in Figure 3.3. The black line in Figure 3.3 shows the type accumulation curve of formations with *–ity* in a 1.4-million-word sample of the British National Corpus. Each tick mark represents the addition of a new

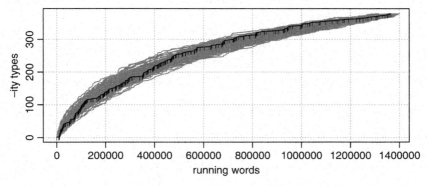

Figure 3.3 A type accumulation curve of formations with *–ity* in a BNC sample.

type such as *curiosity* or *serendipity*. What is apparent is that the density of tickmarks decreases with increasing size of the corpus.

Around the black line, there are 100 overplotted gray lines that represent type accumulation curves from the same BNC sample in which the order of corpus files has been randomly rearranged. The texts are the same, but for each line, the sequence in which they are processed is different. Since not all texts contain the same amount of *–ity* types, some permutations lead to a quicker accumulation of types, whereas other permutations slow down the process. Once all texts are processed, the lines converge on the grand total of 379 *–ity* types, in the upper right corner of the graph. Säily (2014: 55) computes up to a million random type accumulation curves, which allows her to determine whether in a specific subpart of the corpus, formations with *–ity* are significantly underrepresented or overrepresented. The further away a given subcorpus is from the center of the gray lines, the more unusual it is. For instance, the spread of the gray lines in Figure 3.3 shows that a 400,000-word subpart of the corpus should, on average, contain between 200 and 250 different *ity*-types. If we come across a 400,000-word sample with more than 300 types, we can conclude that there is significant overuse. Säily applies this logic to historical data, showing for example that the productivity of *–ity* underwent a significant increase in seventeeth-century English letter writing (2014: 85). She further shows that in Early Modern English, men are more prolific users of *–ity* formations than are women (2014: 78).

In the light of what the preceding paragraphs have discussed, type frequencies and hapax legomena are intimately related to the mental representations of linguistic schemas that speakers have at their disposal for the formation of new coinages and phrasings. The fact that there are multiple ways of measuring productivity already suggests that the exact cognitive correlates of high type frequencies or high hapax ratios are hard to determine, but experimental evidence has been adduced to triangulate between corpus frequencies and the corresponding cognitive processes (e.g. Baayen 1994). Using historical corpus data in order to make inferences about productivity during earlier stages of English is an extremely challenging task, but also here, there are successes we can point to.

3.5   Burstiness/Dispersion

The terms 'burstiness' and 'dispersion' are closely related. Both terms will be treated together in this section, since both refer to the way in which a word is distributed across the text of a corpus. The dispersion of a linguistic unit reflects how evenly it is distributed across the parts of a corpus. If a corpus is divided up into 1,000-word chunks, how many of those contain the unit in question? The burstiness of a linguistic unit captures how regular the intervals are at which the unit appears in a running text. Items with high burstiness appear in dense groups, i.e. 'bursts', at unpredictable intervals. If such a word appears once in a text, chances are high that it will appear again soon, perhaps already in the next sentence, but after a few such occurrences it could be completely absent from the next fifty pages. Once five sentences have gone by without any occurrence of the word, the burst can be assumed to be over. By contrast, items with low burstiness occur regularly and individually at dependable intervals. They are the steady linguistic companions of any speaker or writer.

Figure 3.4 shows that words with very similar frequencies may in fact differ substantially with regard to their burstiness. The four words that are compared are the conjunction *whether*, the preposition *without*, the common noun *council* and the proper noun *London*. The graphs are based on 1.4 million running words from the BNC.

Even to the naked eye, it is apparent that the words in the upper two panels are more evenly distributed across the text than the words in the two lower panels, even though those words have approximately the same text frequencies. In particular, the noun *council* shows nice bursts that alternate with relatively long lulls. Several statistical measurements have been proposed with regard to the quantification of burstiness and dispersion (Gries 2008; Altmann et al. 2009). As a type of frequency, burstiness is not discussed extensively in the linguistic literature on frequency effects. Gries (2010: 197) comments that 'despite the relevance of dispersion for

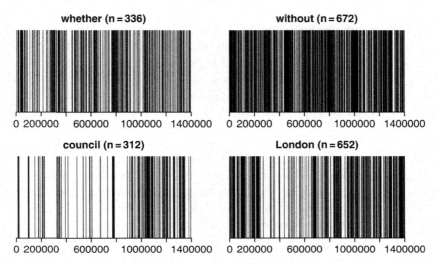

Figure 3.4 Burstiness of four different words in a BNC sample.

virtually all corpus linguistic work, it is still a very much under-researched topic'. Gries further points out that the effects of text frequency, some of which were discussed above, are modulated by burstiness (2010: 198). It is unwarranted to assume that words such as *whether* and *council* will show the same text frequency effects in language processing because the more even recurrence of *whether* has an effect on how easily that word is learned, how familiar it is, how strongly it primes itself, etc. Effects of burstiness on latencies in word naming and lexical decision tasks have been documented by Adelman et al. (2006).

Dispersion can be measured in several different ways. Gries (2008) offers an overview and proposes a measure that he calls deviation of proportions (DP), which is briefly discussed here as an illustration. In order to compute DP, a corpus is first divided into several parts. There is no need for these parts to be equal in size. For example, given a corpus of 1,400,000 words, a first corpus part might hold 7,000 words (0.5 percent), a second part 14,000 words (1 percent) and so on. The linguistic element for which DP is computed (say, *London* or *council*) has to be chosen, and its frequencies have to be determined for the whole corpus and for all the corpus parts. For all corpus parts, observed and expected percentages are compared, and the differences are summed up. Finally, the sum of all differences is divided by two. If DP is calculated in this way, it yields values between 0 and 1, where o indicates a perfectly even dispersion (every corpus part contains the expected number of tokens) and 1 indicates a maximally uneven dispersion (no corpus part contains the expected number of tokens).

Differences in burstiness, such as between *without* (low) and *London* (high), have further been linked to semantic differences, specifically to a hierarchy of increasingly abstract meanings (Pierrehumbert 2012: 104). The more abstract the meaning of a word is, the lower its degree of burstiness. The explanation for this is straightforward: the more general the meaning of a word is, the more contexts are available for its use, and the more regular are its appearances. Altmann et al. (2009: 5) contrast four different types of words (entities, predicates, modifiers and high-level operators) and find that with increasing abstractness, burstiness recedes. However, this effect is mitigated by text frequency. Differences in burstiness are more pronounced in low-frequency items, whereas for highly frequent items, which are less bursty in general, differences in abstractness do not yield a strong effect. Pierrehumbert (2012) follows up on this result, investigating the burstiness of word pairs such as *discuss* and *discussion*. She finds that in a comparison of simplex verbs and derived, de-verbal nouns, the nouns exhibit systematically higher burstiness values. This is explained as a consequence of more specific meanings that develop in the derived nouns. For instance, the derived noun *evolution* has acquired the sense of a scientific theory that is not inherent in the verb *evolve* (2012: 113).

From the perspective of historical linguistics, the relation between reduced burstiness and more abstract meanings is extremely intriguing, not least because grammaticalizing elements are known to undergo semantic changes that commonly involve the 'bleaching' of specific lexical meanings, as in the case of future markers that derive from verbs of coming or going (Hilpert 2008). Conversely, Pierrehumbert's results with regard to derived nouns can be interpreted as the result of lexicalization, in which more-specific meanings develop.

Currently, there appears to be a research gap with regard to the historical dynamics of burstiness. It would be very rewarding to analyze how grammaticalizing forms develop with regard to their burstiness. Gries (2008: 421) shows that the most evenly distributed elements in a BNC sample are highly grammaticalized elements such as determiners, forms of the copula, the negator *not* and deictic elements such as *there*. A plausible prediction would be that grammaticalizing units such as *be going to* show a diachronic decrease in burstiness as they become usable across an increasingly wider set of contexts.

By contrast, lexical elements should not exhibit systematic decreases in burstiness, as on the whole, semantic narrowing and semantic broadening are equally possible career paths for lexical items. Of course, the leveling effect of high text frequency would have to be accounted for in such analyses. Elements that gain in text frequency are, because of that very fact, likely to decrease in burstiness. Another avenue of research might investigate synchronic differences in burstiness between grammatical items and their lexical counterparts, such as the pair of *keep V-ing* and lexical *keep* that was discussed above. Here, the prediction would be that the lexical sources should be relatively more bursty than their grammaticalizing off-shoots, when we control for frequency differences. Applying burstiness measures to the analysis of grammaticalizing and grammaticalized forms might open up the possibility of making grammaticalization more quanti-fiable, which would be a welcome development.

To put the preceding paragraphs into perspective, the dispersion of a linguistic unit captures how evenly it is distributed across the parts of a corpus, while its burstiness describes the regularity of the intervals with which it re-occurs in running text. Like text frequency, burstiness has an impact on the recognizability and processability of linguistic elements. It is furthermore related to meaning, in that more-abstract meanings are found in less-bursty elements. At present, the historical dynamics of burstiness has been only insufficiently addressed, so that further research into this area is called for.

3.6   Behavioral Profile Frequency

An important development in current diachronic corpus linguistics rests on the acknowledgment that variation is fundamental to all aspects of language use. Linguistic units typically have variants, and the speakers of a linguistic community diverge with respect to their experience with these variants. Among the first examples of this that may come to mind are pronunciation differences across different varieties of English, so that, for instance, in Canadian English, the preposition *about* can be pronounced as [əbɛʊt], rather than [əbʌʊt]. Variation can also be observed in the use of morphosyntactic constructions across different language varieties. The relative clause construction in the sentence *There's no-one does that anymore* may strike a speaker of Standard British English or American English as unusual, but subject relative clauses without relativizers are in fact judged as common in varieties such as Hong Kong English or Newfoundland English (Kortmann and Lunkenheimer 2013).

Variation in linguistic units is not limited to cross-varietal contexts, but also occurs within a single language variety, where constructions are routinely realized in different ways. There is variation in pronunciation, as in *going to* vs. *gonna*, and there is morphosyntactic variation. For instance, the sentence *That's the one that I want* expresses an idea that a speaker can also verbalize as the sentence *That's the one I want*. As will be discussed in more detail below, speakers' choices between such variants are guided by the morphosyntactic and pragmatic context in which an utterance is made. The bottom line of these observations is that the linguistic competence of speakers must include probabilistic knowledge of variation, that is, knowledge of the variants that instantiate a given linguistic unit, and knowledge of the contexts in which these variants are appropriately used. Variation can not only be observed in sychrony, but also diachronically, since the conventions of language use are gradually shifting. Hence, speakers' knowledge of linguistic units and their variants is subject to change. If diachronic corpus studies aim to model changes in speakers' linguistic knowledge, as much as possible of this variation has to be taken into account.

What does all of the above mean for the measurement of frequencies in historical corpus data? The idea that speakers build up mental representations of linguistic units and their variants requires that historical corpus linguists examine changes in the so-called behavioral profile of a linguistic unit. Gries and Divjak (2009: 61) define the term 'behavioral profile' as 'a comprehensive inventory of elements co-occurring with a word within the confines of a simple clause or sentence in actual speech and writing'. More broadly construed, the behavioral profile of a linguistic unit such as a presentational object relative clause (*That's the one that I want*) would be an inventory of features such as the ones that are presented in Figure 3.5 below, along with their respective text frequencies, type frequencies and frequencies of mutual co-occurrence.

These features include the presence or absence of the relativizer *that*, but also the pronominality of the subject in the relative clause (cf. *That's the one that John wants*), the type of presentational (*There's the one that I want*), the definiteness of the head (*That's a thing that I want*), the animacy of the head of the relative clause (*That's the man that I saw*) or the verb in the relative clause (*That's the one that I detest*). Not all configurations of these different features are equally likely in actual usage (Wiechmann 2015), so that certain configurations yield very idiomatic object relatives (*That's all I have to say*), whereas others are perceived as less common, though perhaps still acceptable (*That's a hat John wore*).

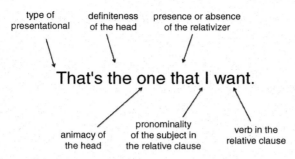

Figure 3.5 Features in the behavioral profile of presentational object relatives.

The fact that speakers entertain very rich and detailed mental representations of the behavioral profiles of syntactic constructions receives support from recent studies on the English dative alternation (Gries 2003; Bresnan 2007; Bresnan et al. 2007), which show that corpus-derived statistics capturing the likelihood of certain constructional variants correspond very closely to acceptability judgments that speakers make under controlled laboratory conditions. In a diachronic extension of this type of work, Wolk et al. (2013: 383) sum up this observation in the following words:

> [T]he likelihood of finding a particular linguistic variant in a particular context in a corpus can be shown to correspond to the intuitions that speakers have about the acceptability of that particular variant, given the same context.

Having heard and remembered hundreds and thousands of ditransitive sentences and prepositional datives over the course of their lifetimes, speakers know with great accuracy how likely it is for them to hear a given variant, such as, for instance, the ditransitive *I wrote him a long letter*, which includes the pronominal subject *I*, the verb *write*, a discourse-given recipient that is expressed through a pronoun (*him*), and an indefinite, three-word theme (*a long letter*). They also know that in the event of a non-given recipient and a short theme (*I wrote the responsible person at the university an email*), they would actually prefer a prepositional dative (*I wrote an email to the responsible person at the university*) over the ditransitive.

Given that behavioral profiles, derived from the frequencies of contextualized constructional variants in synchronic corpora, relate fairly directly to speakers' knowledge of language, it seems to be a viable option to extract behavioral profile frequencies from historical corpus data in order to investigate the grammatical knowledge of speakers who lived in the past. Wolk et al. propose to do exactly this (2013: 384):

> [O]ur work ultimately aims to aspects of the linguistic knowledge that writers in the Late Modern English period must have had, and how this knowledge has evolved over time.

Specifically, Wolk et al. investigate diachronic variability in the dative alternation in the ARCHER corpus, probing whether the probabilistic factors that lead present-day speakers to choose either the ditransitive or the prepositional dative are also active during Late Modern English. The behavioral profiles that Wolk et al. establish for the ditransitive construction and the prepositional dative include factors such as the animacy of the recipient, the length of theme and recipient, and the definiteness of theme and recipient. A mixed-effects logistic regression analysis (Gries 2015), with the choice between the two constructions as the dependent variable and the factors in the behavioral profiles as independent variables, establishes that speakers during Late Modern English used the two constructions according to contextual factors that are very similar to the ones that govern present-day usage (2013: 403). However, there is also evidence of change in speakers' probabilistic knowledge. For instance, ditransitive sentences with inanimate recipients have become more acceptable in the twentieth century.

In a methodologically similar study, Hilpert (2013) investigates diachronic variation in possessive determiner usage in Early Modern English, specifically the alternatives between *mine* / *thine* and their successors *my* / *thy*. Over time, the modern variants oust the older ones, so that there is a shift in relative frequencies that goes to completion. The linguistic knowledge of present-day speakers thus contains a fixed pattern (always use *my*) whereas the knowledge of earlier generations would have been variable and probabilistic (use *my* in context A, use *mine* in context B). A leading question in the investigation of this variability is whether *mine* and *thine* gave way to their respective successors in the same way, at the same time, or if first-person and second-person forms developed in independent ways. In other words, are the behavioral profiles of *mine* and *thine* changing in comparable ways? In order to find that out, Hilpert annotated the uses of possessive determiners in the Corpus of Early English Correspondence (CEEC) for the following language-internal and -external factors:

- the phonological quality of the following word (whether the onset is a consonant, an /h/ or a vowel)

- the prosody of the context (whether the following syllable is stressed or unstressed)
- priming (whether the *n*-less variant occurs in the left context)
- formality (whether the text belongs to a formal or informal genre)
- the writer's gender (female, male, unknown)
- the grammatical person (first person, second person)
- the relative frequency of the following word (Words such as *own* are relatively frequent collocates of possessive determiners; words such as *old* are found less often.)
- the time period during which the text was produced

The respective influences of these factors are assessed through a mixed-effects logistic regression analysis that models the choice between the *n*-variant and the incoming *n*-less variant as a function of all factors and their interactions. Hilpert (2013: 98) finds main effects for all of the listed variables except for the factor person. The insignificance of the latter variable allows the conclusion that speakers of Early Modern English formed a generalization over *mine* and *thine*. Importantly, the variable of time interacts with the factors of the following segment, stress and the relative frequency of the following word. This indicates that the impact of these variables has changed over time, and that a change in speakers' probabilistic knowledge of language has taken place. For example, for speakers with a variable system of *my* and *mine*, a following word that begins in a consonant, such as *father*, used to tip the scale toward the *n*-less variant. This effect is historically dynamic: it was strongest during earlier periods of the CEEC and eventually leveled off, as the *n*-less variant established itself as the default choice.

The cautiously optimistic conclusion that can be drawn from studies of this kind is that frequencies of contextualized constructional variants, which have been called 'behavioral profile frequencies' in this section, can be used to make inferences about the linguistic knowledge of speakers who lived in a relatively distant past. The crucial twist that the analysis of behavioral profile frequencies brings about is that corpus frequencies and frequency changes are not studied in themselves, but rather relative to speakers' choices between alternative linguistic units. As Szmrecsanyi (2013) points out, this approach serves to 'move diachronic corpus analysis beyond mere frequency analysis, exploring instead more or less subtle changes in the probabilistic conditioning of grammatical variation in the course of time'. With regard to frequencies in diachronic corpora and their cognitive correlates, the study of behavioral profiles is thus opening up new ways of using frequency data.

3.7 Concluding Remarks

To summarize the main point of this chapter, the common theme that unites current psycholinguistic research on frequency and historical, corpus-linguistic approaches to frequency is the assumption that language use shapes speakers' knowledge of language and is at the same time an expression of that knowledge (Bybee 2010). To the extent that diachronic corpus linguists aim to investigate cognitive aspects of earlier generations of speakers, they are dependent on psycholinguists' assessments of how frequency of use and the mental representation of linguistic units are related. This relation is multifaceted it cannot be reduced to the correspondence of high text frequency and cognitive entrenchment.

This chapter has surveyed five different expressions of frequency – text frequency, relative frequency, type frequency, burstiness and behavioral profile frequency – and it has discussed a range of cognitive correlates of these frequency types, as well as ways of applying these notions to the analysis of language change. Taking a step back, what this overview suggests is that diachronic corpus linguists need to adopt a more inclusive approach that takes different kinds of frequencies into account, notably frequency types such as burstiness or behavioral profile frequencies, which up till now have not received the attention that they deserve. Another conclusion that can be drawn is that the psycholinguistic study of frequency effects is by no means a fully completed enterprise. For example, Adelman et al. (2006) argue that speedy word recognition, a putative effect of text frequency, is more adequately attributed to even dispersion. Piantidosi et al. (2011) challenge the classic Zipfian idea that word length is a function of word frequency, and instead propose an explanation in terms of informativity. In other words, the ground is shifting under our feet, and it will become necessary to re-assess the way we look at frequency as new findings emerge. All of this is, however, cause for optimism rather than pessimism. As diachronic corpus linguistics will become more well-informed with regard to psycholinguistic insights, we will discover not only limitations, but also new possibilities.

PART II

Salience

CHAPTER 4

Salience in Language Usage, Learning and Change

Nick C. Ellis

4.1 Salience in Psychology, Learning Theory and Psycholinguistics

Psychological research uses the term 'salience' to refer to the property of a stimulus to stand out from the rest. Salient items or features are attended, are more likely to be perceived and are more likely than others to enter into subsequent cognitive processing and learning. Salience can be independently determined by physics and the environment and by our knowledge of the world. It is useful to think of three aspects of salience, one relating to psychophysics and the other two to what we have learned:

1 The physical world, our embodiment and our sensory systems come together to cause certain sensations to be more intense (louder, brighter, heavier, etc.) than others. These phenomena are the subject of research in psychophysics (Gescheider 2013).

2 As we experience the world, we learn from it, and our resultant knowledge values some associations more heavily than others. We know that some stimulus cues are associated with outcomes or possibilities that are important to us, while others are negligible (James 1890a chapter 11; Gibson 1977).

3 We also have expectations about what is going to happen next in known contexts, we are surprised when our expectations are violated and we pay more attention as a result. These phenomena are the subject of research in associative learning and cognition (Anderson 2009; Shanks 1995).

4.1.1 Three Aspects of Salience

4.1.1.1 Psychophysical Salience

Loud noises, bright lights and moving stimuli capture our attention. Salience arises in sensory data from contrasts between items and their context. These stimuli deliver intense signals in the psychophysics of our data-driven perception. Stimuli with unique features compared to those of their neighbors (Os in a field of Ts, a red poppy in a field of yellow), 'pop out' from the scene, whereas they will not in a context of shared features (Os among Qs) (Treisman and Gelade 1980). These are aspects of bottom-up processing (Shiffrin and Schneider 1977).

4.1.1.2   Salient Associations

Attention can also be driven by top-down, memory-dependent, expectation-driven processing. Emotional, cognitive and motivational factors affect the salience of stimuli. These associations make a stimulus cue 'dear'. A loved one stands out from the crowd, as does a stimulus with weighty associations ($500,000.00 vs. $0.000005, however similar the amount of pixels, characters or ink in their sensation), or one which matches a motivational state (a meal when hungry, but not when full). The units of perception are influenced by prior association: 'The chief cerebral conditions of perception are the paths of association irradiating from the sense-impression, which may have been already formed' (James 1890b: 82). Psychological salience is hugely experience-dependent: *hotdog*, *sushi* and 寿司 mean different things to people of different cultural and linguistic experience. This is why, *contra* sensation, the units of perception cannot be measured in physical terms. They are subjective. Hence George Miller's definition of the units of short-term memory as 'chunks': 'We are dealing here with a process of organizing or grouping the input into familiar units or chunks, and a great deal of learning has gone into the formation of these familiar units' (Miller 1956: 91; see also Chapter 6 of this volume).

4.1.1.3   Context and Surprisal

The evolutionary role of cognition is to predict what is going to happen next. Anticipation affords survival value. The Rational Analysis of Cognition (Anderson 1990, 1991) is guided by the principle that human psychology can be understood in terms of the operation of a mechanism that is 'optimally adapted' to its environment in the sense that the behavior of the mechanism is as efficient as it conceivably could be, given the structure of the problem space and the input-output mappings it must solve. We find structure in time (Elman 1990). The brain is a prediction machine (Clark 2013). One consequence is that it is surprisal, when prediction goes wrong, that maximally drives learning from a single trial. Otherwise, the regularities of the usual course of our experiences sum little by little, trial after trial, to drive our expectations. Cognition is probabilistic, its expectations a conspiracy tuned from statistical learning over our experiences (see this volume, Chapters 2 and 3 on frequency and Chapter 6 on chunking).

4.1.2   Salience and Learning

Rescorla and Wagner (1972) presented a formal model of conditioning which expresses the capacity of any cue (conditioned stimulus (CS); for example, a bell in Pavlovian conditioning) to become associated with an outcome (unconditioned stimulus (US); for example, food in Pavlovian conditioning) on any given experience of their pairing. This formula unified over the course of eighty years' research in associative learning, and it elegantly encapsulates the three factors of psychophysical salience, psychological importance and surprisal. The role of US surprise and of CS and US salience in the process of conditioning can be summarized as follows:

$$dV = ab(L - V).$$

The associative strength of the US to the CS is referred to by the letter V, and the change in this strength which occurs on each trial of conditioning is called dV. On the right-hand side, a is the salience of the US, b is the salience of the CS and L is the amount of processing given to a completely unpredicted US. So the salience of the cue and the psychological importance of the outcome are essential factors in any associative learning. As for $(L - V)$, the more a CS is associated with a US, the less additional association the US can induce: 'But habit is a great deadener' (Beckett 1954). Alternatively, with novel associations where V is close to zero, there is much surprisal, and consequently much learning.

This is arguably the most influential formula in the history of learning theory. Physical salience, psychological salience and expectation/surprisal all affect what we learn from our experiences of the world. These factors affect what we learn about language from our language usage too, because linguistic constructions as symbolic form-function pairings are cue-outcome associations (de Saussure 1916; Bates and MacWhinney 1987a; Ellis 2006a; Robinson and Ellis 2008). Linguistic constructions as symbolic units relate the defining properties of their morphological, syntactic and lexical form with particular semantic, pragmatic and discourse functions (Goldberg 1995; Tomasello 2003; Trousdale and Hoffmann 2013).

4.1.3   Measurement and Methodology

4.1.3.1   Psychophysical Salience

Measuring the sensory/psychophysical salience of the linguistic form involves the physical factors that determine how easy it is to hear a particular structure. In his landmark study of first language acquisition, Brown breaks down the measurement of perceptual salience, or 'clarity of acoustical marking' (1973: 343), into 'such variables as amount of phonetic substance, stress level, usual serial position in a sentence, and so on' (1973: 463). Slobin (1973) proposed operating principles for child L1 acquisition suggesting that word-final morphemes are particularly salient. This resonates with the general serial-position curve relating memory to serial position, where items at the beginning and end of a list are preferentially recalled (Greene 1986).

Many grammatical form-function relationships in English, like those associated with grammatical particles and inflections such as the third-person singular -s, are of low salience in the language stream. This is illustrated in my companion Chapter 6 (in this volume) on chunking, in Figure 6.2, panel 2. The reason for this is the well-documented effect of frequency and entrenchment in the evolution of language: grammaticalized morphemes tend to become more phonologically fused with surrounding material because their frequent production leads to lenition processes, resulting in the loss and erosion of gestures (Zuraw 2003; Jurafsky et al. 2001; Bybee 2003, 2010; Bybee and Moder, Chapter 7 of this volume). As Slobin (1992: 191) put it, 'Somehow it's hard to keep languages from getting blurry: speakers seem to "smudge" phonology wherever possible, to delete and contract surface forms, and so forth.'

The basic principles of automatization that apply to all kinds of motor activities and skills (like playing a musical instrument, playing a sport, or cooking) are that, through repetition, sequences of units that were previously independent come to be processed as a single unit or chunk (Ellis 1996, Chapter 6 of this volume). The more frequently speakers use a form, the more they abbreviate it: this is a law-like relationship across languages (Zipf 1935). Zipf (1949) summarized this in the *principle of least effort* – speakers want to minimize articulatory effort and hence encourage brevity and phonological reduction. They tend to choose the most frequent words, and the more they use them, the more automatization of production causes their shortening. Frequently used words become shorter with use.

Grammatical functors are the most frequently used words of a language. In informal and rapid speech, this tendency to give short shrift to function words and bound morphemes, exploiting their frequency and predictability, deforms their phonetic structure and blurs the boundaries between these morphemes and the words that surround them. Of the strong syllables in a corpus examined by Cutler and Carter (1987), 86 percent occurred in open-class words and only 14 percent in closed-class words. The pattern was reversed for weak syllables, with 72 percent in closed-class words and 28 percent in open-class words.

Clitics, accent-less words or particles that depend accentually on an adjacent accented word and form a prosodic unit together with it, are the extreme examples of this: the /s/ of 'he's', /l/ of 'I'll' and /v/ of 'I've' can never be pronounced in isolation. Thus, grammatical function words and bound inflections tend to be short and low in stress, even in speech that is produced slowly and deliberately (Bates and Goodman 1997) and in speech directed to children (Goodman et al. 1990), with the result that these cues are difficult to perceive. When grammatical function words (*by, for, no, you*, etc.) are clipped out of connected speech and presented in isolation at levels where their open-class equivalents (*buy, four, know, ewe*, etc.) are perceived 90 to 100 percent correctly, adult native speakers can recognize them only 40 to 50 percent of the time (Herron and Bates 1997).

Thus, grammatical functors are extremely difficult to perceive from bottom-up evidence alone. Fluent language processors can perceive these elements in continuous speech because their language knowledge provides top-down support. But this is exactly the knowledge that learners lack. It is not surprising, therefore, that in L1 acquisition young children are unable to acquire grammatical forms until they have a critical mass of content words, providing enough top-down structure to permit perception and learning of those closed-class items that occur to the right or left of 'real words' (Bates and Goodman 1997: 51–52). As we will discuss in Section 4.2.3, the low salience of these forms is even more telling for second language learners.

4.1.3.2   Salient Associations
Measuring the psychological salience of linguistic forms is a difficult matter. It is subjective. However, we might start from William James's observations that

> Every nameable thing, act, or relation has numerous properties, qualities, or aspects. In our minds the properties of each thing, together with its name, form an associated group. If different parts of the brain are severally concerned with the several properties and a farther part with the hearing, and still another with the uttering, of the name, there must inevitably be brought about (through the law of association which we shall later study) such

a dynamic connection among all these brain-parts that the activity of any one of them will be likely to awaken the activity of all the rest (James 1890a: 55)

and then try and measure the richness and reliability of association.

Early psychological efforts to measure meaning in these terms (e.g. Osgood 1957) can seem naïve in their focus upon individual lexical items presented out of context. They lack any linguistic analysis of phrasal meaning, sentence-level meaning, pragmatics or usage (Levinson 1995; Lyons 1995; Sinclair 1996). Nevertheless, they provide a starting point. A pioneer was Paivio (1971, 1986), who gathered ratings for words on dimensions of meaningfulness, imageability and concreteness, and then investigated the degree to which these factors affected the learning and memory for words. His ratings were guided by the operationalization that

> The psychological meaning of a stimulus pattern is defined by the total set of reactions typically evoked by it. The reactions may be verbal or nonverbal, so that the potential meaning reactions to a word would include word associations, referent images, non-verbal motor reactions, and affective reactions. (Paivio 1986: 120–121)

His measurement of imagery instructed participants that

> Nouns differ in their capacity to arouse mental images of things or events. Some words arouse a sensory experience, such as a mental picture or sound very quickly and easily ... Any word which, in your estimation, arouses a mental image (i.e. a mental picture or sound, or other sensory experience) very quickly and easily should be given a high imagery rating. (Paivio et al. 1968: 4)

He showed that when people are asked to learn lists of words, the greater the imageability of a word, i.e. the degree to which it arouses a mental image, the more likely it is to be learned and recalled.

Another way of operationalizing the definition of meaning is to measure the 'ease of predication' of the word, i.e. the ease with which what the word refers to 'can be described by simple factual statements' (e.g. a *dog* is a type of animal, a *dog* barks when angry, a *dog* has four legs, a *dog* wags its tail when pleased, a *dog* often lives in a kennel, etc., *vs.* an *idea* . . ., Jones 1985). When Jones (1985) had subjects rate 125 nouns for ease of predication, there was a high correlation ($r = 0.88$) between this measure and imageability as measured by Paivio. Predication time (the mean number of seconds taken to produce two predicates for each word) correlated $r = -0.72$ with imageability (Jones 1988).

Paivio (1971, 1986) developed 'Dual Coding Theory' as an explanation of such findings. In this model, abstract words (words of low imageability and concreteness) have only verbal semantic representations in memory, and only these representations and those for concepts associated in meaning are accessed and activated following an episode of exposure to the word. In contrast, words with high imageability are represented not only in this semantic system but also in an imagery code, as 'sensory images awakened' (James 1890a: 265). 'Concrete terms such as *house* readily evoke both images and words as associative (meaning) reactions, whereas abstract words such as *truth* more readily arouse only verbal associations. The meaning of the latter is primarily intraverbal' (Paivio 1971: 85). His model and his method were quite remarkable, given their roots in behaviorist times. These ideas live on in more modern theories of perceptual symbol systems and grounded cognition (Barsalou 1999, 2008; Bergen and Chang 2013; Lakoff 1987). The idea is illustrated in my Chapter 6 on chunking, in Figure 6.2, panel 4. Cognitive neuropsychological studies confirm the dissociation of imagery and verbal representational systems in cases of agnosia (Warrington 1975). Brain imaging studies confirm how words evoke different modalities of imagery in different regions of the brain (Mitchell et al. 2008; Pulvermüller 1999).

Whatever you might want to add to an operationalization of salience, in terms of individual psychology regarding emotional content, physiological response, subjective report or whatever, or in terms of linguistic theory relating to phrasal meaning, sentence-level meaning, discourse meaning, pragmatics or usage, or whatever, is almost certainly sensible. But these face-valid and fairly simple methods at least allow us a start at measuring the psychological salience of linguistic items in terms of concreteness, imageability and reliability of interpretation.

4.1.3.3   Context and Surprisal

We automatically acquire knowledge of common sequences of events through implicit learning. There is considerable psychological research demonstrating that humans have dissociable, complementary systems for implicit and explicit learning and memory. Explicit learning involves attention and awareness and the generation and testing of hypotheses in a search for understanding. It is the conscious learning that we associate with education and the schoolroom. Implicit learning, in contrast, is the acquisition of knowledge about the underlying structure of a complex stimulus environment by a process which takes place naturally, automatically and without conscious operations.

It happens throughout our waking life. Simple attention to the stimulus suffices for implicit learning mechanisms to induce statistical or systematic regularities in the input environment (Ellis 1994b; Reber 1993; Stadler and Frensch 1998; Rebuschat 2015). Much of the research concentrates upon the implicit learning of sequences of behaviors (Cleeremans and McClelland 1991; Reber and Squire 1998), tones (Aslin and Newport 2012; Saffran et al. 1999) or artificial grammars (Reber et al. 1980), and these experiments show that from repeated experience of sequential behavior, learners automatically acquire knowledge of the underlying patterns of sequential dependencies. From infancy onward, our unconscious learning systems come to predict what is likely to happen next.

Psycholinguistic research demonstrates that language users have tremendous knowledge of the sequential patterns of language at all levels (Ellis 1996, Chapter 6 this volume), despite their never having consciously counted any of these statistics in their language usage. This is true of child language learners, too (Ambridge et al. 2015). The frequency tuning under consideration here is 'computed' automatically by the learner's system during language usage. The statistics are implicitly learned and implicitly stored (Ellis 2002); learners do not have conscious access to them. Nevertheless, every moment of language cognition is informed by these data, as language learners use their model of usage to understand the actual usage of the moment as well as to update their model and predict where it is going next.

Much of the time, language processing, like walking, operates successfully using automatized, implicit processes. We only think about walking when it goes wrong, when we stumble, and conscious processes are called in to deal with the unexpected. From that episode we might learn where the uneven patch of sidewalk is, so that we will not fall again. Similarly, when language processing falters and we do not understand, we call the multi-modal resources of consciousness to help deal with the novelty. Processing becomes deliberate and slow as we 'think things through'. This one-off act of conscious processing, too, can seed the acquisition of novel explicit form-meaning associations (Ellis 2005). It allows us to consolidate new constructions as episodic 'fast-mapped' cross-modal associations (Carey and Bartlett 1978). These representations are then also available as units of implicit learning in subsequent processing. Broadly, it is not until a representation has been noticed and consolidated that the strength of that representation can thereafter be tuned implicitly during subsequent processing (Ellis 2006a, 2006b); thus, the role of noticing and consciousness in language learning (Ellis 1994b; Schmidt 1994).

Surprisal is inversely related to probability. Research operationalizations of surprisal in language involve computing norms in corpora of usage and then looking for violations of those norms. The simplest possible case is the unconditional probability (i.e. relative frequency) of, say, a word in a corpus. '*The* ... ' is less surprising than is '*Discombobulate* ... '. A slightly more complex example is a simple forward transitional probability such as the probability of the word *y* directly following the word *x* (compare '*strong tea*', '*strong computers*', '*powerful tea*', '*powerful computers*') or a conditional probability such as the probability of a particular verb, given a construction ('*give*' is much more likely in a ditransitive than is '*kick*') (Gries and Stefanowitsch, 2004). Gries and Ellis (2015) review such measures. More complex applications include the conditional probability of a word, given several previous words in the same sentence or, to include a syntactic example, the conditional probability of a particular parse tree, given all previous words in a sentence (Hale 2011; Demberg and Keller 2008; Hale 2004; see also Chapter 3 in this volume on the different types of frequency effect).

Boo! However one measures the phenomenon, surprisal calls attention, and attention triggers learning. Surprise is consciousness kicking in. Consciousness is the interface (Ellis 2005). 'Paying attention – becoming conscious of some material – seems to be the sovereign remedy for learning anything, applicable to many very different kinds of information. It is the universal solvent of the mind' (Baars 1997, Section 5).

4.1.4 Acquisition and Processing

4.1.4.1 Psychophysical Salience

For first language acquisition, Brown concluded that 'some role for salience is guaranteed; the child will not learn what he cannot hear' (1973: 463), and that as a determinant of learning, salience is more important than frequency of experience. Pye (1980) found that perceptual salience, 'defined in terms of susceptibility to word and sentence stress and lack of disjuncture caused by a syllable boundary' (1980: 58), was the best predictor of children's order of acquisition of person markers in Quiche Mayan.

Goldschneider and DeKeyser (2001) performed a detailed meta-analysis of the 'morpheme order studies' that, in the 25 years following Brown's (1973) descriptions of first language acquisition, investigated the order of second language (L2) acquisition of the grammatical functors, progressive *-ing*, plural *-s*, possessive *-s*, articles *a, an, the*, third-person singular present *-s* and regular past *–ed*. These studies show remarkable commonality in the orders of acquisition of these functors across a wide range of learners of English as a second language (ESL). The meta-analysis investigated whether a combination of five determinants (perceptual salience, semantic complexity, morphophonological regularity, syntactic category and frequency) could account for the acquisition order. Scores for perceptual salience were composed of three subfactors: the number of phones in the functor (phonetic substance), the presence/absence of a vowel in the surface form (syllabicity) and the total relative sonority of the functor. The major determinants that significantly correlated with acquisition order were perceptual salience $r = 0.63$, frequency $r = 0.44$, morphophonological regularity $r = 0.41$. When these three factors were combined with semantic complexity and syntactic category in a multiple regression analysis, this combination of five predictors jointly explained 71 percent of the variance in acquisition order, with salience having the highest predictive power.

Field (2008) had second-language learners of English listen to authentic stretches of spoken English and, when pauses occurred at random intervals, they had to transcribe the last few words. The recognition of grammatical functors fell significantly behind that of lexical words, a finding that was robust across first languages and across levels of proficiency.

It is clear, therefore, that linguistic forms of low psychophysical salience are both more difficult to perceive and to learn.

4.1.4.2 *Salient Associations*

Child and second language acquisition (SLA) research shows that salience of association, as defined above in terms of concreteness and imageability, is a potent influence upon acquisition and learning. Brown (1973) discussed the salience of a morpheme's associations in terms of its consistency of function and semantic complexity:

> The primary determinant of the order in which mature forms are acquired is semantic complexity, forms making 'concrete' reference less complex than forms making abstract reference. Most difficult of all are the forms lacking any consistent semantic correlate. (1973: 343)

> In semantic terms, the grammatical morphemes appear to modulate the meanings of naming words, like nouns and verbs, and of the relations expressed by combining and ordering naming words. The grammatical morphemes add number, tense, aspect, specificity or nonspecificity, containment or support. These modulations are inconceivable without the major meanings they modify and for this reason alone grammatical morphemes could not be acquired before content words and rules of combination and order. (1973: 454)

Gilhooly and Logie (1980) reported norms for the age of acquisition, concreteness and imageability of 1,944 nouns. Age-of-acquisition and concreteness of a word correlated –0.50, age of acquisition and imageability and words correlated –0.72. This is supported by SLA research: in the learning of foreign language vocabulary, imageable words are learned more easily than abstract words (0.37 < r < 0.53) (Ellis and Beaton 1993).

Language processing research also demonstrates robust effects of semantic richness: words associated with relatively more semantic information are recognized faster and more accurately, due to their possessing richer, better-specified semantic representations (Pexman et al. 2013). For a wide range of current evidence using methodologies including ERP, fMRI, TMS and behavioral approaches in both intact and patient populations, see Pexman et al. (2014).

The European Science Foundation (ESF) crosslinguistic and longitudinal research project (Perdue 1993) examined how 40 adult learners picked up the language of their social environment (Dutch, English, French, German and Swedish) by everyday communication. Analysis of the interlanguage of these L2 learners resulted in its being described as the 'Basic Variety'. All learners, independent of source language and target language, developed and used it, with about one-third of them fossilizing at this level, in that although they learned more words, they did not further complexify their utterances in the respects of morphology or syntax. In this Basic Variety, most lexical items stem from the target language, but they are uninflected.

> There is no functional morphology. By far most lexical items correspond to nouns, verbs and adverbs; closed-class items, in particular determiners, subordinating elements, and prepositions, are rare, if present at all . . . . Note that there is no functional inflection whatsoever: no tense, no aspect, no mood, no agreement, no casemarking, no gender assignment. (Klein 1998: 544–545)

More than half of English spontaneous speech consists of functors such as *the, of, and, a, in, to, it, is, to, was, I, for, that, you, he, be, with, on, by* and *at* (Leech et al. 2001). Their abstractness and semantic lightness makes them more difficult to acquire than concrete, imageable words. They also suffer, as Brown noted, as a result of their lack of consistency of function. Contingency of form-function mapping, as I explain in Chapter 6, Section 6.2, is a powerful determinant of learnability.

4.1.4.3 Context and Surprisal

Contemporary learning theory holds that learning is driven by prediction errors: that we learn more from the surprise that comes when our predictions are incorrect than when our predictions are confirmed (Rescorla and Wagner 1972; Wills 2009; Rumelhart et al. 1986; Clark 2013), and there is increasing evidence for surprisal-driven language acquisition and processing (Smith and Levy 2013; Demberg and Keller 2008; Dell and Chang 2014; Pickering and Garrod 2013; Jaeger and Snider 2013).

In first language acquisition, Brown (1973) considered how predictability worked against the acquisition of grammatical morphemes:

> In a face-to-face conversation between well-acquainted persons the meanings signaled by grammatical morphemes are largely redundant, they are largely guessable from linguistic and non-linguistic context. And so they are dispensable in child speech and in nonliterate adult dialects in a way that content words and word order are not. (Brown 1973: 452)

The same applies in second language acquisition. Grammatical morphemes are often redundant and overshadowed by more salient lexical cues to tense or number (e.g. *Tomorrow*, *I'll* do the shopping; *Yesterday* I walk*ed*; *Seven* boys) (Terrell 1991; Pica 1983). If a learner knows these lexical cues and has processed them, then subsequent processing of the morphological cues in these contexts affords no further information.

In usage-based linguistics, surprisal has been studied in particular in studies of structural priming and of online processing. Surprising structures – e.g. when a verb that is strongly attracted to the ditransitive is used in the prepositional dative – prime more strongly than non-surprising structures (Jaeger and Snider 2013; see also Chapter 8 in this volume, on priming). Analysis of a large corpus of eye-movements recorded while people read text demonstrate that measures of surprisal account for the costs in reading time that result when the current word is not predicted by the preceding context (Demberg and Keller 2008).

Contemporary corpus pattern analysis also focuses upon the tension between predictability in context and surprisal. Hanks (2011: 2) talks of norms and exploitations as the *Linguistic Double Helix*:

> Much of both the power and the flexibility of natural language is derived from the interaction between two systems of rules for using words: a primary system that governs normal, conventional usage and a secondary system that governs the exploitation of normal usage.

The *Theory of Norms and Exploitations* (Hanks 2013) is a lexically based, corpus-driven theoretical approach to how words go together in collocational patterns and constructions to make meanings. Hanks emphasizes that the approach rests on the availability of new forms of evidence (corpora, the internet) and the development of new methods of statistical analysis and inferencing. Partington (2011), in his analysis of the role of surprisal in irony, demonstrates that the reversal of customary collocational patterns (e.g. *tidings of great joy, overwhelmed*) drives phrasal irony (*tidings of great horror, underwhelmed*). Similarly, humor and jokes are based on surprisal that is pleasurable: we enjoy being led down the garden path of a predictable parse path, and then have it violated by the joke-teller.

These various approaches thus converge upon the conclusion that in language processing, surprisal aids acquisition, while redundancy hinders it.

4.2 Salience in Language Change: The Linguistic Cycle, Erosion and Grammaticalization

According to each of the three different aspects of salience considered here – psychophysical salience, salience of associations, and predictability/surprisal – grammatical morphology and grammatical functors score low. Learning theory therefore predicts that these constructions should be more difficult to acquire. These factors can be expected, in turn, to play out in language change.

From patterns of language usage, processing and acquisition, dynamic processes over diachronic timescales and synchronic states, there emerge what de Saussure (1916: 135) termed *Panchronic* principles, generalizations of language that exist independently of time, of a given language or of any concrete linguistic facts. One of these is the 'Linguistic Cycle' (Hodge 1970; Givón 1971; van Gelderen 2011), which describes paths of grammaticalization from lexical to functional category, followed by renewal. Givón (1979: 209) schematized the process as

'Discourse > syntax > morphology > morphophonemics > zero' and, more memorably, as 'Yesterday's syntax is today's morphology'.

Hopper and Traugott (2003, chapter 5) focus upon morphologicalization as 'Lexical item in specific syntactic context > clitic > affix', which leads in turn to 'the end of grammaticalization: loss' (Hopper and Traugott 2003: 140). Sometimes the form alone is lost; more usually, a dying form is replaced by a newer, usually periphrastic form with a similar meaning (Hopper and Traugott 2003: 172). The periphrastic replacement is salient, both psychophysically (it is several lexical items long) and, as an innovation, insofar as it is less predictable and automatic.

Some well-known examples involve negatives, where full negative phrases are reanalyzed as words and affixes and are then renewed by full phrases again. In French, negative statements were originally formed by the use of *ne* before the verb. For emphasis, *ne* often came to be reinforced by particles which once had been independent nouns (e.g. *pas* (step): *Je ne vais pas* (I'm not going), *Il ne marche pas* (he's not walking); *goute* (drop): *Je n'ai goute d'argent* (I have no money)). These particles underwent grammaticalization, with *pas* assuming special status as the default neutral obligatory negative adverb (e.g. *Je ne pense pas* (I don't think so)), though before the twelfth century it was used with verbs of motion where its semantic connection is clear. In modern French, the *ne* is, as often as not, omitted entirely (e.g. *Je suis pas allée* (I didn't go)); its use depends on sociolinguistic factors such as age, gender, style of speech, phonology and clause type (Dewaele 2004), the general pattern emergent from subpatterns of regularities of usage.

Erosion has a particularly dramatic effect in sounds such as suffixes or prefixes that perform important grammatical functions. In this way, while Latin had different forms for all six combinations of person and number in the present tense, French has just three different forms for the present tense of *–er* verbs (four for *–ir, -re* and *–oir* type verbs), and modern English has just two.

The psychological and associative learning processes in usage reviewed in Section 4.1 affect both language learning and language change. In what follows, I summarize a psycholinguistic analysis of these processes, particularly through the lens of second language learners, whose lack of facility accelerates the process.

4.2.1 *Usage Leads to Change: Lower Salience and Homophony*

4.2.1.1 *Usage Leads to Erosion*

Frequently used words become shorter with use. As summarized in Section 4.1.3.1, considerable practice with a particular token results in automaticity of its production and sound reduction, assimilation and lenition – the loss and overlap of spoken gestures (Bybee 2003, 2006; see also Chapter 7 of this volume). Zipf's law describes the law relating frequency and length that occurs in all languages (Zipf 1935; also, see Ellis, this volume, Section 6.7). Salience eventually influences the form of language as a whole, causing some grammatical markers to 'wear away' entirely (McWhorter 2002).

4.2.1.2 Erosion Leads to Homophony

As different words shorten, they meet together into a limited number of monosyllables, so the most frequent words of the language tend also to be the most ambiguous ones (Köhler 1986; Polikarpov 2006). Many of the most frequently used words are ambiguous in their homophony and polysemy (e.g. *to, too, two; there, their, they're; I, eye, aye*): there are a large number of meanings to hang onto a limited number of short sounds. This pattern generalizes across languages: the greater the number of monosyllabic words in the lexicon of a language, the greater the degree of homophony (Ke 2006). Ambiguity is a loss of communicative capacity that arises if individual sounds are linked to more than one meaning, as in homophony and polysemy. If the absence of word ambiguity is a mark of evolutionary fitness, then word formation provides an exponential increase in fitness with length (Nowak et al. 2002; see also Chapters 12 and 13 of this volume).

4.2.2 Change Affects Learning

4.2.2.1 Low-Salience Cues Are Poorly Learned

The Rescorla–Wagner (1972) model of associative learning described in Section 4.1.2 summarizes how low-salience cues are poorly learned. As described in Section 4.1.4, grammatical morphemes and functors are low in all three aspects of salience.

The associative learning phenomenon of 'blocking' entails that the effects will be even greater for second language learners than for first language learners (Ellis and Sagarra 2010, 2011). Blocking occurs in animals and humans alike (Kruschke and Blair 2000; Kamin 1969; Mackintosh 1975; Kruschke June 2006). It describes how learners' attention to input is affected by prior experience (Shanks 1995; Rescorla and Wagner 1972; Wills 2005). Knowing that a particular stimulus is associated with a particular outcome makes it harder to learn that another cue, subsequently paired with that same outcome, is also a good predictor of it. The prior association 'blocks' further associations.

Consider the learning of tense morphology. Infants are learning meanings at the same time as words, and children learning their native language only acquire the meanings of temporal adverbs quite late in development. But adults, with their experience of the world and of their native language, know a variety of pragmatic and lexical means for expressing temporal reference (serialization: presenting events in their order of occurrence; adverbials, e.g. *soon, now*; prepositional phrases, e.g. *in the morning*; calendric reference, e.g. *May 12, Monday*) (Schumann 1987). Thus, adult language learners' expression of temporality exhibits a sequence from pragmatic to lexical to grammatical devices, and the earlier, other means, block the acquisition of the later, morphosyntactic ones: 'Whereas all learners apparently achieve the pragmatic and lexical stages of development, fewer learners achieve the morphological stage of development' (Bardovi-Harlig 2000). Lexical and serialization strategies for expressing temporal reference are salient, constant and simple to apply. Morphological cues to tense are non-salient, they often vary by person and number and typically there are additional irregularities. If, in expression, adult learners can get their message across by using these simpler strategies, they have achieved their goal. In the words of Simon (1962), they have 'satisficed' rather than 'optimized', using the minimum necessary level of formal accuracy to achieve their communicative intention, whereas optimizing upon native-like accuracy would be beyond their current cognitive bounds. Good enough (for the naturalistic world), but not perfect (for the more formal criteria of schooling).

4.2.2.2   Homophonous (Low Form-Function Contingency) Forms Are Poorly Learned

The learning of associations between cues and outcomes is a function of their contingency (Rescorla 1968; see Chapter 8 of this volume). The more reliably a cue predicts an outcome, the better the association is learned. The contingency as measured using, for example, ΔP, the one-way dependency measure of the directional association between a cue and an outcome, predicts difficulty of learning (Shanks 1995) in a wide variety of human and animal learning. This relationship is at the core of connectionist (Chater and Manning 2006; Christiansen and Chater 2001) and competition (MacWhinney 1987a) models of language learning.

Consider an ESL learner trying to learn, from the naturalistic input, the interpretation of –s at the ends of words. Plural –s, third-person singular present –s and possessive –s are all homophonous with each other as well as with the contracted allomorphs of copula and auxiliary be. Therefore, if we evaluate –s as a cue for one of these functional interpretations in particular, it is clear that there are many instances in which the cue is there but that outcome does not pertain; ΔP is, accordingly, low. Evaluate the mappings from the other direction as well: plural –s, third-person singular present –s and possessive –s all have variant expression as the allomorphs [/s/, /z/, /ez/]. Therefore, if we evaluate just one of these, say /ez/, as a cue for one particular outcome, say plurality, it is clear that there are many instances of that outcome in the absence of the cue; ΔP is concomitantly reduced. Thus, a contingency analysis of these cue-interpretation associations suggests that they will not be readily learnable (Ellis 2006a, 2006b; Goldschneider and DeKeyser 2001).

This is just one illustration of the general case. The ambiguity of grammatical functors out of context, their homophony and polysemy that results from high frequency of usage, erosion, desemanticization and extension, entails that they are low-contingency constructions that are difficult to learn.

4.2.2.3   Compounded Prejudices: Low Salience and Low Contingency
These simple analyses have profound consequences. If, as Herron and Bates (1997) demonstrated, fluent native speakers can only perceive grammatical functors from the bottom-up evidence of input 50 percent of the time compared to open-class words, how can language learners hear them, thence to learn their function? If the functions themselves are multiple, ambiguous and redundant, they are difficult to learn for these reasons, too.

4.2.3   Salience and Adult Naturalistic Second Language Acquisition
Consider the following sample of ESL writing, a classic piece from Lightbown and Spada (1999: 74–75) that has introduced many students to the study of SLA. It is a piece of writing intended to describe the cartoon film *The Great Toy Robbery*, written by an ESL French-speaking secondary school pupil: 'During a sunny day, a cowboy go in the desert with his horse. He has a big hat. His horse eat a flour. In the same time, Santa Clause go in a city to give some surprises.' It illustrates a classic ESL difficulty – the omission of third-person singular present tense *-s*. Third-person present *-s* and possessive *-s* are the latest-acquired functors in the morpheme order studies (Goldschneider and DeKeyser 2001; Bailey et al. 1974).

This is a specific example of the more general phenomenon that, although naturalistic second language learners are surrounded by language, not all of it 'goes in', and SLA is typically much less successful than L1A. This is Corder's distinction between input, the available target language, and intake, that subset of input that actually gets in and is utilized by the learner in some way (Corder 1967). Schmidt (1984) described a naturalistic language learner, Wes, as very fluent, with high levels of strategic competence but low levels of grammatical accuracy: 'using 90 percent correct in obligatory contexts as the criterion for acquisition, none of the grammatical morphemes counted

has changed from unacquired to acquired status over a five-year period'
(Schmidt 1984: 5). These grammatical functors abound in the input, but, as
a result of their low salience, the low contingency of their form-function
mappings and adult acquirers' learned attentional biases and L1-tuned automatized processing of language, they are simply not implicitly learned by
many naturalistic learners whose attentional focus is on communication.

4.2.4   Language Use Causes Language Change

Linguistic evolution proceeds by natural selection from among the competing alternatives made available from the idiolects of individual speakers,
which vary among them (Croft 2000; Mufwene 2001, 2008). Since adults are
typically less successful than children at language learning, language use by
a high proportion of adult language learners typically means simplification,
most obviously manifested in a loss of redundancy and irregularity and an
increase in transparency (Trudgill 2002b: chapter 7; Trudgill 2002a).
The 'Basic Variety' of interlanguage (Klein 1998; Perdue 1993) shows similarities with pidgins (Schumann 1978) because pidgins are the languages that
result from maximal contact and adult language learning (McWhorter
2001). Veronique (1999, 2001) and Becker and Veenstra (2003) detail
many parallels between the grammatical structures of French-based creoles
and the Basic Variety of interlanguage of learners of French as a second
language, particularly in the 1:1 iconicity of their mapping of function and
form (Andersen 1984), their controller-first, focus-last constituent ordering
principles, their lack of verbal morphology and the order of development of
their means of temporal reference. Some creoles evolve as the complex-
ification of pidgins resulting from the habitual use by children who learn
them as their native tongue. Others, such as the Atlantic and Indian Ocean
French-related creoles developed from the interactions of adults speakers of
nonstandard varieties of the target language and non-natives (Mufwene
2001). Creoles have systematic grammar, but not so many syntactic features
as do languages like West African Fula, with its 16 grammatical genders, or
morphophonological features such as the complex system of consonant
mutations of Welsh, or phonological features like the tonal languages of
South East Asia, all of these being languages that have had much longer to
evolve their grammatical elaborations and diachronically motivated, but
synchronically obscure, irregularities. Creoles typically have little or no
inflection, they have little or no tone distinguishing words or expressing
grammar, and their prefix/suffix + root combinations are semantically predictable (McWhorter 2001, 2002: chapter 5).

McWhorter argues that the older a language is, the more complexity it has; that is, the more it overtly signals distinctions beyond strict communicative necessity. The most elaborate languages in these respects are those older, more isolated languages that are spoken by groups of people whose interactions are primarily with other speakers of the language, and which thus are learned as native languages by children whose plastic brains are ready to optimally represent them. But their linguistic complexities pose great difficulties to second language learners, prejudiced by L1 transfer, blocking and entrenchment. So some languages are easier for adults to learn, in an absolute sense, than others: 'If one were given a month to learn a language of one's choice, I think one would select Norwegian rather than Faroese, Spanish rather than Latin, and Sranan rather than English' (Trudgill 1983). It is no accident that Faroese, as a low-contact language not subject to adult language learning, has maintained a degree of inflectional complexity which Norwegian has lost. Stasis allows a language, left to its own devices, to develop historical baggage – linguistic overgrowths that, however interesting, are strictly incidental to the needs of human exchange and expression (McWhorter 2001, 2002, 2004). In the same way that, in nature, niche-stability during the flat periods of punctuated evolution allows the continuation of elaborate vestigial forms while competition selects them out, so in language, isolation allows the slow accretion of complexity and its maintenance, while large amounts of external contact and adult language learning select out the less functional linguistic overdevelopments.

Consider again the case in point of third-person present -*s*. It weaves through this stream like a yellow rubber duck, illuminating the flow of the English language and SLA wherever it bobs. English is no longer a language spoken primarily as an L1. The 375 million L1 speakers are in a very definite minority compared to the 750 million EFL and 375 million ESL speakers (Graddol 2000). This preponderance of adult language learning of English is changing its nature. Seidlhofer (2004: 236) describes these changes as English is used across the world as a Lingua Franca. First and foremost on her list of observables is 'dropping' the third-person present tense -*s* (as in 'She look very sad').

So languages are 'streamlined' when history leads them to be learned more as second languages than as first ones, which abbreviates some of the more difficult parts of their grammars (McWhorter 2004). As complex, adaptive systems, languages emerge, evolve and change over time (Larsen-Freeman 1997; Ellis and Larsen-Freeman 2006; Beckner et al. 2009; Croft 2000). Just as they are socially constructed, so too are they honed by use in social interaction. They adapt to their speakers. Because children are better language learners than adults, languages that adults can learn are simpler than languages that only children can learn. Second language acquisition by adults changes the very nature of language itself, in ways that are understandable in terms of the psycholinguistics of salience and general principles of associative learning (for examples in the history of English, see Schneider 2011; Schreier and Hundt 2013).

4.3   Psycholinguistics Meets Historical Linguistics

4.3.1   The Potential

'The mechanisms and principles involved in grammaticalization conform to a complex process of coding and organization of language which is universally applicable to describe the evolution of grammatical forms' (Wischer and Diewald 2002). These universal processes emerge from dynamic processes of cognition and diachrony – 'For a theory of grammaticalization, it is both unjustified and impractical to maintain a distinction between synchrony and diachrony' (Heine et al. 1991: chapter 9) – and of usage and social-interaction – 'Grammar is not absolutely formulated and abstractly represented, but always anchored in the specific form of an utterance . . . Its forms are not fixed templates, but are negotiable in face-to-face interaction in ways that reflect individual speakers' past experience of these forms, and their assessment of the present context' (Hopper 1998: 142).

Complexity arises in systems via incremental changes, based on locally available resources, rather than via top-down direction or deliberate movement toward some goal (see, e.g., Dawkins 1985). Similarly, in a complex systems framework, language is viewed as an extension of numerous domain-general cognitive capacities such as shared attention, imitation, sequential learning, chunking and categorization (Bybee 1998; Ellis 1996; Beckner et al. 2009).

Language is emergent from ongoing human social interactions, and its structure is fundamentally molded by the pre-existing cognitive abilities, processing idiosyncrasies and limitations and general and specific conceptual circuitry of the human brain. Because this has been true in every generation of language users from its very origin, in some formulations language is said to be a form of cultural adaptation to the human mind, rather than the result of the brain adapting to process natural language grammar (Deacon 1997; Schoenemann 2005; Christiansen and Chater

2008). Recognition of language as a complex adaptive system allows us to better understand change across levels and timescales (MacWhinney and O'Grady 2015). That is why enterprises like this, which bring linguists and psychologists together, have potential.

Language and usage are like the shoreline and the sea.

4.3.2   The Difficulties

Of course there are difficulties. Our methods are different. We come from different theoretical traditions. Language on the page, the necessary focus for historical language change, is a far cry from patterns of online language processing in discourse. Indeed, written language bestows salience on matters that are not so in spoken language, and has the power to freeze or slow language change. We cannot track online consciousness on the page. Surprisal, as well as the other operationalizations of salience described in this chapter, is hard to identify in print. Nor do children learn language from books. But scholars of language change, as well as cognitivists, agree that usage matters. We share a focus on corpus analysis. And in this volume, we focus upon the same phenomena. Something useful has to come from this.

4.4   Conclusion

It is always entertaining to hear the reports from the American Dialect Society (ADS), *Merriam-Webster* or the *Oxford English Dictionary* for candidates in their 'Word of the Year' (WOTY) or 'Phrase of the Year'. The new arrivals are current, creative and fun. Favorites of mine include *Recombobulation area* (an area at airport security in which passengers who have passed through screening can get their clothes and belongings back in order), *gate lice* (airline passengers who crowd around a gate waiting to board), *Dracula sneeze* (covering one's mouth with the crook of one's elbow when sneezing, as in popular portrayals of the vampire Dracula, in which he hides the lower half of his face with a cape), *selfie* (a self-portrait photograph, typically taken with a hand-held digital camera or camera phone) and *omnishambles* (a situation that has been comprehensively mismanaged). Words or phonemes can be blended into a portmanteau, with two meanings packed into one word (e.g. *motel*, blending *motor* and *hotel*; *electrocute*, blending *electric* and *execute*). They thrive on witty analogy, 'the fuel and fire of thinking' (Hofstadter and Sander 2013). The ADS WOTY for 2013 was *because* (introducing a noun, adjective or other part of speech (e.g. 'because reasons', 'because awesome')), a language change involving the loss of functors (e.g. 'because *of* reasons', 'because *it's* awesome'). What is unusual is that the passing of these functors was noticed at all. WOTY typically focuses upon the shock of the new, rather than the decline of the old.

At the start of a Linguistic Cycle, highly salient, new constructions enter a language. They are psychophysically intense. They are full of meaning. They are unique in their interpretation. Their novelty charms and surprises.

At the end of a cycle, grammatical constructions exit: by dint of frequency, they have shortened and become psychophysically slight; by dint of shortening, they have become homophonous with low contingency between form and function; by dint of habitual overuse, they have become semantically bleached. Fluent language users expect them to be there and perceive them through expectation. Novice language learners, especially second language learners, tend neither to notice them, nor to understand their function. So morpheme leave the language.

CHAPTER 5

Low Salience as an Enabling Factor in Morphosyntactic Change

Elizabeth C. Traugott

5.1 Introduction

In this response to Nick C. Ellis's Chapter 4, I focus on the role of salience in morphosyntactic change, especially of the type associated with grammaticalization (see, e.g., Lehmann 2002; Hopper and Traugott 2003), but more broadly also with procedural constructionalization (see Traugott and Trousdale 2013). My focus is complementary in several ways: I explore diachrony rather than synchrony and morphosyntactic markers rather than lexical expressions, and I propose that low salience is a factor in enabling morphosyntactic change. By contrast, Ellis addresses mainly synchrony and phonological salience of contentful items and proposes that the relevant factor enabling lexical change is high salience, which he identifies with 'standing out from the rest', intensity and, therefore, prominence.

In Chapter 4, Ellis says that most grammatical items are non-salient (i.e. familiar, and typically unstressed). Assuming this is true synchronically, my question is, how do grammatical items develop and come to be non-salient? Or, more precisely, how do grammatical items come to have low salience? In particular, how do we identify evidence for factors that enable change when the system does not yet include the newly developing 'target' item? For example, what were the 'critical contexts' (Diewald 2002) that preceded the development of *BE going to* developing a 'future' usage, or *all but* developing an 'approximator' usage, and, by hypothesis, what role could salience possibly have had in these developments?

This chapter is organized as follows. I start by characterizing salience as it has been used in synchronic linguistics (Section 5.2). In Section 5.3 I introduce some issues that arise when thinking about salience in historical linguistics, especially the kinds of morphosyntactic change associated with grammaticalization. Section 5.4 is devoted to the question of whether there is evidence that 'expressiveness' (Lehmann 2002) and 'extravagance' (Haspelmath 1999) are onset contexts for grammaticalization. Boye and Harder's (2012) proposal that grammaticalization is associated with non-addressability and nonfocalizability, and that semantic salience decreases after grammaticalization, is the topic of Section 5.5. The chapter concludes with Section 5.6.

5.2 Characterizing Salience in Synchronic Linguistics

Salience has not been a central concept in all areas of linguistics. It has been used largely in connection with synchronic data, especially in usage-based work on phonology, pragmatics and sociolinguistics. It has been used differently by researchers with respect to different domains of grammar (e.g. phonology, morphosyntax) and different aspects of linguistic knowledge (perceptual, cognitive). Indeed, Rács (2013: 25) characterizes it as an 'evasive term'. In phonology, salience may be conceptualized as perceptual, largely prosodic prominence, which is identifiable in experimental phonetics (e.g. Hume et al. 1999). In pragmatics it may be conceptualized as retrieval and accessibility of meaning (Ariel 1990; Giora 2012). As argued in Degand and Simon (2005) and Wagner et al. (2010), because accessible arguments are typically expressed by pronouns (or zero), salience cannot be identified with 'standing out from the rest' as it often is in psychology (Ellis, Chapter 4 in this volume).

Useful distinctions have been made between what is salient to an individual (context-based and short-term) and what is salient to a community (entrenched and long-term) (Giora 2012; Kecskes 2012). Salience to a community, as evidenced by attitudes and stereotypes, is a topic in sociolinguistics (see Montgomery 2012 on cultural salience and Rács 2013 on links between salience in sociolinguistics, cognitive psychology and theories of language variation and change). Overall, however, salience is not a widely used or well-defined concept in linguistics.

It is generally agreed that linguistic salience is gradient and exists on a continuum from high to low salience (Giora 2003). But what is considered 'high' or 'low' has not always been consistent across domains (or researchers). In phonology, high salience is usually correlated with prominent physical cues such as phonological stress, and low salience with perceptually weak cues. Here, high salience and surprisal may go hand in hand. In morphophonology, high perceptual salience has been correlated with a transparency of meaning and form, such as is found in regular suffixation patterns, while low salience has been correlated with maximally idiosyn-cratic and marked inflection or derivation (Chapman 1995). Cognitive salience, by contrast, largely concerns activation associated with the men-tion of animate beings, especially human agents, and the actions in which they engage. In work on discourse and information structure, high salience has been correlated with high cognitive salience and activation by mention of animate beings, and low salience with cognitive familiarity and maximal accessibility, such as is grammatically reflected in use of pronouns, ellipsis and low stress (see Ariel 1990). High token frequency is another factor often cited as inducing familiarity, generalization and similar factors asso-ciated with loss of salience (see Bybee 2010).

Most earlier work focused on a single continuum of high to low salience, largely construed as a perception continuum equally relevant for the speaker/writer and the hearer/reader. There is now a growing body of research suggesting that salience is multidimensional. This is because in interaction, especially intercultural communication, there is a constant interplay of cooperation between interlocutors on the one hand and individual, egocentric production and perception based on different intentions and knowledge bases on the other (Kecskes 2013). Focusing primarily on speakers and production, Kecskes proposes that both linguistic and perceptual salience can take three forms for speakers. One is 'inherent salience', a natural preference built into the speaker's conceptual and linguistic knowledge, based on experience. Another is 'collective salience', which is shared with other members of the com-munity. A third, 'emergent situational salience', may accrue on the fly, in the context of language production. Another proposal regarding reasons for the multidimensionality of salience is that individual speak-ers and addressees have different orientations in interactive situations (e.g. Chiarcos 2011; Chiarcos et al. 2011a). In other words, the question needs to be posed, '"High" or "low" for whom?' Chiarcos (2011) pro-poses that salience for the addressee is backward looking, based on shared knowledge arising from prior discourse. Shared knowledge ('common ground'; see Clark 1992) is easily retrieved; the more it is shared, the more easily it is retrieved, and the 'lower' its salience. For the speaker, however, salience is forward looking. It is 'sensitive to speaker-private intentions' with respect to upcoming discourse, and to what the speaker finds to be 'important'. Salience may therefore be higher for the speaker than for the addressee because the speaker intends a certain direction for the discourse and may actively choose to say something novel in the discourse situation, whereas the addressee interprets it in reference to what has already been said in the discourse situation. Salience can be relatively low for both interlocutors when knowledge is shared.

In addressing the question of how perceptually prominent lexical material becomes grammaticalized and, in Ellis's terms, 'non-salient', I draw on the work cited previously (e.g. Chiarcos 2011) that associates novelty with high salience and associates familiarity and accessibility with low salience.

5.3   Change and Salience

In historical – as in synchronic – linguistics, the concept of 'salience' has been used only occasionally, and then primarily for prosodic prominence. Kerswill and Williams (2002: 81) express concern that when salience is used as an 'explanatory' factor, the argumentation is often *post facto* and circular. Several important issues arise when we think about the relation of psychological work on salience and historical linguistics. Three of these issues are identified here. One is methodological: because speakers from former times cannot be accessed, there is an asymmetry in evidence. The other two are primarily theoretical: distinguishing change from innovation, and characterizing grammaticalization.

5.3.1   *Nonavailability of Direct Evidence for Salience*

As Ellis mentions in Chapter 4, a serious methodological issue for researchers on the relationship between salience and change is found in the impossibility of gaining direct access to speakers of earlier times. This means that we can run no experiments to provide empirical evidence for hypotheses about the role of salience in change. We can assume that present-day practices and perceptual processes are projectable back on the past, guided by the uniformitarian hypothesis that processes remain consistent over time (see Comrie 2003), but we cannot be sure that exactly the same perceptions applied in earlier times. It is likely that they were valued differently. Speakers of, say, ninth-century English lived in a very different world: literacy was the privilege of a tiny few and communication was largely oral (see Kohnen and Mair 2012). Studies of rhythmic alternation in prose (e.g. Schlüter 2005) can give us clues, but since our only historical records are written, we cannot know for certain what was or was not phonologically salient.

5.3.2   *Difference between Synchronic Innovation and Diachronic Change*

In a usage-based approach to change such as is associated with, broadly speaking, functional linguistic work (e.g. Croft 2000; Traugott and Trousdale 2013), 'change' is change in usage.[1] It starts in novel variants (innovation) (Croft 2010: 3) and in speaker interaction (Milroy 1992: 36). But innovation is ephemeral and not stable enough to cause change to occur. Change involves propagation and spread, conventionalization (adoption as a norm among a group of speakers) and entrenchment (mental habituation) of the innovation (Croft 2000, 2010). Propagation and spread are subject to sociolinguistic factors including social salience. They are, presumably, also subject to psychological factors, but to my knowledge, studies of psychological salience are concerned mainly with the individual and therefore with innovation, rather than with change understood as spread and entrenchment in a community.

The distinction between innovation and propagation is made, sometimes explicitly, in the work mentioned earlier in Section 5.2. For Giora (2012), novel meanings (semantic innovations) are low in salience (contrast Ellis's association of novelty with surprise and high salience). For Giora, what is salient is stored in memory, experientially familiar and lexical. Relatedly, Hollmann and Sierwierska (2006) suggest that social salience arises only after entrenchment in a community. Kecskes (2013) proposes that inherent salience and collective salience may change diachronically. An example is the change in meaning of *gay* from 'merry' to 'homosexual' in the mid-twentieth century. Inherent salience changed as the denotation changed, and social salience changed as the word was pre-empted and adopted by the gay community, and then gradually spread to the speakers in general. However, emergent situational salience is, according to Kecskes, synchronic only; it is speaker- and situation-specific. In other words, it is dynamic innovation, such as might occur in a one-off misunderstanding. It cannot be considered change, since true change requires replication (Croft 2000).

5.3.3   *Grammaticalization*

The third issue to be addressed here is that morphosyntactic change is often thought of in terms of grammaticalization. This is true of research by Ellis (this volume) and Hollman and Siewierska (2006). There are currently two rather distinct but still reconcilable views of grammaticalization, so it is important for us to know which one is under discussion.

The 'traditional' view of grammaticalization harks back to Meillet (1958 [1912]). He defines grammaticalization as a change from lexical item to grammatical item and a fixing or automatization ('syntacticization') of word order (see, more recently, Lehmann 2002; Hopper and Traugott 2003). This is a view of grammaticalization as reduction of concrete semantic content ('bleaching'), of syntactic freedom and erosion of morphological brackets and of phonological segments. It is the view of grammaticalization that Ellis refers to in Section 4.2. In this tradition there has for the most part been little attention paid to linguistic contexts for grammaticalization or to the consequences of reduction. On this view, grammaticalization is thought to result in low salience. Grammatical elements are typically not assigned phonological prominence (see Ellis, Chapter 4; Boye and Harder 2012), except when cited metatextually.

In the last few years a different view has developed, with focus on both contexts for and consequences of reduction. The consequence of reduction is typically generalization of meaning, an increase in collocations and token frequency (e.g. Himmelmann 2004; Hilpert 2008; Bybee 2010). From this perspective, there is expansion. Adopting a constructionalist view of change, Traugott and Trousdale (2013) point out that, although reduction and expansion might seem orthogonal on first sight, they are not – they are intertwined, provided change is not considered out of context. For example, a standard example of grammaticalization is the development in the Romance languages of an -r future, as exemplified by *cantare habeo* 'sing-INF have-1SgPRES' > Span *cantaré*, 'I will sing'. In this case, the grammaticalizing phrase was originally periphrastic and free (the parts could occur in either order), but the order became fixed and then reduced to such an extent that the new -r future (derived from the infinitive marker *-re* followed by *habe-*) is structurally an inflection. As an inflection, -r came to be used as the default future in many Romance languages (Roberts and Roussou 2003). It therefore occurred with any verb, whereas the V in a V–INF habe-PRES phrase was highly constrained (Benveniste 1968: 89–90 found that the original contexts were largely passive infinitives of verbs that expressed a course of events that could be regarded as predestined). Its use has since expanded.

One of the types of reduction that Lehmann (2002: 146) cites is scope reduction. Some researchers have argued that certain developments, such as that of pragmatic markers, violate scope reduction and therefore cannot be cases of grammaticalization (e.g. Erman and Kotsinas 1993; Aijmer 1996b). Examples include the development into pragmatic markers of adverbs such as *surely* < 'securely, deliberately', or of a clause such as

I think < adverbial clause types such as *as I think* (Brinton 1996) (and possibly also main clause uses, see Thompson and Mulac 1991). In a view of grammaticalization as expansion, this kind of change can be considered to be grammaticalization (e.g. Traugott 1995; Brinton 1996) because pragmatic markers serve as metatextual and epistemic stance markers; in other words, they cue addressees as to how to interpret the utterance. Like tense and case markers, they are procedural.[2] Like the functors Ellis mentions in Section 4.1.4.2 of Chapter 4 – among them *it, that, you, be* – they are multifunctional and lack 'consistency of function'.

While it is generally agreed that a grammaticalizing element can change only in context (see Bybee, Perkins and Pagliuca 1994: 297; Himmelmann 2004: 31), the exact nature of contexts prior to grammaticalization is an area of some debate. Traugott and König (1991) and Traugott and Dasher (2002) privilege production and 'invited inferences', the kinds of inferential meanings that arise in negotiation of meaning as speakers 'invite' interpretations (usually unconsciously) and hearers infer (usually also unconsciously, and sometimes in ways that do not match the speaker's intended meaning). By contrast, Heine, Claudi and Hünnemeyer (1991: 70) refer to 'context-induced reinterpretation', a term that implies that change results from hearer perception alone. Heine (2002) privileges 'bridging contexts' as enabling factors for grammaticalization. These are inferential contexts that invite pragmatic enrichment and potentials for ambiguity but do not involve change of meaning. Grammaticalization occurs in 'switch contexts' where the new target meaning is isolated from the older one and a new meaning is apparent in the data. Diewald (2002: 109; 2006) envisions the contexts that enable grammaticalization to be not only inferential, but also contexts in which semantic and structural factors have accumulated in specific morphosyntactic 'critical contexts'. Critical contexts are 'highly ambiguous structure[s], which through morphosyntactic opacity' allow several interpretations, among them the new grammaticalizing meaning (Diewald 2006: 20), as *BE going to*, below (Section 5.4), shows. We may infer that opaque, largely non-compositional structures in critical contexts are low in salience and that the lexical items in question (*go, give, mean*, etc.), which are already relatively low in semantic salience (Bybee 2010), become even lower in semantic salience.

Note that Diewald, Heine and others refer to 'ambiguous structures'. Such structures need not be pragmatically or semantically ambiguous, strictly speaking, but need to allow multiple analyses (see Harris and Campbell 1995: 70–72). Denison (this volume, Section 13.1.1) suggests that, in fact, true ambiguity, in which there are discrete analyses and selection of one or the other is of some consequence, occurs so rarely that it is only peripheral and not necessary for change. What does contribute to change, however, is incomplete knowledge that arises largely out of vagueness. In a case of vagueness, interpretations are 'in some relevant respect[s] underdetermined' (Section 13.1.2), and the matter of which exact interpretation one selects is of little or no consequence.

In work on morphosyntactic change, the development of structural ambiguity or vagueness is not considered to be 'a loss of communicative capacity that arises if individual sounds are linked to more than one meaning as in homophony and polysemy' (Section 4.2.1.2), but rather gain of possible new interpretations which may or may not be picked up and enable change.

In the next two sections I discuss the relevance of salience to two interpretations of enabling factors in grammaticalization, understood as reduction.

5.4   Expressiveness or Extravagance at the Onset of Grammaticalization?

To the extent that 'salience' appears in the literature on morphosyntactic change, or more particularly grammaticalization, it has not usually been theorized beyond hypothesized correlations between prosodic and semantic prominence. One issue of debate has been the matter of what it is that motivates change, and in particular whether grammaticalization is motivated by speakers' desire to be different. This can be a construed as a question about whether social, psychological or linguistic high salience are enabling factors.

Examples of grammaticalization frequently occur in which a new grammatical item arises, is used in variation ('competition') with an older one with a similar function and sometimes becomes the new default form. *BE going to* 'future' has some of these characteristics: it is a periphrastic future that competes with older monomorphemic futures *will* and *shall*. It has not, however, become the default future: *will* remains robust, though more so in the UK than in the US (Leech et al. 2009). Another standard example has already been mentioned: the development in the Romance languages of an *-r* future. In this case, the grammaticalizing phrase was originally periphrastic but became reduced in such a way that the new *-r* future is structurally an inflection, as was the old *-b* future. The newer form came to be used as the default future in many Romance languages, where it completely replaced *-b* futures.

In both cases, one could say that the new periphrastic form is more 'expressive' than the older one it competes with. This idea can be found already in Meillet (1958 [1912]: 140), who suggests a spiral development: words are recruited *pour obtenir une expression intense* ('to obtain an intense expression'); they become weaker over time, and are replaced by other, more intense expressions. On this view, encoding by the speaker is the primary enabler of change. Meillet's idea is cited by Lehmann, who later interprets 'expressive' as being 'more transparent, more sumptuous' than extant expressions that are opaque or reduced (Lehmann 2002: 4, 116). An example Lehmann gives is the use of the verb *give* in various languages for adposition *to* or dative inflection. He goes on (2002: 148) to invoke Langacker's (1977: 112 f.) 'correlation between the gradients of semantic content and expressive salience'. For Lehmann, as for Langacker, salience is primarily cognitive.

Haspelmath (1999: 1,057) calls the term 'expressivity' into question, since he associates it with clarity and compositionality. As is well known, in grammaticalization the recruited item loses compositionality and a mismatch arises between the older form and/or meaning (Francis and Yuasa 2008). Drawing on Keller's (1994) maxims of action, Haspelmath suggests that speakers want to signal their difference from others, not by being expressive, in Lehmann's sense, but by being 'extravagant' ('Talk in such a way that you are noticed') (Haspelmath 1999: 1,055). As examples, he gives the introduction of such innovations as *by means of* for *with* (1999: 1,057) and refers to a speaker's desire to achieve social success by means of being imaginative and vivid. In cases like this, a lexical item (e.g. *means*, or *give*) is used for a non-lexical, procedural purpose. Haspelmath associates the new use with high pragmatic salience at first (because it is noticeable) and with high social salience (it identifies the speakers who use it as innovators). However, as frequent replication results in familiarity, the grammaticalizing item could eventually to be assigned low salience. In Haspelmath's terms, 'the loss of pragmatic salience is a natural conse-quence of habituation through frequency of use' (1999: 1,062), because with frequent use of the innovative item, the maxim of extravagance ceases to be relevant and Keller's maxim of conformity becomes 'sufficient reason to adopt the new feature' (1999: 1,058).

Notions such as 'expressiveness' or 'extravagance' seem plausible as enabling factors for grammaticalization[3] when only the decontextualized beginning and ending points of a grammatical change are under considera-tion. If one does not consider context, one might well expect that speakers who recruit an expression to do work similar to that of an extant grammatical item could have a surprise effect on addressees and others in the community. But a close look at the origins of change leads the researcher to evidence that favors variation due to indeterminacy in communication (Croft 2010). This is a discourse-based variant of the proposal that grammaticalization is enabled by structural ambiguity (see Denison, Section 13.3.3 in Chapter 13, this volume).

Where extensive historical data are available and micro-analysis can be done on them, both expressiveness and, especially, extravagance become implausible as enablers of grammatical change.[4] What we find in grammatical change are in many cases very finely modulated, gradual adjustments. Usages are replicated that allow pragmatic implicatures to be strengthened and distributions to be modified in minimal ways, typical of Diewald's (2002) 'critical contexts'. Such changes prior to grammaticalization are not noticeable, or are only barely so. As Croft (2010 and elsewhere) points out, grammaticalization originates in verbalization of experience. New variants arise as the unintended result of the inherent indeterminacy of meaning in use. There is nothing exceptional, extravagant or sumptuous about the onset of grammaticalization. Changes at onset are low in pragmatic, cognitive and social salience. They arise in variation that is 'the normal way of speaking' (Croft 2010: 41).

A case in point is the much-studied and much-cited example of *BE going to* future (see Garrett 2011; Traugott 2012b). In Middle English,[5] *BE going to V* is found only with the meaning 'be in motion for the purpose of *V*ing'. Purpose entails an orientation to future time. The first examples in which, with hindsight, one can detect the possibility that later time is more cognitively salient than purpose appear in the last quarter of the fifteenth century, for example.

(1)   Ther   passed   a theef   byfore alexander that **was goying to** be
       there   passed   a thief   before Alexander that was going to be
       hanged   whiche   said . . .
       hanged   who   said . . .
                              (1477 Mubashshir ibn Fatik, Abu al-Wafa', *The Dyctes and
                              the Sayenges of the Philosophers*, trans. Anthony Woodville
                              [*LION*; Traugott 2012b: 234])

Given the larger scenario and use of *passed* in the immediately preceding context, this is undoubtedly an example of the motion expression, but later time (Garrett 2011 calls it the 'prospective future') is, pragmatically, relatively high in salience because the syntax is passive and therefore the thief is not the agent of the purposed activity (his being hanged). There is no evidence that the author intended to be noticeable or innovative here. Nor is there evidence that authors intended to be noticeable or to give a 'sumptuous reading' in the various other uses of *go* that Garrett suggests were the contexts for the development of the future, most especially adjuncts denoting motion preparatory to action such as

(2)   For Zelmane seeming to strike at his head, and *he going to warde it* ('ward it off'), withall stept backe

(1593 Sidney, *Covntesse of Pembrokes Arcadia* [LION; Garrett 2011: 68])

In such contexts, temporal pragmatics are relatively low in salience, as the interpretation falls out by default from the purpose. Perhaps speakers ranked the pragmatics of later time over motion with intention, and perhaps hearers were more conservative, as Chiarchos's (2011) scenario for salience predicts, but we cannot tell. Even in Example (3), the first likely example of the relative or prospective future 'be about to', there is no evidence that Tourneur intended to be extravagant by substituting BE *going to* 'be about to' for the other plausible future expressions available at the time, *be about to* or *would*:

(3)   [of a man who intended to hang the narrator]
So, for want of a Cord, hee tooke his owne garters off; and as he *was going to* make a nooze I watch'd my time and ranne away.
'So, for lack of a rope, he took his own garters off; and as he was going to make a noose, I watched my time and ran away.'

(1611 Tourneur, *Atheist's Tragedy* [LION; Garrett 2011: 69])

Instead, what we find are a number of examples in which motion with a purpose versus futurity is largely undecidable and, in fact, decidability is somewhat irrelevant in the context. Such examples suggest that the inferential computation of prospective futurity is rendered more or less pragmatically salient depending on the syntax of the sentence in which it occurs and on world knowledge such as what kind of motion is involved in making a noose.

In sum, it appears that neither expressiveness nor extravagance, both of which imply highly salient usage, enables grammaticalization. Rather, enabling factors that accrue in onsets of morphosyntactic change are low in salience and barely perceptible. Once a new pattern has arisen, however, and entrenchment has occurred, they may become socially salient. Once above the level of consciousness, they may be subject to prescription.

Alternatively, they may be the subject of accolade, as in the case of the 2013 American Dialect Society's Word of the Year *because*, used to introduce a noun or adjective, as in *because reasons, because awesome* (see Section 4.4). This expression appears to have been noticed around 2008 and to have become associated with blogs and social media discourse (McCullough 2012). As is typical of many changes, it occurred in contexts semantically coherent with *because*, especially *reasons*, and also commonly used excuses (e.g. *homework*, but not less conventional words such as *racecar*) (McCullough 2013).[6]

5.5 Loss of Availability in Focus Constructions?

Seeking to avoid some of the circularities and problems attendant on earlier definitions of grammaticalization, Boye and Harder (2012) hypothesize that the crucial enabling factor for grammaticalization is 'a structural possibility for competition for discourse prominence in the form of an adequate accompanying expression' (Boye and Harder 2012: 27). An example of an 'adequate accompanying expression' could be the use of *BE going to* in discursive contexts where the purpose (*be hanged* [Example (1)], *ward* [Example (2)]) is semantically more salient than motion, which is thereby backgrounded and loses discourse prominence in favor of purpose. In Boye and Harder's view, the grammaticalizing item (*BE going*, in this case) loses the competition and is assigned a secondary function. They propose that lexical expressions 'are by convention capable of being discursively primary' (2012: 7), the 'point' of the discourse (2012: 12). This means they may be used as focus.[7]

Grammatical expressions, by contrast, 'are by convention ancillary and as such discursively secondary' (Boye and Harder 2012: 7). While they can be the point of the discourse (especially when used by linguists!), they usually are not. Boye and Harder argue that, in themselves, lexical and grammatical expressions are neither discursively prominent nor discursively secondary. It is their use relative to each other in discourse that determines their status. Boye and Harder's hypothesis is that certain lexical items have the semantic potential for enhancing the functional possibilities of an expression to which they are secondary (2012: 28). For an item to grammaticalize, it must be used with sufficient token frequency in a discursively secondary way relative to a lexical expression to become conventionally associated with secondary function (2012: 29). This hypothesis is consistent with Bybee's (2003 and elsewhere) argument that both type and token frequency are primary contributors to grammaticalization.[8] However, there is, to date, scant evidence of frequent use prior to grammaticalization (see Mair 2004 for evidence that token frequency of *BE going to* increased significantly only in the nineteenth century, long after grammaticalization took place).

For Boye and Harder, reduction of the semantic salience of the original lexical item (meaning A) is therefore a prerequisite to grammaticalization (as it is for Diewald, but within a different frame of reference). For them, reduction of semantic salience is also a consequence of grammaticalization: 'a meaning that is by convention secondary . . . must have low salience and must be prone to lose its contours, its semantic specifics' (Boye and Harder 2012: 30). This claim is more questionable than the one regarding loss of salience prior to grammaticalization. We need to be clear that, here: it is the new meaning (meaning B) that is in question. It is true that 'be about to' is more abstract than 'move away', but it has semantic specifics and, as a relative future, is truth-conditional. Grammaticalizing items do not only bleach; they are assigned new meanings (Sweetser 1988). Brems (2011: 111) refers to a 'loss-and-gain model'. Furthermore, like some other auxiliaries, *BE going to* was assigned new semantics after grammaticalization. While it was used as a prospective, relative future in the seventeenth century, it came to be used in the eighteenth century with an additional, and eventually more token frequent meaning: deictic future as well (Nesselhauf 2010).[9] Such a change can hardly be described as loss of semantic contour.

While Boye and Harder's hypothesis that potential for use with secondary discursive prominence, entailing loss of phonological and semantic salience, enables grammaticalization seems to be well supported by standard examples of lexical > grammatical item, the hypothesis excludes several changes that, arguably, involve the development of grammatical meaning, including the development of sentential adverbs like *probably* (Wiemer 2015). Boye and Harder point out that it excludes the rise of demonstratives, which can be focused (though, usually, the focus is metalinguistic, unlike focus on nouns or even pronouns). They justify this on the grounds that demonstratives have been argued to be a third kind of expression, neither lexical nor grammatical, but ostensive (Diessel 1999). The rise of the definite article *the* in English out of demonstrative *that* (Sommerer 2012) is then analogous to the 'lexical > grammatical' change undergone by auxiliaries.

Boye and Harder emphasize that discourse prominence is scalar and therefore gradient (2012: 7). They also emphasize that discourse prominence is distinct from focus, which is information-structuring (2012: 9), and also from lexical status (2012: 11). This is an important distinction for work on prosodic salience. There are many expressions that at least partially meet Boye and Harder's criteria for grammatical items that may be prosodically stressed, among them many adverbs and degree modifiers in English such as *almost, all but*, and pragmatic markers such as *say, look*. These for the most part fail the tests of nonfocalizability and nonaddressability (Boye and Harder 2012: 14–15), but nevertheless many may be stressed (e.g. *We are ALMOST out of salt; That's a ninja turtle, I GUESS*). Adverbs and pragmatic markers are well known to be problematic for rigid categorization. While most manner adverbs like *warmly* have primarily contentful properties and serve as adjuncts in argument structure, degree modifiers and focus adverbs have primarily grammatical properties (Ramat and Ricca 1994). Pragmatic markers are operators on clauses, and their development shows many of the characteristics of grammaticalization (Brinton 1996, 2008). Both degree adverbs and pragmatic markers, then, are on a continuum between contentful and procedural expressions.

For example, and very briefly, *all but* originated as the quantifier *all* 'everything' + the preposition *but* 'except' (De Smet 2012). An early example is

(4)   as these men, *all but* Burgrave, are sent. . .
                         (1585 Walsingham, *Letter* [*CED LEYCESTE*])

This use persists in, e.g. *all-but-dissertation*. *All but* came to be fixed as a down-toning approximator (along with *nearly, almost, far from*) in contexts where literal use of *all* 'everything' is implausible, as in

(5)   Immitate him in ***all but*** his misfortunes
                         (1766 Goldsmith, *Vicar* [*CL I*; De Smet 2012: 611])

Example (5) invites the inference 'nearly everything' (it is implausible that one can imitate someone in literally everything, so the V and the plural NP are critical contexts for the down-toned pragmatics here). In the early nineteenth century, we find *all but* being used with predicate adjectives (i.e. in a syntactic switch context that shows it has been grammaticalized):

(6)   Amidst perils from which escape was ***all but*** miraculous
                         (1838 North American Review, *Sparks Life* [*COHA*;
                                                    De Smet 2012: 612])

There is a degree of indeterminacy and low salience in Example (5). We can hypothesize that the speaker and hearer did not necessarily interpret the same degree of indeterminacy. As the new approximative meaning became familiar and entrenched, it became higher in salience and a distinct semantic contour.

Equally briefly, *look* originated in an imperative (see also Waltereit 2006 on *guarda!* in Italian). From Old English on, it has been used in the non-literal sense 'look to it, take care':

(7) | **loca** | þæt | þu | ne | offrige | þine | lac | on | ælcre | stowe |
     | look | that | thou | not | offer | thy | sacrifice | in | every | place |

    'look to it that you do not offer your sacrifice everywhere possible'

                (10thC Theodulf of Orleans, *Capitula* II.371.1

                              [*DOEC*; Brinton 2008: 189])

In Early Modern English, it begins to appear with an attention-getting function:

(8) ***Looke, looke***, poore Foole, / She has left the Rumpe vncover'ed too

    'Look, look, she has left the rump uncovered too'

                (1630 Middleton, *A Chaste Maid in Cheapside* [*HC*;

                                   Brinton 2008: 194])

The critical contexts appear to be use with *here* and second person (*look you*, sometimes reduced to *lookee*). In these contexts, advice to take care and attention-drawing tend to merge, especially when the complementizer *that* or a *wh-* form like *when* is absent. The salience of 'see with the eye' is lost and a new salience, 'attend to what I have to say', emerges.

What is important in these examples for the current topic is that, by hypothesis, salience is probably higher for the speaker than for the hearer (Chiarcos 2011), especially in cases like *look*. This supports a speaker-production rather than hearer-interpretation model of change. Like other procedural markers, *all but* and *look* are members of sets with similar histories and functions. The approximator *all but* is a member of a set including *almost* and *nearly*. *Almost* has been used as an approximator since Old English, and *nearly* came to be used in the approximator sense in the seventeenth century. Therefore both predate the approximator use of *all but*, and might be expected to have blocked it (see Aronoff 1976) but did not. *Look* is a member of a set including auditory verbs like *hark* and *listen*. Attention-getting uses of *hark* appear at about the same time as those of *look; listen* appears with this use in the MED, but not again until the nineteenth century (US English) (Brinton 2008: 199–200). Again, there is no evidence of blocking. However, in both cases, there is, as in all sets, differential preference for some members over others, and, in the case of *listen*, dialectal differentiation. Such examples suggest that although blocking may have effects in the contentful domain (Section 4.4), in the procedural domain it can be overridden by natural processes of pragmatic inferencing, face-to-face interaction and analogy to sets.

5.6   Conclusion

In answer to the question, 'How do grammatical items develop and come to be non-salient?', I have argued that low salience is an important enabling factor in morphosyntactic change. Procedural, morphosyntactic change is gradual. As critical contexts develop, semantic salience is low for the older 'expression A', since it is familiar and entrenched. The pragmatic inferences and morphosyntactic modulations that occur are also low in salience, as they are essentially background factors, typically unconscious and not noticed by speakers and addressees. Such factors accumulate gradually and may eventually lead to grammaticalization/constructionalization and the development of a new 'expression B'.

After grammaticalization/constructionalization, the new expression may become the object of conscious comment, but in many cases it does not. An example of a construction that came to be stigmatized several decades after it became established is the progressive passive, as in *They were being brought in a cart*, which appeared, if only sporadically, in the 1760s, but was not proscribed until some fifty years later when its token frequency was increasing (van Bergen 2013). I have also suggested that changes in procedural expressions may differ significantly, with respect to salience, from changes in contentful expressions. For example, new word formations and coinages of idioms are usually based on an extant pattern and can be created instantaneously[10] and may have surprisal effects. These are typically conscious and noticeable (e.g. *beautilicious*, based on X-*licious*, 'attractive X').

To the extent that salience is useful as a linguistic concept, it is relevant not only for prosody, semantics and information structuring, but also for morphosyntax generally. There are no easy correlations between prosodic stress, focus and lexical status. In studying language change, we cannot experimentally verify the relevance of salience, but by using the uniformitarian principle we can assume that salience plays a similar role in diachrony as in synchrony. It is useful to think of salience as a multidimensional property of language use that may differ in strength for speaker and hearer. If Chiarcos (2011) is right, and salience for the speaker is forward-looking, speakers may play a more significant role in change than has often been allowed for (but see McDaniel et al. 2015 on the importance of production principles in change).

Notes

Many thanks to Nick Ellis, Laurie Bauer, Graeme Trousdale and especially Marianne Hundt for valuable comments on an earlier version of this chapter.

1. This contrasts with views of change in which 'change' is seen as change in grammars (Kiparsky 1968 and subsequent research in the generative tradition).

2. Procedural expressions are those that 'contribute information about how to combine ... concepts into a conceptual representation' (Terkourafi 2011: 358–59).

3. Indeed, Hopper and Traugott (2003: 73) appeal to the notion of expressivity as one of several initial motivating factors in grammaticalization.

4. The situation is different where lexical innovation is concerned. The development of new contentful items, such as the coining of new words like *Obamadom* (based on the template X-*dom*) or new idiomatic expressions like *orange is the new black* (based on *X is the new Y*), is instantaneous and often ludic, while development of grammatical/procedural items (and of the lexical templates) is gradual and relatively imperceptible (Traugott and Trousdale 2013).

5. The periods of English are usually defined as Old English (c. 650–1100 CE), Middle English (c. 1100–1500 CE), Early Modern English (c. 1500–1700 CE) and Late Modern English (c. 1700 CE–present).

6. Thanks to Arnold Zwicky for this reference.

7. According to Boye and Harter (2012: 18), focus highlights an expression relative to its syntagmatic context. By contrast, contrastive focus highlights the focal expression relative to its paradigmatic alternatives, and therefore Boye and Harder exclude contrastive focus from their empirical test for determining whether a given expression is lexical or grammatical.

8. Hilpert (Chapter 3 of this volume) expands types of frequency from two (type and token) to five, but does not discuss their relevance to the onset of grammaticalization.

9. Traditionally, *BE going to* is thought to have grammaticalized in the seventeenth century, as evidenced by examples such as (3) (e.g. Garrett 2011). The criterion is semantic (new relative future meaning). Traugott and Trousdale (2013: 217–24) suggest that, from a constructionalization perspective, change in form as well as meaning is required, and on this criterion *BE going to* was not constructionalized until the eighteenth century, when use in raising constructions is attested (new syntax) as well as deictic meaning (new semantics). In either case, the semantics of future does not 'lose its contours'. Instead, the contours are changed and elaborated.

10. The pattern or schema itself usually arises gradually, but see endnote 4.

PART III
Chunking

CHAPTER 6

Chunking in Language Usage, Learning and Change: I Don't Know

Nick C. Ellis

6.1 Chunking: The Foundations

6.1.1 Letter Chunks

How many letters can you apprehend from a single presentation? Look at the first of the four stimuli below, just one quick glimpse, and immediately afterwards, write down what you saw. Now do the same for the next three, one at a time.

```
CVGJCDHM
RPITCQET
UMATSORE
VERNALIT
```

I suspect that you perceived more letters from later strings than from earlier ones. But given that each stimulus was the same eight letters long, why should that be?

Miller et al. (1954) showed Harvard undergraduates pseudoword letter strings like those above for very brief presentations (a tenth of a second) using a tachistoscope. The average number of letters correctly reported for the four types of stimuli were, in order, 53, 69, 77 and 87 percent. The pseudowords differed in their 'order of approximation to English' (AtoE). CVGJCDHM exemplifies zero-order AtoE strings – they are made up of letters of English, but these are sampled with equal probability of occurrence (1 in 26). RPITCQET exemplifies first-order AtoE strings – made up of letters of English, but sampled according to their frequency of occurrence in the written language (as in opening a book at random, sticking a pin in the page and choosing the pinned letter [e.g. 'r']; repeat). UMATSORE exemplifies second-order AtoE – these reflect the probabilities of two-letter sequences in English (bigrams) (open a book at random, stick a pin in the page, choose the pinned letter and the one following it in a word [e.g. 'um'], find another random example of the last letter, choose that letter and the one following it [e.g. 'ma']; repeat; . . .). VERNALIT exemplifies fourth-order AtoE – these reflect the probabilities of four-letter sequences in English (4-grams) (open a book at random, stick a pin in the page, choose that letter and the three following it in a word [vern], find another random example of the final trigram, choose that trigram and the one following it in a word [e.g. 'erna']; repeat; . . .).

The fact that we can better perceive higher-order AtoE strings means that our perceptual system is sensitive to the probabilities of occurrence of letters and letter sequences in English. It has expectations about 4-grams and better perceives stimuli which meet those expectations. At a lower level, it has expectations about 2-grams and better perceives stimuli which meet these those expectations. Generally, it has expectations about the relative frequencies of occurrence of English orthographic sequences and better perceives stimuli which meet those expectations. Miller, Bruner and Postman summarized such results, showing that performance can be predicted from knowledge of the statistical structure of English, saying 'the more frequently a trace has been embedded in a trace aggregate, to use the language of Gestalt psychology, the greater the probability that the aggregate will be aroused when the component is activated'.

Two years later, George Miller (1956) introduced 'chunk' as his preferred technical term to replace 'trace aggregate'. In his classic paper, 'The magical number seven, plus or minus two: Some limits on our capacity for processing information', he reviewed the span of short-term memory (STM) – how long a sequence (of digits, letters or words) you can repeat back in order, having just heard it – and observed that for young adults it was 7±2 chunks of information. He noted that memory span is approximately the same for stimuli with very different amounts of information (binary digits have 1 bit of information each; decimal digits have 3.32 bits each; words about 10 bits each). So memory span is not limited in terms of bits of information but rather in terms of chunks, these being the largest units in the presented material that a person recognizes.

What counts as a chunk depends on the knowledge of the person being tested. For example, a word is a single chunk for a speaker of the language, but is many chunks for someone who is totally unfamiliar with the language: compare *breakfast* and *parakuihi*, or *sushi* and 寿司. Chunks are subjective: 'We are dealing here with a process of organizing or grouping the input into familiar units or chunks, and a great deal of learning has gone into the formation of these familiar units' (Miller 1956: 91; see also my Chapter 4 on salience in this volume). The units of perception are influenced by prior association; in William James's words, 'The chief cerebral conditions of perception are the paths of association irradiating from the sense-impression, which may have been already formed' (James 1890b: 82).

6.1.2   Word Chunks

How many words can you apprehend from a single presentation? Look at the first of the four stimuli below, just one quick read through, and immediately afterward, write down what you saw. Now do the same for the next three, one at a time.

> inducted avidity slaughtered renewed dharma authentically
> she that empire the line letter
> any dominant intelligent species to believe
> delivers to the writer a magnificent

I suspect that you recalled more words from later strings than from earlier ones. But given that each stimulus was the same six words long, again, why?

I created these stimuli using the same definitions of order of approximation to English as above, but this time using words as units rather than letters. Instead of a pin and a book, I used the Natural Language Toolkit (Bird 2006; Bird et al. 2009) and searched the Brown corpus (Francis and Kucera 1979). The exercise is inspired by Miller and Selfridge (1950), who built zero- to seventh-order of approximation to English word lists, read them to students and had the students recall as much as they could. Reading from their graph, approximate recall correctness for 10-word lists was 99 percent for seventh-order AtoE, 98 percent for fourth-order, 95 percent for second-order, 62 percent for first-order and 50 percent for zero-order. They concluded that 'when short-range contextual dependencies are preserved in nonsense material, the nonsense is as readily recalled as is meaningful material. . . . [I]t is these familiar dependencies, rather than the meaning per se, that facilitate learning' (1950: 184).

As with letters, the fact that we can better perceive higher-order AtoE word strings means that our perceptual system is sensitive to the probabilities of occurrence of words and word sequences in English. It has expectations about 4-grams, and better perceives stimuli which meet these expectations. At a lower level, it has expectations about 2-grams and better perceives stimuli which meet these expectations. It has expectations about the relative frequencies of occurrence of English words and better perceives higher-frequency words. We have rich knowledge of chunks of words. Generally, our perceptual system is tuned to perceive higher-frequency words and word sequences that are higher in transitional probability. We have never explicitly counted such frequencies, but our perceptual system has automatically tallied their probabilities over our history of using English. The relevant knowledge is induced from usage. It is incidentally acquired while our consciousness is focused upon communication.

Note also, from the comparison of zero-order and first-order word sequence stimuli, another important range of phenomena of usage that we will return to in more detail in Sections 6.4, 6.5 and 6.8. We preferentially process frequent words over infrequent words. Infrequent words are much longer than frequent words. Infrequent words also tend to have unusual orthographic sequences, unusual spelling-to-sound correspondences and unusual pronunciations. Consider for example, *assuage, egregious, epithalamion, inefficacious, internecine, omniscient, puerile, regicidal, synecdoche, terpsichorean.* Usage shapes words.

6.1.3   Grammar Chunks

In 1957, Miller began Project Grammarama at Harvard University in order to study the learning of chunks and rules. Miller (1958) developed a laboratory analogue of grammar learning using an artificial language (AL) consisting of a set of well-formed strings that could be generated by an underlying finite-state grammar shown in Figure 6.1.

This type of finite-state system is formally simple but psychologically complex, since the underlying grammar is not readily apparent from its surface forms. Participants were shown redundant strings of letters (e.g. SSXG, NNXSXG) generated by the underlying grammar. No mention

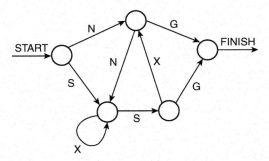

Figure 6.1 Diagram of a finite-state grammar of the type used by Miller (1958).

was made of rules or structure. They were simply asked to memorize the strings. In a comparison condition, they were asked to learn random strings which were drawn from the same letter pool but which did not follow the sequential statistics of the grammar. The results were that, although participants knew nothing of the rules of the language, the redundant, 'grammatical' strings were more easily memorized.

This study was the foundation for what is now the most widely studied paradigm of implicit learning: artificial grammar learning. The standard AL experiment involves two phases: learning and testing. In the learning phase, subjects are shown strings of letters (e.g. MXRMXT, VMTRRR) generated by an underlying grammar or rule system, usually a finite-state system that generate strings of symbols in a left-to-right, non-hierarchical fashion, often referred to as a Markov grammar. The subjects are asked to memorize the strings; no mention is made of rules or structure. After subjects have memorized the list they are informed that the strings conformed to a covert rule structure and are asked to make well-formedness (grammaticality) judgments about a set of novel strings, half of which are grammatical and half of which contain grammatical violations. The typical finding here is that subjects are able to make judgments at significantly better than chance levels without being able to articulate detailed information about what the rules governing the letter strings are, or which ones they were using in guiding their decisions. Thus it has been argued that the task demonstrates implicit learning. The paradigm has been developed and refined over the years and continues to form the basis for a considerable amount of experimental research into grammar and sequence learning (for reviews see Reber 1993; Ellis 1994b; Rebuschat 2015; Stadler and Frensch 1998; and Perruchet and Pacton 2006).

In his very fertile decade of the 1950s, Miller revealed our knowledge of chunks across the scale of language and he showed how this knowledge was used in the learning and processing of language. His work had a profound influence upon both psycholinguistics and the psychology of learning.

6.2   Learning Chunks

Chunking is the development of permanent sets of associative connections in long-term storage. Following Miller's lead, subsequent work in cognitive psychology and in Artificial Intelligence simulations of human learning and cognition in production systems such as ACT-R (Anderson 1983, 1996) and Soar (Laird et al. 1987, 1986) incorporated chunking as the primary mechanism of learning, and chunks as the units of memory.

Newell (1990) argued that chunking is the overarching principle of human cognition:

> A chunk is a unit of memory organization, formed by bringing together a set of already formed chunks in memory and welding them together into a larger unit. Chunking implies the ability to build up such structures recursively, thus leading to a hierarchical organization of memory. Chunking appears to be a ubiquitous feature of human memory. Conceivably, it could form the basis for an equally ubiquitous law of practice. (Newell 1990: 7)

From its very beginnings, psychological research has recognized three major experiential factors that affect cognition: frequency, recency and context (e.g. Anderson 2009; Ebbinghaus 1885; Bartlett [1932] 1967). Learning, memory and perception are all affected by frequency of usage: the more times we experience something, the stronger our memory for it, and the more fluently it is accessed. The more recently we have experienced something, the stronger our memory for it, and the more fluently it is accessed. (Hence your more fluent reading of the prior sentence than the one before.) The more times we experience conjunctions of features, the more they become associated in our minds and the more these subsequently affect perception and categorization, so a stimulus and its interpretation becomes associated to a context and we become more likely to perceive it in that context (hence your recognition of a colleague in their familiar stomping ground, but not unexpectedly in the street). These three aspects of usage drive chunking.

6.2.1 Frequency

The power law of learning (Anderson 1982; Ellis and Schmidt 1998; Newell 1990) describes the relationships between practice and performance in the acquisition of a wide range of cognitive skills – the greater the practice, the greater the performance (including strength of memory, likelihood of recall, and fluency of production or comprehension), although effects of practice are largest at early stages of learning, thereafter diminishing and eventually reaching asymptote. This applies to recognition and recall across our world of experience: people and places, birds and bees, chalk and cheese, and, of course, linguistic constructions, too.

Consider words – though the same is true for letters, morphemes, syntactic patterns and all other types of construction. Through experience, a learner's perceptual system becomes tuned to expect constructions according to their probability of occurrence in the input, with words like *one* or *won* occurring more frequently than words like *seventeen* or *synecdoche*. A learner's initial noticing of a new word can result in an explicit memory that binds its features into a unitary chunked representation, such as the phonological sequence 'wun' or the orthographic sequence *one*. As a result of this, a detector unit for that word is added to the learner's perceptual system, the job of which is to signal the word's presence when its features are present in the input (Morton 1969).

Every word detector has a set resting level of activation and some threshold level which, when exceeded, will cause the detector to fire. When the component features are present in the environment, this increases the activation of the detector; if this takes the level above threshold, the detector fires. With each firing of the detector, the new resting level is slightly higher than the old one: the detector is primed. This means it will need less activation from the environment in order to reach threshold and fire the next time that feature occurs. Priming events sum to lifespan-practice effects: features that occur frequently acquire chronically high resting levels. Their resting level of activity is heightened by the memory of repeated prior activations. Thus our pattern-recognition units for higher-frequency words require less evidence from the sensory data before they reach the threshold necessary for firing. So the perceptual system is tuned by experience of usage.

6.2.2   Recency

Human memory is sensitive to recency: the probability of recalling an item, like the speed of its processing or recognition, is predicted by time since last occurrence. The power function relating probability of recall (or recall latency) and recency is known as the 'forgetting curve' (Baddeley 1997; Ebbinghaus 1885). Language processing also reflects priming effects. Priming may be observed in our phonology, conceptual representations, lexical choice and syntax (McDonough and Trofimovich 2008). Syntactic priming refers to the phenomenon of using a particular syntactic structure, given prior exposure to the same structure. This behavior has been observed when speakers hear, speak, read or write sentences (Bock 1986; Pickering 2006; Pickering and Garrod 2006). (See Chapter 6 of this volume, on priming). Priming is an essential part of conversation partners' aligning and co-constructing meanings.

6.2.3   Context

Human memory is also context dependent: a stimulus (and its interpretation) becomes associated to a context, and we become more likely to perceive it in that context (Baddeley 1997; Godden and Baddeley 1975). A large body of research has shown that memory performance is reduced when an individual's environment differs from encoding to retrieval, as compared to when the two environments are the same (Tulving and Thomson 1973). The context can be environmental (places or cultures), social (speakers or cultures) or linguistic. For an example of linguistic context effects upon processing, Schooler (1993) showed that word fragment completion was faster for the second word of a strong context collocation (as in PROFOUND-IGN____?) than when the word was shown alone (IGN____?). Miller would have talked of this in terms of chunks.

Frequency, recency and context are basic forces in all contemporary psycholinguistic models of language perception and processing (Christiansen and Chater 2001; Jurafsky 2002; Traxler and Gernsbacher 2011; McClelland and Elman 1986; Xu and Tennenbaum 2007; Ellis 1996). We find structure in time (Elman 1990, 2004). Learning is statistically informed, and interpretation is probabilistic: 'Learners FIGURE language out: their task is, in essence, to learn the probability distribution P(interpretation|cue, context), the probability of an interpretation given a formal cue in a particular context, a mapping from form to meaning conditioned by context' (Ellis 2006a). Chunks are probabilistic in their nature and in their processing.

6.3   Chunking Is Rational

Rational analysis (Anderson 1990) aims to answer *why* human cognition is the way it is. Its guiding principle is that the cognitive system optimizes the adaptation of the behavior of the organism to its environment in the sense that the behavior of the mechanism is as efficient as it conceivably could be, given the structure of the problem space or input-output mapping it must solve. Determining optimality for rational behavior requires a quantifiable formulation of the problem. For the case of memory, the criterial factor is the optimal estimation of an item's need probability. Rational analysis considers the way that human memory corresponds to this needs function. Anderson's (1990) rational analysis implicated three factors in determining *information need*. You met them before in the previous section, describing the forces of learning: frequency, recency and context. Consider the relative availability of items in the mental lexicon.

6.3.1   Frequency

The probability of a word occurring in a particular source is predicted by its past frequency of occurrence in that source. It works for all sorts of information. Whether organizing a library, a mental lexicon or a tool shop, you should have the most-used items nearer to hand. The power law of learning is rational in that it follows this trend. Memory performance is tuned to the world.

6.3.2   Recency

There is a power function relating the probability of a word occurring on day *n* to how long it has been since the word previously occurred. The probability of a word occurring in, say, speech to children (from the CHILDES database), or the *New York Times*, or the e-mail a person receives is predicted by its past probability of occurrence – there is a power function relating the probability of a word occurring in the headline in the *New York Times* on day *n* to how long it has been since the word previously occurred there. The forgetting curve is rational in that it follows this trend. Things happen in bursts (Barabási 2005, 2010). You can see this in your e-mail – you do not hear from someone for a while, then there is a flurry of correspondence, and then things quiet down on that front again.

6.3.3   Context

A particular word is more likely to occur when other words that have historically co-occurred with it are present. In analysis of the *New York Times* and the CHILDES databases, Schooler (1993) showed that a particular word was more likely to occur when other words that had occurred with it in the past were present. For instance, a headline one day mentioned Qaddafi and Libya, and sure enough a headline the next day that mentioned Qaddafi also mentioned Libya. I am sure you could think of parallel examples from this week's news. Schooler collected likelihood ratio measures of association between various words in order to assess the effect of this local context factor on memory and processing. As already described, in both the child language and the *New York Times* databases, a word was more likely to occur if it had occurred previously, but additionally a word was more likely to occur in a headline if a string associate of it occurred, and these effects are additive in the way predicted by Bayesian probability.

See how these three aspects of *information need* in the problem space are satisfied by their *cognitive* counterparts in learning, memory and perception summarized in Section 6.2. Chunking provides a rational representation of usage. It both builds the representations and organizes their relative availability according to need.

6.4 Psycholinguistics: Everything in Language Comes in Chunks

Ellis (2002) reviewed how the 50 years of psycholinguistic research from 1950 onward demonstrated language processing to be exquisitely sensitive to chunk frequency at all levels of language representation: phonology and phonotactics, reading, spelling, lexis, morphosyntax, formulaic language, language comprehension, grammaticality, sentence production and syntax. Usage shapes *every aspect* of language. There is space here for just a few illustrative examples.

6.4.1 Phonotactic Chunks

Frisch et al. (2001) asked native speakers to judge, using a 7-point rating scale, non-word stimuli for whether they were more or less like English words. The non-words were created with relatively high- or low-probability legal phonotactic patterns, as determined by the logarithm of the product of probabilities of the onset and rime constituents of the non-word. The mean wordlikeness judgments for these non-word stimuli had an extremely strong relationship with expected probability ($r = .87$).

6.4.2 Lexical Chunks

High-frequency words are named more rapidly than low-frequency ones (Balota and Chumbley 1984), they are more rapidly judged to be words in lexical decision tasks (Forster 1976) and they are spelled more accurately (Barry and Seymour 1988). When naming pictures, people are more successful and faster on items with higher-frequency names (Oldfield and Wingfield 1965).

Auditory word recognition is better for high-frequency than low-frequency words (Luce 1986; Savin 1963). There are also cohort effects in spoken word recognition. Hearing the initial phoneme of a word activates the set of all words in the lexicon that have this same phoneme. Then, as the speech signal unfolds over time and more information is received, the set is narrowed down. In the cohort model of speech recognition

(Marslen-Wilson 1990), activation in the cohort varies so that items are not simply 'in or out'. Rather, higher-frequency words get more activation from the same evidence than do low-frequency words. This underlies lexical similarity effects whereby a whole neighborhood of words is activated but the higher-frequency words get more activation and so listeners are slower to recognize low-frequency words with high-frequency neighbors because the competitors are harder to eliminate (Lively et al. 1994). Thus, the language processing system is sensitive both to the frequency of individual words and to the number of words which share the same beginnings (at any length of computation).

6.4.3   Orthographic Chunks

English spelling-to-sound mapping is a 'quasi-regular' domain. Words consisting of orthographic chunks with regular or consistent mappings to pronunciation are read better than those with irregular or inconsistent mappings. For the case of adult fluency in English, after controlling for overall word frequency, words with regular spelling-sound correspondences (like *mint*) are read with shorter naming latencies and lower error rates than words with exceptional correspondences (cf. *pint*) (Coltheart 1978); in development, exception words (*blood, bouquet*) are acquired later than are regular words (*bed, brandy*) (Coltheart and Leahy 1996).

Similarly, words which are consistent in their pronunciation, in terms of whether this agrees with those of their neighbors with similar orthographic body and phonological rime (*best* is regular and consistent in that all *-est* bodies are pronounced in the same way), are named faster than inconsistent items (*mint* is regular in terms of its grapheme-phoneme conversion (GPC) rule, but inconsistent in that it has the deviant *pint* as a neighbor) (Glushko 1979). The magnitude of the consistency effect for any word depends on the summed frequency of its friends (similar spelling pattern and similar pronunciation) in relation to that of its enemies (similar spelling pattern but dissimilar pronunciation) (Jared et al. 1990). Adult naming latency decreases monotonically with increasing consistency on this measure (Taraban and McClelland 1987). Because of the power law of learning, these effects of regularity and consistency are more evident with low-frequency words than with high-frequency ones, where performance is closer to asymptote (Seidenberg et al. 1984).

In development, Laxon et al. (1991) have shown that within regular words, consistent (*pink*, all *-ink*) and consensus (*hint*, mostly as in *mint*, but cf. *pint*) items are acquired earlier than ambiguous ones (*cove* vs. *love, move*) and that within irregular words, those in deviant gangs where the several items sharing that rime are all pronounced in the same irregular fashion (like *look, book, cook*, etc., or *calm, balm, palm*) are acquired earlier than ambiguous ones (*love*). As with the learning of other quasi-regular language domains, these effects of consistency/ambiguity of spelling-sound correspondence within a language have been successfully simulated in connectionist models (Harm and Seidenberg 1999; Seidenberg and McClelland 1989).

6.4.4   *Morphological Chunks*

Morphological processing, like reading and listening, also shows effects of neighbors and false friends where regular inconsistent items (e.g. *bake-baked* is similar in rhyme to neighbors *make-made* and *take-took*, which have inconsistent past tenses) are produced more slowly than entirely regular ones (e.g. *hate-hated, bate-bated, date-dated*) (Daugherty and Seidenberg 1994; Seidenberg and Bruck 1990).

Psycholinguistic studies of the statistical patterning of chunks and their associations have been central in connectionist models of morphological processing and acquisition. These models capture the regularities that are present (1) in associating phonological form of lemma with phonological form of inflected form and (2) between referents (+past tense or +plural) and associated inflected perfect or plural forms (Cottrell and Plunkett 1994; Ellis and Schmidt 1998), simulating error patterns, profiles of acquisition, differential difficulties, false-friends effects, reaction times for production and interactions of regularity and frequency that are found in human learners (both L1 and L2), as well as acquiring default-case-allowing generalization on 'wug' tests.

Token frequency counts how often a particular form appears in the input. Type frequency, on the other hand, refers to the number of distinct lexical items that can be substituted in a given slot in a construction, whether it is a word-level construction for inflection or a syntactic construction specifying the relation among words. For example, the 'regular' English past tense *-ed* has a very high type frequency because it applies to thousands of different types of verbs, whereas the vowel change exemplified in *swam* and *rang* has much lower type frequency. The productivity of phonological, morphological and syntactic patterns is a function of type rather than token frequency (Bybee and Hopper 2001). This is because (1) the more lexical items that are heard in a certain position in a construction, the less likely it is that the construction is associated with a particular lexical item and the more likely it is that a general category is formed over the items that occur in that position; (2) the more items the category must cover, the more general are its criterial features and the more likely it is to extend to new items; and (3) high type frequency ensures that a construction is used frequently, thus strengthening its representational schema and making it more accessible for further use with new items (Bybee and Thompson 1997). In contrast, high token frequency promotes the entrenchment or conservation of irregular forms and idioms; the irregular forms only survive because they are high frequency.

6.4.5   Collocation Chunks

Reading time is affected by collocational and sequential probabilities. Durrant and Doherty (2010) used lexical decision to assess the degree to which the first word of low-frequency (e.g. *famous saying*), middle-frequency (*recent figures*), high-frequency (*foreign debt*) and high-frequency and psychologically associated (*estate agent*) collocations primed the processing of the second word in native speakers. The highly frequent and high-frequency-associated collocations evidenced significant priming.

The British linguist Firth emphasized the importance of collocational knowledge in our understanding of word meanings: 'You shall know a word by the company it keeps' (Firth 1957). Forty years later, Landauer and Dumais (1997) presented a computational analysis of this maxim. Their Latent Semantic Analysis (LSA) model simulates a language learner's acquisition of vocabulary from text. The model simply treats words as being alike if they tend to co-occur with the same neighboring words in text passages. By inducing global knowledge indirectly from local co-occurrence data in a large body of representative text, LSA acquired knowledge about the full vocabulary of English at a rate comparable to that of school children. After the model had been trained by exposing it to text samples from more than 30,000 articles from *Groliers Academic American Encyclopedia*, it achieved a score of 64 percent on the synonym portion of the Test of English as a Foreign Language (a level expected of a good ESL learner). The performance of LSA is surprisingly good for a model which had no prior linguistic or grammatical knowledge and which could not see or hear, and thus could make no use of phonology, morphology or real-world perceptual knowledge. In this model, lexical semantic acquisition emerges from the analysis of word co-occurrence. Figure 6.2 panel 6 compares *butterfly* and *don't* for the information latent in their collocational contexts.

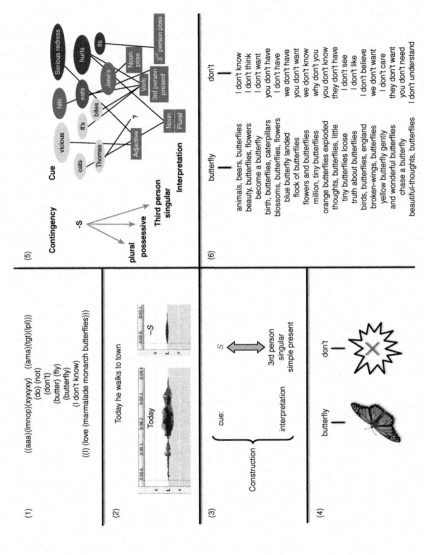

Figure 6.2 Some factors affecting language chunking. (See text for details.)

6.4.6 Phrasal Chunks

Arnon and Snider (2010) used a phrasal decision task (Is this phrase possible in English or not?) to show that comprehenders are also sensitive to the frequencies of compositional four-word phrases: more-frequent phrases (e.g. *don't have to worry*) were processed faster than less-frequent phrases (*don't have to wait*), even though these were matched for the frequency of the individual words or substrings. Tremblay, Derwing, Libben and Westbury (2011) examined the extent to which lexical bundles (LBs, defined as frequently recurring strings of words that often span traditional syntactic boundaries) are stored and processed holistically. Three self-paced reading experiments compared sentences containing LBs (e.g. *in the middle of the*) and matched control sentence fragments (*in the front of the*) such as *I sat in the middle/front of the bullet train*. LBs and sentences containing LBs were read faster than the control sentence fragments in all three experiments.

Maintenance of material in short-term memory and its accurate subsequent production is also affected by knowledge of formulaic sequences. Bannard and Matthews (2008) identified frequently occurring chunks in child-directed speech (e.g. *sit in your chair*) and matched them to infrequent sequences (e.g. *sit in your truck*). They tested young children's ability to produce these sequences in a sentence-repetition test. Three-year-olds and two-year-olds were significantly more likely to repeat frequent sequences correctly than to repeat infrequent sequences correctly. Moreover, the three-year-olds were significantly faster to repeat the first three words of an item if they formed part of a chunk (e.g. they were quicker to say *sit in your* when the following word was *chair* than when it was *truck*). Tremblay, Derwing, Libben and Westbury (2011) similarly used word and sentence recall experiments to demonstrate that more sentences containing LBs (the same ones as in their earlier-mentioned comprehension experiments) were correctly remembered by adults in short-term memory experiments.

What about L2 learners? Jiang and Nekrasova (2007) examined the representation and processing of formulaic sequences using online grammaticality judgment tasks. English as a second language speakers and native English speakers were tested with formulaic and non-formulaic phrases matched for word length and frequency (e.g. *to tell the truth* vs. *to tell the price*). Both native and non-native speakers responded to the formulaic sequences significantly faster and with fewer errors than they did to non-formulaic sequences.

Ellis and Simpson-Vlach (2009) and Ellis, Simpson-Vlach and Maynard (2008) used four experimental procedures to determine how the corpus linguistic metrics of frequency and mutual information (MI, a statistical measure of the coherence of strings) are represented implicitly in native and non-native speakers, thus to affect their accuracy and fluency of processing of the formulas of the Academic Formulas List (AFL, Simpson-Vlach and Ellis 2010). The language processing tasks in these experiments were selected to sample an ecologically valid range of language processing skills: spoken and written, production and comprehension, form-focused and meaning-focused. They were (1) speed of reading and acceptance in a grammaticality judgment task where half of the items were real phrases in English and half were not; (2) rate of reading and rate of spoken articulation; (3) binding and primed pronunciation – the degree to which reading the beginning of the formula primed recognition of its final word; and (4) speed of comprehension and acceptance of the formula as being appropriate in a meaningful context. Processing in all experiments was affected by various corpus-derived metrics: length, frequency and mutual information (MI). Frequency was the major determinant for non-native speakers, but for native speakers it was predominantly the MI of the formula which determined processability.

Repetition also leads to automatization and fluency of production (Segalowitz 2010; DeKeyser 2001; Anderson 1992). Forms that are used highly frequently become phonologically eroded. 'Words used together fuse together' (Bybee 2003) (after Hebb's (1949) research often summarized by the phrase 'Cells that fire together, wire together') (see also Ellis, this volume, Chapter 4, Section 4.2).

6.4.7   Chunks in Sentence Processing

There is a substantial literature demonstrating sensitivity to such sequential information in sentence processing (see MacDonald and Seidenberg 2006 for review).

Consider sentences (1) beginning 'The plane left for the ...' Does the second word refer to a geometric element, an airplane or a tool? Does the third imply a direction, or is it the past tense of the verb leave in active or in passive voice?

(1)   a. The plane left for the East Coast.
         b. The plane left for the reporter was missing.

What of the likelihood of the past tense passive interpretation of leave in the sentence beginning 'The note left for the . . .' as in (2). Is it greater or less than that for the plane sentence (1b)?

(2)   The note left for the reporter was missing.

Psycholinguistic experiments show that fluent adults resolve such ambiguities by rapidly exploiting a variety of probabilistic constraints derived from previous experience (Seidenberg 1997). There is the first-order frequency information: *plane* is much more frequent in its vehicle meaning than in its other possible meanings, *left* is used more frequently in active rather than passive voice. The ambiguity is constrained by the frequency with which the ambiguous verb occurs in transitive and passive structures, of which reduced relative clauses are a special type (MacDonald 1994; MacDonald et al. 1994). On top of this there are combinatorial constraints: sentence (2) is easier to comprehend as a reduced relative clause than sentence (1b) because it is much more plausible for a note to be left than for it to leave (Trueswell et al. 1994).

These psycholinguistic studies of sentence processing show that fluent adults have a vast statistical knowledge about the behavior of lexical items and the chunks they inhabit in their language. Fluent comprehenders know the relative frequencies with which particular verbs appear in different tenses, in active vs. passive and in intransitive vs. transitive structures, the typical kinds of subjects and objects that a verb takes, and many other such facts. This information is relevant at all stages of lexical, syntactic and discourse comprehension (Seidenberg and MacDonald 1999). Frequent analyses are preferred to less-frequent ones.

Eye-movement research shows that the fixation time on each word in reading is a function of the frequency of that word (frequent words have shorter fixations) and of the forward transitional probability (the conditional probability of a word given the previous word $P(w_k|w_{k-1})$: for example, the probability of the word *in*, given that the previous word was *interested*, is higher than the probability of *in* if the last word was *dog*) (McDonald and Shillcock 2003a, 2003b). Parsing time reflects the more-frequent uses of a word (e.g. the garden-path effect caused by *The old man the bridge*, in which *man* is used as a verb). Phrase-frequency affects parsing in a similar way. For example, ambiguity resolution is driven not only by how often a verb appears as a past participle and how likely a noun is to be an agent, but also by the exact frequencies of the noun-verb combination. Reali and Christiansen (2007) demonstrate such effects of chunk frequency in the processing of object relative clauses. Sentences such as *The person*

who I met distrusted the lawyer, are easier to process when the embedded
clause is formed by frequent pronoun-verb combinations (*I liked* or *I met*)
than when it is formed by less-frequent combinations (*I distrusted* or
I phoned).

Generally, analyses of large corpora of eye-movements recorded when
people read text demonstrate that measures of surprisal account for the
costs in reading time that result when the current word is not predicted by
the preceding context. Measuring surprisal requires a probabilistic notion
of linguistic structure (utilizing transitional probabilities or probabilistic
grammars). The surprisal of a word in a sentential context corresponds to
the probability mass of the analyses that are not consistent with the new
word (Demberg and Keller 2008).

6.4.8   Hierarchies of Chunking

This research demonstrates that associative learning from usage results in
chunking at all levels of language. Language knowledge involves statistical
knowledge, so humans learn more easily and process more fluently high-
frequency forms and 'regular' patterns which are exemplified by many
types and which have few competitors. Usage-based perspectives of acquisition thus hold that language learning is the implicit associative learning of
representations that reflect the probabilities of occurrence of form-
function mappings. Frequency is a key determinant of acquisition because
'rules' of language, at all levels of analysis from phonology through syntax
to discourse, are structural regularities which emerge from learners' lifetime
unconscious analysis of the distributional characteristics of the language
input.

6.5   Connectionism and Statistical Language Learning

Psycholinguistics demonstrates the ubiquity of chunking in language;
connectionism and statistical language learning approaches investigate
chunking in acquisition and processing. Connectionist theories are data-
rich and process-light: massively parallel systems of artificial neurons use
simple learning processes to statistically abstract information from corpora
of representative input data (Elman et al. 1996; Christiansen and Chater
2001; Rumelhart and McClelland 1986). The work of Elman (1990) on
'finding structure in time' was influential in demonstrating the types of
syntagmatic and semantic structures that are emergent from linguistic
sequences.

6.5.1   *Phonological Sequences*

Elman (1990) used a simple recurrent network (SRN) to investigate the temporal properties of sequential inputs of language. The network was fed one letter at a time and had to predict the next letter in the sequence. It was trained on 200 sentences where there was no word or sentence boundary information. The network abstracted a lot of information about the structure of English. It learned about orthographic sequential probabilities; it learned that there were common recurring units (which we might identify as morphemes and words); it extracted word sequence information, too. At times, when the network could not predict the actual next phoneme, it nonetheless predicted the correct category of phoneme: vowel/consonant, etc. Thus it moved from processing mere surface regularities to representing something more abstract, but without this being built in as a pre-specified constraint: linguistically useful generalizations emerged. Simple sequence learning processes learned regular chunks like words, bound morphemes, collocations and idioms; they learned regularities of transition between these surface chunks; and they acquired abstract generalizations from the patterns in these data.

Such chunks are potential labels, but what about reference? The more any word or formula is repeated in phonological working memory, the more its regularities and chunks are abstracted, and the more accurately and readily these can be called to working memory, either for accurate pronunciation as articulatory output or as labels for association with other representations (e.g. Ellis 1994a). It is from these potential associations with other representations that other interesting properties of language emerge. I will return to this is Section 6.6.

6.5.2   *Syntactic Sequences*

Learning the grammatical word-class of a particular word, and learning grammatical structures more generally, involves the automatic implicit analysis of the word's sequential position relative to other words in the learner's stock of known phrases which contain it. Elman (1990) trained a recurrent network on sequences of words following a simple grammar, the network having to learn to predict the next word in the sequence. At the end of training, he cluster-analyzed the representations that the model had formed across its hidden unit activations for each word+context vector. This showed that the network had discovered several major categories of words – large categories of verbs and nouns, smaller categories of

inanimate or animate nouns, smaller-still categories of human and nonhu-
man animals, etc. (e.g. 'dragon' occurred as a pattern in activation space in
the region corresponding to the category animals and also in the larger
region shared by animates, and finally in the area reserved for nouns).
The category structure was hierarchical, soft and implicit. The network
moved from processing mere surface regularities to representing something
more abstract, but without this being built in as a pre-specified syntactic or
other linguistic constraint and without provision of semantics or real-
world grounding. Relatively general architectural constraints gave rise to
language-specific representational constraints as a product of processing
the input strings. These linguistically relevant representations were an
emergent property of the network's functioning (see Redington and
Chater 1998 for larger analyses of this type on corpora of natural language).
Learning the grammatical categories and requirements of words and word
groups reduces to the analysis of the sequence in which words work in
chunks.

6.5.3   Statistical Language Learning

Saffran, Aslin and Newport (1996) demonstrated that eight-month-old
infants exposed for only 2 minutes to unbroken strings of nonsense
syllables (e.g. *bidakupado*) are able to detect the difference between three-
syllable sequences that appeared as a unit and sequences that also
appeared in their learning set but in random order. Statistical language
learning has since become a major research field, demonstrating, in infant
language acquisition (Molnar and Sebastian-Galles 2014) and child language acquisition (Rebuschat and Williams 2012), how language learners
implicitly learn the statistics of the language to which they are exposed,
and how the representational chunks that emerge from this implicit
learning form a rich system that, through 'repeated cycles of integration
and differentiation' (Studdert-Kennedy 1991), associates phonology, syntax and semantics 'in richly structured and productive ways'
(MacWhinney and O'Grady 2015).

   There is much research into the types of statistical learning that are
possible, both implicitly and explicitly. Figure 6.2 panel 1 illustrates some
of the factors that affect sequential associative learning, including the
transparency of the underlying structure and the units over which learning
is taking place. In particular, while sequential dependencies can be implicitly learned, discontinuous dependencies are more problematic and may
require working memory representation and explicit learning (Rebuschat

and Williams 2012). Figure 6.2 panel 2 illustrates how some units in the speech stream are much more salient than others, and therefore are more likely to enter into implicit learning (see my Chapter 4 in this volume, Section 4.1.3.1 – Psychophysical Salience).

6.6 Chunks, Symbols and Constructions

Chunking does not only take place within the sequences of language form. Chunking binds form with meaning in symbolic constructions. Many of the examples in Section 6.4 related to cross-modal association between, for example, print and sound in reading, or form and meaning in sentence processing. Constructions are form-meaning mappings, conventionalized in the speech community, and entrenched as language knowledge in the learner's mind. They are the symbolic units of language relating the defining properties of their morphological, syntactic and lexical form with particular semantic, pragmatic and discourse functions (Croft and Cruise 2004; Robinson and Ellis 2008; Goldberg 1995, 2003, 2006; Croft 2001; Tomasello 2003; Bates and MacWhinney, 1987; Langacker 1987; Lakoff 1987; Bybee 2008b).

Broadly, Construction Grammar argues that all grammatical phenomena can be understood as learned pairings of form (from morphemes, words and idioms, to partially lexically filled and fully general phrasal patterns) and their associated semantic or discourse functions. Figure 6.2 panel 3 illustrates such a form-function mapping. Whereas sequential learning may well take place implicitly, at least for adjacent elements, the seeding of cross-modal associations is usually a result of conscious, explicit processing, although thereafter, the strengths of these associations are also implicitly tuned during usage.

6.6.1 *Learning Novel Form-Meaning Associations*

Research on explicit learning (e.g. Ellis 2005) has shown how conscious processing promotes the acquisition of novel, explicit, cross-modal, form-meaning associations. These breathe meaning into the processing of language form. Form-meaning chunks are symbolic constructions. Learning a new symbol, for example a lexical construction, as an explicit declarative memory from a sound-image episode such as 'étoile'-★ involves explicit learning (Ellis 1994a). The primary conscious involvement in language acquisition is the explicit learning involved in the initial registration of pattern recognizers for constructions that are then tuned and integrated into the system by implicit learning during subsequent input processing.

Neural systems in the prefrontal cortex involved in working memory provide attentional selection, perceptual integration and the unification of consciousness. Explicit learning results in explicit memories.

Neural systems in the hippocampus bind disparate cortical representations into unitary episodic representations (Ellis 2005: 305). By forming unitized memory representations, the hippocampal region performs the information-processing function of forming pattern-recognition units for new stimulus configurations and of consolidating new bindings; these are then adopted by other brain regions in the neocortex where they subsequently partake in implicit tuning (Gluck et al. 2003). Once such cross-modal chunks have been consolidated, these representations are also then available as units of implicit learning in subsequent processing, allowing statistical learning and tallying of form-meaning contingencies. Some of the cross-modal associations are much richer in their perceptual imagery than others (see my Chapter 4 in this volume, Section 4.1.3.2, Salient Associations). Figure 6.2 panel 4 illustrates this.

The function relating strength of association and frequency of experience is the power law of practice. Like other stimuli, linguistic forms are typically ambiguous. The same form can attract different meanings. So there is competition between the different meaning candidates when it comes to interpretation (see Chapter 12 in this volume, on ambiguity). As described in Section 6.4.7, parsing and comprehension are probabilistic processes. The resolution of this competition depends upon the contingency of form and functions in prior experience.

6.6.2   Contingency

Because linguistic forms are ambiguous and carry multiple meanings with varying strengths of association, it is not just the frequency of encounter of a construction that determines its acquisition. The degree to which animals, human and other alike, learn associations between cues and outcomes depends upon the contingency of the relationship as well. In classical conditioning, it is the reliability of the bell as a predictor of food that determines the ease of acquisition of this association (Rescorla 1968). In language learning, it is the reliability of the form as a predictor of an interpretation that determines its acquisition (MacWhinney 1987a). The last thirty years of psychological investigation into human sensitivity to the contingency between cues and outcomes (Shanks 1995) demonstrates that when, given sufficient exposure to a relationship, people's judgments match quite closely the contingency specified by ΔP (the one-way dependency statistic, Allan

Table 6.1 *A contingency table showing the four*
possible combinations of events, showing the presence
or absence of a target cue and an outcome

	Outcome	No outcome
Cue	a	b
No cue	c	d

1980), which measures the directional association between a cue and an outcome, as illustrated in Table 6.1.

In the table, a, b, c and d represent frequencies, so, for example, *a* is the frequency of conjunctions of the cue and the outcome, and *c* is the number of times the outcome occurred without the cue.

$$\Delta P = P(O|C) - P(O|\neg C) = \frac{a}{a+b} - \frac{c}{c+d}$$

ΔP is the probability of the outcome, given the cue (P(O|C) minus the probability of the outcome in the absence of the cue ($P(O|\neg C)$). When these are the same, when the outcome is just as likely when the cue is present as when it is not, there is no covariation between the two events and $\Delta P = 0$. ΔP approaches 1.0 as the presence of the cue increases the likelihood of the outcome and approaches -1.0 as the cue decreases the chance of the outcome – a negative association.

Some cues, especially grammatical functors, are ambiguous in their interpretations, and this makes them difficult to learn (Figure 6.2, panel 5). Connectionist and psycholinguistic research shows that the strength of association between a linguistic form and an interpretation is also updated implicitly from usage, and the likelihood that a particular interpretation comes to mind is a function of the relative strengths of association of the various possible outcomes.

6.7 Chunking in Language Change

I have described the learning theory and psycholinguistic evidence of chunking: how each episode of usage strengthens the relevant associations, and how these effects cumulate into syntagmatic frequency effects whereby more-frequent linguistic forms are preferentially recognized and more fluently produced, as well as associative frequency effects whereby

interpretation and expression of form-function mappings reflect the
satisfaction of statistical constraints. Chunking provides a rational representation of usage. It both builds the representations and organizes their
relative availability and fluency according to need.

6.7.1   The Principle of Least Effort Shapes an Artisan's Tools

The work of Zipf (1935, 1949) provides comprehensive empirical evidence
of the effects of these processes in language structure, usage and change.
Zipf's (1949) groundbreaking analysis of the ecology of language centers
upon communicative function, where linguistic constructions are tools for
sharing meanings. He laid the foundations by carefully crafting a tool
analogy to illustrate the operation of the *principle of least effort*. It is
a productive and provocative metaphor:

> An artisan works at his bench, with *n* different tools of various sizes and
> weights arranged on a straight board in front of him as he sees fit. His
> occupation is to perform for us certain jobs using his tools as economically as
> possible. We do not care how many tools he uses, nor how he alters their
> shape, weight, and usage, nor how he arranges them upon the board.

The work of using a tool consists of transporting it from its place on the
board to the artisan's lap and then back again after its use. Over time, he
adapts the arrangement of his tools according to their usage, taking
account of the mass *m* of the tool, the distance *d* away on the board and
the frequency of use *f* (Zipf 1949: 59). In order to use his tools with the
maximum economy *'he must arrange the n tools of his shop in such a way that
the sum of all of the products of f × m × d for each of the n tools will be
a minimum'* (1949: 59). You will be reminded now of rational analysis as
discussed in Section 6.3.1 – clearly, the most frequently used tools should
be kept closer to hand. But various additional economic principles apply.
Ideally, there should be a 'close packing' of tools, for then *d* is reduced.
From this follows the *principle of the abbreviation of the size* – the smaller
the size *s* of the tools and their mass *m* can become, the more closely they
can be packed together – as well as the *principle of the abbreviation of mass* –
reducing the mass *m* of the tools will also lessen the work (*m × d*) (1949: 61).
The redesigning of tools according to these principles should take account
of their frequency of use: 'the artisan will lay a premium upon the reduc-
tions of the sizes of all of the tools in proportion to their nearness to him'
(1949: 61). The arrangement aims to more closely pack together the tools as
well as to reduce their *n* number.

So much for the forms of the tools. But what of their functions? The more functions a tool can perform, the fewer the total necessary number *n* of tools. In their redesign, it is economical to adapt the easiest tool so that it absorbs the jobs of other less-easy tools and thereby increase its own frequency of use still more. In increasing the frequency of the easiest tool, the easier its use is made by abbreviation – and the easier the tool's use is made by abbreviation, the more frequently it is used. *'In short, greater frequency makes for greater ease which makes for greater frequency and so on'* (1949: 62).

> As a result of the artisan's redesignings, every one of the tools can have been altered in form and function from its original state beyond all present recognition. Some tools may have changed their form but preserved their usage; By definition, this is a *formal change*. Some tools may have preserved their form but changed their usage; by definition this is a *semantic change*. And some may have done both and others may have done neither.
>
> Nevertheless, whatever alterations were or were not undertaken from moment to moment in the course of the shop's history, they were all undertaken, or not undertaken, as a response to the minimizing of the total work of the shop, according to the 'minimum equation', which directly or indirectly refers to all form, function, and arrangement. Therefore we may say that, from moment to moment, the shop was seeking to preserve by definition a *formal-semantic balance in the forms or usages of its tools.* (1949: 63)

Over time, the more frequent tools tend to become lighter, smaller, older, more versatile and more thoroughly integrated with the action of other tools because of their permutations of use with them. They are also the most valuable tools in the system, in that their permanent loss would cause the relatively greatest cost of redesigning and retooling. Hence, it is most economical to conserve the most frequent tools.

6.7.2   *The Principle of Least Effort Shapes Linguistic Tools*

Zipf's artisan's board is straight in order to allow his tool analogy to parallel the one-dimensionality of the serial speech stream. (*Get it?* – How bland are these two words individually, but how potent in the holophrase, in the context.) In the next 150 pages, he extends the principle of least effort to the economy of language and how this shapes language change. In the evolution of human behavior and 'all trades, their gear and tackle and trim' (Hopkins 1918), flint, bone and rocks have undergone formal and semantic changes, emerging as spades, Swiss-Army knives, Brown (#4) Robertson-head screwdrivers and all manner of specialist tools. Likewise the evolution of language involves formal changes – for example, *telephone, gasoline* and

omnibus have become *phone, gas* and *bus* – and semantic changes where
shorter words have been substituted for longer ones – for example, *car* for
automobile, or *juice* for *electricity* – and the shorter substitutions have taken
on the specialized meaning of the longer word: *juice* now means 'electricity', among other things (Zipf 1949: 67).

His theoretical insights are matched by admirable empirical effort and
precision. He reports extensive analyses of many corpora of some thousands
of words from different authors, genres, languages and eras. He counts words
as tools, measuring their frequency, their packing as a function of length and
other aspects of psychophysical mass, their semantic versatility, their degree
of collocation or permutation with other words and their age in the language. This work is particularly impressive, given that it was performed
when *computer* meant 'a person who makes calculations', well before the
digital age. His analyses reveal several *universal laws of language*.

6.7.3   *Universal Laws of Language*

The most fundamental of these laws, now eponymous as *Zipf's law*,
describes the frequency distribution of words: the frequency of words
f decreases as a power function of their rank *r* in the frequency table.
Thus the most frequent word (in English, *the*, with a token frequency of
~60,000/million words) occurs approximately twice as often as the second-
most-frequent word, three times as often as the third-most-frequent word,
etc. The rank-frequency relationship, since $r \times f = C$, 'appears on doubly
logarithmic chart paper as a succession of points descending in a straight
line from left to right at an angle of 45°' (Zipf 1949: 24[1]). Zipf demonstrated
that this scaling law holds across a wide variety of language samples. It has
been confirmed repeatedly since.

Next is the *law of abbreviation of words*:

> Every language is demonstrably undergoing formal and semantic changes
> which act on the whole in the direction of shortening the sizes of longer
> words, or of increasing the frequency of shorter words. Moreover, as far as
> we know, every language shows an inverse relationship between the lengths
> and frequencies of the usage of its words. (Zipf 1949: 66)

The longer the period of usage over which this shortening can apply, the
shorter the resultant word. Zipf (1949: 111) shows graphs relating word
length (number of syllables, 1–6), period (Old English, Middle English,
15th, 16th, 17th, 18th, 19th centuries) and percentage coverage of the
newspaper text, whereby the sizes and frequencies of words are inversely

related to their age, with the result that the longer and less-frequent words tend to be the younger ones.

The *principle of the economical versatility of words* describes how the number of different 'meanings' of a word decreases according to the square root of its frequency, i.e. $mr = \sqrt{Fr}$. His first demonstration of this, figure 2.2 (Zipf 1949: 29–30), concerns how the average number of different meanings of the twenty successive sets of 1,000 words in the Thorndike Frequency Count of English, when ranked in order of decreasing frequency, decrease in proportion to the square root of the rank.

The *principle of the economical permutation of words* describes how the number of different permutations into which a word enters, as along with the frequencies with which the permutations occur, is directly related to the frequency of the word. Thus, for example, the more frequently a word appears in the language, the ever more frequently it is used in holophrases.

Many of these principles work at other sizes of grain. For example, the *Economical Permutation of Morphemes in Words* describes how the magnitudes of morphemes decrease as their frequencies increase.

The impulse behind these various principles is the economy that comes from the 'close packing' of tools and the reduction of their *n* number. Because of this influence,

> there is a tendency for old age, small size, versatility of meaning, and a multiplicity of permutational associations all to be directly correlated with high frequency of usage . . .
>
> All the Principles are all constantly operating simultaneously, for the preservation of a dynamic equilibrium with a maximum of economy. That is, in dynamic processes, words are constantly being shortened, permuted, eliminated, borrowed, and altered in meaning. (Zipf 1949: 121)

These are serious linguistic universals. Zipf's work is astonishing in so many ways: it pioneered the ubiquity of power law relationships in complex systems, corpus analysis and empirical linguistics, dynamic systems theory, rational analysis and the recognition that psycholinguistic processes and the structures and functions of language are inextricably linked in usage.

6.7.4   *A Zipfian Analysis of Contemporary English*

For the case of language change in English as it relates to chunking, it is instructive to update his law of abbreviation analysis using more-modern corpora and statistical techniques. Figure 6.3 shows the relation between length in phonemes (top) and alphabetic letters (bottom) and log frequency of occurrence for the 54,447 word form types constituting more than

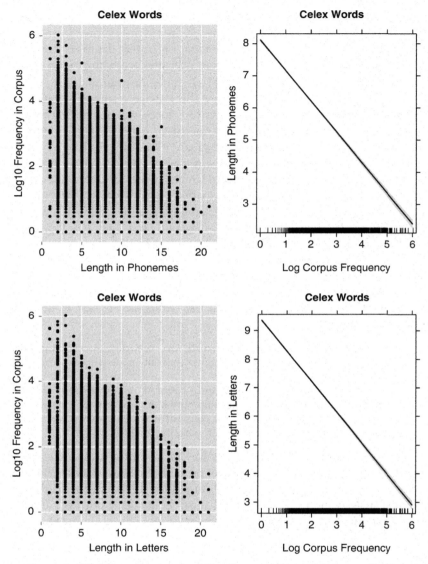

Figure 6.3 The relation between length in phonemes *(top)* and in letters *(bottom)* and log frequency of occurrence for English words in the CELEX database. Note that in each column there are many more observations at lower frequencies than at higher ones. Indeed, in each column there is a Zipfian frequency distribution (though you cannot see the long tail here). So these figures are driven by two of Zipf's universals. The right-hand plots show the regression line relating length and log frequency.

18 million word tokens in the CELEX lexical database of English. The law of abbreviation of words clearly applies equally to spoken and written word forms.

Figure 6.4 shows the relation between length (in letters) and log frequency of occurrence for the top 5,000 words, 2-word, 3-word, 4-word,

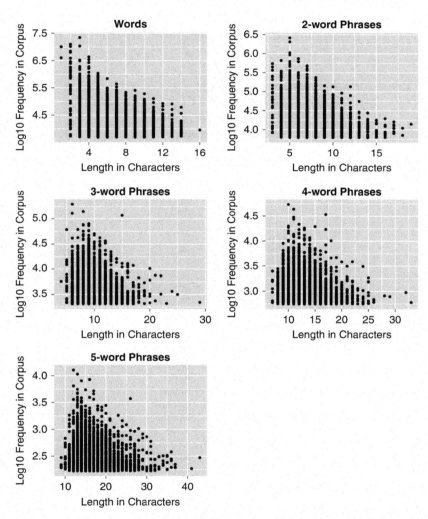

Figure 6.4 The relation between length (in letters) and log frequency of occurrence for the top 5,000 words, two-word-, three-word, four-word and five-word phrases of English from COCA.

and 5-word phrases from the largest publicly available, genre-balanced corpus of English: the 450-million-word Corpus of Contemporary American English (COCA)[2]. I use letter length here rather than phoneme length for convenience, given the same effects upon spoken and written form in Figure 6.3. Again, the law of abbreviation of words clearly applies. The inverse association of length and frequency clearly holds for 2- to 5-gram phrases, too. The shaping of these words is clearly shown in Table 6.2, which shows the top six along with six examples from the

Table 6.2 *Rank, frequency, example ngram and length of 1-, 2-, 3-, 4- and 5-grams in the 450-million-word Corpus of Contemporary American English (COCA)*

Rank	Frequency	Ngram	Length
Words (1-grams)[1]			
1	22,038,615	The	3
2	12,545,825	Be	2
3	10,741,073	And	3
4	10,343,885	Of	2
5	10,144,200	A	1
6	6,996,437	In	2
. . ..			
99,914	17	Septicaemia	11
100,033	17	slum-dwellers	13
100,112	16	Mistily	7
100,200	16	ill-bred	8
100,223	16	Spackle	7
100,439	16	Reappointed	11
2-grams[2]			
1	2,586,813	of the	5
2	2,043,262	in the	5
3	1,055,301	to the	5
4	920,079	on the	5
5	737,714	and the	6
6	657,504	to be	4
. . .			
1,020,318	23	zoo Atlanta	10
1,020,319	23	zoo director	11
1,020,337	23	zoom is	6
1,020,348	23	zooms out	8
1,020,375	23	zulu nation	10
1,020,380	23	Zurich to	8

Table 6.2 *(cont.)*

Rank	Frequency	Ngram	Length
3-grams			
1	198,630	I do n't	6
2	140,305	one of the	8
3	129,406	a lot of	6
4	117,289	the United States	15
5	79,825	do n't know	9
6	76,782	out of the	8
. . .			
1,011,682	25	youth may be	10
1,011,694	25	youths who had	12
1,011,726	25	Zero to Three	11
1,011,736	25	zip code and	10
1,011,750	25	zone is the	9
1,011,760	25	Zoning Board of	13
4-grams			
1	54,647	I do n't know	10
2	43,766	I do n't think	11
3	33,975	in the United States	17
4	29,848	the end of the	11
5	27,176	do n't want to	11
6	21,537	the rest of the	12
. . .			
1,001,168	13	you've got to get	13
1,001,170	13	Yugoslav republic of Macedonia	27
1,001,177	13	zero in New York	13
1,001,191	13	Zoe Baird and Kimba	16
1,001,200	13	zucchini and yellow squash	23
1,001,201	13	Zukerman joins us now	18
5-grams			
1	12,663	I do n't want to	12
2	10,663	at the end of the	13
3	8,484	in the middle of the	16
4	8,038	I do n't know what	14
5	6,446	I do n't know if	12
6	5,551	I do n't think it	13
. . .			
989,575	6	Zero Tolerance Approach to Punctuation	34

Table 6.2 *(cont.)*

Rank	Frequency	Ngram	Length
989,576	6	zest cup fresh lemon juice	22
989,577	6	Ziggy Marley and the Melody	23
989,579	6	zinc oxide or titanium dioxide	26
989,586	6	Zukerman joins us now to	20
989,587	6	Zulu nationalist Inkatha Freedom Party	34

[1] Word frequencies www.wordfrequency.info/100 k_samples.asp (Retrieved November 28, 2014)
[2] 1 million most frequent 2-, 3-, 4- and 5-grams in the largest publicly available, genre-balanced corpus of English – the 450-million-word Corpus of Contemporary American English (COCA) www.ngrams.info/ Retrieved November 28, 2014

bottom of ranks of the approximately 100,000 most-frequent words in the corpus. Indeed, there is a tendency for old age, small size, versatility of meaning and a multiplicity of permutational associations all to be directly correlated with the highest frequency of usage here. These are the words which take the most pages of explanation of their many meanings and functions in major dictionaries (e.g. Simpson and Weiner 1989) and grammars (e.g. Biber et al. 1999). These are the words which enter the majority of different colligational permutations with other words, as well as the frequencies with which the permutations occur. These are the words which, if lost as a whole, would cause the relatively greatest cost of redesigning and retooling the grammar of English.

Note that the use of orthography blunts the shortening effects at highest frequencies, where words like *the* and *and*, which have three orthographic segments, are spoken as fewer phonemes, *the* as two and *and* being usually produced with only one. Jurafsky et al. (2001) used a phonetically hand-transcribed subset of 38,000 tokens from the Switchboard corpus to gauge the role of frequency, measuring word length on an acoustic representation of small subsets of words. They show that function words that are more predictable are shorter and more likely to have reduced vowels, supporting a probabilistic reduction hypothesis whereby the conditional probability of the target word, given the preceding word and given the following one, plays a role on both duration and deletion.

Table 6.2 also illustrates the top six as well as a sample of lowest 1,000,000th-order 2-, 3-, 4- and 5-grams (the lower-frequency examples are also from the end of the alphabet, since the lists are sequenced first by frequency, then by alphabetical order). The higher-frequency phrases are much shorter than the lower-frequency ones, and they tend to serve distinct grammatical or discourse functions. So too, the higher-frequency phrases illustrate the dynamics of chunking and contraction in process, with the multiple exemplars of *I don't* and *you've got*, as described in Bybee (2006). *I* is by far the most frequent pronominal subject of *don't* (210,940) and *you* is the most frequent pronominal subject of *'ve got* (*you* 25,765, *I* 17,535 as I search in COCA now).

Zipf's theoretical and empirical influences are very much in evidence in present-day research (e.g. Ferrer i Cancho and Solé 2003; Kello et al. 2010; Wiechmann et al. 2013; Williams et al. 2014; Thurner et al. 2015; Corral et al. 2015; Ellis et al. 2016).

6.7.5   Grammaticalization

Bybee (2010, 1998, this volume, 2003) and Bybee and Hopper (2001) have developed a model of grammaticization as the process of automatization of frequently occurring sequences of linguistic elements. With repetition, sequences of units that were previously independent come to be processed as a single unit or chunk. This repackaging has two consequences: the identity of the component units is gradually lost, and the whole chunk begins to reduce in form. As described above, these basic principles of automatization apply to all kinds of motor activities: playing a musical instrument, cooking or playing an Olympic sport. They also apply to grammaticization. A phrase such as *(I'm) going to (verb)* which has been frequently used over the last couple of centuries, has been repackaged as a single processing unit. The identity of the component parts is lost (children are often surprised to see that *gonna* is actually spelled *going to*), and the form is substantially reduced.

Thus, in Bybee's model, frequency and chunking are driving forces of language change: (1) frequency of use leads to weakening of semantic force by habituation; (2) phonological changes of reduction and chunking/fusion of grammaticizing constructions are conditioned by their high frequency; (3) increased frequency conditions a greater autonomy for a construction, which means that the individual components of the construction (such as *go, to* or *-ing* in the example of *be going to*) weaken or lose their association with other instances of the same item (as the phrase reduces to *gonna*); (4) the loss of semantic transparency accompanying the rift between the components of the grammaticizing construction and their lexical congeners allows the use of the phrase in new contexts with new pragmatic associations, leading to semantic change; and (5) autonomy of a frequent phrase makes it more entrenched in the language and often conditions the preservation of otherwise-obsolete morphosyntactic characteristics (Bybee 2003).

6.7.6   Other Domains

Section 6.4.4 described how productivity of phonological, morphological and syntactic patterns is a function of type rather than token frequency (Bybee and Hopper 2001), whereas high token frequency promotes the entrenchment or conservation of irregular forms and idioms. The irregular forms only survive because they are high frequency.

For type and token frequency, and the effects of friends and enemies in the dynamics of productivity of patterns in language evolution, Lieberman, Michel, Jackson, Tang and Nowak (2007) studied the regularization of English verbs over the past 1,200 years. English's proto-Germanic ancestor used an elaborate system of productive conjugations to signify past tense, whereas Modern English makes much more productive use of the dental suffix, '-ed'. Lieberman et al. chart the emergence of this linguistic rule amidst the evolutionary decay of its exceptions. By tracking inflectional changes to 177 Old English irregular verbs, of which 145 remained irregular in Middle English and 98 are still irregular today, they showed how the rate of regularization depends on the frequency of word usage. The half-life of an irregular verb scales as the square root of its usage frequency: a verb that is 100 times less frequent regularizes 10 times as fast.

There is a rich literature on frequency effects in the chunking of compound morphology as well. Baayen et al. (2010) analyzed the processing times of English and Dutch compounds in word naming, lexical decision and eye-tracking as a function of the compound token frequency, head and modifier token frequency and head and modifier compound family sizes (type frequencies) in the reading of English and Dutch compounds to show effects of these frequency measures independently as well as in many complex dynamic interactions.

Constructions are nested and overlap at various levels (morphology within lexis within grammar, hierarchical semantic organizations, etc.).

Sequential elements can be memorized multiple times as wholes at these different levels. So there is no one direction of growth, but rather continuing interplay between modalities, between top-down and bottom-up processes and between memorized structures and more-open constructions. Constructions develop hierarchically by repeated cycles of differentiation and integration. This is why we need to go beyond univariate statistics, beyond multivariate statistics still, toward computational modeling (richly informed by corpus data), and why there is sense in viewing language as a complex adaptive system (Beckner et al. 2009).

As usage frequencies affect processing, so they affect language change. In the orthography, lower-frequency compounds are transcribed as two words, whereas higher-frequency compounds become individual lexical entities in their own right (compare *goat herd, pig man, shepherd, cowboy*). These are results of associative learning too. According to the *Shorter Oxford English Dictionary*, the word *pineapple* (from *pine* + *apple*) was originally used in late Middle English to refer to the reproductive organs of conifer trees (now known as *pine cones*). When European explorers discovered the tropical fruit *Ananas comosus* in the Americas, because they looked like (what we now call) pine cones, they named them *pineapples* (first referenced in 1664). Zipf would appreciate the dynamics of the formal-semantic balance through which has evolved, in contemporary English, pineapple coming in chunks.

Notes

1. Not only the computations, but the graphs were drawn by hand too.
2. www.ngrams.info/ Retrieved November 28, 2014.

CHAPTER 7

Chunking and Changes in Compositionality in Context

Joan L. Bybee and Carol Lynn Moder

7.1 Introduction

Recent studies of morphosyntactic change have been influenced by the upsurge in interest in grammaticalization and the view that syntactic patterns are governed by constructions, which can change over time in various ways. The underlying mechanisms that lead to grammaticalization and constructionalization have been sought in general cognitive processes, including the formation of chunks, but also the processes by which chunks acquire meaning from the context. As a process that occurs within an individual speaker as she or he uses language, chunking is a covert change which does not necessarily lead to overt changes in structure or meaning. However, as chunks become more entrenched in a community of speakers, certain overt indicators arise, including distributional tendencies or morphosyntactic restrictions, and, later, changes in meaning and contexts of use.

Chunking comes about through repetition; common word combinations are more easily accessed as a whole rather than through word-by-word access. The most commonly studied changes resulting from chunking, such as those taking place in grammaticalization, tend to occur as the construction gains extremely high frequency. However, chunking also has an impact on word combinations repeated with much lower frequency. It is one such lower-frequency chunk that we study here, the phrase *beg the question*. By examining this phrase over time, we are able to identify rather subtle changes in form and distribution that are the result of chunking. More importantly, however, this phrase helps us understand the role of the local and broader social context in determining the interpretation of the phrase. While most studies of chunks have been focused on the loss of compositionality – that is, the change from a transparent meaning derived from the sum of the parts – the phrase we study reveals both the loss of

148

compositionality and the re-establishment of at least partial compositionality as the broader context of use changes.

7.2   Chunking

Ellis (Chapter 6 of this volume) has made a strong case for chunking as a primary process at all levels of language and grammar. While linguists love to break utterances down into their smallest units, from phonetic segments to morphemes to words, language users have a natural tendency to group such small units into larger combinations for easier access and memory storage. This natural and completely unconscious process is evident in all categories of human activity: units that are repeated in sequence lead to the creation of a cognitive sequence and the more the sequence is repeated, the stronger the cohesion among the contiguous cognitive elements becomes. This process affects linguistic units and forms the basis of constructions and constituents (Bybee 2002; Beckner and Bybee 2009).

While the question has probably never been put to historical linguists, it is likely that most would not consider the formation of a chunk by an individual speaker to be an instance of language change. The speaker's initial formation of a chunk has very little impact on language structure or meaning. However, the habitual use of a chunk in a community can change distributional tendencies, and once the chunk becomes associated with a particular context, it can be identified as such by distributional criteria (Erman and Warren 2000). For instance, how do we know that *in the morning* is a chunk and *at a morning* is not?

First, chunks or prefabricated sequences of words are higher in frequency than phrases formed more freely. The chunk *in the morning* has 16,681 occurrences in the Corpus of Contemporary American English (COCA) compared to only 27 occurrences of *at a morning*. Second, the phrase *in the morning* is fixed, in the sense that changes in the preposition, the nominal number, the definiteness of the article or adjectival modification all yield a different chunked or non-chunked expression. These criteria demonstrate that the chunked expression is conventionalized.

7.3   Meaning and Context

Like lexical items, most chunks form and are maintained because they express a meaning or pragmatic function that speakers find useful. Thus *in the morning* takes on the specific meaning of 'every morning' or in some cases 'tomorrow morning' because these are concepts that are useful to speakers. We call the concepts that seem to attract expression, by lexical items, grammatical constructions or pre-fabricated chunks, 'niches' in conceptual space. As chunks come to be used in certain niches, the whole chunk is directly associated with the niche, and at times this leads to a loss of transparent meaning.

Langacker (1987) proposed distinguishing between two related properties of morpheme or word combinations: analyzability and compositionality. Analyzability refers to the ability of language users to identify the component units in a word or phrase. Thus *in the morning* is perfectly analyzable because any English speaker can recognize and identify the component parts. Compositionality refers to the transparency of the meaning of the whole word or phrase; a compositional combination has a meaning predictable solely from the sum of the meaning of the component parts. The phrase *in the morning*, while analyzable, is not completely compositional when used in the sense of 'tomorrow morning' because nothing in the phrase itself supplies the interpretation of 'tomorrow'.

Historical linguists as well as psycholinguists have been interested in the loss of compositionality over time. The semantic changes that take place in grammaticalization, for example, lead to the loss of compositionality. The meaning of a tense/aspect form such as *has written*, which expresses 'past with current relevance', cannot be derived from combining the meanings of the morphemes comprising it, which are PRESENT + *have* + VERB + PAST PARTICIPLE. Rather, in grammaticalization, uses of the construction in a growing and changing range of contexts lead to the establishment of a new meaning (Carey 1994). Such meaning changes have been carefully studied in a number of works such as Heine et al. (1991), Bybee et al. (1994) and Traugott and Dasher (2002), just to name a few.

Loss of compositionality also occurs in derivational morphology. It is common for a derived form to move away semantically from the meaning of its base. Clear examples are *awful*, which does not mean 'full of awe' as it would if it were compositional. Instead it has an added negative sense. The adverb derived from it *awfully* has also lost its compositionality, especially when used as an intensifier, as in *awfully good*. Hay 2001, using a psycholinguist's methodology, argues that loss of compositionality is due to the derived form gaining frequency of use and exceeding the frequency of the base form. Her proposal is that the more often the combined derived form is used, the easier it is to access as a whole and the less that access activates the representations of the component parts.

The Hay model is useful for understanding the relation between chunking and compositionality, but it does not explain how the meaning change occurs. The role of context must be included in the explanation (Bybee 2014). Indeed, use in context may be what determines the relative frequencies of the base and derived forms. Consider the example of the two related words *dirt* and *dirty*. We conjecture that the derived word is fairly compositional to native speakers, though not nearly as transparent as other relations, such as that between *legible* and *illegible*. *Dirt* and *dirty* have very similar frequencies, occurring in the COCA 13,844 and 12,975 times respectively. However, their contexts of use are somewhat different. The noun has relatively concrete uses, occurring often in the discussion of roads and also in conjoined phrases such as *dirt and dust, dirt and oil, dirt and grease* and *dirt and sawdust*. The adjective occurs more often in metaphorical uses, in phrases such as *dirty words, dirty details, dirty looks, dirty messages, dirty work, dirty joke, dirty little secret* and *dirty bomb*, none of which involves dirt in the sense of the noun examples. Such contexts detract from the clear compositionality of the derived form. Compare this situation to a more compositional pair: *legible* and *illegible*. In COCA they occur 436 and 282 times respectively, and an examination of the contexts shows that both are used in similar ways, modifying *handwriting, letters, notes, words* and so on. These examples suggest that context of use may be the primary determinant of the maintenance or loss of compositionality. Our case study laid out below demonstrates the power of context in determining both loss and re-establishment of compositionality.

As mentioned above, Langacker argues that morpheme or word combinations also have degrees of analyzability, by which he means varying degrees to which language users recognize the component morphemes or words as instances of units occurring in other combinations. From a diachronic point of view, we find that chunks maintain some degree of analyzability despite loss of compositionality. Language users may not identify the stem of *awful* as an instance of *awe*, but *–ful* is fully recognizable. Also, the presence of *awful* in *awfully* is clear enough, despite the loss of compositionality. Analyzability is only fully lost when phonetic changes obscure the integrity of the component parts, as when phonetic changes make it difficult to find *dis-* and *–ease* in *disease* or *busy* and *–ness* in *business*. The reduction of *have* in the combinations *would have, could have* and so on, obscure its etymology and some language users spell these combinations as *would of* and *could of*. The phrase to be studied here undergoes no such phonetic reduction; therefore, our study can be restricted to examining changes in compositionality.

7.4   The Causes of Change: Rational Analysis and Zipf's Law

The perspective taken on chunking by psychologists as presented in Ellis'
contribution (chapter 6, this volume) allows us to highlight an important
difference between the search for explanation by psychology versus historical linguistics. Ellis writes,

> Rational analysis (Anderson 1990) aims to answer *why* human cognition is
> the way it is. Its guiding principle is that the cognitive system optimizes the
> adaptation of the behavior of the organism to its environment in the sense
> that the behavior of the mechanism is as efficient as it conceivably could be
> given the structure of the problem space or input-output mapping it must
> solve.

In applying this principle to language, Ellis, citing Anderson, proposes
a measure of 'information need' and then concludes that chunking occurs
because it optimizes efficiency. Since high frequency sequences are
chunked, and since recency and context contribute to chunking, a more
efficient language processing is achieved, as items that are needed more
often in the particular context are easier to process.

Such 'rational analyses' would be viewed by scholars of language change as
teetering dangerously on the verge of teleology. A teleological explanation is
one that cites the end result of the change as the motivation for the change.
For instance, if one were to assert that *shall* and *will* grammaticalized into
future markers because Old English had no future marker, the explanation
would involve goal-oriented acts on the part of speakers or on the part of the
language as a whole. Certainly, the language can have no goals or plans, and
speakers are simply trying to communicate, not create new grammatical
categories. Thus, historical linguists are generally disposed to provide explanations that do not cite goals, but rather cite mechanisms that occur during
language use for the purpose of communicating (Croft 2000).

Thus, linguists would be cautious in applying 'rational analysis' to
language structure. However, Anderson and Ellis are asking why the
human cognitive system is the way it is. As chunking is a domain-general
process (not restricted to language, but applying to all types of cognitive
experience), the ability to chunk certainly evolved gradually (and very
early, as most if not all animals are able to use chunked behavior) and
had a selectional advantage. In that sense, we can say that humans chunk
because they have evolved to be able to do this and it facilitates interaction
with the environment. This general ability is behind the chunking that
occurs in language, but it is not a specific reaction to 'information need'.
So our view would be that linguistic chunks develop because humans

automatically chunk all of their experience, not because it creates more efficient communication.

A similar difference between the psychologist's and historical linguist's points of view arises in the evaluation of Zipf's 1949 account of the correlation between brevity and frequency of use. As Ellis notes in his chapter, Zipf documented the correlation between the length of words and their frequency of use as well as their propensity to be polysemous. To explain these correlations, Zipf elaborates the 'principle of least effort', which, he argues, is a general principle of human behavior. Ellis extols Zipf's principles by calling them 'serious linguistic universals'. We certainly agree that Zipf's principles are powerful and important to the understanding of lexical structure. In addition, we agree that some form of 'least effort' may apply to the explanation of these universals. However, as mentioned above, explanations should rest on understanding the mechanisms that actually create the correlations. Zipf also writes that an understanding of mechanisms is crucial (1949: 65–66), but the particular mechanisms he cites will seem to the historical linguist to have missed the mark.

In his 1949 book, Zipf develops the tool analogy as a way of understanding how language users shape words to achieve least effort. Ellis gives a fuller account of this analogy, so here we refer briefly to three points: an artisan working in his shop will arrange his tools so that the ones needed more often are closer at hand; he will reduce their size and mass in proportion to their frequency of use, so that the more-frequently used tools can be placed closer together; and he will use the tools that are closer at hand (the more frequently used ones) in new functions to avoid reaching for the less-frequently used tool. This metaphor is useful to some extent, but the question arises as to the extent to which ordinary language users are like the artisan. A major difference is that the artisan intentionally arranges and modifies his or her tools, while the bulk of language change occurs without the users intending to change it at all.

Let us consider the mechanisms that Zipf cites for the shortening of words and the development of polyfunctionality of words. For shortening of high frequency words, he cites the mechanism of clipping or truncation, by which *telephone* becomes *phone*, *gasoline* becomes *gas* and so on. The problem with this mechanism is that these clippings are more or less intentional at the beginning, and they do not represent the way most higher-frequency words grow shorter. Most shortenings of words take place by gradual phonetic reduction, which tends to operate opportunistically on high-frequency words. Thus OE *hlafweard, hlaford* 'loaf keeper' gradually changes to *lord* and *hlafdie* 'loaf kneader' gradually changes to *lady.* The vast number of variants of these words in Old and Middle English attest to the gradual reduction in length. Similarly, grammaticalizing phrases such as *be going to* undergo gradual phonetic reduction producing a wide range of variation. Language users are not intentionally shortening these phrases; rather the tendency to automate production of common sequences, as well as the lack of stress or other prominence on high frequency items leads to a gradual, unconscious phonetic reduction (Bybee 2001: 60–62).

The mechanism that Zipf cites for the development of polysemy of high-frequency words is the substitution of a short word for a longer one. His examples are the use of *juice* for *electricity* and *car* for *automobile*. These are two very different sorts of examples (one a metaphorical substitution, the other the use of what was earlier the generic term for 'vehicle' for what has become the generic vehicle). The more common type of change that leads to more frequent words becoming polysemous applies in English much more to verbs. More frequent verbs have very generalized meanings and can thus move into new contexts more freely. Thus consider all the senses of *go* or *run* in phrases such as *go crazy, go bump, go sour; run a business, run a machine, run a red light*. These verbs are not chosen because they are short or high frequency necessarily, though these may be factors in their easy access, but because their meanings are general and malleable in context.

These examples of the psychologist's vs. the historical linguist's search for explanation demonstrate a major difference in approach: the psychologist seems to assume that change is guided by a goal of optimal efficiency, while the historical linguist sees that language change occurs unintentionally and unconsciously as language users, equipped with cognitive abilities developed mostly for other domains, apply these abilities while they are trying to communicate. The following case study, which examines in detail changes in degrees of chunking and compositionality, shows how language users grapple with matching the meaning of a chunk to context. It also shows that chunking and changes in compositionality occur in phrases that are not necessarily of high frequency.

7.5   Case Study: *Beg the Question*

To explore in more detail the role of context of use in the loss **and** gain in compositionality that can take place in language change, we turn to the examination of the expression *beg the question*. The pathway of development of *beg the question* is an apt case to consider for our purposes, owing to its mid-twentieth-century shift to a new context of use, illustrated in (1).

(1)   Mr. Obama, speaking at the White House, said pro-Russian separatists have blocked investigators from the scene, fired their guns in the air, removed physical evidence and delayed or impeded the collection of the bodies. *'All of which begs the question: what exactly are they trying to hide?'* he asked.
(Obama Denounces Russia and Separatists for Obstructing Crash Site, *New York Times*, July 21, 2014)

In (1), *beg the question* means 'compels us to raise the following question'. This contemporary use of the expression is quite distinct from its sixteenth-century form and context, illustrated in (2).

(2)   And I say this is still to **begge the question**, and not to answere the Argument. So your doctrine is sufficiently overthrown.
Nowell (1583)

In (2), one of the parties in a disputation is accusing the other of not following prescribed rules of logic. The assertion is that the argument the speaker has advanced does not provide an independent reason, ground or piece of evidence for the truth of the original premise, but that he instead does nothing more than re-state the original thesis or question. We trace the pathway of development of the expression *beg the question* by examining its form and context in the databases and corpora listed in Table 7.1.

We chose to use Early English Books Online and Eighteenth Century Collections Online to represent uses in the early period because these collections allow for extensive consideration of semantic and pragmatic contexts. For the nineteenth-, twentieth- and twenty-first-century uses, we used the COHA and COCA corpora, but in some instances we had to go beyond the limited contexts provided there by locating and examining the

Table 7.1 *Usage databases*

1472–1700	1810–1900
Early English Books Online (EEBO)	Corpus of Historical American English (COHA)
130,305 texts	132,214,194 texts
1701–1800	1900–1990
Eighteenth Century Collections Online(ECCO)	Corpus of Contemporary American English (COCA)
207,632 texts	221,997,147 texts
	1990–2012
	Corpus of Contemporary American English (COCA)
	190,000+ texts

original texts. We searched these databases and corpora for all variations of the phrase *beg the question*. We analyzed the expressions found for evidence of chunking, using the following structural correlates: choice of lexical items, grammatical forms of the words, flexibility of grammatical structure and possibility of modifiers or other items intervening.

7.5.1   Beg the Question: Pathway of Development

The Original Niche
Beg the question has its origins in the Latin term for a specific Aristotelian logical fallacy, *petitio principii*. It was introduced in the sixteenth century as a technical term of logic with a precise semantic/pragmatic niche in the system of logical reasoning taught to a specific community of speaker/writers – the educated classes from the medieval period onward. The Latin term for the fallacy is first attested in English texts in 1548, seen in (3).

(3)   *Petitio principii, that is when a man wyl proue a thynge to be true, by the same thinge, or wyth another, that is as doubtfull as that is, which is called into question.*
                                                                    Turner (1548)

   Note that this first occurrence already makes use of the term *question*. In the context of the Aristotelian logical argumentation taught in medieval schools, the term *question* typically refers to *the thing in question* or 'the question' that the parties agree is under debate in a particular argument. The earliest English form of *petitio principii* rendered it as *petition of principle*, as shown in this phrase from 1574: *These be all petitions of principles*. However, this expression largely drops out of the EEBO database after 1589, and the niche is ceded to *beg the question*.

   The verb *beg* first appears in this contextual use in the database in 1582: *That is, the **begging** or taking of that as granted: which is in controversie.* Because the use of *beg* in *beg the question* has been described as resulting from a 'cavalcade of misleading translations' (Liberman 2010), it is worth noting the extent to which the sixteenth- and seventeenth-century texts show evidence of mapping the then primary meaning of *beg* – 'to ask for alms' – into this semantic niche. The examples you will see in (4) show the collocation of *beg* in *beg the question* with words associated with 'asking for alms'. The frequent use of modifiers, such as *poore, mean, pitiful, shamefull* or *beggarly*, suggest that the sixteenth- and seventeenth-century community of speaker/writers drew heavily on the existing meaning of the word *beg* to enhance the insult inherent in accusing an opponent of faulty reasoning.

Chunking of the Phrase

The examples in (4) illustrate that in the early uses, the phrase is not fixed. *Question* appears often in phrases like *that in question* or *that which is questioned*, showing variation in the category and form of the term *question* and the frequent appearance of intervening items. In a number of cases, we find synonyms for *question* following *beg*; in (4) *that you should prove* is an example of this. These variations in lexical items, the grammatical forms of the words and grammatical structure indicate that *beg the question* is not yet a fixed chunk. We also see evidence that the items in the phrase maintain their categoriality. Both *beg* and *question* appear in verb and nominal forms with a variety of inflections, modifiers and intervening items. The items also maintain predictable compositional meanings: the phrases in which they appear can easily be interpreted based on the common meanings of the items in this context. Thus, in the sixteenth and early seventeenth centuries, we can say that *beg* and *question* collocate frequently in the logical niche, but *beg the question* has not yet become an established chunk.

(4)   Compositionality 1579–1624
       *Alas, this is such a poore **begginge of that in question*** 1579
       *a shamefull **begging** of that which is **questioned*** 1580
       it is onely a pitifull begging of that you should proue 1601
       *by **a pitifull begging of the cause in question*** 1601
       *you **beg an Argument from your selfe**, drawne from a **beggerly** fallacy* 1624

By the late seventeenth century, *beg the question* shows strong evidence of chunking. In (5), the verb *beg* is followed immediately by *the question*. *Question* is thus fixed as a noun, and most typically a singular, definite noun, because in the logical context, the participants have identified a single question that is known and agreed upon in prior discourse. Although we still see uses of phrases like *the thing in question*, *beg* most frequently collocates with the exact phrase *the question* immediately following. The chunked form *beg the question* is far and away the most frequent form in the logical context for the educated community of writers. Whereas *the question* is fixed with little inflectional variation, *beg* maintains its categoriality as a verb. It continues to appear as either a verb or a nominal, as the variation in the forms of *beg* in (5) illustrates. The chunked phrase *beg the question* can take a variety of subjects and modifiers, but only those appropriate within the constraints of its logical niche. Because of the fixing of the phrase and its frequently associated meaning within its logical niche, the meaning of the phrase begins to be less broadly interpretable in terms of the general meaning of its component parts. The chunk appears to be moving toward a reduction in compositionality.

(5)   Chunking 1670–1700
 . . . *Petitio Principij,* **a shameful <u>begging</u> the Question**
 . . . **it is a meer <u>begging</u> the Question**
 . . . *or a more mean <u>begging</u> the Question*
 . . . **It's but a <u>begging</u> the Question in this case**
 . . . **which** *is* **meerly <u>begging</u> the Question**
 . . . **He would sometimes have been <u>begging</u> the Question**
 . . . *is to <u>beg</u> the question without saying any* . . .
 . . . *in which* **you all along <u>beg</u> the Question**
 . . . **they <u>beg</u> the Question**
 . . . **But this <u>begs</u> the Question**
 . . . **He <u>begs</u> the Question of the Dissenters** . . .
 . . . **herein he has but <u>begged</u> the Question**

Broadening the Niche

In the first half of the eighteenth century, the Aristotelian context and meaning of *beg the question* remain predominant, and we find the same chunking and variation seen in (5). However, from the mid-eighteenth century onward, *beg the question* begins to move outside its narrow niche, appearing more widely in magazines, plays, travel writing and memoirs in contexts less clearly concerning disputes. This shift in contexts and uses might be expected, given social and historical changes in the period. The mid- to late eighteenth century in England was characterized by a rapid increase in the availability and distribution of texts of various types to greater numbers of people in disparate social groups (Spufford 1981).

Increased industrialization and urbanization also led to a proliferation of educational institutions, many of which were targeted to the poor and middle class. These institutions had widely disparate curricula, though most at least promoted basic literacy. Formal training in Aristotelian logic continued, but only in elite schools and universities (Vincent 1993). Given the increase in text types and the more varied readership, the form-meaning pairing associated with *beg the question* within its original Aristotelian niche was no longer in the common ground of all readers. Uses of *beg the question* by the educated community of writers were now being read and interpreted by readers outside that community. In the more popular genres, a reader who was not already familiar with the logical fallacy that *beg the question* was intended to highlight would have a great deal of difficulty determining what question might be under discussion and exactly how it might be being begged. One clear difficulty for such unschooled readers was that in most texts the chunk *beg the question* did not occur immediately after 'the question' was stated, as seen in (6).

(6) *Beg the question*: lack of contiguity
The count did not carry matters thus far: He said, that I was certainly right in some of my principles, but that the kingdom we were then in, proved against me in others. He desired me to consider the difference in the trade of England, or any other country at different periods. You had more wool in Henry the eighth's reign, than you have now, but what comparison is there between the benefit resulting to the kingdom in the two periods? Then look at your corn trade, you had as many acres of land in the time of the ancient Britons as now; but proper attention, and putting all the springs of industry in motion, have changed the possibility in one case, to a certainty in the other. **You also beg the question**, by stating as products, what are received by different nations from colonies or fisheries.

Marshall (1772)

This example comes from an eighteenth-century travel narrative. The question under consideration in the reported discussion is: How can commerce and manufacture flourish? The protagonist/author asserts that governments that promote a more equitable tax burden have more flourishing trade. However, the statement of this 'question' occurs several pages before the Count's use of *beg the question*, making an inference about its meaning from context complex at best.

The movement of the phrase *beg the question* out of strictly logical contexts of confutation, disputation and argumentation in this period opened the way for readers to make discourse-based inferences which generalized the meaning of the chunk to broader contexts. Indeed, we find evidence that such shifts were occurring in a 1752 text by Jonathan Edwards, an excerpt of which appears in (7).

(7) 'Illiterate readers' 1752
Among the Particulars of Mr. W-m's Method of disputing, I observed, that he often causelessly charges me with **begging the Question**, *while he frequently* **begs the Question** *himself, or does that which is equivalent.*
But that it may be determined with Justice and Clearness, who does, and who does not **beg the Question**, *I desire it may be particularly considered, what that is which is called* **Begging the Question** *in a Dispute. –* ***This is more especially needful for the sake of illiterate readers.***

Edwards (1752: 117)

In what follows this excerpt, Edwards attempts to clarify for 'illiterate readers' what the true meaning of *beg the question* within the context of a dispute should be. Of particular interest for our purposes is what Edwards says it is not, since his proscriptions against these uses give us an indication of how *beg the question* had begun to shift its meaning within its broader contexts of use. Edwards describes three incorrect uses: (1) 'merely to suppose something in a Dispute, without bringing any Argument to prove it'; (2) 'offering a weak Argument, to prove the Point in Question'; and (3) 'missing the true Question, and bringing an Argument that is impertinent, or beside the Question' (Edwards 1752: 117–118).

Pathways to New Uses

Before we trace the shifts in meaning Edwards describes, it is helpful to review examples that explain the meaning of *beg the question* within the original niche. In the sixteenth and seventeenth centuries, it was quite common for a writer charging another with begging the question to explicitly and painstakingly demonstrate in the text exactly how the argument did so. The examples in (8) illustrate the seventeenth-century meanings of *beg the question*. In the first example, we see the prototypical definition of *beg the question*. A writer is accused of committing precisely that fallacy which one is taught in Aristotelian logic not to commit, asserting or assuming as evidence the very question in dispute, proving that something is so by asserting that it is so. The second example shows that one could also beg the question by presupposing an argument with which one's opponent might disagree without offering any independent proof.

(8)   Supposing and begging the question
       *Will this be admitted of as excellent Logick in your Schooles, **to prove an assertion by the same assertion, and to beg the question in controversie?** If so, then in all points asserted and disputed of, it is so because it is so, will serve for proof.*

                                                                     Whitehead (1672)

       *For the former of these he offers **no manner of proof beyond his own affirmation**, and therefore it is sufficient to deny it as he knowes we do, and evidently **begs the question in assuming and not offering any proof to the contrary**.*

                                                                     Tombes (1657)

If we examine the uses of *beg the question* across a variety of texts from the late eighteenth through the early twentieth century, we find in theological and scientific texts a continued use of the Aristotelian meanings. However, outside of this narrow niche, we also find examples of how the 'problematic' uses Edwards describes extend the meanings of *beg the question*. The example in (9) illustrates the meaning of 'supposing, using a faulty assumption'.

(9)　Supposing, using a faulty assumption
　　　*Mr. Blame **begs the question** when he says that carpets are cheaper now than they were thirty years ago. So is everything; but taxing people did not reduce the price, or give the carpet-workers better wages, as he contends.*
　　　　　　　　　　　　　　　　　　　　　　　　　　　　Mills (1890)

This meaning can be seen as an extension of the original Aristotelian meaning, in that it highlights a problem with an argument supposed by another person. The nineteenth-century use carries over the meaning of supposing we saw in (8), but it broadens its application from supposing the question in dispute to presenting evidence which subsequent writers believe to be faulty.

The 'missing the true question' meaning, shown in (10), moves a step further from the original meaning of *beg the question*. This example comes from a spoof published in 1798 in a magazine called the *Weekly Entertainer*. The tongue-in-cheek text is in the form of a letter addressed to a politician requesting that he propose a bill in Parliament to regulate time more effectively by turning day into night.

(10)　Missing the true question, arguing beside the point
　　　To this plan [of turning day into night], *I am aware of many objections, but they are easily answered. It will be said, in the first place, how can you alter the course of the sun? This is really **begging the question**. Let it first be proved that the light of the sun is necessary, convenient, or even proper for the meetings of people of fashion. Is not the moon a better planet to preside on such occasions?*
　　　　　　　　　　　　　　　　Proposal for the Regulation of Time, 1798

Here the spoof writer raises possible objections to his plan in the form of a question and then dismisses the question because it fails to adequately grasp the proposal and is thus beside the point. This use is quite removed from the Aristotelian meanings in (8). Although this fictitious context of debate about a Parliamentary proposal could evoke a context in which strict logical reasoning might be relevant, here the questions are not dismissed because they assume a point as evidence or because they reassert the question. They are dismissed because the writer construes the arguments they raise as irrelevant to the proposal and thus inadequate.

The contemporary example in (11) demonstrates that this meaning is not restricted to eighteenth-century spoofs.

(11)   Missing the true question

If racism, homophobia, jingoism, and woman-hating have been features of national life in pretty much all of modern history, it rather **begs the question** *to spend a lot of time wondering if right-wing radio is a symptom or a cause.*

Hate Radio (Williams 1994)

Both of these meaning extensions, and indeed all three of the problematic meanings proposed by Edwards, can be subsumed under a more general meaning of 'failing to adequately address the issue in question'. This meaning preserves part of the Aristotelian niche, continuing to associate *beg the question* with contexts that involve argumentation, but it loses the specificity of the kind of problem in argumentation that the expression originally denoted. However, this broader interpretation is more likely to be inferable in general contexts of use, especially by the new wider community of users – readers not schooled in logical fallacies. These broader uses continue into the twentieth century.

An additional meaning, shown in (12), appears in the nineteenth century, further extending the ways in which *beg the question* relates to argumentation. In the 1888 example, one can *beg the question* by failing to address it all. This use also continues, as the 1949 example shows.

(12)   Evading the question

Now you're at it again; **begging the question, and dodging the argument.**

Bird (1888)

A quarrel couldn't even grow between him and Emma. And she would be unfair, **beg the question**, *if a quarrel did spring up; she would cry.*

Welty (1949)

A Changing Social Context

We have suggested that the Aristotelian niche in which *beg the question* developed was common to the educated community of writers and prevalent in sixteenth- and seventeenth-century texts. Then environmental changes subsumed the niche into a larger world of readers and text types. The posited constriction of the original niche can be supported by examining the frequency of words that denote logical contexts – *sophistry, fallacy, confutation* and *animadversions*. These numbers are seen in Table 7.2. For EEBO, COHA and COCA, the table shows the token frequency of the word, the

Table 7.2 *Loss of semantic/pragmatic niche*

1472–1700 (EEBO) 130,305 records					1810–1899 (COHA) 132,214,194 records		
	f	# records	ratio		*f*	# records	ratio
Sophistry	3,309	1649	.013	Sophistry	348	233	.000000100
Fallacy	4,890	2123	.016	Fallacy	568	297	.000000100
Confutation	7,717	2690	.059	Confutation	34	26	.000000010
Animadversions	4,884	1711	.013	Animadversions	0	0	

1701–1800 (ECCO) 130,305 records				1900–1999 (COHA) 221,997,147 records			
		# records	ratio		*f*	# records	ratio
Sophistry		6,499	.031	Sophistry	161	126	.000000060
Fallacy		11,626	.056	Fallacy	703	444	.000000200
Confutation		8,969	.043	Confutation	5	4	.000000001
Animadversions		8,401	.041	Animadversions	0	0	

number of records or texts in which it occurs, and the ratio of the number of records in which the word appears divided by the total number of records in the database or corpus. For ECCO, the database search provides only the number of records in which the word appears, but does not provide a separate token frequency. Because the early text databases do not provide an overall word count, the ratio of the number of records in which a form occurs divided by the total number of records in the database is used to allow a comparison of the relative occurrence of these forms.

As Table 7.2 shows, words denoting the Aristotelian logical contexts increase from 1472 through 1800. These numbers suggest that the niche in which *beg the question* might occur was relatively common during this early period. By the nineteenth century, we see a precipitous drop in the relative frequency of occurrence of these words. The two specialized terms for the discourse in which one writer would critique or prove another to be wrong by logical argument or proof, *animadversions* and *confutation*, largely disappear. The remaining two terms, *sophistry* and *fallacy*, also show a sharp decline from the earlier period in the number of texts in which they occur, though *fallacy* appears to be more robust in twentieth-century texts than in nineteenth-century ones.

The decreasing frequency of the terms in Table 7.2 provides support for our observation that by the nineteenth century the original niche of *beg the question* had begun to constrict. As the chunk begins to occur regularly outside its niche, it is adapted by the larger community of speakers. 'Illiterate' readers, no longer commonly trained in the system of logic, encounter the chunk in its new contexts of use and must interpret its meaning. These readers appear to have developed initially non-compositional interpretations of the chunk, in which *beg the question* referred to some behavior within an argument or discussion. We see further uses that reflect a loss of compositionality through the early twentieth century.

Reanalysis and Restoring Compositionality

The path of development of *beg the question* is not, however, simply a story of chunking, loss of niche and loss of compositionality. One of the most interesting facets of the development of this chunk occurs in the mid-twentieth century, where we see evidence of a reanalysis of the chunk to restore compositionality. This reanalysis led to the new construction exemplified above in (1): *All of which begs the question: what exactly are they trying to hide?*

One of the forerunners of this use first appears in 1961. In (13), we see how *beg the question* has shifted. The phrase *the question* no longer refers anaphorically to a premise given or assumed in the prior discourse. Rather it refers cataphorically to a new question that develops from the prior topic. This shift in reference co-occurs with a shift in the form of the construction, in which *beg the question* is immediately followed by an actual question. *Question* thus takes on its broader compositional meaning.

(13)   Assumption raises the question
        the President said that 'were it not for the necessity to devote so much of the national resources to defense, a strong case could be made' for larger federal participation in the joint federal-state-local effort to meet 'the growing problems of community development in cities and towns'. That statement is sound, but it **begs the question**. Does the country not have adequate resources to do both?

                                                        The New Republic (1961)

This re-establishment of the compositional meaning of *question* facilitates the movement of *beg the question* from its restricted niche in Aristotelian logic to a much larger niche, as a new construction that is employed as part of a discourse strategy for introducing a new question or topic.

This reanalysis was made possible by features of form and context present in the older construction. With respect to form, within its Aristotelian niche, *beg the question* could occasionally occur in a context in which it was immediately followed by a question, but the questions that followed were not 'the question' or premise, which was already given in the prior context and understood to be in the common ground. The questions following the chunk in these cases were typically quotations from the opponent's discourse, used to illustrate the inadequacy of the argument, as seen in (14). This text responds to an argument constructed by a Dr. Whitby, who has asserted that the plague is resistant to cold. Throughout the text, the author cites verbatim extracts from Whitby's argument in italics and then refutes them. The questions that follow *beg the question* here are quotations that illustrate the weakness of the opponent's argument.

(14)   Questions following *beg the question* in Aristotelian niche
       Now follows a better answer, *Cold Water is known to resist it (the Plague) very much*. This is begging the Question. *Did not the Plague stop very much last Winter in France, so that at Marseilles they thought themselves very nigh clear of it? And did it not break out again, when the Weather grew hot?* In general, we may oppose to these single Instances three great Plagues, that have been in the North within these Dozen of Years, all of them in the Winter.

                                                                    The Explainer (1722)

In later extended uses outside the Aristotelian niche, we also occasionally find *beg the question* immediately followed by questions, as in (15). In this excerpt from a novel, *beg the question* has the broader meaning of 'making a faulty assumption'. The following questions illustrate what the protagonist identifies these faulty assumptions to be. Though the examples in (14) and (15) establish precursors to the form of the new construction in which a question follows the chunk *beg the question*, they maintain the original referent of *the question*; the following questions designate highlighted premises or assumptions that explicate how 'the question' given previously in the common ground has been begged.

(15)   Questions following *beg the question* in popular novel
       No doubt many excellent, solid people would regard Lottie's spiritual condition with grave suspicion, and ask, disapprovingly, 'What business have two such DIFFERENT loves to be originating in her heart at the same time?' But, in the term 'different', **they beg the question**. Where is the antagonism? Where is even the dissimilarity? Are not these two impulses of the heart near akin, rather?

                                                                           Roe (1875)

Though examples such as these were interpretable by the elite community of speakers, they could easily facilitate inferences by the broader readership outside that community that the phrase *the question* referred to the actual question or questions that followed *beg the question* in the text.

A Formal Shift

A second shift in the formal features associated with the chunk may also have allowed for reinterpretation. In its original Aristotelian niche in the sixteenth and seventeenth centuries, *beg the question* often appeared with human subjects. The use of a human subject is closely related to the dialogic nature of the niche; the opponent whose reasoning was deemed faulty was often designated by name, or directly accused in the second person of begging the question. In Table 7.3, we see that such uses of human subjects accounted for about half of the uses of *beg the question* from 1500 to 1700. In the eighteenth century the use of human subjects declines and the use of abstract subjects increases to nearly 70 percent. This may be a key development, since uses with abstract subjects require greater contextually based inferencing to identify the aspects of the common ground needed to interpret *beg the question*.

To illustrate this distinction, we compare the examples in (16) and (17).

(16)   Human Subject: Aristotelian niche
       A college was founded this year in Newton, which for that reason was called Cambridge; and the importance of receiving learning at that or like places, to qualify men for the ministry, has been much insisted upon ever since; and those who have not been educated at such places have commonly been called *laymen*. And among many reflections that have been cast upon them, one is, that **they often beg the question** in argument. But who are guilty of this mean sort of conduct now?

                                                                            Backus (1777)

Within the Aristotelian niche, both human and abstract subjects occur within discourse contexts that elaborate the meaning of *beg the question*. The example in (16), which uses human subjects, can be clearly understood as a comment about an individual's purported reasoning.

Table 7.3 *Subjects of* beg the question

Subjects	1500–1700	1791–1800	1801–1899	1900–1949	1950–1999	1990–2012
Human	368 (48%)	58 (31%)	18 (49%)	10 (37%)	15 (24%)	20 (5%)
Abstract	399 (52%)	132 (69%)	19 (51%)	17 (63%)	48 (76%)	376 (95%)

(17) Abstract Subject: literary magazine

The other argument that would trace back this fable to the time of Plato is equally inconclusive, namely that Plotinus and Syncaius would not borrow from Apulcius, being a Latin Writer, as the Greek philosophers had all the sources of perfection among themselves. **This is completely begging the question**; it is supposing that the fable of Cupid and Psyche were known to the Greeks before Apulcius wrote, and that consequently the two writers had no occasion to borrow from him. This however, is the fact to be proved, and if it be taken for granted, what occasion is there to have recourse to any argument to prove it.

The European magazine (1782)

In (17), the abstract subject *this* and the meaning of *begging the question* might be considerably less interpretable if the context did not elaborate what the question was and how the matter was being argued.

As the chunk moves out of its niche and into more popular contexts, the use of either a human or abstract subject may make a larger difference in the interpretability of *beg the question*. In the example from a late eighteenth-century novel in (18), we see that the precise antecedent of *this* and the meaning of *begging the question* are highly ambiguous.

(18) Abstract Subject: popular novel

Sydney said, 'If the business is of a nature not to require much brains, he could recommend a young man now in Paris, but from his skill, or address, nothing was to be expected. Simple matter of fact was his talent.'

This was begging the question, though in the handsomest manner, solely from a wish to serve him.

Elvira (1792)

By contrast, in the example in (19) from another late eighteenth-century novel, the use of the human subject *you* renders the meaning of *begging the question* clearer. Though the reader may or may not be able to identify the precise referent of *the question*, it is clear that Fanny's comment takes Sir Charles to task for his reasoning.

(19) Human Subject: popular novel

I told him, laughing at the same time as this strange fancy, that I was too proud to love a man who had chosen another woman.

'That is to say, Fanny,' replied he, 'you would have loved him, had he addressed you instead of my sister.'

'**You are begging the question, Sir Charles**', said I; 'it is the most improbable thing in the world, that he should ever think of addressing a girl who has neither fortune nor family to recommend her.'

The Way to Lose Him (1773)

In the period from 1900 to 1949, which immediately precedes the shift to the new construction, the percentage of abstract subjects is 63 percent. It rises to 76 percent from 1950 to 1999, the period in which the new construction is developing. In the period from 1990 to 2012, we find an almost complete shift to the use of abstract subjects with *beg the question* (95 percent). The small percentage of human subjects (5 percent) occurs in uses of *beg the question* to mean 'evade the question', which also permits the interpretation of *question* in a compositional meaning.

Other Formal and Distributional Shifts

In addition to the overwhelming use of abstract subjects, the new meaning is associated with a variety of formal changes that reflect a reanalysis and renewal of the compositionality of the chunk, shown in Table 7.4. First, since the term *question* refers forward to actual questions the author wishes to pose, the term can be plural and multiple questions may follow. Second, *question* can take modifiers, which intervene in the chunk. Third, *question* can take indefinite modifiers, since it no longer refers to a question already in the common ground.

A correlate of the shift to the contemporary meaning of *beg the question* is the increased frequency of the chunk. It is important to note, however, that this frequency change does not precede the shift; it follows it. As Table 7.5 shows, the frequency of the chunk *beg the question* per million words in COHA is relatively low in the first half of the twentieth century, but it increases from 1950 to 1999, with the first spike

Table 7.4 *Formal changes associated with contemporary meaning*

Formal change	*f* in COCA	Example
Plural	6	*But when the magic's done, reality **begs the questions**: How does it taste? And how healthy is it?*
Modifiers	71	*So, those high scores **beg the politically incorrect question**, are Asians naturally more intelligent?*
Determiner *a*	13	*The conditions in which these hogs must live and die **beg a question** about our own species: What kind of creatures are we that would subject other beings to such a life?*
some	2	***beg some fundamental questions, begs some larger questions***

Table 7.5 *Frequency of* beg the question *in COHA 1900–1989*

	1900–1909	1910–1919	1920–1929	1930–1939	1940–1949	1950–1959	1960–1969	1970–1979	1980–1989
f	6	5	7	10	7	9	14	5	14
f per million words	.27	.22	.27	.41	.29	.37	.58	.21	.55

Table 7.6 *Frequency of* beg the question *in COCA*

	1990–1994	1995–1999	2000–2004	2005–2009
Frequency	72	84	104	101
f per million words	.69	.81	1.01	.99

in the 1960s when the new use appears. An examination of the contexts of use shows that the low frequency in the early part of the century may have been due to the constriction of the niche discussed above. In this period, *beg the question* continued to occur within its logical niche, but the occasions for its use were limited. The relative frequency of these logical uses remains low but fairly constant, even in the contemporary corpora. The increase from the 1960s forward is in the occurrence of the new construction.

Table 7.6 shows that the increase in frequency continues from 1990 through 2009, as the new meaning becomes more established. This increase is a product of the greater number of contexts in which the new meaning may be used. Unlike its narrow, restricted function within the Aristotelian niche, the new discourse function of *beg the question* may apply to a greater variety of contexts.

7.6   Conclusions

The case study of *beg the question* has demonstrated that the compositionality of a chunk waxes and wanes based on the context of use. Chunking occurs when a form develops as the common way of realizing a meaning within a niche, resulting in the fixing of a particular form. For *beg the question*, this occurred in the late seventeenth century. The process of chunking may result in some loss of compositionality, but in lower-frequency forms, like *beg the question*, the items in a chunk can maintain their analyzability. When the context itself changes, as it did for the *beg the question* in the late eighteenth century, the chunk may develop less compositional meanings, but it may also undergo reanalysis that will restore the compositionality of the chunk as it moves into a new niche, as occurred in the mid-twentieth century. Thus, compositionality can be renewed in ways supported by the discourse context. Most importantly, neither frequency nor chunking necessarily disrupts analyzability and compositionality; the pathway of development depends entirely upon the context.

As we mentioned earlier, chunking itself would not traditionally be considered a linguistic change; however, the consequences of chunking for a community of speakers – changes in compositionality in particular – do constitute semantic/pragmatic change and can lead to grammatical change. It is important to note that changes in compositionality are not intentional: speakers are not trying to make the language optimal in any way. As we have shown, language users are trying to extract meaning from words as they occur in context. As a result, they provide new meanings for old phrases, which then turn out to be useful in the new contexts. The new meaning of *beg the question* is useful, but a way of saying the same thing, *raise the question*, not only already existed, but was and still is more frequent than *beg the question*. Of course, the prior existence of *raise the question* means that the functional niche already existed. Creating a new way of saying something so similar seems to belie the proposed optimality of vocabulary and grammatical structure and suggests that the motivations of speakers and the mechanisms employed in language change cannot be guessed at by simply examining patterns in the outcome.

PART IV
Priming

CHAPTER 8

Priming and Language Change

Martin J. Pickering and Simon Garrod

8.1 Introduction

Much psychological research demonstrates that speakers imitate each other's linguistic choices. They also persist in their own choices over both the short and the long terms. Although such choices may sometimes reflect deliberate or conscious decisions, they are much more commonly the result of *priming* – a largely non-conscious or automatic tendency to repeat what one has comprehended or produced. Much of the time, priming causes people to decide between already-available alternatives, but it can also lead people to use new words, expressions or constructions, and moreover to remember them for subsequent use. If this process occurs in a population rather than in an individual, it should lead to language change. In this chapter, our goal is to demonstrate that priming could underlie aspects of language change. Priming has strong effects on language use (microgenesis) and almost certainly language development (ontogenesis); it is the task of the historical linguist to determine its actual role in language change and, perhaps, evolution (phylogenesis).

The first part of the chapter discusses the claim that interlocutors tend to *align* their linguistic representations in a way that supports a central goal of conversation – to align their understanding of the situation under discussion. Such linguistic alignment, on occasion, persists beyond the conversation and can lead to long-term linguistic changes in the individual. Moreover, such changes can occur between native-speaking adults and learners, such as children or adult learners (such as immigrants). Our discussion draws on different aspects of language, such as words and conceptual frameworks. The second part then focuses on structural priming – the tendency to repeat abstract linguistic structure across utterances – as an important component of alignment. We review the extensive literature, primarily concerned with syntax, to show the nature and extent of such priming, the factors that appear to enhance (or inhibit) it, its occurrence across groups such as children and non-native speakers and the evidence concerning its longevity. Finally, we consider the construction of routine expressions. Our conclusion suggests that alignment in general, and alignment of syntax in particular, is likely to be a major historical mechanism of language change (as discussed in detail by Mair, Chapter 9 of this volume). We now introduce alignment, priming and routinization, and suggest how they can apply to language change within a linguistic community of adults, to adults entering the community and to children growing up in the community.

8.2 Psychological Mechanisms of Language Change

Pickering and Garrod (2004) argued that communication is successful to the extent that interlocutors align their models of the situation under discussion. Such situation models include information about people, space, time, causality and intentionality (e.g. Zwaan and Radvansky 1998), so aligned interlocutors will share similar understandings of who did what to whom, where, when and why. To achieve such alignment of situation models, interlocutors do not extensively reason about each other's mental states, but rather align at other linguistic (and indeed non-linguistic) levels of representation, such as choice of words, pronunciation and grammar, in a largely automatic fashion. Essentially, interlocutors prime each other to speak about things in the same way, and people who speak about things in the same way are more likely to think about them in the same way as well. Importantly, interlocutors do make use of more conscious and deliberate strategies on occasion, but do so as a 'last resort' when automatic alignment breaks down. Work on alignment has looked at tendencies for interlocutors to repeat each other at many different linguistic levels, and has, to some extent, considered when such linguistic alignment relates to enhanced understanding. The focus of this work is generally on short-term alignment, for example within a particular conversation, but the research suggests that alignment can sometimes persist.

A rather separate tradition has considered the extent to which people tend to produce utterances with the same linguistic structure as an utterance that they have just produced or comprehended. Most of this work is concerned with syntax and is referred to as syntactic or structural priming. Bock (1986) found that participants tended to produce sentences such as passives after having produced another otherwise unrelated passive, without being aware of the relationship between the sentences. This suggested that the linguistic representations associated with passives were primed, just as words can be primed. Bock et al. (2007) found equivalent priming when the participant heard but did not produce the prime sentence. Importantly, strong priming effects also occur in dialogue and constitute one of the motivations for Pickering and Garrod's (2004) interactive-alignment account. The focus of such work is primarily on short-term effects, but effects can also persist (Kaschak, Kutta and Schatschneider 2011).

Finally, many researchers have discussed people's tendency to establish novel expressions or novel interpretations of established expressions – which we call *routines*. These can emerge during conversations, for example when interlocutors repeat each other's expressions and their interpretation. However, most discussion of routines refers to the long-term development of fixed expressions that come to behave like words in many respects (e.g. Aijmer 1996a; Kuiper 1996; Nunberg et al. 1994; Bybee 2006). These three phenomena of alignment, priming and routinization are likely to reflect similar psychological mechanisms. For example, priming appears to under-lie alignment and almost certainly contributes to the development of routines.

These phenomena could be relevant to language change if their effects can be large and pervasive. As we demonstrate, there is good evidence for these claims. But additionally, they must be very long-lasting and stable. In other words, speakers must make essentially permanent changes to their linguistic representations in ways that affect how they say things over their lifetimes. Our discussion is rather speculative because psycholinguistic studies tend to be fairly short-lived and it is very hard to know whether effects demonstrated in the laboratory persist over people's lifetimes, or could lead to even longer-term changes across generations. Therefore, our goal is primarily to demonstrate how permanent changes could come about. But in addition, we need to focus on groups of people that are particularly relevant to language change. In this paper, we refer to three groups: adults within the linguistic community, adults entering the community and children growing up in the community.

8.2.1 Alignment

Alignment was first motivated by Garrod and Anderson (1987), who had pairs of participants play a cooperative maze game in which they took turns to describe their positions to each other. They tended to align on the same description scheme. For example, if one player said *I'm two along, four up*, her partner tended to say *I'm one along, five up*; but if she said *I'm at B4*, her partner tended to say *I'm at A5*. These players aligned on a 'path' or a 'coordinate' description scheme, rather than specific words. In other cases, they aligned on a 'figural' scheme (e.g. referring to shape in the maze as a *right indicator*) or a 'line' scheme (e.g. *second row, two from the end*). They also aligned on the interpretation of these descriptions, for example, both treating the origin as the bottom left corner of the maze. When this alignment was 'local' (i.e. between adjacent turns), Garrod and Anderson referred to it as 'output-input coordination' – essentially, use the same words or description schemes that your partner had just used. But alignment was also 'global', in the sense that pairs of participants often began by using different description schemes but subsequently converged on the same scheme as each other (usually the coordinate or the line scheme). This suggests that they set up a conventional way to refer to positions.

For alignment to affect language change, it must of course persist over conversations. Garrod and Doherty (1994) had participants repeatedly play the maze game over a period of weeks, with either the same or different partners. In both cases, participants tended to persist with the description scheme that they had established across conversations. Most interestingly, the persistence was strongest when participants played with new partners, but specifically when those partners were drawn from the same community as themselves (i.e. those partners would each play with each other) rather than from different communities (those partners would not play with each other). So alignment on description schemes was long-lasting, was not partner-specific and was particularly enhanced by community member-ship. This means that such alignment is a good candidate for language change for adults within a linguistic community.

Garrod and Clark (1993) found that children (aged 7–8 years) would converge on referring expressions and description schemes to refer to maze positions to at least as great an extent as adults. But they were much less happy than adults to abandon those referring schemes when it became clear that they were leading to misunderstanding. Garrod and Clark interpreted this result as showing that the natural tendency for the children is to converge (as predicted by interactive alignment) and that the ability to inhibit this tendency as required has to develop over time. Most impor-tantly, the study shows that alignment is not limited to mature language users.

Other work has addressed the tendency to persist in choice of referring expressions. Brennan and Clark (1996) had directors describe a set of cards depicting common objects to matchers so that they could reconstruct the directors' array. One set of trials contained multiple objects from the same category. Directors and matchers settled on subordinate terms to refer to the objects (e.g. *pennyloafer*) because basic-level terms (e.g. *shoe*) would not discriminate between these objects. A subsequent set of trials included one object from each category, so basic-level terms would now be sufficient. However, participants often continued to use the subordinate terms. In another study, Branigan, Pickering, Pearson, McLean and Brown (2011) told participants that they were playing a similar game with an apparent interlocutor (who they believed to be either a person or a computer, whereas in fact responses were pre-programmed). Participants were very likely to adopt their apparent partner's choice of object name, even if that name was strongly dispreferred (e.g. *seat* for a bench). Both studies show that interlocutors' tendency to align is very strong and occurs even if the expression would almost certainly not be used otherwise.

8.2.2 Structural Priming

We have noted that people tend to repeat the syntactic structure of utterances that they have just produced (Bock 1986) or comprehended (Bock et al. 2007). But more importantly, there is a strong tendency to repeat syntax in dialogue. For cross-speaker priming to play a major role in language change, it must be widespread and have large effects, and this appears to be the case. Importantly, not all structural priming appears to be specifically due to syntax. For example, speakers repeat abstract aspects of meaning relating to thematic roles and discourse emphasis. Such effects do tend to be smaller than syntactic priming (see Pickering and Ferreira 2008); for reasons of brevity, we focus on syntactic effects in this discussion.

Levelt and Kelter (1982) asked Dutch shopkeepers *Om hoe laat gaat uw winkel dicht?* ('At what time does your shop close?') or *Hoe laat gaat uw winkel dicht?* ('What time does your shop close?'). In the former case, replies tended to include the preposition (e.g. *Om vijf uur*, 'At five o'clock'); in the latter, replies tended to exclude the preposition (e.g. *Vijf uur*, 'Five o'clock'). Perhaps surprisingly, this effect did not persist when a clause intervened between prime and target.

Branigan, Pickering and Cleland (2000) had participants take turns to describe and match picture cards, and found that they tended to use the form of utterance just used by their interlocutor. For example, they tended to use a prepositional object form such as *the pirate giving the book to the swimmer* following another prepositional object sentence, but a double-object form such as *the pirate giving the swimmer the book* following another double-object sentence. In other words, the study showed structural priming between interlocutors similar to the type of structural priming that occurs within an isolated speaker (Bock 1986). Branigan et al. (2000) found that the participant repeated the confederate's choice of construction 77 percent of the time when the verb was repeated and 63 percent of the time when the verb differed.

Many other studies have shown priming in dialogue for these constructions in English and other languages (e.g. Bernolet, Hartsuiker and Pickering 2007; Schoonbaert, Hartsuiker and Pickering 2007), with similar effects occurring whether participants were using their native language or a well-learned second language. Other studies have extended the effects to different constructions such as actives/passives (Bernolet, Harsuiker and Pickering 2009) and possessive alternations (*the girl's apple/the apple of the girl*; Bernolet, Hartsuiker and Pickering 2012).

Branigan, Pickering, McLean and Cleland (2007) found that interlocutors were more likely to repeat grammatical forms when they had just been addressed than when they were part of the conversation but had not been addressed (a side-participant). This effect occurred whether they responded to the previous speaker or the previous addressee. It may be that participants encode more deeply when they are directly addressed, perhaps as a result of acting on the prime (or preparing potential responses). Interestingly, it did not matter whether an addressee responded to the previous speaker or a previous side-participant. This suggests that the tendency to repeat grammar is not due to simple reciprocity. Most importantly, it suggests that addressees are more likely to be the instigators of language change than other people such as side-participants or (presumably) overhearers. Language change is more likely to be the result of direct interaction rather than mere exposure (e.g. listening to a debate).

8.2.2.1   Long-Term Priming

Language change of course also requires long-term effects of priming. The emphasis of most priming work, and the theoretical account of alignment due to Pickering and Garrod (2004), focuses largely on short-term effects, either from one utterance to the next or within the context of an individual conversation. However, long-term priming does occur. Hartsuiker and Kolk (1998) found evidence that priming was not limited to adjacent prime-target pairs, and that the likelihood of a rare construction increased during a session. More strikingly, Kaschak et al. (2011) found that priming persisted over about a week. In their study, one group of participants completed (written) sentence stems that were designed to elicit a prepositional object completion, and another group completed stems that were designed to elicit a double-object completion. Participants returned to the laboratory a week later and were presented with stems that could be completed with either construction. They tended to persist in the construction that they used. Such effects may require that the experimental task stay the same across sessions (Kaschak, Kutta and Coyle 2014).

Of course, long-term between-speaker effects are more important for accounts of language change. Hartsuiker, Bernolet, Schoonbaert, Speybroeck and Vanderelst (2008) investigated whether participants would repeat grammatical forms in dialogue after a lag of zero, two or six intervening utterances. They found persistence at all lags, but the lexical boost (the tendency for priming to be considerably enhanced by lexical repetition; see below) did not occur after lags of two or six utterances. These results support other demonstrations of 'long-term' priming from production-to-production and comprehension-to-production in monologue (Bock and Griffin 2000; Bock et al. 2007). They in fact investigated written as well as spoken dialogues, and found similar results. Such long-term between-interlocutor effects of course support the role of priming and alignment in language change. However, it is important to note that language change could also come about via immediate alignment effects that are then remembered (I immediately copy your form and then remember the form that I have just used).

8.2.2.2 *Priming Ungrammatical Structures*
Importantly, priming can lead speakers to produce forms that they hitherto regarded as ungrammatical. In comprehension, a number of studies have demonstrated processing facilitation or increased acceptability of ungrammatical sentences after brief exposure to similar exemplars. For example, Kaschak and Glenberg (2004) found that reading times for a construction that is ungrammatical in Standard English (the needs-construction, as in *The meal needs cooked*) decreased with consecutive presentations. These results generalized across modalities (spoken to written language) and to different verbs (Kaschak and Glenberg 2004) and sentential contexts (Kaschak 2006). In addition, Luka and Barsalou (2005) showed that grammaticality ratings for moderately ungrammatical sentences (e.g. *Armanda carried Fernando the package* or *Rachel needs to get a tattoo as colourful as Bob has*) were higher for those participants who had read them previously than for those who saw them for the first time. This effect was induced by as little as a single presentation and was also obtained for sentences which shared only structure and no content words with those presented during initial exposure. In all, these findings suggest that people process ungrammatical sentences in ways that yield persistent effects in the

linguistic system as a result of limited exposure. Such persistence generalizes across different words and types of sentences.

Ivanova, Pickering, McLean, Costa and Branigan (2012) had participants read sentences and decide if they matched pictures of transfer events,
and then describe an unrelated picture of another transfer event with
a particular verb. Participants occasionally used ungrammatical sentences
such as *The dancer donates the soldier the apple* after they had read another
ungrammatical sentence with the same verb, such as *The waitress donates
the monk the book*. They did not produce such sentences on other occasions, for example when the prime verb was different or when *donates* was
used appropriately. This suggests that adult native speakers can be primed
to produce ungrammatical sentences – something which will lead to
language change within adults.

8.2.2.3   *Boosts to Priming*

As we have noted, Branigan et al. (2000) found that the participant
repeated the confederate's choice of construction around 77 percent of
the time when the verb was repeated, and over 63 percent of the time when
the verb differed. The enhanced tendency to repeat grammar in the context
of lexical (verb) repetition is known as the *lexical boost* and supports the
claim of the interactive-alignment account that repetition at one linguistic
level (the lexicon) leads to repetition at another level (grammar).
Importantly, similar effects occur in second-language users (Schoonbaert
et al. 2007). The lexical boost also occurs within speakers (Pickering and
Branigan 1998) and has been extensively replicated (see Pickering and
Ferreira 2008).

Cleland and Pickering (2003) had participants describe pictures of
colored objects to each other in a dialogue game similar to Branigan
et al. (2000). Participants were more likely to use a complex noun phrase
like *the sheep that's red* after hearing *the door that's red* than after hearing *the
red door*. This tendency was enhanced when the prime was *the sheep that's
red* rather than *the door that's red*. Interestingly, it was also enhanced,
though to a smaller extent, by *the goat that's red*, where *goat* and *sheep* are
semantically related (*the semantic boost*). This study showed that interlocutors align on the form of noun phrases and also that alignment occurs
with comparatively rare constructions. Hence, repetition of content-word
heads (verbs or nouns) enhances syntactic priming.

We should note, however, that the lexical boost appears to be largely or
entirely short-lived. Hartsuiker et al. (2008) found a strong boost when
prime and target were adjacent (lag 0) but not when they were separated

(lag 2 or lag 6). This is perhaps surprising, because a long-term combination of syntactic form and lexical content would have been compatible with the establishment of routines containing fixed words and syntax. It is possible that long-term lexically specific priming does occur under some circumstances (and indeed Kaschak and Borreggine 2008 reported such an effect for one verb, *lend*). But the relationship between the lexical boost to priming and the establishment of routines remains unclear.

Another finding is that priming tends to be larger for constructions that are less frequent than for constructions that are more frequent (Bernolet and Hartsuiker 2010; Jaeger and Snider 2013). One account of such data is that speakers are less likely to expect rarer than more frequent forms, and so when they encounter a rare form, they are surprised, and learn from this event. Whatever the explanation for this finding, the strong priming of rare forms may reinforce the memory for such forms and hence promote language change.

8.2.2.4　Corpus Work

With or without repetition, the tendency to repeat is sufficiently strong that it is easy to understand how it could have an extensive effect on everyday language use. Importantly, some corpus-based studies have reported similar effects, with Gries (2005) finding a strong tendency to repeat choice of dative structure and a lexical boost (see also Szmrecsanyi 2006). And a recent corpus study (Reitter and Moore 2014) has shown a strong tendency for short-term repetition of syntactic rules in both a task-oriented and a more spontaneous dialogue corpus (the Map Task and the Call Home Telephone corpus). Overall, the data from corpora are remarkably consistent with the data from experimental work, and strongly reinforce the claim that alignment is strong enough to affect everyday language use and hence language change.

8.2.2.5　Priming in Children

Structural priming in children appears broadly similar to structural priming in adults and therefore can serve as a basis for language change within children. For example, Rowland, Chang, Ambridge, Pine and Lieven (2012) had 3- to 4-year-olds, 5- to 6-year-olds, and adults play a describe-and-match dialogue game based on Branigan et al. (2000) and found similar verb-independent priming at all ages. However, they did not find a lexical boost in children (a finding replicated in Peter, Rowland, Chang and Blything 2015). There are also studies showing priming of young children in monologue (e.g. Huttenlocher, Vasilyeva and Shimpi 2004; Shimpi,

Gámez, Huttenlocher and Vasilyeva 2007) and some suggestion that such effects can persist (Savage, Lieven, Theakston and Tomasello 2006).

8.2.2.6   Priming and Alignment between Languages

Language change can of course occur as an effect of language contact. So long as a speaker of one language can understand some utterances in a second language, those utterances might influence his or her native language, and those influences may persist. Alternatively, the speaker's native language may influence another language that he or she is learning and comes to use regularly (e.g. as an immigrant). Such influences may work by cross-linguistic (between-language) structural priming, which is the well-established tendency for a speaker's choice of utterance in one language to be affected by utterances that he or she has encountered in another language.

Loebell and Bock (2003) found between-language priming within a speaker in a monologue task. Hartsuiker et al. (2004) had Spanish-English bilinguals describe cards to each other in a version of Branigan et al.'s (2000) dialogue game. Participants first heard a prime description in their first language (Spanish) and then had to describe the subsequent picture using their second language (English). The experiment showed cross-linguistic priming for passive sentences: Spanish-English bilinguals tended to produce English passive sentences more often following a Spanish passive than following a Spanish active.

Many other studies have found between-language priming, and indicate that it shares many properties with within-language priming. For example, Schoonbaert et al. (2007) showed both within- and between-language priming for native Dutch speakers of English. In the absence of verb repetition, priming was very similar from Dutch to English, English to Dutch, within Dutch and within English. Some other studies have also shown similar within- and between-language priming (e.g. Kantola and Van Gompel 2011) but others have shown reduced between-language priming, for example from Cantonese to Mandarin (Cai, Pickering, Yan and Branigan 2011). Some studies suggest that between-language priming requires the two languages to form the construction with the same word order (Bernolet et al. 2007), but priming may also occur between constructions that are formed slightly differently in the two languages (Bernolet, Hartsuiker and Pickering 2009, 2013). Finally, between-language priming may be enhanced when prime and target verbs are translation equivalents (Cai et al. 2011; Schoonbaert et al. 2007). This boost is smaller than the within-language lexical boost, and suggests that the locus of the boost is the semantic relationship between the sentences across languages. There is also evidence of between-language priming in bilingual children (Vasilyeva et al. 2010).

8.2.3 Routinization

Conversation is extremely repetitive, and the comparison with carefully crafted monologue (as in texts) is very striking indeed (Tannen 1989). Pickering and Garrod (2004) argued that expressions that are repeated become routines for the purposes of the dialogue. By routine we mean an expression that is 'fixed' to a relatively large extent. Extreme examples include repetitive conversational patterns such as *How do you do?* and *Thank you very much.* Many examples are idioms, such as *kick the bucket* (where all the words are fixed) or *keep/lose one's cool* (where some words are fixed but others can vary). However, many common fixed expressions such as *I love you* have literal interpretations. Note that groups of people often develop particular types of routine. Thus, Kuiper (1996) described the fixed language used by auctioneers and sportscasters. For example, radio horse-racing commentators produce highly repetitive and stylized speech, which can consist of entirely fixed expressions (e.g. *they are coming round the bend*) or expressions with an empty slot that has to be filled (e.g. *X is in the lead*). He argued that such expressions are stored in long-term memory, and are then accessed when needed, in a way that reduces processing load and aids fluency.

Most discussion of routines refers to the long-term development of fixed expressions that come to behave like words (e.g. Aijmer 1996a; Kuiper 1996; Nunberg et al. 1994; Bybee 2006). But we propose that they often originate in the context of a particular interchange. If one speaker starts to use an expression and gives it a particular meaning, the other will most likely follow suit – clearly an effect of priming. Thus routines are set up 'on the fly' during conversation.

Such routines can of course be elicited experimentally, as we illustrate from Garrod and Anderson (1987). Table 8.1 gives a brief transcript of an interaction in which *A* and *B* are trying to establish their respective positions in the maze (indicated by arrows in Figure 8.1). Consider the use of *right indicator*, which takes on a specific meaning (referring to a particular configuration within mazes). Once the players have fixed on this expression and interpretation, they do not describe the configuration in alternative ways. Although we can be less certain of what happens during comprehension, the responses to references to *right indicator* strongly

Table 8.1 *Transcript of an extract from a maze-game dialogue taken from Garrod and Anderson (1987)*

8	——A: You know the extreme right, there's one box.
9	——B: Yeah right, the extreme right it's sticking out like a sore thumb.
10	——A: That's where I am.
11	——B: It's like a right indicator.
12	——A: Yes, and where are you?
13	——B: Well I'm er: that right indicator you've got.
14	——A: Yes.
15	——B: The right indicator above that.
16	——A: Yes.
17	——B: Now if you go along there. You know where the right indicator above yours is?
18	——A: Yes.
19	——B: If you go along to the left: I'm in that box which is like: one, two boxes down O.K.?

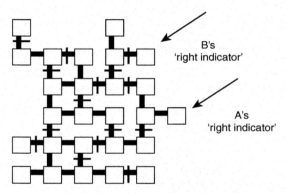

Figure 8.1 The maze arrangement seen by each participant in the game transcribed in Table 8.1. The arrows point to the two 'right indicators' being described by *B* in utterances 13 and 15/17.

suggest that they also understand the expression in its special sense. Similar processes occur when interlocutors agree on a 'shorthand' description of unfamiliar objects, as when referring to a tangram as an ice skater (Clark and Wilkes-Gibbs 1986).

As we have argued, interactive alignment involves the priming of particular levels of representation and the links between those levels. Producing or comprehending any utterance leads to the activation of those representations, but their activation gradually decays. However, when interactive alignment leads to sufficiently strong activation of the links between the levels, routinization occurs. Routinization involves the setting down of new memory traces associated with a particular expression. The expression therefore becomes lexicalized, with a particular semantics, phonology and syntax, in a way that is compatible with the conception of the lexicon assumed by Jackendoff (2002; chapter 6). Routines are comparatively long-lasting and involve a kind of implicit learning. Not surprisingly, the new representations do not normally come about by explicit agreement (for related discussion, see Bybee and Moder, Chapter 7 of this volume; Ellis, Chapter 6 of this volume).

Jackendoff (2002) proposed that linguistic representations (i.e. containing phonological, syntactic and semantic/conceptual components) may either be stored and accessed directly, or constructed online. He treated anything that is stored and accessed directly as a lexical item. Hence, lexical items can range from morphemes to whole constructions or even stretches of text that have been memorized (e.g. speeches). To explain his account, we need to describe the representation of both traditional lexical items (i.e. words) and more complex lexical items.

Traditional lexical items have a phonological representation linked to a syntactic representation, both of which are linked to a conceptual/semantic representation. Figure 8.2 illustrates the arrangement for the word *right* (in 2.1). The phonology is shown on the left, the syntactic representation in the middle and the conceptual/semantic representation on the right. The three representations are all linked to each other through the subscript 'i'. More complex lexical items, such as fixed or semi-productive idioms, are represented as having phonological, syntactic and conceptual/semantic components, but with only partial mappings between

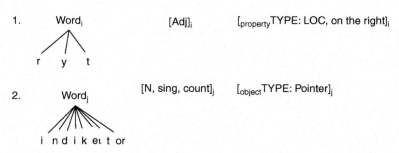

Figure 8.2 Schematic drawing of Jackendoff's (2002) lexical representation for *right* and *indicator*.

the three components. For example, the idiomatic construction *take NP to task* involves separate mappings between the phonological words and the syntactic structure and between the syntactic structure and the semantic structure. These complex lexicalizations provide a suitable framework for formalizing routines because they represent the fixed aspects of the routines but at the same time allow for variables (in this case, NP).

We assume that routines are not simply recovered from long-term memory as complete chunks (in contrast to Kuiper 1996, for example). There are a number of reasons to suspect that producing routines involves some compositional processes. First, it can straightforwardly explain how people produce semi-productive routines with a variable element, as in *take NP to task*, where NP can be any noun phrase referring to a person or people. Second, the structure of non-idiomatic sentences can be primed by idiomatic sentences in production (Bock 2004). Third, it is consistent with the production of idiom blends such as *That's the way the cookie bounces* (Cutting and Bock 1997). Note that evidence also suggests syntactic processing of routines in comprehension. For example, Peterson, Burgess, Dell and Eberhard (2001) found that syntactically appropriate continuations to phrases are responded to faster than syntactically inappropriate ones when the phrase is likely to be the beginning of an idiom (e.g. *kick the . . .*).

Let us explain routinization in dialogue by examples from the maze-game transcript in Table 8.1. First, consider the use of *right indicator*. When B says *it's like a right indicator* (11), the expression *right indicator* is not a routine, but is composed of two expressions whose interpretations are relatively standard, and whose meaning involves normal processes of meaning composition. So, B accesses the lexical entries in Figure 8.2 and creates a phrase with the structure in Figure 8.3(1). Importantly, however, B does not simply use *right indicator* to refer to any object that can be referred to as a right indicator, but instead uses it to refer to a particular type of object that occurs within this maze (see Figure 8.1). A accepts this description with *yes* (12), presumably meaning that he or she has understood B's utterance correctly. B then interprets A's utterance at this stage using the normal processes of meaning decomposition corresponding to the compositional processes that A has used in production. The expression *right indicator* now keeps recurring, and is used to refer to positions in the maze. Whereas initially it was used as part of a simile [*it's like a right indicator* in (11)], subsequently it is used referentially [*that right indicator you've got* in (15)]. At some point (we cannot be certain when, but presumably fairly rapidly), it becomes a routine.

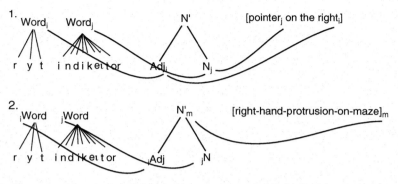

Figure 8.3 Illustrations of the lexical representation of (1) the literal and (2) the routine version of the expression *right indicator*.

How does such routinization occur? We propose that the activation of *right* and *indicator* plus the specific meaning that *right indicator* has in this context leads to the activation of the phonological representation and syntactic representation together with the activation of the specific meaning ('right-hand-protrusion-on-maze'). Therefore, the links among the phonology, syntax and semantics are activated (as specified in the interactive alignment model). That increases the likelihood that the interlocutors are going to subsequently use *right indicator* with that specific meaning.

But in addition to this basic interactive-alignment process, the activation of the links 'suggests' the positing of a new long-term association, essentially that *right indicator* can have the meaning 'right-hand-protrusion-on-maze'. We propose that when activation is strong enough, a new lexical entry is constructed, as illustrated in Figure 8.3(2). In this representation, the phonology of *right* and *indicator* are linked to the syntactic categories Adj and N in the syntactic component, but crucially there is no direct link between the phonology of the two words and the semantic/conceptual representation at the right of the figure. Instead, a new link is established between the N' (which is the mother node for Adj and N) and the local meaning 'right-hand-protrusion-on-maze'.

This automatic account of routinization does not require speakers to take into account what they assume their addressees believe about the meaning of *right indicator* in order to determine when they can use this term. There is no need to reason that the addressee would be able to understand *right indicator* before deciding whether to use this expression in contrast to a longer alternative.

Routinization therefore involves the positing of links between the levels, with routines being objects that have partly or completely fixed interpretations at multiple linguistic levels. For instance, a particular lexical item gets a particular interpretation for a specific conversation, or a particular combination receives a particular interpretation (as in *right indicator*). This combination then gets stored and can be accessed as a routine, thereby reducing choice. One prediction is, therefore, that the difficulty that is associated with determining which expression to use when more than one are available will disappear or at least be greatly reduced when it has become a routine. For example, pictures that have more than one name take longer to describe than pictures that have one dominant name (e.g. Griffin 2001). But when a particular name has been routinized, accessing that name should be straightforward even if there is an alternative.

We now consider the implications of routinization for language change. A key issue in the study of language change is explaining how changes in the language can spread within and across generations of speakers. Kirby (1999) refers to this as the *problem of linkage*. In biological evolution, linkage occurs through the inheritance of genes from one generation to the next. The traditional linguistic analogy is to explain linkage through the passing down of a language from one generation to the next during its acquisition (see Lieven, Chapter 14 of this volume; López-Couso, Chapter 15 of this volume). It is then assumed that language change is determined by constraints (which Kirby calls the linguistic bottleneck) that apply to the language-learning mechanism. However, interactive alignment and routinization offer an alternative linkage mechanism associated with language use. In the same way that experimental communities of speakers establish their own routines over the course of repeated interactions, so real communities of speakers can establish and maintain routines as well. Hence, one kind of language variation is found in what Clark (1996) calls *communal lexicons* – particular sets of expressions associated with different communities. For example, skiers talk of *piste*, physicists of *quarks* and statisticians have a special interpretation of *significance* and *normal distribution*. This kind of variation would be expected if each community were establishing their own routines.

As we have argued, routines can be considered lexicalizations, bits of language stored and accessed directly from memory. One important topic in the study of language change is the emergence and maintenance of simple and complex lexicalizations. Take, for example, the process of grammaticalization in which lexical elements increasingly take on grammatical functions. A good example of this is the evolution in English of the complex future auxiliary *going to* from the simple lexical verb of motion *going*, which may even become reduced to the simple *gonna* (Hopper and Traugott 2003). This historical process follows a similar pattern to that of routinization in dialogue. Initially, an expression takes on a contextually determined interpretation (in this case with reference to a future action presumably involving motion). This expression-meaning mapping then becomes fixed and eventually generalizes to other analogous future actions that do not involve motion. As soon as it becomes fixed in this way, it becomes a routine which can be reduced like any other lexicalization with repeated usage (e.g. becoming the simple lexical item *gonna*). The important distinction between this account of language change and the more traditional acquisition-based account is that the evolutionary process arises from usage rather than constraints on learning, because the linkage is through interactive alignment and routinization. For a more detailed discussion of how frequency of usage relates to processes of grammaticalization, we refer the reader to Bybee (2006); see also Mair (this volume, Section 9.4).

Another evolutionary phenomenon in English concerns the steady loss of irregular verb forms. Here the problem is somewhat different from that of the *going to*-auxiliary. Over the years, irregular past tense verbs (e.g. *mown*) have been replaced by their regular counterparts in English (*mowed*). Interestingly, this regularization process is sensitive to the frequency of use of the verb, with recent research suggesting that verbs regularize at a rate that is inversely proportional to the square root of their usage frequency (Lieberman et al. 2007). How can this be explained? If we consider irregular expressions as lexicalized routines, this may help to explain the circumstances in which they are lost. On our account, speakers use routines because they can be accessed directly from memory, thereby bypassing the complex decisions of non-routine language production. However, this is only beneficial if the routine is readily accessible. In other words, if accessing the routine (e.g. *mown*) takes longer than formulating the full form (e.g. *mow + -ed*), or if speakers fail to access it at all on occasion, then it will fall out of use to be replaced by the non-routine regular form. Again Bybee (2006) gives a detailed account of how the process of regularization can be explained in terms of the probability of retrieving stored representations.

8.3 Conclusions

Languages reside in the minds of those who speak and understand them, so it would be surprising if historical language change were not subject to psycholinguistic principles applying to those minds. One such principle is priming, the fact that people tend to repeat the structure and meaning of what they have recently used or encountered. Here we argued that priming, which strongly influences language processing, may also play an important role in language change.

First, we showed how priming in dialogue leads to alignment of linguistic representations, which supports the ultimate goal of aligning conversationalists' understanding of the situation under discussion. We then discussed the extensive literature on structural priming among native and non-native adults and children. Finally, we considered processes by which expressions become routinized. These effects are pervasive in laboratory experiments and are also observed in corpora. We propose that they serve as a basis for processes of language change in English and elsewhere.

CHAPTER 9

From Priming and Processing to Frequency Effects and Grammaticalization? Contracted Semi-Modals in Present-Day English

Christian Mair

9.1 Introduction

In their contribution to the present volume (Chapter 8), Pickering and Garrod respond to the editors' invitation to assess the relevance of psycholinguistic research on priming for historical linguistics. At first glance, this seems a long shot indeed. Priming studies work with time frames of seconds and minutes, whereas historical linguistics deals with centuries and millennia. The data in priming experiments are obtained through systematic elicitation in tightly controlled laboratory environments, whereas historical linguists have to work with textual evidence which has come down to us more or less accidentally, is always selective and biased, and – especially for older stages of the language – insufficient in quantity and poor in quality. Pickering and Garrod make it clear from the start that, given the task they are facing, priming must be a mere starting point, serving as a feeder mechanism for more long-term processes such as interactive alignment and routinisation. The link between priming and language change is thus indirect and sometimes precarious. But their chapter also shows that it is certainly worth exploring in greater depth, because it is only through specific language-historical case studies that the concrete relevance of psycholinguistics for historical linguistics can be established.

There is a sense in which historical linguistics and psycholinguistics have been integrated comfortably for more than a century, namely at the level of what Aitchison (2003: 736) refers to as '"top layer" causation', the acknowledgement of the fact that ultimately all language change has to proceed in conformity with general properties of human cognition and the human mind. In practice, this acknowledgment has had little impact, though. When studying specific instances of change, historical linguistics has tended to limit its scope to the sociolinguistic dynamics of the spread of innovations in the community and to the impact they have on the linguistic system (e.g. in terms of increasing/decreasing transparency and restoring equilibrium).

Leading figures of the Neogrammarian movement, such as Hermann Paul, held that the intergenerational transmission of language in acquisition must be a privileged site of linguistic innovation, but empirical studies testing this claim have been rare (see the discussion in Aitchison 2003: 737; also Lieven and López-Couso, Chapters 14 and 15 in this volume). Similarly general constraints have been invoked to account for the distribution of information in utterances[1] or a crosslinguistically attested dispreference for centre embedding (i.e. the nesting of constructions in a matrix of the same constructional type[2]).

Historical psycholinguistics, as understood in the present volume and in the contribution by Pickering and Garrod, is about more than such a general acknowledgment of cognitive and psychological constraints on language change. It is about testing, if possible through statistical quantification, the effect of specific psycholinguistic processes (such as, for example, priming) in order to shed light on the actuation and the spread of individual changes in specific languages. Pickering and Garrod summarise their research agenda as follows:

> Our conclusion suggests that alignment in general and alignment of syntax in particular is likely to be a major historical mechanism of language change. We now introduce alignment, priming and routinization, and suggest how they can apply to language change within a linguistic community of adults, to adults entering the community and to children growing up in the community.

This quotation goes far beyond the general acknowledgment of cognitive constraints on language change because it mentions specific mechanisms in acquisition, production and processing and identifies specific groups of speakers who could be targeted in investigations. Among the three psycholinguistic mechanisms they discuss, they place the emphasis on alignment as the one most likely to bridge the two gaps which currently separate psycholinguistics and historical linguistics. These are (1) the gap between the subjective micro-time of language acquisition, production and processing and the objective macro-time of structural change in language systems and (2) the associated gap between the mind of the speaking individual and the usage norms of the group or community.

Understood in this way, historical psycholinguistics can complement historical pragmatics and historical sociolinguistics in order to produce a more comprehensive and fine-grained model of the origin and spread of linguistic innovations (and the converse development of obsolescence).

9.2 Language History: Changing Language Systems, Changing Traditions of Speaking and Writing and the Lifespan of the Speaking Individual

The default way of writing the history of a language is to focus on the long-term historical evolution of the structure of the linguistic system. This perspective backgrounds the individual speaker, the community and the contexts of use. To give an example, Middle English initial [kn] in words such as *knife* and *know* is said to 'become' [n] in Modern English – when in fact the situation was rather more complex. We can assume a natural envelope of variation for initial [kn] clusters which will always produce a limited number of simplified realisations. Forms such as [ni:] or [tni:] (for [kni:]) are regular but transient stages in acquisition and may be present as performance slips in small numbers in adults. In the case of English, at a particular time and in a particular community of speakers, this natural envelope of variation developed an imbalance which started a diachronic development that had effects beyond the micro-time of the individual lifespan.

It is such macro-historical changes in the norms of community usage which have been at the centre of attention in the great philological histories of the English language (e.g. Jespersen 1909–1949, Visser 1963–1973). They assemble and aggregate large numbers of citations from (usually) written works by numerous authors to illustrate the characteristic usage of a period and changes across periods. Investigations focusing on the changing usage of historical individuals across the lifespan, by contrast, are exceptional even today (but see Adamson 1998; Petré 2009). In fact, the individual idiolect is explicitly eliminated from language history in at least one seminal theoretical treatment which has had enormous influence in shaping the methods of modern historical linguistics. As Weinreich, Labov and Herzog argue, the site of language change is the community and not the individual:

> The grammars in which linguistic change occurs are grammars of the speech community. Because the variable structures contained in language are determined by social functions, idiolects do not provide the basis for self-contained or internally consistent grammars.
>
> Linguistic change is transmitted within the community as a whole; it is not confined to discrete steps within the family. Whatever discontinuities

are found in linguistic change are the products of specific discontinuities within the community, rather than inevitable products of the generational gap between parent and child. (Weinreich, Labov and Herzog 1968: 188)

The focus on changing community norms explains why corpus linguistic methods were adopted early and successfully in historical linguistics. Little conceptual effort was required to integrate them into the standard models. Corpora and the associated tools for concordancing and statistical analysis enabled language historians to work on essentially familiar problems – but much faster, more efficiently and with more statistical sophistication. Nor was it much of a conceptual challenge to extend the sociolinguistic apparent-time methodology developed for the study of ongoing change to cover older stages of the language, as is witnessed by the rapid rise of historical socio-linguistics (Nevalainen and Raumolin-Brunberg 2003) and historical prag-matics (Jucker 1995). Both historical sociolinguistics and historical pragmatics are perfect ways of putting social factors and communicative contexts back into the language historical picture. Formality, politeness and gender effects certainly did not play themselves out in precisely the same way in medieval England that they do today, but it is nevertheless safe to assume that – then as now – politeness, formality and gender were factors to consider in the spread of linguistic innovation.

Pickering and Garrod propose useful ways of complementing historical pragmatics and historical sociolinguistics in order to establish a comprehensive, usage-based model of language change, thus releasing historical psycholinguistics from the 'no-person's-land between language universals and more general psychological ones' (Aitchison 2003: 736) in which currently it is still stuck. In current work on language history it is corpus linguistic studies which show potential affinity to psycholinguistics because of their rich quantification (though, of course, historical corpus studies are typically concerned with changes in community norms in historical macro-time, and not with intra-speaker or intra-writer variability). As Pickering and Garrod point out, however, there are studies such as Szmrecsanyi (2006), which bring back subjective-individual micro-time into corpus linguistics. In addition to the cumulative overall frequencies (typically expressed in measures such as 'frequency per million words'), this study also gives local frequency measures covering persistent and repeated use of a form for a defined length of text (corresponding to a defined interval of time) by one speaker, or by small groups of speakers in conversational interaction. Persistence in the use of forms in the short term is plausibly related to long-term entrenchment:

Along somewhat different lines, persistence may be thought of as a type of short-term entrenchment. 'Entrenchment' (originally a Cognitive Grammar term) is a mechanism due to which the effect of discourse frequency on mental representations is such that these representations are strengthened through their activation in use (cf. Langacker 1987: 59 f.). It is true that entrenchment is understood as being a mechanism operating over longer intervals of time, possibly a speaker's lifetime – in contrast, persistence is a phenomenon that probably dissipates after a few minutes. Yet, persistence as well is due to linguistic patterns, or representations thereof, being activated through use; in this way, it may make sense to refer to persistence as 'micro-entrenchment', and to entrenchment as 'macro-persistence'. (Szmrecsanyi 2006: 141)

This way of linking the micro-time of speech production to the build-up and transformation of the language faculty over the lifespan[3] is compatible with the pathway from priming via alignment to routinisation as proposed by Pickering and Garrod. Szmrecsanyi does not comment on the final step in the extension, from the lifespan to macro-historical time in the history of the speech community. Alignment has the potential to link the two, as by definition the site of interactive alignment is not the mind of the individual but the conversational dyad or group.

Two other promising avenues for exploring the interface between psycholinguistics and language change deserve mention here. The first is Hawkins's (1994) performance theory of order and constituency, and in particular his claim that, other things being equal, speakers' preference for 'Early Immediate Constituents' drives grammatical change and accounts for the status of typologically dominant orders in the languages of the world.

The second is even more directly related to priming, the focus of the present chapter. In a 2008 special issue of *Theoretical Linguistics*, the target article (Jaeger and Rosenbach 2008) points out the homology between unidirectional priming and the assumed unidirectionality (or irreversibility) of grammaticalisation processes. The target paper is commented on from a variety of perspectives, the most relevant one for the present purpose being the contribution by historical linguist Elizabeth Traugott (2008a), who explicitly advocates the use of corpus data as a complement to and potential corrective for experimental priming data:

If priming is a factor in change, which seems plausible, at least at the phonological level, then we would hope to be able to find evidence for its effects in contemporary language use, outside of experimental situations (some of them with visual input of pictures). Spoken corpora should be used to test the hypothesis, but since our historical data are almost all written until the twentieth century, comparative investigation of written corpora is essential as well. (Traugott 2008a: 136)

As a corpus linguist hardened by long experience, I am very happy to endorse this exhortation, but feel obliged to add the self-critical caveat that most 'spoken' corpora are available only as orthographic transcriptions. Many interesting processes of morphosyntactic change – including the spread of *wanna*, which will serve as a case study below – involve a phonological dimension which eschews conventional spelling. In such cases the faithfulness of the transcription is generally in inverse proportion to the amount of material transcribed.

After this brief survey of relevant research by others, let us return to Pickering and Garrod. Priming, alignment and routinisation – though invoked by them chiefly in order to account for syntactic changes – are probably even more directly relevant to the rather trivial phonetic changes such as the one mentioned above ([kn] → [n]). Occasional simplification of consonant clusters is expected in **microgenesis**, the seconds-to-minutes time frame which matters in the study of the production and perception of utterances in live conversation. Investigating the role of self- or other-priming in variable consonant-cluster simplification in the present-day language thus presents itself as one way of shedding light on what happened in the past. In acquisition (**ontogenesis**, in Pickering and Garrod's terms), the ability to produce initial [n] precedes the ability to produce the [kn] cluster, with the homorganic [tn] cluster providing an intermediate form for obvious physiological reasons. Acquisition data from German, a West-Germanic language historically related to English which has preserved initial [kn] clusters, therefore become relevant to an understanding of what happened in the history of English. After all, language change in macro-historical time (or **phylogenesis**, in Pickering and Garrod's terms) in this particular case reversed the process of acquisition in the individual ([kn] > [(t)n] > [n], rather than [n] > [(t)n] > [kn]).

Physiology, psychology, cognition and language history in macro-historical time are not usually in such an uncomplicated relationship with each other when it comes to lexical and grammatical change, the domain on which Pickering and Garrod focus. For example, claiming that French 'was in contact with' English in the later Middle Ages or that English 'borrowed' a lot of words from French is not harmless and convenient shorthand, but a potentially misleading metaphor, which personifies languages as independent agents and also highlights the structural sediments of change rather than the psychological and social processes which brought them about. Some kind of historical-psycholinguistic approach is clearly needed in order to shed light on how bilingual minds performed during the type of conquest diglossia which arose in England after the Norman Conquest (always taking note of the fact, of course, that we are dealing with two different kinds of bilingual minds: the minds of the English-dominant peasant majority, who found it necessary or desirable to accommodate prestige vocabulary from their conquerors' language into their communicative repertoires, and the minds of the French-dominant elite who eventually shifted to the language of the majority, taking along a fair portion of French vocabulary in the process).

Still more controversial is the role of contact in accounting for some changes in Middle English grammar, for example the establishment of analytical comparison of adjectives (*more polite – most polite*) alongside the synthetic type (*politer – politest*). If historical psycholinguistics, and in particular concepts such as (cross-linguistic) priming, routinisation and alignment, were able to get us closer to an understanding of how a small selection from the large number of the ever-present 'borderline grammatical' (Pickering and Garrod, this volume) experiments turn into diachronic innovations in the community norm, this would represent a definite advance in language history.

9.3 'Linkage': How to Extrapolate from Psycholinguistic Evidence to Language Change beyond the Lifespan

The natural diachronic horizon for psycholinguistics is the human lifespan. On such a view, historical change in languages can only come about through successive adjustments during acquisition, as part of the intergenerational transmission of language. Doubtless, there are grammatical changes which can be handled within this model; for example, simple cases of syntactic reanalysis. Thus, it is realistic to assume that a learner of early nineteenth-century English heard late and rare instances of the *be*-perfect (e.g. *she is gone*) and reanalysed them as copula sentences of the type *she is away/off* in acquisition.

Focussing on acquisition as the exclusive site of language change may tally well with the axioms of Generative Grammar (Lightfoot 1979, 2006; Warner 1993 on English modal verbs), but the language-historical mainstream – based as it is on traditional philology and more recent influences from sociolinguistics and usage-based linguistics – has always chafed at this very narrow conception, which moreover seems difficult to square with considerable amounts of experimental and corpus data. In particular, the model fails

Table 9.1 *Contrasting research designs in corpus-based linguistics and psycholinguistics*

	Corpus-based/usage-based linguistics	Psycholinguistic priming studies
Aim of investigation	retrospective documentation of variation and change in community norms	analysis of 'online' dynamics of language processing in the individual
Data source and quantity	naturalistic setting: mass of pooled performance data; produced under naturalistic conditions by large numbers of speakers/writers on whom we typically have sparse metadata	laboratory setting: smallish number of informants, providing data in rigorously controlled 'laboratory' conditions
Data collection and analysis	collected, analysed and statistically profiled retrospectively and aggregated 'in bulk'; typical measurements speaker-independent ('frequency per million words')	observed in subjective/psychological 'micro' time, to study production/perception or acquisition in the individual

with gradual processes of change, the long-term drifts of language history, such as the establishment of SVO as default word order, and grammaticalisation processes, which typically run their fairly consistent course over several centuries and through ordered stages in which outgoing and incoming forms coexist in successive stages of functional differentiation ('layering', in the terms of Hopper and Traugott 2003).

As Table 9.1 shows, corpus-based historical linguistics, with its focus on the long term and the community, and psycholinguistics, with its focus on the short term and individual cognition, are still very far apart:

There are two ways of reconciling the micro-time of individual language production, processing and acquisition and the macro-time of community history. From Hermann Paul to the Generativist-inspired model of language change proposed by Lightfoot (1979, 2006), scholars have assigned the crucial role to intergenerational transmission during acquisition. Pickering and Garrod, however, favor a different kind of 'linkage':

> A key issue in the study of language change is explaining how changes in the language can spread within and across generations of speakers. Kirby (1999) refers to this as the *problem of linkage*. In biological evolution, linkage occurs through the inheritance of genes from one generation to the next. The traditional linguistic analogy is to explain linkage through the passing

down of a language from one generation to the next during its acquisition. It is then assumed that language change is determined by constraints [which Kirby (1999) calls the linguistic bottleneck] that apply to the language learning mechanism [. . .]. However, interactive alignment and routinization offer an alternative linkage mechanism associated with language use. In the same way that experimental communities of speakers establish their own routines over the course of repeated interactions, so real communities of speakers can establish and maintain routines as well. Hence, one kind of language variation is found in what Clark (1996) calls *communal lexicons* – particular sets of expressions associated with different communities. For example, skiers talk of *piste*, physicists of *quarks*, statisticians have a special interpretation of *significance* and *normal distribution*. This kind of variation would be expected if each community was establishing their own routines.

Language acquisition takes place in the group but is often studied in its effects on individual cognition and maturation. Routinisation can be studied as a cognitive process in the individual, but the lexical and grammatical routines which result from it are the collective property of large and small speech communities – generally referred to as *grammaticalisation, lexicalisation* or *constructionalisation* (Traugott and Trousdale 2013). Interactive alignment, finally, starts out with the conversational dyad or small group, thus providing the missing link which allows the easy extension of the perspective both to the individual speaker's mind and the community and society at large. As Pickering and Garrod put it,

> Our conclusion suggests that alignment in general and alignment of syntax in particular is likely to be a major historical mechanism of language change. We now introduce alignment, priming and routinization, and suggest how they can apply to language change within a linguistic community of adults, to adults entering the community and to children growing up in the community.
> [. . .]
> Our discussion is rather speculative because psycholinguistic studies tend to be fairly short-lived and it is very hard to know whether effects demonstrated in the laboratory persist over people's lifetimes, or could lead to even longer-term changes across generations. Therefore, our goal is primarily to demonstrate how permanent changes could come about. But in addition we need to focus on groups of people that are particularly relevant to language change. In this paper, we refer to three groups: adults within the linguistic community, to adults entering the community, and to children growing up in the community.

Table 9.2 differs from Table 9.1 in that it highlights the potentially shared interests between corpus linguistics and psycholinguistics which emerge on such a view.

Table 9.2 *Research topics in corpus linguistics and psycholinguistics – contrasts and overlap*

	Corpus linguistics/usage-based linguistics	Psycholinguistics
Priming	largely disregarded	core topic
Persistence	synchronic genre-specific and text-type specific frequency peaks; diachronic frequency bursts in objective historical 'macro-time'	speaker-related frequency peaks in subjective 'micro-time'
Alignment	receives some interest in qualitative conversation analysis and studies on 'emerging syntax'	core topic
Routinisation	core topic: focus on products of routinisation (chunks, collocations, fixed expressions and idioms)	core topic: focus on process
Entrenchment	term used loosely to refer to establishment of new option in group norm	technical term used to refer to representation of linguistic forms and constructions in the individual mind
Usage norm	core topic	largely disregarded
Structural ambiguity/ reanalysis	studied as point of entry for innovation in the system	studied as a problem in language perception
Grammaticalisation	core topic	disregarded

9.4   Case Studies

A promising rapprochement between historical linguistics and psycholinguistics has been achieved in the Freiburg-based doctoral research training group on 'Frequency Effects in Language' (DFG GRK 1624, http://frequenz.uni-freiburg.de/abstract&language=en), which has encouraged projects combining corpus analysis and psycholinguistic experimentation (not necessarily focussed on priming in all cases). Thus Lorenz (2013) studied 'the emancipating effects of frequency' in the creation of monomorphemic contractions such as *gonna, wanna* and *gotta.* Corpus data covering the past two centuries and perception and production experiments in the lab were shown to provide mutually supporting evidence and thus a more comprehensive analysis of aspects of these well-known grammaticalisation processes. Krause (2017) investigated analogical leveling of German imperatives with irregular [iː] (e.g. *stehlen: stiehl → stehl(e), sich ergeben:*

ergib dich → ergeb(e) dich). Apparent-time analysis of the experimental data again sheds light on important aspects of a change which has its roots in the Early Modern period.

Pickering and Garrod point out further directions for inquiry which I find very promising. For example, they show that priming may lead to greater acceptance of moderately ungrammatical structures in individual speakers in the short term. This observation is clearly relevant for historical linguistics, as many innovations start out as moderately ungrammatical extensions or reconfigurations of existing rules. In two recent studies (Mair 2012, 2014), I have used corpus data to document the origin and spread of *do*-support (i.e. main-verb syntax in questions and negations) with *(have) got (to)*. Examples (1) and (2) provide illustrations and are marked with an asterisk to signal unacceptability in Standard British English:

(1) *Do you got the time? [possessive]

(2) *Who do I got to see? [modal]

However, such forms are well established in certain non-standard varieties of North American English. Absence/loss of auxiliary *have*, on the other hand – as in (3) and (4) below – is more widely current in varieties of English around the world.

(3) I got the time.

(4) I got to see Mr Smith.

Note that speakers who assign strong negative acceptability ratings to examples such as (1) and (2) are more tolerant when the use of auxiliary *do* with *got* is presented in 'bridging contexts' such as the following:

(5) ?I got to obey the law, and so **do** you.

(6) ??I've got to obey the law, and so do you.

It seems reasonable to design priming experiments to test whether absence of the prime *('ve* or *have)* in the first part of example (5) facilitates use of the pro-form *do* in the second:

(7) I**'ve** got to obey the law → and so **have** you.

(8) I got to/gotta obey the law → and so **do** you.

If this priming-related correlation holds, loss of the prime is a factor in destabilising the older construction and creating a systemic point of entry for the new one. As it happens, this particular bridging context fits mono-logic and dialogic situations and is therefore a suitable variable to study the question whether interactive alignment promotes the spread of this particular innovation to other speakers, who then, by further routinizing it, will help spread it throughout the community:

(9)   A: I've got to obey the law.   B: So **have** we all.

(10)   A: I got to obey the law.   B: So **do** we all.

In a similar vein, local frequency bursts in corpora (*persistence*, in Szmrecsanyi's (2006) terms) is a phenomenon which has remained understudied and deserves more thorough investigation from a psycholinguistic perspective. Of course, it is tempting to handle such clusterings of forms in certain passages of text as trivial discourse factors: one portion of text is narrative in structure and hence contains a lot of past tense, whereas the following portion makes predictions and therefore contains a lot of future forms. Such top-down analysis of discourse macro-structure, however, is not able to explain persistence in the choice of realisational variants of forms which have the same or similar function, such as *going to, gonna, will* and *'ll* or, to add a slightly less hackneyed example, *want to* or *wanna*. Consider the following examples from the Corpus of Contemporary American English (COCA):

(11)   GEORGE-STEPHANOPOU# (Off-camera) Odds you run?
       DONALD-TRUMP-1CEO# Well, I **don't wanna** say odds. I **don't wanna** put myself in that position. I **don't wanna** put you in that position. But I will tell you, I love this country. I hate what's happening to it. And you may very well be surprised. (COCA Spoken 2011)

(12)   . . . that coach is **gonna** hurt a lot of women who are **gonna** wanna take that time off, which I think they should after having that baby. (COCA Spoken 2007)

(13)   . . . has high blood pressure, so they're gon**na** wan**na** check to make sure that blood pressure is in good shape. (COCA Spoken 2010)

In examples (11) and (12), the first instances of *wanna* and *gonna*, respectively, may be said to prime the following ones. Examples (12) and (13) raise the additional possibility that *gonna*, as the older and better established form, primes the less well-established *wanna*. Again, alignment (or lack of it) can be demonstrated in the dialogic passages of the corpus:

(14)   ACTRESS-1FEMALE2# It is not your last hope. No daughter of mine is getting her stomach stapled, absolutely not.
       JOHN-QUIONES-1-# (Voiceover) And who better to provide insight for this scenario than renowned heart surgeon and TV host Dr. Mehmet Oz.

Table 9.3 Want to *and* wanna *in COCA (spoken material)*[4]

	WANT TO	WANNA
total frequency	103,466	2,144
→ of which preceded by *want** -9L	5,352	39
→ of which preceded by *want* -9L	5,035	33
→ of which preceded by *wan* -9L	24	98
→ of which preceded by *-na* -9L	83	147

JOHN-QUIONES-1-# (Off-camera) Doctor, welcome to 'What Would You Do?' Good to see you. Why do you **wanna** do this? DOCTOR-MEHMET-OZ-# I **wanna** learn from people intervening, what they're thinking, because I think it reflects what's happening around the country when people hear these stories about the usefulness of gastric bypass surgery or the fears that you may have about it. (COCA Spoken 2011)

Table 9.3 above shows some suggestive local frequency concentrations involving various combinations of *wanna* and other contracted and non-contracted forms. The search window includes the time before the production of *wanna* (operationalised as up to 9 words to the left = -9L):

In this 'spoken' corpus, which is made up of orthographic transcriptions and therefore likely to under-report the contraction, *want to* is vastly more frequent than *wanna*. The figures in Table 9.3 show that, out of a total of 103,466 instances of *want to*, 5,376[5] (or 5.2 per cent) have another form of the lemma *want* occurring within a span of nine words to the left. For the 2,144 forms of *wanna*, the corresponding figure is 137 (or 6.4 per cent) – a contrast which proves significant in a chi-square test ($p=0.02$). Of course, such local frequency bursts found in corpora are not proof of priming, but they define the envelope within which priming effects may play a role. This envelope, it should be noted, is thus significantly greater for *wanna* than for the full form *want*.

If the specific effect of lexical priming remains hard to define precisely, that of formal priming emerges rather more clearly. *Want to* is preceded by *wanna* in only 0.0002 per cent of all relevant cases, whereas the corresponding figure for *wanna* is 4.6 per cent (which is significant at $p<0.001$ in the chi-square test). As similar distributional tendencies can be observed for the form *-na* alone (covering *gonna* and *wanna*), we could go further and argue that *wanna* can be primed not just by previous mention of itself, but by a preceding *gonna*, too.

One environment which could be used in a laboratory experiment to test possible priming effects of the contraction *gonna* on the use of *wanna* is the construction *X is going to want to do Y*, where *going to* and *want to* (or their reduced forms *gonna* and *wanna*) do not just co-occur within a predefined span of words, but are used in syntactic integration. Of the four logically possible combinations, one is statistically dominant, two are attested at relatively low frequencies and one is not found at all in the spoken material from COCA:

– *going to want to*:   561
– *gonna want to*:   24
– *gonna wanna*:   13
– *going to wanna*:   0

As has been hinted above, full forms of *gonna* and *wanna* are very likely to be over-reported in orthographic transcriptions of spoken material, so that *gonna want to* and even *gonna wanna* are not as rare as they are made out to be in the transcribed material. Consider the following example:

(15)   Way too soon, because we're still **going to** be working it out right then. I think we're **going to** have disagreements about democracy, again, the same fundamental issues. We're **gonna** have disagreements about approaches to Israel, because as the public voice becomes much more pronounced in this part of the world, likely to be quite anti-Israeli, we'll probably have some disagreements about working against terrorism. The old guard was a real partner. These guys aren't. Also, we're **going to want to** give help to them, but only on certain conditions.

(COCA, spoken, 2011)

Here the general stylistic informality of the passage – with uses of *gonna*, with contracted negations, with informal vocabulary such as *these guys* – creates an expectation that in 'we're going to want to give help' at least *going to*, if not both forms, would be contracted, and this expectation is in fact borne out when listening to the original broadcast.[6]

Having noted the existence of such local bursts of frequency even in a corpus environment which would tend to systematically underreport them,[7] the next important step is to relate them to the more established global frequency effects usually invoked in corpus linguistic explanations of language change, such as the well-established correlation between overall token-frequency in a corpus and the likelihood of phonetic reduction. Scheibman (2000) has demonstrated this particular frequency effect exhaustively for *I don't know* → *dunno* in American English conversation, to mention an example outside of the range of the more common illustrations provided from cases of grammaticalisation (such as *wanna*, the study case used here). Table 9.4 gives combinations of *want to* + VERB in the order of frequency, detailing ranks 1 to 10 and 41 to 50.

It should be noted that the ten top-ranked verbs combining with the full form *want to* are also the top ten combining with the reduced form *wanna*, with the deviations in the rank order being trivial on the whole.[8] High token frequencies obviously make for statistically robust patterns. Ranks 41 to 50 in the list of *want to*-combinations are less frequent by broadly the power of ten and, with the exception of *believe, think* and *add*, the verbs in the *wanna* list are not found among the top 50 in the other group. Medium token frequencies make for less robust statistical patterns.

If the token frequency of the *want to* + VERB combinations is a major factor (or even one of several factors) accounting for the reduction to *wanna*, then contraction rates should be lower in the 41 to 50-bracket than in the 1 to 10-bracket. This is the case on the whole. The average contraction rate for the top-ten combinations is 2.4 per cent, whereas it is only 1.5 per cent for ranks 41 to 50.[9] This finding should be taken with a grain of salt, however, as it is obtained on the basis of amateur transcription of the original spoken data, which considerably under-reports contraction (as has been demonstrated). Unfortunately, turning to corpora with more professional and fine-grained transcription is not a solution, because these generally tend to be too small for heavy-duty statistical trawling for frequency effects.

Contraction rates for conversational American English obtained in the Santa Barbara Corpus (SBC) by Lorenz are 276 out of 364 relevant tokens, i.e. 75.8 per cent (Lorenz 2013: 99). This figure gives us a realistic idea about the true prevalence of *wanna*-contraction in informal American speech. The British National Corpus (BNC) contains ca. 10 million words of mixed-genre spoken material which was transcribed by secretarial staff under expert linguistic guidance and may thus be a better match for the spoken portion of COCA (which comprises media broadcasts spanning a broad range of formality). It generally has *wanna*-contraction rates of around 25 per cent for high-frequency verbs: e.g. 140 out of 556 (=25.2 per cent) for *be*, and 204 out of 802 (25.4 per cent) for *do*. However, even in this fairly large sample of spoken English, the verbs occupying ranks 41 to 50 in COCA are so infrequent that it is not possible to calculate meaningful average contraction ratios. For example, *miss* (rank 49) happens to be used three times with *want to* and twice with *wanna*, whereas all nine instances of *continue* (rank 50) have *want to*. In the Santa Barbara Corpus, with a total below 400 relevant tokens, an analysis of the verbal collocates of *want* is not feasible at all.

Table 9.4 *Most frequent combinations of full and reduced forms of* want to + *VERB (COCA, spoken)*

Rank order / VERB		want to	Frequency	wanna	Frequency	Contraction rate (%)
(1)	BE	want to be	8,032	wanna be	231	2.8
(2)	DO	want to do	6,288	wanna do	157	2.4
(3)	GO	want to go	4,814	wanna go	110	2.2
(4)	GET	want to get	4,697	wanna get	115	2.4
(5)	KNOW	want to know	4,073	wanna know	105	2.5
(6)	SEE	want to see	3,839	wanna see	98	2.5
(7)	MAKE	want to make	3,313	wanna make	61	1.8
(8)	SAY	want to say	3,156	wanna say	72	2.2
(9)	TALK	want to talk	2,897	wanna talk	68	2.3
(10)	HAVE	want to have	2,489	wanna have	52	2.0
...						
(41)	POINT	want to point	353	wanna point	3	0.8
(42)	RUN	want to run	340	wanna run	4	1.2
(43)	BELIEVE	want to believe	340	wanna believe	18	5.0
(44)	THINK	want to think	320	wanna think	7	2.1
(45)	PAY	want to pay	319	wanna pay	1	0.3
(46)	CUT	want to cut	303	wanna cut	2	0.7
(47)	ADD	want to add	296	wanna add	6	2.0
(48)	JOIN	want to join	278	wanna join	3	1.1
(49)	CONTINUE	want to continue	271	wanna continue	1	0.4
(50)	MISS	want to miss	260	wanna miss	2	0.8

Table 9.5a *Most frequent combinations of contracted negation and* want to/wanna + *VERB (COCA, spoken)*

Rank order / VERB	n't want to	Frequency	n't wanna	Frequency	Contraction rate (%)
BE	n't want to be	2,122	n't wanna be	61	2.8
DO	n't want to do	1,093	n't wanna do	33	2.9
GO	n't want to go	945	n't wanna go	28	2.9
GET	n't want to get	774	n't wanna get	40	4.9
SEE	n't want to see	686	n't wanna see	33	4.6
HAVE	n't want to have	608	n't wanna have	14	2.3
TALK	n't want to talk	547	n't wanna talk	25	4.4
HEAR	n't want to hear	412	n't wanna hear	16	3.7
SAY	n't want to say	411	n't wanna say	19	4.4
GIVE	n't want to give	400	not in top 10		n.a.

But the reservations against assuming an all-too-dominant role for token frequency as the dominant factor in accounting for *wanna*-contraction are not merely based on transcription quality. Even a cursory look at the global statistics, which can be seen as a metric for routinised contraction of high-frequency chunks, shows that context-dependent local frequency bursts remain relevant, too, and hence open a window for the possible additional influence of priming and alignment. The results of Table 9.4, for example, look different for the top-ten-ranked verbs when we focus on negated forms, in which the possibility of using a full or contracted form of the negative particle allows for potential priming effects. As the contracted negative is the statistical default, the baseline for comparison is provided by the top ten forms of *n't want to* + VERB.

The average contraction rate[10] now is 3.3 per cent, which suggests a facilitative influence on *wanna*-contraction of a preceding contracted negation particle.

In Table 9.5b we note the reverse effect to the one observed in Table 9.5a. For a total of 949 full forms of *not want to*, we only have 8 reduced realisations as *not wanna*, that is 0.8 per cent: an uncontracted negative particle works against the *wanna* contraction.

As can be seen, global token frequencies are not sufficient for an account of what is going on in the data. Questions and complications are raised at every turn in the interpretation of the data. Since the diachronic change we are looking at is still ongoing, the fascinating possibility arises of investigating

Table 9.5b *Most frequent combinations of uncontracted negation and* want to/wanna + *VERB (COCA, spoken)*

Rank order / VERB	*not want to*	Frequency	*not wanna*	Frequency
BE	*not want to be*	282	*not wanna be*	4
DO	*not want to do*	98	*not wanna do*	–
GO	*not want to go*	97	*not wanna go*	2
GET	*not want to get*	95	*not wanna get*	1
SEE	*not want to see*	148	*not wanna see*	1
HAVE	*not want to have*	92	*not wanna have*	–
TALK	*not want to talk*	55	*not wanna talk*	–
HEAR	*not want to hear*	41	*not wanna hear*	–
SAY		[not in top 10]		–
GIVE	*not want to give*	41	*not wanna give*	–

these further through appropriately designed experiments in laboratory conditions.

9.5   Conclusion

The above argument has presented a corpus linguist's positive response to an invitation from two psycholinguists to start working together more closely to understand language change in macro-historical time.

Priming in speech production is reflected in persistence of forms (that is, temporary 'bursts' in token frequency) in the corpus data. These bursts feed into the overall corpus frequencies and thus into any classic 'Bybee-type' usage-based account of the emergence of grammatical structure, as one factor among many others. On close inspection, the local bursts also highlight the fact that the supposedly linear and straightforward diachronic pathways of change – such as the development from the lexical verb *want* to the semi-auxiliary *wanna*, which was the study case used in the present chapter – unfold in a complex web of unexpected additional influences. Thus, speakers' choice of *wanna* is not merely conditioned by the status of *want* in their underlying grammars; additional influence can be shown to be exerted by the presence in the immediate context of analogous forms such as *gonna* (which is not entirely unexpected), but also of grammatically unrelated elements such as contracted negators (which is surprising). Theoretically, such unexpected connexions could have been revealed by the tools of traditional corpus linguistics, for example through a careful and systematic analysis of collocational patterns. In practice, however, the collocational profiles of grammatical morphemes such as *-na* or *-n't* tend to be suppressed at the expense of lexical patterns in such analyses, so that the approach through the concept of priming, at least in this case, has certainly sharpened analytical awareness.

A particular difficulty is that priming effects are very short-term. The gap between the short-term effects documented in psycholinguistic priming studies and the macro-historical time of language change in the community can be bridged by taking priming as a first step in interactive alignment and routinisation. Alternative ways of bridging the gap would be to propose a chain of the following type:

> very short-term (automatic) priming
> → medium-term (attentional) priming
> → long-term effects of implicit learning

Phenomena which deserve particular attention are (1) the role of cross-linguistic priming in language contact and (2) the possible diagnostic value of priming experiments to find out whether a change in progress has stalled or is still active.

The default approach to language history has been to focus on the diachronic development of the decontextualized system, with the roles of speakers, listeners and contexts being banished to the margins. Much recent progress in historical linguistics has been due to successful campaigns to put speakers, the community, and the social and cultural contexts of communication back into the picture. Historical pragmatics and historical discourse analysis have enabled us to rethink language history as the history of changing traditions of speaking and writing. Historical sociolinguistics has helped us understand how synchronic regional, social and stylistic variability interacts with historical change. What has been missing is an equally detailed and fine-grained analysis of the cognitive/psychological factor. Pickering and Garrod encourage us to work toward a 'historical psycholinguistics', which – as they demonstrate with several of their examples – has a place alongside historical pragmatics and historical sociolinguistics in a comprehensive, usage-based theory of language change.

While I fully endorse the research programme they propose, I would like to end with a caveat on terminology. I have used the term 'historical psycholinguistics' because of its analogy to 'historical sociolinguistics' and 'historical pragmatics', to emphasise the fact that the psycholinguistic perspective is needed alongside the sociolinguistic and discourse-pragmatic ones in order to develop a truly comprehensive, usage-based model.

The analogy holds with regard to the overall aim, but it can be challenged when it comes to the nature of the data.

Sociolinguistic and pragmatic research on the present is generally based on spoken data, whereas we usually rely on written evidence for the past. In sociolinguistic and pragmatic research, however, the different modality does not fundamentally change the epistemological nature of the evidence. Just as we can apply sociolinguistic analyses to certain types of present-day nonstandard writing, we can use some of the written evidence which has come down to us from the remote past as proxy for the reconstruction of speech (Culpeper and Kytö 2010). In historical pragmatics and historical sociolinguistics, extending the time-depth thus creates procedural problems, but does not pose any major conceptual challenges.

This is different for psycholinguistics, for which the primary data needed for historical research are lost and proxy evidence from writing, though possible in principle,[11] will generally be too poor for systematic research. However, as we have no reason to assume that the cognitive mechanisms underlying priming, routinisation and alignment have changed during the period covered by the extant 5,000 years of documented linguistic history and the 2,000 or 3,000 additional years made accessible through the methods of historical-comparative reconstruction, we can safely assume the uniformitarian principle. But to avoid misunderstandings, the best designation for the type of psycholinguistically informed language history that Pickering and Garrod advocate is 'cognitive historical linguistics'. It is a budding field of study which has already derived some inspiration from traditional cognitive and construction grammar (e.g. Hilpert 2013) and will benefit even more from future cooperation with experimental psycholinguistics. Like many other products of human activity – from our great historic cities to institutions such as economic markets, structures of government, codes of conduct and artistic traditions – languages outlast the lifetimes of their myriad creators, and yet they keep evolving – in orderly and systematic ways which can at least partly be traced to countless individuals' preferences, habits and routines.

Notes

1. Cf., e.g., Behaghel's laws (1909, 1923–32), in particular his 'Gesetz der wachsenden Glieder' [Law of Increasing Constituent-Length], which was one of the foundations of the Prague School's theory of Communicative Dynamism (Firbas 1992).

2. One textbook illustration of the phenomenon is provided by relative clauses embedded within relative clauses: *a reviewer who many authors fear* → *a reviewer who many authors who most readers like fear*. Such structures are not dispreferred on grammatical grounds alone, but more so because of their processing complexity and, beyond a certain length, also because of limitations on short-term memory.

3. There is enormous literature on first- and second-language acquisition. More recently, changes in linguistic competence and cognitive faculties in the adult lifespan have begun to receive serious attention (e.g. Ramscar et al. 2014).

4. COCA treats the form *wanna* as two 'words' (*wan* + *na*) – in all but two of the 5,196 attestations of the graphic form <wanna> in the corpus (the two mistakenly unanalysed ones being in the fiction section). The spoken material contains 2,198 forms of *wan*, composed of 2,177 which are tagged as verbs and a further 21 which are tagged as adjectives. While tagging in the first and more important group is reliable, the 21 'adjectives' also contain nonstandard spellings for *one* and uses of the form as a proper name. This potential noise is largely irrelevant, however, as searches for the bigram 'wan na' ensure perfect precision and near-perfect recall (i.e. the 2,144 cases listed in Table 9.3), so that further checking and manual post-editing of the concordance output becomes largely unnecessary.

5. This figure is composed of 5,352 tokens of *want* to* and 24 of *wan*.

6. Accessed on 7 October 2015 at http://abcnews.go.com/ThisWeek/video/round table-revolt-revolution-15231001. The crucial passage occurs at two minutes forty-five seconds into the broadcast. Contraction is helped by the fact that several rhetorically gifted experts are interviewed at the same time and all talk very fast to get their soundbites' worth in.

7. For more realistic contraction rates, see the discussion of *wanna* in the Santa Barbara Corpus, below. As the COCA data were not manually post-edited, they contain a small number of cases of the following type: 'none of the things you want to be done have been done' (COCA, spoken, 1990). These are derived from underlying 'raising' or 'Empty Case Marking' (ECM) constructions of the type 'I want something to be done' and are not available for contraction in most dialects, even if *want* and the *to*-infinitive end up in adjacent positions in relative clauses and questions (cf. Pullum 1997). The number of such cases is statistically negligible, though.

8. The rank order for the top-ten combinations with *wanna* being *be, do, get, go, know, see, say, talk, make* and *have, thank* holds rank 20 in the list of *wanna* + VERB combinations (20 occurrences). Rank 15 in the list of *wanna* + VERB combinations is occupied by *tell*, which holds rank 17 in the *want to* list (1,181 occurrences).

9. Top-ten combinations: total occurrences of the variable 44,667 (of which 43,578 are full and 1,089 are contractions); 41–50 bracket: total 3,127 (of which 3,080 are full and 47 are contractions). The chi-square test shows this distribution to be very highly significant (p=0.0009).

10. For the calculation of the average contraction rate, the 6 instances of *n't wanna give* were included: the total occurrences of the variable thus stand at 8,213, of which 7,938 are uncontracted and 275 are contracted. In a comparison of the ten generally highest-frequency verbs (Table 9.4) and the ten highest-frequency *negated* verbs (Table 9.5a), the contrasts emerge as very highly significant in the chi-square test (p=2E–06).

11. For the recent past, examples which come to mind are false starts and related phenomena recorded in our oldest corpora of spoken languages or in archival sound recordings. Some older manuscript sources might contain instances of self-correction or misspellings which reflect language production processes during the writing.

PART V

Analogy

CHAPTER 10

The Role of Analogy in Language Processing and Acquisition

Heike Behrens*

10.1 Introduction

Analogical reasoning is a powerful processing mechanism that allows us to discover similarities, form categories and extend them to new categories. Since similarities can be detected at the concrete and the relational levels, analogy is in principle unbounded. The possibility of multiple mapping makes analogy a very powerful mechanism, but leads to the problem that it is hard to predict which analogies will actually be drawn. This indeterminacy results in the fact that analogy is often invoked as an explanandum in many studies in linguistics, language acquisition and the study of language change, but that the underlying processes are hardly ever explained. When checking the index of current textbooks on cognitive linguistics and language acquisition, the keyword 'analogy' is almost completely absent, and the concept is typically evoked *ad hoc* to explain a certain phenomenon. By contrast, in work on language change, different types of analogical change have been identified and have become technical terms to refer to specific phenomena, such as *analogical* leveling when irregular forms become regularized or *analogical extension* when new items become part of a category (see Bybee 2010: 66–69; for a historical review of the use of the term in language change and grammaticalization, see Traugott and Trousdale 2013: 37–38).

In this chapter, I will discuss the possible effects of analogical reasoning for linguistic category formation from an emergentist and usage-based perspective, and then characterize the interaction of different processes of analogical reasoning in language development, with a special focus on regular/irregular morphology and argument structure. The focus on language acquisition is chosen because, in longitudinal studies on language development, we can trace the effect of analogical reasoning on a certain linguistic state over time.

I will conclude with a discussion on the similarities and differences between acquisition and change.

10.2   Definition: What Is Analogy?

10.2.1   Analogical Reasoning from a Cognitive Science Perspective

Analogy is a domain-general form of structure mapping between a source and a target (Gentner 1983). Such mappings can be based on perceptual *similarity* when one notices the similarity between two blue objects, or they can be *relational* when one sees two rows of three different objects each and notices that two of these objects share the position as the middle one without being physically similar. Markman and Gentner (1993) demonstrate this with the example of two sets of three geometrical objects in a row (see Figure 10.1). The squares in Set (a) are bigger than those in Set (b): the medium-sized square in Set (b) is identical in size to the smallest square in Set (a): they are object matches because they share the same perceptible attributes. By contrast, the analogy between the smallest square in Set (a) and the small square in Set (b) is a relational one: they are different in size, but both are the smallest in their set (Markman and Gentner 1993).

To give a linguistic example, mappings can be based on physical similarity or on abstract relations: In morphology, we find patterns based on physical similarity in allophonic variation, where a stem with a certain coda is inflected with a particular allomorph.

Gentner and Smith (2012: 131) state that **analogical reasoning** involves three processes:

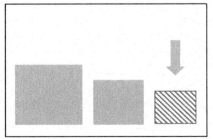 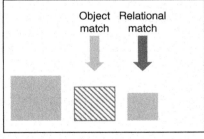

Figure 10.1 Perceptual similarity and relational analogy. The relevant squares are distinguished by their pattern.

- **Retrieval** Given some current topic in the working memory, a person may be reminded of a prior analogous situation in the long-term memory.
- **Mapping** Given two cases present in the working memory (either through analogical retrieval or simply through encountering two cases together), mapping involves a process of aligning the representations and projecting inferences from one analogue to the other. The mapping is *structure consistent* and *systematic* because it concerns large relational systems.[1]
- **Evaluation**: Once an analogical mapping has been done, the analogy and its inferences are judged.

10.2.2   The Effect of Analogy on Perception

Analogical reasoning is not just triggered by the situations we perceive, but it is an active process that can shape our perception. The ability needed to draw comparisons is *structural alignment*, i.e. the ability to notice the correspondences between elements. Alignment has three cognitive effects (Gentner et al. 2016):

(a) It makes the similarities more salient and leads to abstraction and transfer (Gentner and Markman 1997).

(b) It promotes the noticing of alignable differences. For example, most people are not aware of a basic principle in engineering, namely that diagonal braces render a construction more stable. Gentner et al. (2016) had adults and children construct skyscrapers, most of which collapsed when they had reached a certain height. In one experimental condition, children were asked to tell which of two buildings (one with and one without diagonal strengthening) was stronger, first by just looking at them, then by shaking the buildings. In the subsequent observational study of their building activities, they had aligned the perceptual difference without explicit instruction: the building with diagonal braces was more stable than that without. This effect was even stronger when the critical difference was the only difference between the two constructions.

(c) It invites the projection of inferences from the base (or source) domain to the target domain, and is thus instrumental for the understanding of metaphors, for example.

Hofstadter and Sander (2013) argue that the potential for analogical reasoning is indeed unbounded, which makes them the 'fuel and fire of thought'. They demonstrate the versatility of analogical reasoning for words, many of which (like *band* or *chair*) carry multiple meanings and many associations from their contexts of use. In dictionary approaches to meaning, such associations and meaning extensions cannot be considered, yet they are relevant for our understanding of these words in context. Hofstadter and Sander argue that the flexibility in using linguistic units and in understanding such flexible usage would not be possible if meaning were fixed:

> And the fact is that ordinary words don't have just two or three but an *unlimited number* of meanings, which is quite a scary thought; however, the more positive side of this thought is that each concept has a limitless potential for variety. (Hofstadter and Sander 2013: 5)

What follows from these cognitive approaches to analogy is that analogical reasoning is not only unconstrained in principle, but also happens on the fly (Skousen 2002; see Section 10.3, below). But if alignment is so flexible, how can we predict or ascertain which analogies are actually drawn in language processing? At least two questions arise:

(a)   Do we draw all possible comparisons? At least in language acquisition research, it seems that children generalize rather conservatively. How relational and abstract are the generalizations that we make? Do we draw on abstract relational principles or rules to generate new sentences, or do we exploit constructional patterns with some degree of surface regularity and lexical specificity as well as semantic grounding?

(b)   What guides or constrains the comparisons we make? There is evidence that we 'overlook' a lot of possible analogies. What influences the likelihood with which we make a particular comparison?

The findings from psychology suggest that the analogies we draw spontaneously are rather limited and often based on surface similarity. First, there is evidence that children are strongly surface-oriented even when comparisons are directly presented to them (Gentner 1988). For example, if a 4- to 5-year-old is asked to interpret 'How is a cloud like a sponge', they might say 'both are round and fluffy'. A 9-year-old or an adult might say 'both hold water and later give it back'. Gentner (1988) used the term 'relational shift' to describe this shift from property-based interoperation to relational interpretation. Second, in research on analogical transfer in adults, we find that remindings are strongly based on overall similarity, especially surface similarity. Even adults fail to notice and use past analogues that only share relational similarity (Gentner, Rattermann and Forbus 1993; Gick and

Holyoak 1980) unless they are frequent enough to form a schema. Bybee (2010: chapter 4) supports the importance of local and similarity-based generalizations when reviewing research on the acquisition of syntax that shows that children's 'new' utterances differ only slightly from the constructions they have produced before.

In the following, I will focus on analogical processes in morphology and syntax. The studies reviewed here focus on category-internal changes (e.g. spread of regular morphemes). The focus will be on theories and studies in language acquisition

10.3   Analogical Processes in Language

Analogical processing is needed when assigning new exemplars to a category or when extending the range of a category. While some theories make a sharp delineation between symbolic and rule-based processes that rely on binary category assignment (see Section 10.4.1, below), others assume that categories are emergent, dynamic and – importantly – also malleable. Such frameworks include connectionist models (Skousen 1989, 2002; Skousen, Lonsdale and Parkinson 2002), exemplar models (Pierrehumbert 2001), some versions of construction grammar (Croft 2001) and usage-based or constructivist models of language (Beckner et al. 2009; Bybee 2010; Langacker 1987; Tomasello 1998). They describe how categories are formed when a new item is associated with an existing category. Analogical relationships play a crucial role in this process:

> Analogical modeling, on the other hand, does not have a training stage except in the sense that one must obtain a database of occurrences. Predictions are made 'on the fly', and all variables are considered apriorily equal (with certain limitations due to restrictions on short-term memory). The significance of a variable is determined locally – that is, only with respect to the given context. Gang effects are related to the location of the given context and the amount of resulting homogeneity within the surrounding contextual space. (Skousen 2002: 3)

The internal structure of such categories can be seen as one of more-or-less closely related items:

> In an exemplar model, each category is represented in memory by a large cloud of remembered tokens of that category. These memories are organized in a cognitive map, so that memories of highly similar instances are close to each other and memories of dissimilar instances are far apart. (Pierrehumbert 2001: 140)

This clustering of related exemplars can give rise to prototype effects for those members that are most central to the category because they share the most features (Ibbotson 2013), or – in non-feature-based terminology – are high-frequency representatives of the typical function of a category (O'Donnell, Römer and Ellis 2013). Prototypes facilitate the association of new members with a particular category, and may serve as models for the extension of that category (Goldberg 2006; Ibbotson and Tomasello 2009). For example, *give* is the most frequent verb used in the ditransitive, double-object construction (*give John a book*), and it denotes transfer of possession, while *get* is the most frequent verb used in ditransitive constructions with prepositional objects, and denotes caused motion/change of location (*get the ball over the fence*). Corpus analyses as well as association experiments and language development data show that this relationship holds, although it is not completely deterministic, since it is possible to encode transfer in a prepositional construction (*give the book to John*). Goldberg (2006: 89) calls this the *cognitive anchoring effect*, where one high-frequency exemplar can serve as the salient standard for comparison.

10.3.1   *The Role of Analogy in Category Formation and Extension*

Analogical reasoning leads to *learning* in terms of categorization, abstraction and category extension. Langacker (2000) describes these processes as follows:

> The cognizer needs the ability to compare two structures and notice discrepancies as well as similarity or overlap. When source and target (the new item) match in the relevant respects, the target is categorized as an item belonging to the source category. (Langacker 2000:4)

This definition entails that each comparison allows for multiple mappings, which in turn leads to categorization in multiple dimensions. For example, when interpreting a novel verb form like *gorped*, it can be classified as a past tense verb based on its position and meaning in an utterance, as well as by its overlap or surface similarity with the *–ed* suffix of other past tense forms. Another form like *glam* can also show analogy with other past tense forms in terms of its position and meaning, though not in surface similarity with the regular past tense suffix, but rather with a smaller pattern of irregular forms (e.g. *swim-swam-swum*). Such slight mismatches between source and target lead to an *extension* of the category. Ultimately, the past tense category should encompass all forms and the analogical mappings that hold between them. Moreover, such a category should be flexible because new markers can be integrated, and the weight of the mappings can change. Such a dynamic model of categories and categorization is proposed by so-called exemplar models (Barsalou, Huttenlocher and Lamberts 1998). The example of the past tense category also shows that analogical mapping goes beyond surface similarities, even if they are available in that speakers make choices between different possibilities (*glum* vs. *glimmed*).

According to Langacker, analogy leads to categorization. For language acquisition, I will link the concept of analogy to the concepts of schematization and granularity as proposed by Langacker (1987). In this view, children need to direct their focus from detail to similarities on higher levels in order to discover schemas and more abstract relationships. Gentner and Medina (1988) trained children to make such *progressive abstractions* by drawing their attention to literal similarity matches first, and then highlighting similarities across dimensions.

In historical linguistics, two aspects of analogical reasoning are prominently studied: proportional analogies and analogical leveling (to my knowledge, these terms are not prominently used in the acquisition literature). *Proportional analogies* describe the induction by exploiting the parallelism of three examples to fill the gap of item 4 (*walk : walked : go : goed*). This regularization can also be an example of analogical leveling, when phonological or morphological distinctions are diminished due to a more general regularization process. Bybee and Beckner (2014) argue that these cases can be subsumed under frequency-induced processes of categorization. However, De Smet and Fischer (Chapter 11 in this volume) correctly point out that while analogy is part of any categorization process, it is a much wider concept because analogy allows for multiple mappings, not just mappings onto existing categories (see the discussion on relational analogies above). They follow Traugott (2011), who distinguishes analogy as a mechanism or process of thought, from analogization as the product of analogical reasoning that is visible as a new stage in language change.

While both historical linguistics and language acquisition deal with change in language use, they also differ in important dimensions: In language change, the linguistic conventions or structures themselves change as a function of changing preferences in the language community, whereas in language acquisition, the language use of the individual child changes as she or he gradually approximates the form-function correspondences of the ambient language(s). Hence, the outcome is quite different. Yet, some of the fundamental questions are the same. They concern the theoretical debate on when and whether speakers process language by 'rule', which would allow them to make far-reaching generalizations, using relational analogies, or whether developmental change is a rather local and gradual abstraction. In the past decades, usage-based studies on acquisition have accumulated converging evidence from a number of different phenomena and languages to show how local generalizations can lead to a more wide-ranging, rule-like change. In the following sections, I will discuss the theoretical foundations for this research and demonstrate such a process with data from German plural acquisition. In Sections 10.6 and 10.7, I will try to systematize similarities and differences between language acquisition and language change, and identify some open questions for further research.

10.3.2   Similarity Matches versus Relational Matches

Linguistic relations can be complex, or – in the terminology of usage-based approaches to language development – 'abstract'. While 'concrete' relations are based on the (partial) physical identity of linguistic sequences, 'abstract' linguistic relations are underlying relations. Even infants are able to recognize recurrent patterns in nonsense syllables. Marcus, Vijayan, Bandi Rao and Vishton (1999) exposed 7-month-old infants to syllable sequences of the pattern ABB (e.g. *ga ti ti)* or ABA (e.g. *la ni la*). After two minutes of familiarization (that is, hearing the same pattern again and again), they were exposed to new stimuli with the same or a different pattern. Infants paid more attention to the new pattern. Experiments like these show that infants are able to recognize familiar patterns and distinguish them from new patterns, even if the concrete elements have changed.

In principle, syntactic rules could be based on such patterns. The following sentences do not share a single concrete realization of a morpheme, i.e. they have no surface similarity, but they have the same underlying structure, e.g. Agent Action Patient:

(1)   *Kim loves Anna.*
(2)   *Sophie kissed Jack.*
(3)   *They see John.*

This example illustrates that relational analogies exist at various levels. One could also group the words by their part-of-speech category (pronouns, proper names and verbs). Depending on the language, thematic roles like Agent, Action and Patient are systematically linked to grammatical functions like Subject, Verb and Object. This openness makes analogy powerful but also unbounded. Since analogical reasoning relies on the discovery of both physical similarities and relational ones, multiple analogical mappings are possible between any set of items or structures. Consequently, one of the big debates in language acquisition, and to a lesser extent in linguistic theory and psycholinguistics, is at what level such structures are represented (see Section 10.4.1, below). In sum, Gentner and Colhoun (2010) and Gentner and Smith (2012) see analogy as an invitation to compare and to draw inferences from such a comparison.

> Reasoning by analogy involves identifying a common relational system between two situations and generating further inferences driven by these commonalities. The commonalities may also include concrete property matches between the situations, but this is not necessary for analogy; what is necessary is overlap in relational structure. (Gentner and Smith 2012: 130)

10.4　The Role of Analogy in Constructivist Theories of Acquisition

Usage-based, emergentist and constructivist theories of acquisition do not assume a genetic predisposition for linguistic categories, or *a priori* linguistic representations. Crosslinguistic research on adult linguistic categories has shown that there are no principled constraints on grammatical categorization (Slobin 1997a). Crosslinguistic research has also shown that the influence of language on children's emerging categories starts early. While very general prelinguistic concepts or *biases* exist that influence children's early perception and categorization before language-specific categorization sets in (Mandler 2008), the process of 'tuned attention' (Ellis 2006a, 2006b; Freudenthal, Pine and Gobet 2009) leads children to discover the form-function relationships that are relevant in their target language(s). This entails that children's linguistic categories are emergent, malleable and shaped by the input language (Bowerman and Choi 2003; Majid, Bowerman, Kita, Haun and Levinson 2004).

Construction Grammar has become the dominant syntactic theory for modeling such usage-based acquisition processes, and it is also applied to language change (e.g. Bybee and Beckner 2014). While there is typically no commitment to a particular version of construction grammar, acquisition research draws on the general assumptions that linguistic units are symbolic units with a phonological and a semantic side, and that similarities hold at these levels (Croft and Cruse 2004). Croft and Cruse distinguish between *phonological* alignment, *conceptual* alignment and *symbolic* alignment. Language learning, then, is based on generalization from one instance or a few instances to many. It requires *intention reading* and *pattern finding* (Tomasello 2003). Pattern finding requires entrenchment or reinforcement of items based on their token frequency. This memorization is the prerequisite for noticing similarities between items. Conceptual and symbolic alignment require detecting the form-function alignment of symbolic linguistic units, as well as similarities between units on the conceptual level. Conceptual similarity does not require or entail formal similarity.

In the following, I will discuss two domains with a rich body of research in terms of analogical reasoning. First I will discuss the acquisition of regular and irregular morphology with respect to the power of analogical reasoning: is it possible to acquire linguistic rules bottom-up based on analogy, or do linguistic rules require top-down declarative processing? Second, the acquisition of verb-argument structure will serve to demonstrate how different analogical mappings lead to a refinement of the form-function correspondences in syntax.

10.4.1   Linguistic Rules without Analogy? Learning the German Plural

According to Langacker (2000: 219 ff.), linguistic rules can be conceived of as schemas with few constraints. For schema formation, the resemblance of the new structure to the source structure is essential, it is a bottom-up process (Langacker 2008). Langacker (1987: 447) argues that if rules are conceived as schemas, and if the analogy is made explicit, there is no difference between rule-based and schema-based explanations, e.g. when generalizing from *search/searcher, lecture/lecturer* and so forth to *strive/striver* (cf. the relational shift in analogical reasoning in general cognitive processing discussed in Section 10.3.1).

This view contrasts with the top-down processing of symbolic rules, as proposed, for example, by Clahsen (1999), Marcus et al. (1992), Pinker and Prince (1988) and Pinker and Ullman (2002). In the so-called Dual-Mechanism Model of inflection (DMM), symbolic rules apply to categories as a whole and are independent of other processing factors such as frequency or analogy (Pinker and Ullman 2002). This leads to a difference in the processing of regular inflection, where the regular affix or default affix is added to the root of the noun or verb to be inflected, and irregular forms, which are stored in memory. The DMM thus reduces the memory load by generating regular forms through the generation of the intended form by a symbolic, top-down rule. In order to explain why not just every noun will receive the regular plural, an additional memory component is needed in which all irregulars are stored. Due to their holistic storage, irregular forms are subject to associative processing and show frequency and analogy effects, whereas frequency and analogy are irrelevant in the processing of regular morphology, if there is a strict distinction between holistic processing by memorization for irregulars, and combinatorial processing for regular forms ('item and process model' or 'words and rules'; cf. Pinker 1999; Huang and Pinker 2010). Supposedly, the human language processor is innately set up to process symbolic rules by different means than irregular items (Clahsen 1999: 1007).

By contrast, as noted above, constructivist and usage-based approaches to acquisition rely heavily on the storage of forms for entrenchment, and automatization of the stored form, as well as for schematization: comparison between forms is only possible when forms are stored. Dual-mechanism accounts propose that learning can take the form of top-down and memory-independent processing when the child can identify a regular affix.[2] The acquisition of German plural morphology provides a good testing ground for these processing models, because productivity and frequency are not confounded (Clahsen 1999; Clahsen et al. 1992). The low-frequency -*s* plural, one of eight plural markers, shows the fewest constraints in its occurrence and is productive with new and nonce nouns. And it is well attested that the German -*s* plural is overgeneralized early, despite its relative low frequency. To decide between the validity of the two proposals, the critical evidence is whether all German plural markers are overgeneralized by analogy, or whether there is a difference between the -*s* plural and the other affixes. If the -*s* plural is indeed a default marker that is applied whenever the child cannot rely on stored forms, -*s* should be overgeneralized to a wide range of noun stems and not be constrained by analogy.

As in many other languages, the plural system in German is determined by phonotactic features (syllable structure, final sound) and gender (Ravid et al. 2008). German has four plural affixes (-(*e*)*n*, -*e*, -*er* and -*e*), which can be combined with vowel raising or umlaut, as well as a substantial group of nouns that do not mark the plural (notably masculine and neuter nouns ending on -*el* and -*er*). The -*s* plural is taken by 16.5 per cent of nouns, mainly neuters and strong masculines, but rarely occurs with feminine nouns (Wegener 1999). Mugdan (1977) estimates that about 75 per cent of German plurals are predictable by phonotactics, declension class and gender, but there is a certain degree of variation between possible markers, some of which also show up in dialectal variation.

The DMM makes the claim that the -*s* plural is 'morphonologically free (Marcus, Brinkmann, Clahsen, Wiese and Pinker 1995: 229) and that it represents the elsewhere condition: it 'appears when the phonological environment does not permit any other plural allomorph' (Marcus et al. 1995: 229; see also Bornschein and Butt 1987: 142). But do the linguistic facts of the -s plural really fulfill this condition? It turns out that the default conditions in their current formulation provide an insufficient characterization of the elsewhere condition. A review of the linguistic facts reveals that the -s plural alternates with other markers in all domains. The -s plural can occur in almost all phonological surroundings with ordinary nouns, but has two main sets of applications. First, there is a large group of mostly monosyllabic nouns that end in plosives (*Deck-s, Dock-s, Trick-s, Stopp-s, Tipp-s*; please note that these words are not borrowed from English, but are part of the common ancestry). In this phonological condition, -s alternates with the (umlaut)-e plural (e.g. *Zug > Züg-e* 'train-s'; *Boot > Boot-e* 'boat-s'). Second, the -s plural is commonly used when the noun root ends in an unreduced vowel which does not carry the main stress (e.g. *Oma-s* 'grandma-s'; *Auto-s* 'car-s'; cf. Bornschein and Butt 1987: 141). However, feminine nouns ending with -a often take the -n plural, sometimes in alternation with -s (e.g. *Firma > Firm-en / Firma-s* 'company-s'; *Diva > Div-en / Diva-s* 'diva-s'). Such alternations are also found in default conditions like proper names (e.g. *Corsa > Corsa-s / Cors-en*; a product name of a car) or truncations (e.g. *Sozi-s* or *Soz-en* from *Sozialist-en* 'socialist-s'). Finally, when the noun root ends with a stressed full vowel, the -s plural alternates with -n or -e (e.g. *Café-s* vs. *Phantasie-n* 'fantasy-s' vs. *Knie-e* 'knee-s'; cf. Köpcke 1993; Mugdan 1977; Wegener 1999).

Most importantly, there is also a true phonological constraint for the -s plural: because it is non-syllabic, it is blocked when the stem itself ends in sibilants like -s. This constraint holds in all default conditions like proper names (e.g. *die Thomas-se* 'the Thomas-es'; *der Klaus > die Kläuse* 'the Klauses'), loan words (*die Boss-e* 'the boss-es'), nominalizations (*die Etwas-se* 'the something-s') or acronyms (*die MAZ-en;* see Goebel and Indefrey 2000: 194). Further exceptions to default processing are found with foreign words ending on the pseudosuffix -er. They do not receive -s marking, but are zero-marked as common for native nouns ending in -er. This holds even if they preserve their English pronunciation as in *Manager-0, Computer-0, Surfer-0* or *Jogger-0.*

The participant of this study is a monolingual German boy, Leo, who grows up in Leipzig, Germany. His parents have higher education and speak dialect-free, clearly articulated standard High German. Leo's language development was recorded from age 1;11.13 (age in years; months.days), the onset of multi-word speech, until age 4.[3] Analyzed here are the transcripts of 317 one-hour recordings made between ages

2;0.0 and 4;0.0, as well as the diary utterances from 1;11.15 to 3;0.00. The corpus contains 134,614 utterances from the child (including 6,249 diary utterances) with a total of 76,612 nouns. The MLU (mean length of utterance) in words increased from 1.1 at age 2;0 to 3.9 at age 3;11 (for comparison, adults have an MLU of about 5). For the purpose of this analysis, all nouns were coded with respect to the plural class and number. In addition, errors were coded in terms of the target class and the error made. There is a total of 367 errors, 117 of which are errors involving the wrong use of the -*s* plural. The following analysis tests whether the -*s* plural shows the fewest constraints, as predicted by the dual-mechanism model.

The second and major argument for the DMM is that default markers should be freely generalizable and should not be constrained, by analogy, like irregular markers. Furthermore, they should be used on default conditions whenever access to memory is blocked. In concrete terms, this means that -*s* errors should apply to nouns of all other plural classes and they should not be constrained by gender. The -*s* plural is indeed over-generalized to nouns of several other plural classes, as predicted by Clahsen et al. (1992). However, this holds for -*en* and -*e* plurals as well. In order to show that -*s* has a special status, one needs to show that it is not constrained by analogy to existing -*s* plurals. This will be tested by analyzing the phonotactic properties of nouns with -*s* errors.

The 117 error-tokens with -*s* affect 44 different noun roots. It turns out that -*s* is not overgeneralized to all kinds of stems, but rather to four groups of nouns which can be characterized by their final sound (see (1), below): nouns ending in liquids (1.a) or nasals (1.b), as well as nouns ending in stops (1.c) or unreduced vowels (1.d). In addition, there is an early-isolated error on a noun ending in a sibilant, which had been transcribed with a question mark (1.e).

(1)   Distribution of -*s* errors with respect to the final sound of the noun root
       (a) Nouns ending in liquids
       -*er*   *Bagger-s* 'excavator-*s*'; *Zimmer-s* 'room-*s*'; *Lautsprecher-s* 'loud+speaker-*s*'; *Käfer-s* 'bug-*s*'; *VW+Käfer-s* 'VW+beetle-*s*'; *Marienkäfer-s* 'lady-bug-*s*'; *Teller-s* 'plate-*s*'; *Stopper-s* 'stopper-*s*'; *Roller-s* 'scooter-*s*'; *Koffer-s* 'suitcase-*s*'; *Laster-s* 'truck-*s*'; *Lokführer-s* 'engine+driver-*s*'; *Tiger-s*; *Hänger-s* 'trailer-*s*'; *Anhänger-s* 'trailer-*s*'; *Eimer-s* 'bucket-*s*'; *Container-s* 'container-*s*'; *Blinklicht-er-s* 'flashlight-*s*'
       -*el*   *Wirbel-s* 'swirl-*s*'; *Pinsel-s* 'paint brush-es'; *Onkel-s* 'uncle-*s*'; *Löffel-s* 'spoon-*s*'; *Kamel-s* 'camel-*s*'; *Deckel-s* 'lid-*s*'; *Äpfel-s* 'apple-*s*'

-r   Tür-s 'door-s'; Stinktier-s 'skunk-s'; Stör-s 'sturgeon'; Dinosaurier-s
      'dinosaur-s'
-l   Ball-s 'ball-s'; Wohnmobil-s 'motor home-s'; Strahl-es 'beam-s';
      Steckerl-s 'pin-s (in a game)'
(b) Nouns endings in nasals
-en   Güterwagen-s 'freight car-s'; Kesselwagen-s 'tank+waggon';
      Modellwagen-s 'model car-s'; Maenneken-s 'little+men-s';
      Bilderrahmen-s 'picture frame-s'; Düse-n-s 'nozzle-s'; Buchstabe-
      n-s 'letter-s'
-n   Strassenbahn-s 'street car-s'; Trambahn-s 'street car-s'; U+Bahn-s
      'subway-s'; S+Bahn-s 'street-car-s'; Modell+Eisenbahn-s 'model
      railroad-s'; Eisenbahn-s 'railroad-s'
-ng   Verpackung-s 'packaging-s'; Schmetterling-s 'butterfly-s'
-m   Form-s 'form-s'; Muffinform-s 'muffin form-s'
(c) Nouns ending in velar stops
      Fabrik-s 'factory-s'; Zug-s 'train-s'
(d) Nouns ending in stressed full vowels
      Papagei-s 'parrot-s'; Geweih-s 'antler-s'
(e) Others
      Bussas (?) 'busses'

Contrary to the hypothesis that -s errors should not be constrained to
analogy, these phonotactic patterns correspond to existing -s plurals. In the
plural nouns produced by the child, the -s plural is found with liquids (e.g.
Hotel-s, Onkel-s, Tunnel-s), nasals (Clown-s; Bonbon-s 'candy-s'; Tram-s
'street car-s'; Tandem-s), plosives (Lok-s) or stressed full vowels (Café-s).
The only error pattern which apparently cannot result from analogy is the
overgeneralization of the -s plural to nouns ending in -(e)r. However, the
final -r is not pronounced [ty:ɐ̯], and it is possible that children misanalyze
the ending as a full vowel (Szagun 2001; for theoretical support see
Vennemann 1972 and Wiese 1996: 252 ff.). In sum, this rather narrow
distribution does not suggest that -s is scattered across the whole morpho-
nological space by rule, as claimed by Marcus et al. (1995: 245). Also, the
data do not suggest that the -s plural instantiates the 'elsewhere condition'
of being used when no other marker can apply. Instead, -s errors are
not exclusive in these conditions, but compete with -(e)n or -e errors
(cf. (1)(a)–(e), above).

  It is also informative to look at the time course in which different types
of -s errors appear. Initially, there are mainly errors on nouns ending on -er
and -el, where -s errors alternate with -n errors. Errors on nasals, the second
major group, come in only eight months later at age 2;8, and errors on
plosives follow at 2;9. The gradual extension of error domains suggests that

the child acquires the phonological freedom of the -*s* plural in a stepwise fashion.

The acquisition data presented here support claims that type frequency is not the sole determinant of productive inflection, but that analogy is another critical factor (cf. Goebel and Indefrey 2000 and Hahn and Nakisa 2000 for related results in connectionist modeling of the German plural, and Dąbrowska 2001, 2004, 2012 for analogical processes in acquiring the Polish genitive, as well as individual differences in older speakers).

The research on the acquisition of inflectional morphology also shows that children draw on different sources of information for their generalizations: They gather information about allomorphic variation (within one month after his first plural production, the German boy Leo had identified and overgeneralized all German plural affixes, cf. Behrens 2002). Like all other German children whose plural acquisition was studied, his overgeneralization errors were not coincidental, but fell in the realm of the errors that can be expected based on the phonological and prosodic properties of the stem (Ravid et al. 2008), and the resulting errors correspond to the prototypical plural schemas or Gestalt (Bittner and Köpcke 2001; Köpcke 1998). In sum, the German plural system is not determined by a single generalization, but is a system with internal variability and a number of more-or-less reliable subregularities. Children make use of analogies on several levels when learning the system: they have to identify the functional equivalence of the different allomorphs (*affix-orientation*); they identify the phonotactic properties of the stem and form predictions about appropriate plural markers (*stem-orientation*); and they derive knowledge about the prosodic and phonotactic properties of the resulting inflected form (*product-* or *schema-orientation*). This allows them to identify the highly regular aspects of the system with very low error rates and to make non-random choices in the less-regular domains of the system (Behrens 2011). Given the complexity of the system, a continuing process of calibration can be observed, since children also have to learn to disentangle the interaction of plural marking with case and gender marking (Behrens 2011; Szagun 2001, 2006; Szagun, Stumper, Sondag and Franik 2007).

10.5 The Acquisition of Argument Structure: From Concrete to Abstract Representations

Another domain in which there is rich research on the nature of generalization is argument structure, or the contingency between semantic and syntactic information as well as the influence of concrete strings of linguistic units and their frequency.

In usage-based linguistics, the key finding is that children do not operate with general 'rules' and abstract categories, but learn by making generalizations over the input they receive. In the terminology used in this framework, children proceed from concrete to abstract representations. 'Concrete' here refers to the replication of strings of words or chunks without having analyzed their internal structure. Abstraction results from repeatedly registering commonalities between exemplars such that these commonalities are reinforced (Langacker 2000: 5). For example, forms like *faked, borrowed, hated, burped* and so forth have a dental suffix (*–ed*) to denote past tense that has three phonologically conditioned allomorphs. The repeated encounter of forms inflected with *–ed* will lead to the analysis and segmentation of the inflected forms and will allow speakers to then integrate new items into a morphological paradigm. Schematization is a special form of abstraction, since we can compare items at different levels of specificity or granularity when we notice analogies at different levels of abstractness (Langacker 2000). In contrast to abstract rules, schemas always start out with concrete similarities in the expression, as they are based on concrete usage events (Langacker, 2008: 219–20). Tomasello (1992) analyzed the early verb use of an English-speaking child and demonstrated that early verb syntax was item-specific and did not generalize to other verbs of the same argument structure class. The argument structure of such 'verb-islands' is thus better characterized by thematic roles such as *hitter/hittee* or *kisser/kissee* than by more abstract roles such as agent/patient or subject/object. In the initial phase of syntax acquisition, no transfer of knowledge between syntactically similar verbs seems to take place, and abstract categorical links between constructions seem to be absent (but see Naigles, Hoff and Vear 2009).

Subsequent research has employed a number of methods both in experimental investigations and in corpus analyses of naturalistic data to explore the extent to which children generalize over the form-function correspondences in the input. Although these studies rarely use the term 'analogy', the findings can nonetheless be framed in terms of analogical reasoning, as Ibbotson (2013: 10) states:

> A key part of responding to this challenge will be to specify in greater detail the mechanisms of generalization, specifically a mechanistic account of the dimensions over which children and adults make (and do not make) analogies. As usage-based approaches have argued, relational structure and mapping between representations is a fundamental psychological process that underpins forming these abstract connections.

Analogy thus plays a central role in the acquisition of language, because children have to develop from mappings based on observable similarities. For example, activities in which an agent manipulates an object are typically encoded by transitive verbs (Slobin 1985a). Languages differ as to which cues encode that relationship: morphology (case marking), semantics (agency) or syntax (word order). Research within the competition model has shown that the order in which children acquire the different facets of argument structure generalizations depends on the availability and reliability of these cues in the input (Bates and MacWhinney 1987; Bates et al. 1984; MacWhinney 2004). In the following, I will present a selection of the rich acquisition literature to demonstrate how children develop from string-oriented, concrete units to more abstract generalizations based on the syntax or semantics of certain constructions, and how this accumulated knowledge prevents them from making possible generalizations when there is a well established alternative (pre-emption).

10.5.1   *String-Based Processing*

The hypothesis that early child language is item-based emphasizes the role of concrete linguistic strings. Such strings can mark the beginning of utterances and determine their pragmatics, or they can take the form of slot-and-frame patterns with open slots, also in middle position. I call these processes 'string-based' because the linguistic units that serve as the anchor for developing constructions may not have been fully analysed by the children. Utterance-initial strings are important in question formation and in the acquisition of auxiliaries. Here, children start out with very few utterance-initial patterns (*wh*-word+pronoun or pronoun+auxiliary) that encode certain semantic functions before acquiring the complete paradigm (Cameron-Faulkner, Lieven and Tomasello 2003; Lieven 2008; Rowland, Pine, Lieven and Theakston 2003). Similar processes can be observed when children acquire complex sentences. Again, they start out with a few strings (e.g. *I think, you know*) that are not used with their full semantics but serve as an evidentiality marker instead. Gradually, children acquire the full paradigm as well as the full semantics, with independent propositions in the matrix and the complement clause (Brandt, Kidd, Lieven and Tomasello 2009; Diessel 2004).

But not only sentence onsets are relevant for detecting syntactic patterns and their functions. Children also detect stable frames with variable slots that can be filled by increasingly variable material. Such slot-and-frame patterns (Braine and Bowerman 1976) or low-scope formulae (Pine and Lieven 1993) can also act as anchors for future development. In morphology, such patterns are referred to as *frequent morphological frames* (Erkelens 2009; Mintz 2003). They can serve as the basis for developing word classes.

10.5.2   Syntax-Based Processing

A major research question concerns the productivity of children's emerging linguistic knowledge. In corpus analyses of naturalistic developmental data, one typically studies the degree of overlap between syntactically related constructions: the more overlap, the more lexical-specificity; the less overlap, the more variability and productivity. This relationship has also been explored experimentally. In a training study with low-frequency verbs, Childers and Tomasello (2001) found that it is easier for children to acquire new structures if the frame of the construction is kept constant (by pronouns rather than variable full NPs). In a priming study with passive sentences, Savage, Lieven, Theakston and Tomasello (2003) showed that younger children were only able to produce new passives with the same verb (lexical priming), whereas older children were also able to produce passives with new lexical material (syntactic priming). A similar reliance on similarity in priming for 4-year-olds, but not older children, was found by Goldwater and Echols (2011).

Similar evidence for the growing abstractness of children's syntactic generalizations comes from studies in the so-called 'weird word order paradigm'. When children hear a new verb as a description of a transitive action, the 2-year-olds tended to copy the attested frame even if the word order was atypical (VSO: *dacking Elmo the car*, or SOV: *Elmo the car gopping*), whereas the 4-year-olds consistently corrected the utterances to SVO word order (Akhtar 1999). Studies like these show the development from exemplar-based processing to more abstract generalizations in which form-function correspondences have been learnt.

To trace form-function correspondences also helps to learn semantics. In their *syntactic bootstrapping hypothesis*, Gleitman (1990) and Fisher (1996) argued that children need to keep track of different uses of a verb in order to come to a fine-grained understanding of its meaning. Such form-function correlations can also be exploited in a different direction. *Coercion* describes the process by which a verb assumes the meaning of the construction, as in *sneeze the napkin off the table* (Goldberg 2006).

10.5.3   Semantics-Based Processing

The vast body of first language acquisition research focuses on the formal productivity of particular inflectional paradigms or argument structure constructions. It is less clear which mechanisms help the child to generalize across constructions (but see Abbot-Smith and Behrens 2006; Elman 2003). To this end, a functional analysis is required as well. In particular, the child needs to work out in what respect the constructions differ from one another, and whether and how the transfer of knowledge between constructions is constrained (cf. the research on argument structure overgeneralizations, e.g. Bowerman and Brown 2006a). Put in terms of analogy, this means that children will have to work out what is the same or different between similar constructions in order to avoid overgeneralization errors. This question relates to a much-debated topic in the usagebased language change literature that studies how certain constructions emancipate themselves from their source construction through changes in the usage pattern (see, for example, Hilpert's visualization of verb-to-noun conversion in English, Hilpert 2011: 445 and 447). Here, speakers have to become aware of the range of uses of the new constructions, as opposed to the form-meaning pairing of the old construction. Regarding language acquisition, I will focus on two research paradigms that explore the semantic basis of generalization: research on functional equivalents in socalled variation sets and research on novel verb learning in the Artificial Language Learning paradigm.

In so-called *variation sets*, the function held is constant but the formal encoding varies (Küntay and Slobin 2002). Such sequences are used as reformulations or recasts when the child does not seem to understand the utterances in (2):

(2)   Father to son, age 2;3
        Who did we see when we went to the store?
        Who did we see?
        Who did we see in the store?
        Who did we see today?
        When we went out shopping, who did we see?

Typically such variation sets keep some elements stable and vary others, which can help the child to discover the formal and functional relationships between different constructions. In addition, the contextual embedding of such variation sets helps the child to identify the form-function pairings. Ibbotson (2013: 19) calls variation sets 'powerful cross-sentential cues to generalization' and reports findings from Waterfall (2006) that about 20 to 80 per cent of English child-directed speech consists of variation sets (the percentage depends on the criteria of the distance between items that are considered to be part of a 'set') and that children's use of verbs that occurred in variation sets was more appropriate. These findings stress the importance of syntactic variation for specifying verb meaning(s) (see the discussion of syntactic bootstrapping above).

While studies on variation sets exploit the effect of variation in naturalistic data, experiments in the Artificial Language Learning paradigm with children and adults investigate what constrains speakers' generalizations when they are confronted with novel verbs in a familiar construction, or with novel verbs in novel constructions. How readily do they transfer their existing knowledge to new items or constructions? In recent studies, Suttle and Goldberg (2011) and Robenalt and Goldberg (2015) provided further evidence for the influence of semantics on learner's generalizations. Suttle and Goldberg (2011) found that speakers are more confident about new uses of words when they fall within the semantic space typically encoded by that construction. Robenalt and Goldberg (2015) demonstrated that learners are less likely to accept a new use of a high-frequency verb if there is an alternative expression (pre-emption). This suggests that speakers tend to prefer familiar phrases, but accept creative uses more readily when there is no established alternative (see also Abbot-Smith and Behrens 2006 for related findings on the generalization of auxiliaries in present perfect, passive and future constructions).

10.6 Conclusions

Psycholinguistics deals with online processing in comprehension and production. Experiments such as the ones reviewed in Section 10.2 can inform us about the inferences that participants can draw, given the evidence they get. Analogical reasoning is considered to be a very fundamental process that contributes to human categorization in general, and – more specifically – to the lines along which we extend categories. Thus, analogy has also become a prominent concept in explaining the processes by which grammatical categories or lexical items change over time (Section 10.3). However, studies on the structure of language are typically offline, as they can only compare synchronic varieties and their change. In order to study the mechanisms that lead to developmental change, language acquisition data could provide insights into the online processing of linguistic information by language learners, as well as the effect of this processing on the developing system.

Regarding language acquisition, the focus of usage-based research on language development lies on the social and general cognitive learning mechanisms children use to detect and abstract the grammatical patterns found in their input language (Behrens 2009; Ibbotson 2013; Tomasello 2003). Research has shown that children tend to start out with local, item-based generalizations, but acquire more abstract relations readily when the form-function relationships are transparent. In doing so, they exploit analogy at the item-based, syntactic and semantic level.

First, there is reason to assume that analogical reasoning is a major driving force both in acquisition and change, because it allows speakers to integrate new items into existing categories, or extend the category based on similarities and perhaps even relational analogies. This leads to certain similarities between language change and language acquisition: children are better with regular form-function mapping, and in historical development we often observe regularization processes, for example in the change from forming past tense by vowel shift to forming it with a dental suffix (see above). In German plural formation, highly predictable classes do not pose problems for children, whereas error rates are high when the system allows several markers, as is the case for monosyllabic masculine and neuter nouns (e.g. the contrast between *Park-s* or *Pärk-e* 'park-*s*' or *Tunnel or Tunnel-s* 'tunnel-*s*', where *Tunnel-s* is typical for Southern varieties of German, and *Pärk-e* is the Swiss German variety). Thus, it seems that the range of overgeneralization errors resembles the outcome of historical change, as evidenced in current variation.

Second, change seems to be small and gradual, and often item-specific in the beginning. Bybee (2014, chapter 4) discusses how children's generalizations stick closely to the established categories. This is confirmed by the data presented above: although the same plural errors are found in several acquisition corpora, children in the end coalesce with the adult system. However, their errors provide evidence for possible lines of generalization by analogy. It seems that in order for a change to take effect in the system itself, the conventions of a speech community have to be changed. In language history, this, too, is an extended and gradual process. Rosemeyer (2016) analyses the change in the auxiliary selection in Spanish between 1270 and 1699, when an increase of *haber* 'have' at the expense of *ser* 'be' was observed. Mixed-model analyses that take the aspectual properties of verbs as main variables show that non-directional and non-telic verbs are first affected by the change, before it affects directional and telic verbs. In the end, only a few verbs with high token frequency withstand the change. Rosemeyer argues that this change in auxiliary selection preferences is first driven by salience, because the new usages are very notable, until well-attested frequency mechanisms set in (cf. Hilpert, Chapter 3 in this volume): Increasing type frequency for the new patterns drives the change further, whereas high token frequency leads to *remanence* or 'the temporary persistence of a replaced construction in a usage context due to processes of social conventionalization' (Rosemeyer 2016: 183). Fischer (2007: chapter 3) argues that analogical change is a reanalysis of form-function associations that takes place within an analogical grid:

> I would argue that analogy is primary or at least stands on an equal footing with reanalysis since a reanalysis, both a semantic-pragmatic and a structural one, takes place within the contours of the communicative situation *and* the grammatical system in which a structure operates. The reanalysis will therefore also be confined and shaped by the formal structures that already exist. My hypothesis is that a reanalysis of a structure will not as a rule result in a totally new structure, but in one that is already in use elsewhere. (Fischer 2007: 123)

Despite these similarities in the processes that lead to change in the linguistic system of the individual or the language community, there are critical differences between acquisition and change (see Diessel 2011, 2012 for additional evidence). In grammaticalization processes, lexical items become grammatical functors, such as the verb *go* in English, which went through semantic bleaching such that its progressive form became an auxiliary to denote intention (*going to*). But although children tend to acquire lexical items before function items, it is not the case that their ontogenetic development has to mirror historical development; i.e. they do not need to acquire the full lexical semantics before they can learn the bleached and grammaticized meaning. Instead, whether children learn the lexical verb *go* before the future marker depends on the distribution of these forms in the input. In German, *gehen* is still a lexical verb, and its use as an intention marker is relatively rare and still involves motion (i.e. it has a smaller functional range than its English or Dutch counterpart). Consequently, children acquire *gehen* as a lexical verb first (Behrens 2003). But a comparison with Dutch (Behrens 2003) and English data (Theakston et al. 2002) shows that children do not learn the auxiliary sense from the lexical verb. In these languages, *gaan* and *go* are predominantly used as auxiliaries, and the auxiliary use is early. *Go/gaan/ gehen* are polysemous and polyfunctional verbs in these three closely related languages, and each language shows a different distribution of these functions. If language development mirrored historical change, we would expect similar developmental trajectories. Instead, we find language-specific and verb-island-like development: children acquire different form-function clusters or constructions in their respective target language, depending on the frequency and function as attested in the target language.

Furthermore, historical language change changes the system used by the linguistic community, whereas in the individual's ontogenetic language change through language acquisition, the learner typically approximates that system. So how can we try to integrate this discrepancy between supposedly similar processes that account for different outcomes? In the following section, I will review two strands of research that may help to identify the crucial processing factors further.

10.7 Discussion and Outlook

One line of research that tries to explain the mechanisms of change is social, since language change is a process that is mediated between the individual and his or her speech community. Here, the major difference between language learning and historical language change seems to be the *target* of development, because language change concerns the changing linguistic preferences of a language community, whereas first language acquisition looks at the change within an individual as she or he tries to approximate his or her language to the way it is used by his or her environment. Although many children make the same errors (e.g. *go-ed* for *went*) and may resist counterevidence or even corrections for a while, they ultimately give in to the conventional language use of the majority. The case is more complex with children growing up multilingually, because they actually have a choice and can, for example, refuse to speak one of the languages they are exposed to (de Houwer 2007). Motivational aspects and questions of identity thus have a big influence in language use and learning outcome of second-language learners and bilinguals. However, there is no evidence that children seem to drive language change (see Lieven, Chapter 14 in this volume).

A second line of research looks at the effect of time or experience on processing. So far, I have focussed on analogy. But the kinds of analogies we draw are not determined only by degrees of similarity, but also by other processing factors such as frequency and recency, and also perceptual salience. Furthermore, there is developmental change in the individual mind as well as in the system used by the speech community. What could this possible interaction between analogical reasoning, salience and frequency look like?

The contribution of analogy is twofold: it lets us categorize new experiences with existing ones, but also observe similarities to other categories and form the relation of an element to several categories (e.g. in the case of plural development, we do not see errors on the 100 per cent predictable nouns on schwa, but a lot of variation on those groups of nouns that have similar phonotactics properties of the noun stem, but with different plural markers. Here, the child has observed the analogy of a certain noun to several plural classes. Analogy also leads to innovation if a speaker creates a new form (but note that that innovation does not need to be based on analogy). As discussed in the cognitive science literature cited above (see Section 10.2), a spread of such an analogy-based innovation will be particularly successful if the analogical link is promoted and made salient.

The contribution of salience is twofold, too: first, items can have lower or higher *perceptual* salience, the ease with which an item can be observed, for example because of its prosodic highlighting and its phonetic substance. Unreduced segments are easier to perceive than reduced ones (see Traugott and Ellis, Chapters 5 and 4 in this volume). But salience also relates to expectancy, or frequency-based inferences: surprisal refers to the fact that an item may be salient because we do not expect it in this context. Whereas perceptual salience seems to pertain to the psychophysical prominence of a segment, surprisal seems to pertain to the semantic salience, since it is context dependent (cf. Section 10.5, and the discussion in Traugott, Chapter 5 in this volume and Ellis, Section 4.1.3, in Chapter 4 of this volume).

Frequency effects, finally, are multifold, too: The differential effect of type and token frequency (entrenchment versus learning and change from variation) has been much discussed (Bybee 2010), but becomes more complicated because this is a dynamic relationship over time. Time plays a role in the dispersion of the tokens over time (cf. the discussion of *dispersion* and *burstiness* in Hilpert, Section 3.5 of Chapter 3 in this volume), but also in the accumulated experience of an individual over time (see Baayen et al., Chapter 2 of this volume), where growing experience leads to a continuous change in the type and token relationships that have been registered.

It follows that the interaction between analogical reasoning, salience and frequency are complex, but can be modelled with new theories and methods. In recent years, researchers from different fields proposed models that see both the individual and the collective linguistic systems as dynamic or complex adaptive systems (Beckner et al. 2009; van Geert and Steenbeek 2005; de Bot, Lowe, Thorne and Verspoor 2013). They argue that all processing factors interact, and that the outcome of this interaction depends on the individual's current cognitive state. Hence, the initial state in the language learner is not knowing the language. Over time she or he accumulates more and more evidence based on the input they hear (typically a relatively stable synchronic state), and approximates that state. Thus, successful first language acquisition typically consolidates the state of the system. In language change, however, a relatively stable state disintegrates over time and consolidates on a new state because more and more speakers use the new form-function patterning.

By combining methods like analyses of complex developmental/historical databases and insights from language learning as well as language changes, we can specify the outcome of the interaction of different processing factors on a given state. This is the aim of current models that try to explain language evolution and change as well as first and second language acquisition (see also MacWhinney 2012; Christiansen and Chater 2016).

Notes

* I would like to thank Dedre Gentner, Marianne Hundt and Sandra Mollin for their thorough and insightful comments on the previous versions of this manuscript. My sincere thanks also go to Catherine Diederich for proofreading the first version of this chapter and to Julia Voegelin for drawing Figure 10.1.

1. Dedre Gentner (personal communication) explains mapping as follows: the mapping is structurally consistent (that is, it has one-to-one correspondences and parallel relational structure). It favors larger and deeper common relational systems over isolated matches (the systematicity principle).

2. There is a rich debate on the exact nature of this process. Marcus et al. (1992) as well as Clahsen, Rothweiler, Woest and Marcus (1992) proposed that there are so-called default conditions which help the child to identify the default marker. In case of plurals, the default marker is applied, for example, to proper names and certain types of nominalizations or conversion, but see Goebel and Indefrey (2000) and Dąbrowska (2004: 116–58) for a rebuttal of the so-called default conditions.

3. For more detail, see Behrens 2006. The data are part of the public CHILDES archive: MacWhinney (2000).

CHAPTER 11

The Role of Analogy in Language Change: Supporting Constructions

Hendrik De Smet and Olga Fischer

11.1 Introduction

In this chapter, we will adhere to a broad view of analogy, following Behrens's twin chapter on the role of analogy in language acquisition. Briefly, by 'analogy' we understand both the recognition of simple item similarity as well as relational (structural analogy), as described for instance in the work of Gentner and associates (2011). It is clear from the literature on language variation and change that analogy is difficult to capture in fixed rules, laws or principles, even though attempts have been made by, among others, Kuryłowicz (1949) and Mańczak (1958). This is probably one of the reasons why analogy has not been prominent as an explanatory factor in generative diachronic studies. More recently, with the rise of usage-based grammar, construction-grammar (CxG) and probabilistic linguistic approaches, the interest in the role of analogy in linguistic change – already quite strongly present in linguistic studies in the nineteenth century (e.g. Paul 1886) – has been revived. Other studies in the areas of language acquisition, cognitive science and language evolution have also pointed to analogical reasoning as a deep-seated cognitive principle at the heart of grammatical organization.[1] In addition, the availability of increasingly larger diachronic corpora has enabled us to learn more about patterns' distributions and frequencies, both of which are essential in understanding analogical transfer.

Despite renewed interest, however, the elusiveness of analogy remains. For this reason, presumably, Traugott (2011) distinguishes between analogy and analogization, with the intention to separate analogy as (an important) 'motivation' from analogy as (a haphazard) 'mechanism'. The distinction is deemed necessary since 'much analogical thinking never results in change' (Traugott 2011: 25). Analogization thus focuses on the *results* of analogical thinking.

Another attempt to mitigate the unruliness of analogy is found in Bybee and Beckner (2014), who consider categorization more important than analogy. This goes against most psycholinguists' conviction that categorization itself can only be the result of analogical thinking (see, e.g., Chalmers et al. 1992; Gentner 2010; Gentner et al. 2011). Bybee and Beckner note, nevertheless, that 'the much rarer change of analogical extension' is 'not accomplished by analogical reasoning but rather by changes in existing categories' (2014: 506). Examining 'a wide range of changes that have been called "analogical"', they find that 'all [changes] fall under the umbrella of changes in categorisation and that a separate mechanism of change dubbed "analogical" is not necessary'. They illustrate this with the case of the past tenses of *strike* and *dig*, for which 'no proportional model [. . .] is possible' because these two verbs do not share the phonological characteristics that are deemed necessary to make the analogy. That is, they do not share 'the property of ending in a velar [nasal] consonant' of the wider *cling, swing* class (with past tense *-ung*), to which new members were added (*sling-slung, hang-hung*) (Bybee and Beckner 2014).

It seems to us that analogy is interpreted too narrowly here. Analogy not only concerns a similarity between concrete (in this case phonological) forms, on the one hand, and abstract patterns (in this case verbs and their past tenses), on the other, but also *local* similarities in function/meaning (cf. the idea of 'structural mapping' (Gentner and Namy 2006; Gentner and Smith 2012)). As Anttila (2003), Itkonen (2005) and others have made clear, and as proponents of CxG emphasize, analogy always involves a *combination* of form and function. The new past tenses of *strike* and *dig* can be explained by analogy when one looks more closely at the full synchronic circumstances operating at the time of their first occurrence. When we look at it in terms of analogy, the new past could well have been supported *semantically* by the past tenses of *cut* and *stick* 'stab' (i.e. *cut* and *stuck*), which like *strike* and *dig* convey a cutting or stabbing movement. As to form, they share the short vowel and the plosives. Like *struck, stuck* and *dug* are attested in the OED from the sixteenth century onward. In addition, it must be mentioned that it is quite likely that *struck* was an *independent* phonetic development (cf. Ekwall 1965: §§81, 215; Hogg 1988): the ME form was [strɔːk] (from OE [ɑː]) but with a variant [stroːk], which with other ME [oː]-sounds developed to [uː] in the Great Vowel Shift and was later shortened to [u] > [ʌ] before plosives. If this is correct, the form *struck* itself could have strengthened the analogy. And finally, a more general iconic principle may also have played a role, that of the 'principle of quantity'. It is noteworthy that *cut, struck, dug* and *stuck* all convey a highly telic, brief movement, which is more appropriately conveyed by a phono-logically shorter form (cf. also the 'ideophonic' argument put forward in Hogg (1988), where he considers the past tense *snuck* in relation to *dug* and *struck*). This development shows that one need not always have a very frequent pattern for analogical extension; a local pattern, if strengthened semantically, may do the job too.[2]

Another example of interaction between multiple local analogies – this time affecting syntactic structure – can be observed in Dutch and involves the extension of a reflexive pronoun in verbs denoting psychological activities. The category contains verbs such as *zich*[REFL] *herinneren* 'to remember', *zich*[REFL] *realiseren* 'to realise' and *zich*[REFL] *ergeren* 'to be annoyed', and has been joined quite recently by verbs such as *beseffen* 'to realise' and *irriteren* 'to be irritated', which are now also used reflexively by younger speakers. The analogy here concerns not only the semantic simi-larity but also the fact that some of these verbs share a causative structure. Thus, there is both causative *dit herinnert me*[OBJ] *eraan dat . . . / dit ergert me*[OBJ] 'this reminds me that . . . / this annoys me', and reflexive *ik herinner me*[REFL] *dat . . . / ik erger me*[REFL] *eraan dat . . .* 'I remember that . . . / I am annoyed that', resulting in the causative verb *irriteren* (*dit irriteert me*[OBJ] 'this irritates me') to also develop a reflexive con-struction: *ik irriteer me*[REFL] 'I am irritated'. Thus a network of analogies, involving both causative and reflexive verbs expressing mental activities, may lead to local change (see also Van der Horst 2008: VII, 9.6).

What these examples show is that if analogy is to be properly under-stood, its operation must be seen against the background of complex constructional networks capturing the myriad relations between individual constructions. In this respect, Abbot-Smith and Behrens (2006) propose the notion of 'supporting constructions' in language acquisition, to explain why German children, for instance, learn some constructions earlier than others. Abbot-Smith and Behrens (2006: 1,019) find that a 'supported construction' was acquired earlier and faster than a non-supported one if the source and target constructions 'share[d] lexical or morphological subparts' [see also López-Cuozo, Chapter 14 in this volume]. They show that the *sein*-passive (i.e. the perfect passive corresponding to English HAVE-*been*+past participle) is acquired earlier than the *werden*-passive (the non-perfect passive corresponding to English BE+past participle) due to the fact that a lexical-morphological and highly frequent subpart of the construction is already familiar to German children in the form of the perfect construction with *sein*+past participle. Interestingly, they also show that the acquisition of a target construction can be *hindered* if two constructions 'share an identical semantic-pragmatic function', as is the case for the future construction with *werden*, which is hindered by the fact that the future may also be expressed by the present tense in German (Abbot-Smith and Behrens 2006: 1,002).

We believe that the notion of 'supporting construction' may also help to explain how constructions spread analogically in diachrony. As we will show, the 'construction conspiracy hypothesis' – the term Abbot-Smith and Behrens use – can be extended to language change. It has been observed, for instance, that an analogical extension is the more likely, the more its outcome resembles one or more already existent patterns (Bybee and Slobin 1981; Fischer 2011, 2015; De Smet 2012, 2013). The role of those existent patterns in language change is much like that of Abbot-Smith and Behrens's (2006) supporting constructions. They facilitate the emergence of an innovative pattern, presumably because shared phonological, functional or morphosyntactic components are already entrenched and give the 'innovative form'[3] a selectional advantage. In language change, this has the effect of obscuring the novelty of the innovative form – a characteristic feature of change that has been pointed out by many observers before (e.g. Warner 1982; Aitchison 1991; Denison 2001, and Chapter 13 in this volume). In that light, it can be hypothesized that the likelihood of an innovation depends on the set of supporting constructions facilitating the innovative form.

From this it follows that the course of change is highly contingent. Because every (potential) new expression has a unique set of supporting constructions, as determined by its specific form, syntax and function, the chances for an item to extend its range of use vary from item to item and from grammatical context to grammatical context. Indeed, whereas the grammaticalization literature has initially revealed recurrent pathways of change (e.g. Heine and Kuteva 2002), more recently attention has moved to the ways in which each specific grammaticalization is *also* uniquely conditioned by the form and function of the source item and by similarity relations to other constructions (e.g. Fischer 2007; Breban 2010; Ghesquière 2014; Van de Velde 2015). The 'construction conspiracy hypothesis', applied to diachrony, is well suited to explaining the contingency of change.

To be sure, direct application of a concept from the field of language acquisition to that of language change is not completely unproblematic. There are clearly a number of differences between the data in the two fields. First, frequency in the acquisition case relates to both input frequency of the adult and output frequency of the child.[4] In a diachronic study we only have output frequencies as data (cf. the types of frequencies noted by Hilpert, Chapter 3 in this volume), but it is likely that a distinction between input and output frequencies is less relevant here, since we are dealing with much less-limited adult language utterances and fully developed adult grammars, and a range of generations.

Second, a problem in the Abbott-Smith and Behrens study was that they could only rely on the acquisition data of one child, providing homogeneous and dense data but limited to only one speaker (although the findings were supported by less-dense data from three other children), while the historical data are problematic, as we mentioned above, in that they are typically quite (or possibly, too) diverse, coming from many different sources involving many types of variation (genre, dialect, age, sex, education, social class, etc.).

Third, the construction(s) that offer(s) 'support' to a particular innovation in diachronic studies may be more numerous and may provide support of both a substantive (lexical-morphological) as well as of a more abstract/structural or semantic-pragmatic type. After all, in change we are dealing with adults rather than children.[5] Adults have already acquired the full range of constructions possible, and pay attention not only to low-level phenomena but also to high-level ones (cf. Chalmers et al. 1992), involving 'structure mapping' (cf. Gentner et al. 2011; Behrens, Chapter 10 in this volume). Children, on the other hand, concentrate on substantive elements in the early years of acquisition (cf. Goldwater et al. 2011).[6]

Fourth, it seems also quite likely that we will not find the kind of 'speed' noticed in Abbott-Smith and Behrens because we are dealing with a very diverse number of 'speakers', constituting a mix of generations per period, and a very diverse number of genres, etc. Therefore, the 'construction conspiracy' hypothesis applied to language change must primarily focus on frequency and chronological order of appearance of new patterns. Conceivably, though, there is also a difference in speed between the way more *substantive* analogies spread in language change compared to more abstract/structural ones.

Fifth, we also expect that there may be a difference concerning Abbott-Smith and Behrens' finding that the acquisition of the target construction can be *hindered* if other constructions *share an identical semantic-pragmatic function*. Whereas children are still in the process of learning as many constructions as possible and trying hard to make distinctions between them (i.e. they are busy extending their language and their grammar), adults are confronted with a plethora of constructions that have already been entrenched (cf. Ellis, Lieven, Chapters 6 and 14 in this volume) and they may therefore be more likely to shift relatively infrequent or new constructions toward already-existent ones (or mix them up), especially when the expressions are quite similar in form and meaning. They might be more likely to simplify the grammar where possible for the sake of economy. In addition, as already indicated above, young children are more aware still of low-level rather than high-level distinctions, thus privileging substantive forms (cf. note 4) over more-abstract structural patterns which they are still in the process of acquiring. By contrast, as adults we 'learn' to see only those substantive differences which are functional or relevant, gradually ignoring non-functional ones. In other words, we do not learn, remember and process more than is absolutely necessary. This is what Hawkins (2004: 40) has called the principle of 'Minimize Forms':

> Minimizations in unique form-property pairings are accomplished by expanding the compatibility of certain forms with a wider range of properties [meanings]. Ambiguity, vagueness and zero specification are efficient, inasmuch as they reduce the total number of forms that are needed in a language.

Hawkins notes that this minimization is connected with the frequency of the form and/or the processing ease of assigning a particular property to a reduced form. The ambiguity that arises is no problem, since '[t]he multiple properties that are assignable to a given form can generally be reduced to a specific P[roperty] in actual language use by exploiting "context" in various ways' (Hawkins 2004: 41). Thus, it seems likely that in language change, in contrast to language acquisition, *pragmatic-semantic similarity* may in fact 'support' the 'acquisition'[7] of a new construction out of earlier, analogically similar, source constructions.

To find out how the 'construction conspiracy hypothesis' may apply to language change, and how it may differ from the way it functions in language acquisition, we will briefly discuss two diachronic cases in the history of English, partly based on existing literature (investigated in Fischer 1994, 2015; De Smet 2012). The changes include the development of semi-modal HAVE-*to* (Section 11.2) and the development of the new degree modifier *as good as*, compared to that of other degree modifiers (Section 11.3). We will also note, where appropriate, what happened to similar source constructions in other languages to find out possible differences in analogical outcome.

There is an inevitable methodological disadvantage to arguing the case for analogy on the basis of specific historical case studies. Analogy operates inside language users' heads and is only indirectly visible in the historical textual evidence on which we have to rely. Therefore, its operation can be made plausible, at best. However, the more observations are added to support it, the more plausible a hypothesis becomes, and this is what the two case studies below contribute to.

11.2   The Grammaticalization of HAVE-*to*

The development of HAVE in combination with a *to*-infinitive has long been considered a typical case of grammaticalization following the characteristics as traditionally defined in the framework, i.e. bleaching, chunking, phonetic reduction and generally comprising a gradual change steered semantically and by pragmatic inferencing, which is followed by a syntactic reanalysis into, in this case, a semi-auxiliary (Fleischman 1982; Brinton 1991; Heine 1993; Krug 2000; Łęcki 2010). Fischer (1994) countered the essentially semantic-pragmatic view of the development, arguing instead that a change in basic word order from SOV to SVO taking place in the course of the Middle English period played a primary role. Fischer (2015) returns to the case in order to find out to what extent analogy of both a structural and a substantive type may have been involved, and how this may have supported the development of HAVE-*to* into a semi-auxiliary expressing necessity. The only way to ascertain the strength of this support, and hence its influence, is by looking at the dates and frequencies of occurrence of the support construction(s) and establishing similarities in both form and meaning with the target structure. On the basis of the Corpus of Middle English Verse and Prose,[8] it can be shown that a (partly) substantive formal pattern (the adjacency of HAVE and the *to*-infinitive) became increasingly frequent across texts, serving as a possible analogical model for a later semi-auxiliary HAVE-*to*, and that other analogies of a substantive, structural and semantic-pragmatic type may have helped to establish the later necessity meaning of the phrase.[9]

One of the problems with the traditional account is that there is no evidence for a *gradual semantic* change in the verb HAVE from 'possess' via a more general or bleached meaning to a necessity sense before *to*-infinitives. Problematic, too, is that both bleached HAVE (see (1)) and *occasional* necessity meanings were already present in Old English (cf. Fischer 1994), as seen in (2). (Note that in (3)–(5), the meaning cannot be one of necessity, in contrast to (2)). The new semi-modal construction with a *regular* necessity meaning is only firmly attested from Early Modern English onward, and is not really common until the nineteenth century (Krug 2000: 89–90). A general problem in grammaticalization studies is that the investigation typically concentrates only on the construction that is changing, and hence on the *diachronic* development, and not on the constructions that may provide support, i.e. the *synchronic* situation current at the time (cf. Noël 2012).[10]

(1) *And   her   beoð swyþe genihtsume weolocas . . . Hit hafað eac þis land*
And here are very abundant whelks . . . It has also this land
sealtseaþas, and hit hafaþ hat   wæter   (Bede 1, 026.9)
salt-springs, and it has hot water
'And there are plenty of whelks . . . the country also has (or: 'there are also')
salt springs and hot water'

(2) *hæfst   ðu   æceras   to   erigenne*   (ÆGram. 135.2)
have you acres to plow
'do you have acres you could/should plow? / are there acres for you to plow?'
(necessity possible)

(3) *hwile þu   hefdest   clað   to werien. and to etene and to*
'while you had clothes to wear, and to eat and to
*drinken *
drink' (necessity unlikely)
(Old English Homilies, series 1, EETS, Morris 1868:33)

(4) *Ic   hæbbe mete to   etene þone þe   ge   nyton*   (Jn (WSCp)4.32)
I have food to eat that that you not-know
'There is food I (may/can) eat that you know nothing of/There is food
for me to eat that . . . ' (necessity highly unlikely since *Ic* refers to
Jesus/God)

(5) *þe   Sægeatas selran   næbban   to geceosenne cyning ænigne*
the Seagates better [ACC] not-have to choose king any [ACC]
(Beowulf 1850–51)
The Seagates do not have any better man to choose (which they can
choose) as king/ For the Seagates there wasn't a better man to choose as
king' (necessity impossible)

The questions that arise with respect to this particular grammaticalization scenario, then, are

- Why were there such long time gaps between the various stages of the development (cf. Heine 1993: 67: 'grammaticalization is a continuous process that does not stop at a certain point')?
- Why did HAVE-*to* develop a meaning of necessity rather than e.g. future (as could happen elsewhere)?
- Why did it become a modal (semi-)auxiliary?

- If grammaticalization pathways are seen as potentially universal (cf. Haspelmath 1989), and steered by deep universal cognitive mechanisms (cf. Heine 2014),[11] then why did similar source constructions in other related languages containing a verb like HAVE and an infinitive not undergo a similar development?

In Dutch, for instance, the same cognate construction did not become a (semi-)auxiliary nor develop a consistent sense of necessity (Fischer 1994; Van Steenis 2013), its use being pretty much as it was in Old English. One of the reasons is that Dutch did not change into a consistent SVO language like English; SOV order remained the rule in subordinate finite and non-finite clauses. This meant that a fixed structural adjacency of the finite verb and the infinitive did not develop as a support construction for a (semi-)auxiliary status of the finite verb (cf. Fischer 1994, and see below).[12] In the Romance languages, which did become more strictly SVO, the cognates of Latin *habere* following an infinitive acquired future sense, which might also have been a possibility in English, cf. Yanovich (2013).[13] A very interesting case is the grammaticalization of Spanish *tener que/de* and Portuguese *ter que/de*, where the possessive verb *tener /ter* 'to hold' did develop a meaning of necessity. In many ways, the situation is similar to the one in English, due to similarities in basic word order and analogical support from other 'necessity' constructions with *tener de, haber de, deber (de)*, but here, too, there are important differences due to the presence of other support constructions (cf. Fischer and Olbertz, forthcoming).

There are good reasons to assume that the developments that ultimately led to the semi-auxiliary status of HAVE-*to* are the result of a complex of factors which are all of the supported and thus synchronic kind, i.e. the changes are not driven construction-internally or unidirectionally by the process of grammaticalization itself. First, there is the increasing adjacency of HAVE and the *to*-infinitive already noted above, which led to their being interpreted as a chunk [for chunking, see Ellis, chapter 6 in this volume and Bybee and Moder, chapter 7 in this volume, and for frequency see Baayen, Tomaschek, Gahl and Ramscar, chapter 2 in this volume]. This adjacency already emerged earlier, in constructions with preposing of the NP$_{OBJ}$ via *wh*-movement (as e.g. in (6), cf. also Krug 2000: 98–99) or topicalization (e.g. (7)), or heavy NP shift (e.g. (8)), all quite frequent, as seen in rows 1, 4 and 5 of Table 11.1.

(6)   Lord! ***what nede*** *shulde Crist have to lepe doun þus fro þe pynacle*
                                                      (ME Corpus, Wyclif)
        'Lord, what need should Christ have to leap down thus from the pinnacle'

(7)　　. . . *Na **clathes** þai salle have to gang in* (ME Corpus, *Pricke of Conscience*)
　　　' . . . No clothes they shall have to walk-about in'

(8)　　a. . . . *Þat has to stere **bath se & land**.* (ME Corpus, *Altenglische Legenden*)
　　　　' . . . who has to govern both sea and land'
　　　b. *And qua so will has to wete **how it worthid eftir*** (ME Corpus, *The Wars of Alexander*)
　　　　'And who has [the] desire to know how it will become afterwards'

Table 11.1 *Occurrences of* have, haue, hast, has *etc. followed immediately by a* to-*infinitive in* The Corpus of Middle English Prose and Verse *(from Fischer 2015)*

Subtypes	Interpretation	(Sub)total
Two NP objects		
1. preposed object + HAVE + *to*- inf. + object	Old interpretation only[14]	49
2. HAVE + *to*-inf. + object *(inf)* + object *(have)*	Old interpretation only	1
3. object(*inf*) + object(*have*) + HAVE + *to*- inf.	Old interpretation only	1
	Subtotal	51
Shared object[14]		
4. preposed shared object + HAVE + *to*- inf.	Mostly old, new possible	74
5. HAVE + *to*- inf. + shared object	Mostly old, new possible	14
6. HAVE + *to*- inf. + object (shared?)	Mostly old, new possible	10
	Subtotal	98
No explicit object		
7. HAVE + *to*- inf. (passive, intransitive (?))	Mostly old, new possible	33
	Total: with *to*-infinitive	182
Other types		
8. HAVE (as perfect or possessive) + *to* + NP		931
to = *too/two*		32
hast as a form of the verb *haste(n)*		13

Table 11.1 only looks at frequencies of the *adjacency* of HAVE and *to* in Middle English. Quite clearly, more corpus research making use of syntactically tagged corpora is necessary to find out how this relates to *non*-adjacent cases of HAVE and *to* in the period (cf. Hilpert, Chapter 3 in this volume). From Fischer (1994), which was based on *all* instances of HAVE and *to*-infinitives in the Helsinki Corpus, it was already clear that *overall* the use of HAVE and a *to*-infinitive increased in the course of the Middle English period. It is also

important to note that topicalization, e.g. of the object, was much more frequent in Old and Middle English (as it still is in Dutch and German) compared to Modern English because it has an important discourse role marking 'given' from 'new' (see the studies in Meurman-Solin et al. 2012).

Second, next to this increase in adjacency, there is a steep rise in Middle English of *to*-infinitives as a replacement for *that*-clauses, so that we see more and more patterns of VPs consisting of a verb followed by a *to*-infinitival complement. Manabe (1989: 21) shows that the ratio of *to*-infinitives to *þæt*-clauses in Old English is 20.1 per cent as against 79.9, whereas in the fourteenth century this has changed into 62.3 and 37.7 per cent, respectively, and in the fifteenth century to 72.5 and 27.5 per cent, almost a complete reversal (Manabe 1989: 165–6). Also of interest is the fact that the greatest increase occurs after the verbs of 'Cause-Allow' (92.7 per cent of infinitives), followed by 'Command-Desire' (73.4 per cent). All the other possible categories ('Perception', 'Love-Fear', 'Teach-Help', 'Say-Declare') score much lower. The verbs that score high are much more closely connected to modality, and more likely to become auxiliary-type verbs; indeed, verbs expressing 'Cause' or 'Command' are easily connected with modal necessity. It may not be surprising, therefore, that the modal *to*-infinitive after HAVE, which also began to function as a causative around this time (see Hollmann 2003; Los 2005; and Table 11.2), also followed this tendency.

Third, another, somewhat more abstract structural analogy that may have played a role is the already-regular use in Old English of inanimate subjects with weak possessive/existential HAVE, paving the way for inanimate subjects in constructions with HAVE-*to*. An example of this was already given in (1). The weak semantic link that exists in such existential constructions between the subject of the clause and the object in terms of transitivity (cf. Hopper and Thompson 1980) may have played a role too, as we will see below.

Fourth, in addition to these *structural* analogies, more *substantive* types of analogical support constructions were probably also influential in the process, such as the very high frequency of the construction with the infinitive DO, with or without[15] an explicit direct object of HAVE, as seen in Table 11.2 (cf. (9)a and (b), respectively), and the relatively frequent occurrence of the construction HAVE + *nede* + *to*-inf. (cf. 10) (see also Table 11.3).[16]

Table 11.2 *Occurrences of* have, haue, hast, has *etc. followed by* to do(n)(e) *in The Corpus of Middle English Prose and Verse (from Fischer 2015)*[17]

Subtypes	Interpretation	(Sub)total
Two NP objects		
1. HAVE + object + (*for*)*to*-DO + object	Old interpretation only	144
2. HAVE + object + objec + (*for*)*to*-DO	Old interpretation only	17
3. preposed object + HAVE + *to*-DO + object	Old interpretation only	9
	Subtotal	**170**
Shared object		
4. HAVE + shared object + (*for*) *to* DO	Mostly old, new possible	91
5. preposed shared object + HAVE + (adverb) + (*for*)*to*-DO	New meaning is possible	58
6. HAVE + (*for*)*to*-DO + shared object	New meaning is possible	13
7. HAVE + (*for*)*to*-DO + adverb/implicit object	New meaning is possible	2
	Subtotal	**164**
'Have dealings with'		
8. HAVE *with* NP (*for*)*to*-DO; *with* NP HAVE (*not* etc.) (*for*)*to*-DO	Implicit object, only old meaning possible	89
Causative HAVE		
9. HAVE + object + *to*-DO	Causative	6
	Total: with (for)to-infinitive	**431**
Other types		
10. HAVE (as perfect or possessive + *to* + NP; *to* = *too/two*	not applicable	225

(9) a. *and **I have mych to do** with myn owne mat[ers]. . . (so that in good ffeyth I can nat make an end lightly)* (ME Corpus, *Stonor Letters*)
   'and I have much to do/there is much to do concerning my own business (so that in good faith I cannot finish things easily)'

   b. *and your Maystyrshepe seyde to me that ye wolde nott **have to do** with hytt in no wyse* (ME Corpus, *Stonor Letters*)
   ' . . . that you would not have [any dealings/anything] to do with it in any way'

(10) a. *ʒif þei **had nede to ride in þat contrey*** (ME Corpus, *Three Kings of Cologne*)
   'if they had (a) need to ride in that country'

   b. *I wat þou **nede has to be hale*** (ME Corpus, *Cursor Mundi*)
   'I know (that) you have (a) need to be whole (e.g. bodily sound)'

Table 11.3 *Occurrences with* HAVE, MUST *and impersonal* BE *and the noun/adverb* nede(s), *in The Corpus of Middle English Prose and Verse (from Fischer 2015)*[19]

Subtypes	Totals
HAVE + *nede* + inf.	
(a) HAVE + *nede* + PP/NP + *to*-inf.	9
(b) HAVE + *nede* + (*for*)*to*-inf.	78
(c) *to*-inf. + HAVE + *nede*	54
(d) HAVE + *nede* + NP-object	54
(e) HAVE + *nede* + *to*-inf. OR NP-object (unclear)	7
Subtotal	195
MUST + *nede(s)* + zero inf.	
(f) *mot(e)(n)* etc. + *nede* + zero (/*to*) inf.	131
(g) *mot(e)(n)* etc. + *nedes* + zero inf.	96
Subtotal	227
Impersonal BE + *nede* + *to*-inf.	
(h) *is, was, war,wer(e)(n), be nede* + *to*-inf.	188
Total of all *nede* constructions with inf.	410

The analogical pattern with *nede* is crucial as a support, since it answers the question of where the later, strong and fixed meaning of necessity comes from, if it is not seen as the result of a unidirectional, construction-internal grammaticalization process as in the traditional explanation. The other support patterns mentioned above provided only formal similarities (both of a substantive and structural kind), their semantics always being 'weakly possessive' as in the Old English period.

The influence of HAVE + *nede* + *to*-infinitive on the grammaticalization of HAVE-*to* has to be seen in the light of yet other constructions with *need*, providing further analogical support. Table 11.3 indicates a highly frequent co-occurrence of *nede* with both HAVE and an infinitive (195 instances) and with MUST *nede(s)* and an infinitive (227 instances).[18]

Similarly, the impersonal construction with BE + *nede* in the last row of Table 11.3 may also have been an influence, since the empty verbs BE and HAVE are also to some extent interchangeable (as referred to above in their use in existential constructions), and, perhaps more importantly, since impersonal constructions were disappearing in the late Middle English period. This latter fact would have favored (personal) HAVE, which takes a nominative subject for the experiencer role, over (impersonal) BE, where the experiencer, if present, is found in the dative:

Table 11.4 *Constructions with the (im)personal verb* NEED
(from Fischer 2015)[21, 22, 23]

Subtypes	Totals
Nedeth (impersonal verb)	
(a) pronoun[DATIVE] + *nedeth* etc. + NP-object	173
(b) full, lexical NP[DATIVE?] + *nedeth* + NP-object	20
(c) pronoun[DATIVE] + *nedeth* + *(for)(to)*-infinitive	105
(d) full lexical NP[DATIVE?] + *nedeth* + *(for)(to)*-infinitive	39
(e) Prepositional NP *(for/to)* + *nedeth* + *(for)(to)*-infinitive/NP-object	13
Subtotal	350
Neden (personal verb)	
(f) active construction (NP[NOM] *nedeth* + complement (nominal or infinitival))	39
(g) passive construction (NP[NOM] BE *neded* (+ *to*-infinitive))	45
Subtotal	84

(11)   That yow[DAT] were nede / to resten hastily (ME Corpus, *Shipman's Tale*)

All three constructions in Table 11.3 may well have helped the semantic change, strengthening the notion of necessity, which plays a primary role in them. The fact that MUST with the adverb *nedes* occurs as a kind of fixed idiom (also in the presumably mixed form MUST *nede*, without the genitive adverbial *-s*), both strongly conveying necessity, may in turn have influenced the interpretation of the form HAVE *nede*, making it look like a fixed phrase with a similar modal meaning. Interesting in this respect, too, are a few occurrences of MUST *nede* followed by a *to*-infinitive rather than the usual zero-infinitive (row (f) in Table 11.3). Furthermore, *neden* also appears by itself as a verb in an impersonal construction: *me nedeth/ nedyth/neded* etc. (+ *to*-infinitive), next to BE *nede*, which may also have helped establish a pattern of HAVE + *nede* as a composite predicate (cf. Table 11.4, below).

As already hinted at, the *im*personal verb *neden* disappeared, together with impersonal BE *nede* and other impersonal constructions in late Middle English, thus providing a kind of 'negative support'. (Or, to put it differently, the presence of impersonal *neden* expressing 'external necessity' may have hindered the development of this sense for HAVE *(nede)-to* because the two expressions would have shared 'an identical pragmatic-semantic function' in terms of Abbott-Smith and Behrens, referred to in Section 1). Overall, impersonal constructions became replaced by personal ones. In the case of *me/him/her nedeth* and *him was need* the 'replacement', i.e. the new personal form *he nedeth* etc. with an animate, and hence more transitive subject,[20] expressed more clearly an 'internal need' on the part of the subject rather than some external need or necessity. The latter was typically the case in the impersonal construction, where the dative experiencer in the by-now regular object position after the verb (due to the SOV> SVO change mentioned before) expresses an entity that is affected by *external* circumstances rather than one actively involved in it. This relates the *im*personal structure (when accompanied by an infinitive, which is the more frequent pattern, see Table 11.4) more closely to necessity because when there is an external need for someone *to do* (infinitive) something, he, as it were, 'has to' do it.

What this shows is that, with the loss of impersonal (more external) *nedeth* and the rise of personal (more transitive) *neden*, a gap arose regarding the expression of external necessity. It is quite possible that this gap was filled by the development of HAVE-*to* into a modal semi-auxiliary of (external) necessity. This was possible because the construction with HAVE-*to* already allowed occasional modal interpretations connoting necessity, and it was already a frequent combination with the noun *nede* (followed by a *to*-infinitive), which was likewise tinged with necessity. Note furthermore that HAVE-*to*, when it occurs by itself without the noun *nede*, loses transitivity because there is no longer a NP object present. In fact, the subject of HAVE-*to* can now be said to be without a *theta*-role, as is the case with passive and existential constructions, which cannot assign a *theta*-role to their subject.[24] This weakens the involvement of the subject and hence strengthens the sense of *external* necessity.

Once HAVE-*to* became part of the modal auxiliary system, it could also develop a narrower semantic role within this closed system, in which there was no place for the looser kind of relational verb that it was before, since it could no longer indicate any relation between a subject and an object, as it had before. No doubt other developments involving the core modals, in which they lost some of their forms and functions (e.g. their inability to be used in the past tense, as a participle or infinitive) also contributed to the rise of HAVE-*to* as a modal semi-auxiliary because of its usefulness as a gap filler.[25]

Finally, in connection with the historical link between impersonal *neden* and the development of HAVE (*nede*)-*to* (if indeed our story is correct), it is perhaps of interest to mention that the present-day semi-modals HAVE-*to* and NEED, unlike MUST, still share the lack of an authoritative voice (Coates 1983: 56), and when used in the negative, they both convey, again unlike MUST, that 'there is *no* necessity to do something', rather than that 'there *is* a necessity to *not* do something' (Coates 1983). In addition, the fact that HAVE-*to* allows 'habitual aspect, while MUST does not' (Coates 1983) is also of interest because it may well be related to the fact that HAVE was also in use as a weak *possessive* in existential clauses.

11.3   The Grammaticalization of *as good as*

By virtue of their function, Present-Day English expressions such as *a bit, as good as, far from, more or less* or *somewhat* can all be classified as degree modifiers. Despite their functional similarity, however, the expressions in question show only partly overlapping grammatical behavior. Example (12), below, lists and illustrates some of the main grammatical slots in which degree modifiers are found. Focusing by way of example only on the five items listed above, one finds that all five can modify predicative adjectives, as in (12i), but only *far from, more or less* and *somewhat* can modify attributive adjectives as well, as in (12ii). While *far from* cannot modify finite verb forms, *a bit, as good as, more or less* and *somewhat* can, yet they do so in different positions. *As good as* always precedes the finite (lexical) verb, as in (12iii), whereas *more or less* and *somewhat* can either precede or follow, as in (12iv). Then there is *a bit*, which can only follow the verb. When modifying a noun phrase, *a bit* and *somewhat* are linked to the noun phrase by *of*, as in (12v), unlike *far from, more or less* and *as good as*, which directly precede the noun phrase, as in (12vi). The differences are summarized in Table 11.5.

(12)   Main grammatical slots for degree modifiers
    (i) [*is* __ ADJ] This wedding of yours is *a bit inconvenient* for me, actually. (1991, BNC)
    (ii) [*a* __ ADJ N] But I think you will also see, sir, as the details unfold, that it is in its nature a *far from simple* case. (1986, BNC)

Table 11.5 *Grammatical distribution of five degree modifiers*

		a bit	as good as	far from	more or less	somewhat
(i)	*is* __ ADJ	+	+	+	+	+
(ii)	*a* __ ADJ N	–	–	+	+	+
(iii)	N __ V_{fin}	–	+	–	+	+
(iv)	N V_{fin} __	+	–	–	+	+
(v)	*is* __ *of a* N	+	–	–	–	+
(vi)	*is* __ *a* N	–	+	+	+	–

(iii) [N __ V$_{fin}$] Oh, it's all right, she didn't even hesitate, she *as good as popped the question* herself. (1993, BNC)

(iv) [N V$_{fin}$ __] Being one-sided, the interest of this correspondence *depends somewhat* on what one thinks of Maud. (1992, BNC)

(v) [*is __ of a* N] Sorry – problem's *a bit of a silly word* to use in the light of what's happened to you. (1991, BNC)

(vi) [*is __ a* N] and secondly you presented what the County Councillors do as *more or less a rubber stamping* of what the officers put before them. (s.d., BNC)

If the net is cast wider to include more grammatical contexts and more degree modifiers – say, *a lot, any, hardly, kind of, much, pretty, rather, some* – differences only accumulate. In fact, on closer inspection, hardly any two degree modifiers can be found that have the same grammatical distribution.

Where, from a synchronic point of view, this situation is difficult to explain, a diachronic approach offers some hopes of disentangling the distributional chaos. Some of the differences are explained by the different lexical sources from which degree modifiers developed. Take *a bit* as an example. *A bit* started out as a noun that initially meant 'a bite', hence 'a small morsel of food', underwent semantic generalization to indicate any small quantity, and eventually developed (among other things) into a degree modifier marking low degree (Traugott 2008; Claridge and Kytö 2014). Knowing this, we can account for some of the grammatical behavior *a bit* displays as a degree modifier. For instance, that *a bit* follows rather than precedes the verb it qualifies naturally reflects its use as direct object to transitive verbs when it was still a noun phrase – compare (13a–b). In other words, the syntactic versatility of the source item goes some way toward explaining the eventual distributional behavior of the degree modifier.

(13)   a. She *worried a bit* if he had got back safely, but not enough to ask anyone if he had. (1993, BNC)

   b. they looked eagerly at each other, they both changed Countenance, and neither of them offer'd to *taste a Bit*. (1765–70, CLMET3.0)

There is a complication, however. (12i), above, shows that *a bit* can also premodify predicative adjectives – a position its lexical source could not occupy. Such distributional discrepancies between source item and degree modifier point to historical extensions. Indeed, *a bit* started regularly appearing with predicative adjectives well after it had become established as a degree modifier in other contexts – compare (14), where *a bit* modifies a verb, to (15), where it modifies a predicative adjective (Claridge and Kytö 2014: 251).

(14)   Ax him some deep question, that he may *shew himself a bit.* (1779, CLMET3.0)

(15)   and if she is *a bit fractious* at times, remember what she has gone through. (1848, CLMET3.0)

However, if degree modifiers could extend to new grammatical contexts, they should – given enough time – eventually all end up with very similar, even identical, grammatical distributions. But this does not seem to happen. The items in Table 11.5 all had degree modifier uses from Early Modern English onward – at the latest – yet distributional differences remain. This implies that extension must be constrained. The construction conspiracy hypothesis may be able to account for these constraints.

To illustrate the role of supporting constructions, we consider here in some more detail the history of the degree modifier *as good as* and contrast it with that of two other degree modifiers, its near-synonym *all but* and its Dutch cognate *zo goed als* (all three are what Quirk et al. 1985: 597 call 'approximators', meaning 'almost, virtually'). Not only do the three expressions have divergent histories, the emergent differences between them can be linked to distinct (i.e. item-specific or language-specific) sets of supporting constructions.

From Late Middle English, *as good as* could be used as a degree modifier, as in (16a) and (16b).[26] As the examples show, its use was at this point syntactically restricted to modifying predicative adjectives (including secondary predicates) and past participles. It was also collocationally restricted, usually combining with elements that denoted death or destruction.[27]

(16)   a. and hys son fell downe be fore hym *as good as dede.* (1448, IMEPCS)
        b. Yerelonde ... myghte not be forborne But if Englond were nyghe *as gode as lorne.* (a1450-1500(1436), MED)

From its use with predicative adjectives and past participles, the degree modifier use of *as good as* underwent a number of extensions. It started co-occurring with nouns, as in (17a). Also, it came to combine with more verb forms, initially with active perfect verbs (17b), later with bare infinitives with *do*-support (17c), bare infinitives with modals (17d) and finally with finite past and present forms (17e, f). Note in these examples also a loosening of the collocational constraints that characterized Middle English usage.

(17)   a. Afterward by the [construction – our insertion] of the neighbours of the places there aboutes, which [. . .] builded them houses to dwel among them, at lengthe there was such a resort of men thither, that it was euen *as good as a city*. (1564, EEBOCorp1.0)

b. Yea excellent, we *haue as good as won* the wager. (1573, EEBOCorp1.0)

c. And Bellarmine *does as good as confesse* this one [. . .]. (1617, EEBOCorp1.0)

d. but he will deale kindly with him, he *will as good as giue* them to him, if he will but make a legge [i.e. 'bow'], and thanke him for them. (1618, EEBOCorp1.0)

e. Neither needs their any proofe; for the common people *as good as thought so* before. (1638, EEBOCorp1.0)

f. for he *as good as confesseth* that we are bound to [. . .]. (1641, EEBOCorp1.0)

The historical extensions seen in *as good as* only partly resemble those of its near-synonym *all but*. As described in De Smet (2012), *all but* developed into a degree modifier with nouns in the late eighteenth century.[28] By the early nineteenth century it could be found with nouns (18a), predicative adjectives (18b), past participles (18c) and perfect verb forms (18d).

(18)   a. he considered it *all but a just punishment* for their attempted mesalliance. (1834, COHA)

b. as if the works of nature were not *all but infinite*. (1821, COHA)

c. The Morea, in 1775, was *all but desolated*, by letting loose upon it twentyfive [sic!] thousand Albanians, after its desertion by the Russians. (1827, COHA)

d. even in the very instant it appeared within his gripe, he *had all but clutched* it, when his wife [. . .] hastily stepped forward. (1827, COHA)

That much is familiar, yet two differences with *as good as* stand out. First, *all but* also extended to attributive adjectives (19a). Second, *all but* appeared with past and present tense verb forms (19b, c) before it started combining with bare infinitives (19d).

(19)   a. and the celestial spaces are continually strewed with this highly rarified, and *all but immaterial* substance. (1836, COHA)

b. true, she *all but consented* – and did consent in a sort. (1835, COHA)

c. he turns his head and gives me a look that *all but says*, How d'ye do, Will? (1836, COHA)

d. an occasional squall of sleet or snow *would all but congeal* his very eyelashes together. (1851, COHA)

How to account for the extensions in *as good as* and *all but*? Figure 11.1 proposes diachronic trajectories of extension for the two degree modifiers that are consistent with the available data.[29] Importantly, both trajectories

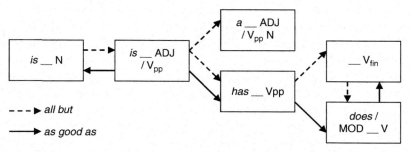

Figure 11.1 Diachronic trajectories of extension in *as good as* and *all but*.

consist exclusively of extensions between contexts sharing some formal or syntactic element. The similarities include the following: (1) nouns and adjectives can both occur in predicative position following copular *be*; (2) adjectives and past participles are near-perfect paradigmatic alternates; (3) past participles occur in predicative copular constructions as well as in the perfect tense; (4) most past tense finite forms are phonologically identical to the past participle; (5) past tenses and present tenses are paradigmatic alternates, as are affirmative *do*-support constructions, (6) which in turn resemble modal constructions in taking a bare infinitive. It can be argued, then, that every step in the extension process draws on similarities to established use. Put differently, every grammatical context to which a degree modifier spreads can become a 'supporting construction' for the following extension.

However, this cannot suffice to explain the divergences between *as good as* and *all but*. To account for these, we must consider the broader constructional networks in which each item features. For a start, why did *as good as* extend to *do*-support and modal constructions before it appeared with finite verb forms, whereas *all but* took the opposite trajectory? There is evidence to suggest that, for *as good as*, extension to *do*-support contexts happened to be supported by a range of additional patterns – all related to the degree modifier by more or less incidental lexical and syntactic correspondences. First, there was adverbial *as good*, meaning 'to the same effect'. The pattern derived from a construction that had a bare or *to*-infinitive as postposed subject and an optional dative benefactive, as in (20a). It survived into Early Modern English, now with the benefactive reinterpreted as subject, but still with a bare or *to*-infinitive, as in (20b).

(20) a. A man were *as good to be dede As smell* therof the stynk. (c1500, MED)
      b. we had *as good loose* somewhat, *as vndoe* our selues by law, and then loose that too. (1615, EEBOCorp1.0)

Second, there was *as much as*, which could appear in the sequence *do as much as* V, where *much* and the bare infinitive jointly functioned as direct object to transitive *do*, integrated by the similative *as . . . as* construction. The use is illustrated in (21).

(21)   for he that amid pleasant discourses and mery talke mooveth a speech that causeth bending and knitting of browes [. . .], he *doth as much as overcast* faire weather with a blacke and darke cloud. (1603, EEBOCorp1.0)

Third, *do* already frequently combined with *good* in the expression *do good*, as in (22), where *good* was presumably a noun and the object of transitive *do*.

(22)   one moment in hell will bee worse then all the pleasure in the world *did good* (1630, EEBOCorp1.0)

All these were supporting constructions that could facilitate the extension of *as good as* into *do*-support contexts. For lack of formal similarities, none of these supporting constructions were available to *all but*, whose trajectory of extension consequently took another course.

The other discrepancy between *as good as* and *all but* is harder to explain. Why did *all but* extend to attributive adjectives, while *as good as* never did? A (tentative) argument can, again, be made by relying on supporting constructions. *All* (as a quantifier) had always been felicitous as the first element of a noun phrase, and (as an intensifier) it could even occur following determiners, as in (23a). *But* could already precede attributive adjectives, as in (23b).

(23)   a. It is an *all* potent restorative – a sovereign antidote against the blue devils, and an infallible driver out of black ones. (1811, COHA)
       b. on the 28th of June [they] came in sight of the town of Apalache, of which they took possession with *but* slight opposition. (1821, COHA)

Even the surface sequence *all but* ADJ N occurred regularly. Typically, this was with *all* functioning as quantifying pronoun, and *but* as preposition introducing a dependent noun phrase, but just occasionally, a single context would allow both the pronoun-cum-preposition reading and the degree modifier reading, as in (24a, b).

(24)   a. the King's intention appeared to be a pardon to *all but actual regicides*. (1753, CLMET3.0)
       b. After having endured *all but real suffocation* for above a quarter of an hour in the tub, I was moved to the bed and wrapped in blankets. (1771, CLMET3.0)

If only through homophony, all these patterns could predispose degree modifier *all but* to extend into attributive adjective contexts. In contrast, they would not have borne on the development of *as good as*. Regarding the latter, speakers of Early Modern English who wanted to use *as good as* with a nominal attribute may have been inclined to another solution, since *as good as* would appear modifying postposed adjectives, as in (25a). Here we can suspect another supporting construction, seeing that similative *as* could easily introduce postmodifiers, as in (25b).

(25) a. the Turks [... disdained] that they [...] should be so derided of a handfull of men *as good as alreadie vanquished* [...]. (1603, EEBOCorp1.0)

b. O blessed Virgin, deliuer me out of this danger, and J will offer vnto thee [...] a candle *as bigge as the maine maste of my ship.* (1609, EEBOCorp1.0)

Where *as good as* and *all but* diverged because of differences in very local, item-specific constructional networks, divergences between *as good as* and its Dutch cognate *zo goed als* arose because of structural differences between the grammars of English and Dutch. *Zo goed als* started out as a degree modifier in the same grammatical contexts as *as good as* – i.e. with predicative adjectives, such as the secondary predicate in (26a), and with predicative past participles, as in (26b).[30] But from there the items entered different trajectories of extension.

(26) a. Hy beloofd [...] het aldus ... *zo goed als splinternieuw* voor den dag
he promises it this way as good as brand-new to the day
te doen komen (1731, WNT)
to make come
'This way he promises to make it appear as good as brand-new.'

b. Uwen Horatius, die ik, al eenigen tijd geleden, getoond heb
your Horace which I already some time ago shown have
dat *zo goed als uitverkocht* is [...] (1738, WNT)
that as good as sold-out is
'Your Horace, which I have some time ago shown to be as good as sold out ...'

Let us consider two areas of divergence, both showing how innovation is steered by existing synchronic structures. First, attributive adjectives and past participles can take much more elaborate premodification in Dutch than in English (which has to resort to postmodification to allow for the same complexity), as in (27a). This explains why *zo goed als*, unlike *as good as*, but like any other Dutch degree modifier, easily spread from predicative into attributive contexts, as in (27b).

(27) a. de   *in het openbaar*   *afgelegde*   verklaringen   (2002, TNC)
         the   in public   made   statements
         'the statements made in public'

      b. de   vrijverklaring der   toch   *zoo goed als* *verlorene* Amerika[an]sche
         the   release   of the anyway   as good as   lost   American
         bezittingen   (1824, CHK)
         possessions
         'the release of the American possessions that had been as good as lost anyway'

Second, Dutch has a large class of 'separable' verbs whose first element
will appear preceding the verbal stem in most contexts, including with past
participles, but takes clause-final position in main clauses when the verb is
finite. *Vaststellen* 'fix, arrange' is such a verb, consisting of a separable
element *vast* 'fast/firm' and a verbal stem *stellen* 'put'. In (28a) *vast* and
stellen appear as a single complex word, while in (28b) they behave as two
separate words.

(28) a. over   een periode die   in overleg   wordt *vastgesteld* (2002, TNC)
         during a   term   that in consultation is   fast-put
         'for the duration of a term that is fixed by mutual agreement'

      b. Het akkoord   *stelt* de   voorwaarden *vast* waarop [...]. (2002, TNC)
         the agreement puts   the conditions   fast   on which ...
         'The agreement fixes the conditions on which ... '

In the development of *zo goed als*, these separable verbs acted as a bridge
between adjective modification and verb modification. When *zo goed als*
appeared with past participles, it also appeared with the past participles of
separable verbs, as in (29a). Next, *zo goed als* began to appear with finite
forms of separable verbs. The extension was facilitated by the resemblance
of the separable first elements to secondary predicates – indeed, *zo goed als*
simply continues to precede the separable element whenever it takes clause-
final position, as in (29b) (conveniently avoiding violation of the V_2 rule in
Dutch main clauses). Later still, *zo goed als* appeared with other types of
complex predicates, whose positional behavior is the same as that of
separable verbs, as in (29c).

(29) a. Men   meld [...] dat   de   Huwelyks Verbintenis   van   een   Noordschen
         one   reports   that   the wedding   of   a   Northern
         Prins   met   een   Nabuurige   Princes   tegenwoordig *zo goed als* *vastgesteld*
         prince with   a   neighbouring princess   presently   as good as   fixed
         is   (1765, CHK)
         is
         'It is reported that the wedding of a Northern prince with a neighbouring princess has
         been as good as fixed.'

b. Vermits   men   geene Matroozen voor   de Koopvaardy Scheepen Kan
because   one   no   sailors   for   the merchant ships   can
krygen [. . .], *staat* de   Koophandel *zoo goed als* *stil* (1777, CHK)
get   stands the   commerce   as good as   still
'Because no sailors can be found for the merchant ships, commerce has virtually come to a standstill.'

c. [. . .] geloof ik, dat wij den opstand *zoo goed als* *meester* *zijn.*
believe   I   that we the   uprising as good as master   are
(1826, CHK)
'I believe we have the uprising almost under control.'

The expected final step is extension to simple finite verbs. However, in Present-Day Dutch, *zo goed als* is still only marginally acceptable with simple finite verbs, and only so in subordinate clauses, as in (30a) – as opposed to (30b). In comparison to English *as good as*, the restriction to subordinate clauses looks bizarre. The reason is the regularities emergent from prior-established patterns, which dictate that *zo goed als* must follow the finite verb in main clauses, but should always precede at least part of the predicate in its scope, exactly as in (42)–(44) above.

(30) a. Deze   boeren veranderden zoveel   aan   het slot   dat het zijn
These   farmers changed   so much to   the castle that it   its
karakter als   herenhuis *zo goed als* *verloor* (s.d., Google)
character as   manor house as good as lost
'These farmers made so many changes to the castle that it as good as lost its original character as a manor house.'

b. Het slot   (*zo goed als) *verloor* (*zo goed als) zijn karakter als
the castle   (as good as)   lost   (as good as) its   character as
herenhuis   (*zo goed als).
manor house (as good as)
'The castle as good as lost its original character as manor house.'

It appears, then, that Dutch *zo goed als* finally ran out of luck – or rather, out of supporting constructions.

11.4 Conclusions

The critique often levelled against analogy – that analogy is too unconstrained and too unpredictable to have any true explanatory power – can at least in part be countered by studying changes within their broader synchronic context(s). The two case studies presented above show that the timing and context of analogical change is not random, but is instead determined by the synchronic state of the grammatical system of a given language at a given time. In each case, the timing and/or contexts of change can be linked to the absence or availability of constructions, both substantive and structural, on which an innovation can be modeled. For HAVE-*to*, decisive factors of change included (among others) chunking of HAVE and *to* in Middle English, the rise of the *to*-infinitive, particularly with verbs expressing modal notions, and complex interactions between HAVE-*to* and the verb and adverb *nede(n)*. For *as good as*, analogical extension has been shown to be to some extent a self-feeding process, with one extension facilitating the next. But the process was also steered by the synchronic availability of various supporting constructions.

The notion of 'supporting construction' (Abbot-Smith and Behrens 2006) allows a more explicit operationalization of analogy. Its transfer from language acquisition to language change appears basically unproblematic, bearing in mind various differences in how the effect of supporting constructions can be expected to play out in the two domains (as discussed above). The notion does raise new issues, however. For one thing, supporting constructions potentially range from fully substantial chunks to highly abstract patterns (comparable to the micro-, meso- and macro-constructions distinguished in CxG). Not only may the respective impact of either type of supporting construction vary between acquisition and change, it is also conceivable that different types of supporting constructions bear differently on change as such. For instance, it is striking that analogical change proceeds faster in the case of *as good as* than in the case of HAVE-*to*. Perhaps this is because the supporting constructions involved are all highly substantial in the former case but more mixed in the latter.

Another question – also raised by Abbot-Smith and Behrens (2006) – is whether existing constructions can also negatively impact on potential changes. As argued above, Abbot-Smith and Behrens's (2006) argumentation on this point transfers less easily to diachrony. In the history of *as good as* there is no hint of hindrance from other constructions: synonymy is perfectly tolerated – witness the later emergence of *all but*. In the case of HAVE-*to*, the situation is more complex, since part of the success of HAVE-*to* can be linked to the decline of impersonal *need* – which could be interpreted to mean that *need* hindered HAVE-*to* until it declined. In general, modal verbs, constituting a closed class, might be less tolerant of synonymy than degree modifiers, forming an open class.

Notes

1. For the use made of analogy in usage-based approaches, see, e.g., Tomasello (2003), Bybee (2010); for construction-grammar, see Croft (2001), Goldberg (1995, 2006); for probabilistic linguistic approaches, see Bod et al. (2003), Bod

(2009); for language acquisition, see Slobin (ed. 1985), Abbot-Smith and Behrens (2006), Behrens (2009); for cognitive science, see Holyoak and Thagard (1995), Gentner et al. (2001), Gentner (2003, 2010), Hofstadter (1995), Hofstadter and Sanders (2013); and for language evolution, see Deacon (1997, 2003).

2. Barðdal (2008) makes clear that analogy may occur even with low type frequency, provided there is strong semantic coherence.

3. By 'innovative form' we here mean both ontogenetically innovative (in acquisition) and phylogenetically innovative (in change).

4. Most studies of L1 acquisition are based on the CHILDES Corpus, which contains both the children's utterances as well as those of the caregivers. Since the recordings are almost exclusively with children under the age of 3 (cf. Ninio 2011: 64), the influence of peers on their speech is negligible. Ninio (2011) also makes clear that at this age, children have learned the core grammar of English. In another study (2006), Ninio shows that this learning takes place via 'lexical-specific combinatory rules' and 'item-specific syntactic schemas' (2011: 4), and he emphasizes all along the importance of 'similarity matching and transfer' (2011: 38), i.e. learners make use of the common features of the source and target of the analogy, concentrating on concrete items and ignoring irrelevant features.

5. As we saw above in the case of *strike/struck* etc. and Dutch (*zich*) *beseffen* etc., where both formal/structural and functional/semantic similarities formed the 'support' for the new (analogical) structures. Behrens, chapter 5 in this volume, notes that analogy in children's early acquisition is item-based.

6. Goldwater et al. (2011) summarize this as follows: 'Because the ability to map relationally complex structures develops with age, younger children are less successful than older children at mapping both semantic and syntactic relations. Consistent with this account, 4-year-old children showed priming only of semantic relations when surface similarity across utterances was limited, whereas 5-year-olds showed priming of both semantic and syntactic structure regardless of shared surface similarity. The priming of semantic structure without syntactic structure is uniquely predicted by the structure-mapping account because others have interpreted structural priming as a reflection of developing syntactic knowledge.'

7. We have put 'acquisition' in quotes because, as Deacon (1997: 74) has convincingly shown, analogy is in fact a default; it concerns our inability to see a difference between two constructions due to inattention, laziness etc. (economy). This explains how innovations leading to change may sneak into the language imperceptibly (cf. Ellis, Chapter 4 in this volume, on the importance of *absence* of saliency).

8. See http://quod.lib.umich.edu/.

9. The meaning that HAVE-*to* develops in the course of time can best be described as 'external necessity' or, a term used by Narrog (2005: 685 ff.), 'event-oriented' necessity. According to Coates (1983), HAVE-*to* differs from MUST and HAVE-*got-to*, in that in the former 'the speaker is never involved'

(1983: 53); 'the speaker is neutral' and 'never the source of obligation' (1983: 56). Here we will simply use the term 'necessity' to refer to the developing meaning of HAVE-*to*.

10. Concerning Bybee's (2010: 107) view on grammaticalization, which is seen as 'involv[ing] the creation of a new construction *out of* an existing construction', Noël (2012: 5) remarks that it is strange, especially for a usage-based linguist, that the creation of a new construction '*into* an existing construction' is not considered 'equally important'.

11. Heine (2014) writes in connection with the unidirectionality of grammaticalization: 'It is *only the cognitive dimension that is sensitive to directionality*: it accounts for the cross-linguistically regular transfer from movement in space to prediction – a transfer that can be interpreted meaningfully only in terms of *an elementary metaphorical capacity* recruited to bridge the gap between two contrasting domains of human conceptualization' (emphasis added).

12. One of the anonymous reviewers mentions that fixed structural adjacency would not be the case in intransitive constructions where there is no object to intervene between the auxiliary and the infinitive. The point is, as shown by Steenis, that intransitive constructions do not really occur in Dutch.

13. Yanovich (personal communication) also mentioned that future sense still occurs in English but only in sentences in combination with *yet*, as in: *I have yet to find a solution to this problem*.

14. 'Old interpretation' means that the main verb HAVE can still be interpreted as a possessive, or a weak existential verb with a relation to the subject. This interpretation always obtains when the object is 'shared', i.e. in clauses such as *I have a book to read*, which means either 'I possess a book which I can/must read' or 'There is a book for me to read'.

15. Cases without an explicit object may well have prepared the way for the later use of intransitive infinitives with *have to*.

16. The increase in use of HAVE and *need* in Middle and Early Modern English was already quite noticeable in the corpus investigated in Fischer (1994), giving grounds for looking at this combination in more detail.

17. *To do(n)(e)* occurs 2,976 times in the Corpus; roughly 14 per cent of these are in some combination with HAVE. It is important to note that the construction with *to do(n)(e)* in row 8 only provides a formal substantive analogy for the later modal necessity usage (the infinitive usually followed HAVE immediately, since the direct object of HAVE was mostly left implicit). Semantically, it was close to the original Old English 'weak possessive' sense; it never conveyed necessity, as is indeed still the case (as in e.g. *This book has to do with the divisions within the church*).

18. It is important to mention that *nede* was originally a noun, of which the genitive and instrumental cases (*nedes* and *nede*, respectively) came to be used adverbially. It thus became impossible for the speaker to make a clear distinction between adverb (when used with *must*) and noun usage (when used with *have*). This explains the equation in the speaker's mind of *must*

nedes with *have nede to*. This confusion becomes particularly clear from mixed usages as commented on below.

19. Exact word order of elements in the constructions is not indicated. Only combinations with *nede(s)* have been counted, other spellings (*neod(e)*, *need(e)*) being rare. The form *nede* occurs in total 4,442 times in the Corpus, of which at least 174 are verbs, leaving roughly 4,268 nouns. This means that about 10 per cent of occurrences of the noun *nede* occur in the type of constructions collected in Table 11.3. Also noteworthy is that the construction with HAVE + *need* is rare in Old English. Only 10 examples were found in the Dictionary of Old English corpus, only one of which has an infinitive, making it likely that it was indeed replacing an impersonal construction as argued here.

20. According to Hopper and Thompson (1980), animacy is one of the parameters that increases the overall transitivity of the clause.

21. The order given in (a) (row 1) is the usual order, but the dative pronoun may also follow the verb.

22. Coordinate constructions are not counted because the case of the 'subject' is not clear in this case.

23. It is to be noted that the personal verb appears only in late Middle English, almost all instances in Table 11.4 coming from the fourteenth and fifteenth centuries. The table does not include the impersonal constructions with empty subjects (*hit/there*), of which there are many (adding, by the way, to the high number of constructions with infinitives), since the (dative) experiencer is usually missing here (this construction, too, disappears).

24. In generative linguistics, this is called 'Burzio's generalization': the observation that a verb can assign a *theta* (or semantic) role to its subject position if and only if it can assign an accusative case to its object. This pertains to passives and unaccusatives like *the ice melted*. Typical for both these categories is that the subject argument is not a semantic agent, which means that the syntactic subject does not actively initiate, or is not actively responsible for, the action of the verb. Similarly, the combination HAVE-*to* lacks an object and an 'active' subject. It is perhaps no accident that external or event-oriented necessity is often linked in language to impersonal, passive and existential constructions (cf. Payne 2011; Ba 1995; and various reviews in Hansen and de Haan 2009).

25. Another interesting development that may have helped further the use of HAVE-*to* is the loss of non-finite forms with the semi-modal BE-*to* construction, which also expresses necessity. Hundt (2014b) argues that the loss of these (never very frequent non-finite constructions) may have left a gap for HAVE-*to*, showing on the basis of corpus evidence that the HAVE-*to* and BE-*to* constructions could be used in similar syntactic contexts and shared enough semantic ground (even though they were not semantically equivalent) for such a replacement.

26. The history of *as good as* is described here on the basis of various sources. For Middle English, these are IMEPCS and the quotation database of the MED. For Early Modern English, which is when all the relevant extensions take

place, use has been made of EEBOCorp1.0 (Petré 2013). EEBOCorp1.0 was compiled from the *Early English Books Online* archive and contains over half a billion words of running text, covering the period 1480–1700.

27. The origin of the degree modifier use is not completely clear. It stands to reason that it is historically related to the similative *as . . . as*-construction, which grades a property, introduced by the first *as*, with respect to a reference value, introduced by the second, e.g. *I neuer met with no knyght but I was as good as he / or better* (1485, IMEPCS). Our Middle English data do not contain bridging contexts that link the similative construction to the degree modifier. Even so, a historical link between the two constructions could explain the negative connotation typical of the degree modifier in its earliest use. The reference value in the similative *as . . . as*-construction is typically a minimal level on a scale that the 'comparisee' either matches or emulates (e.g. *he muste proue that hym selfe was prophecyed vppon to be the fore goer of some newe Cryste as good as euer was the olde* (1533, EEBOCorp1.0)). In other words, similative *as good as* tended to imply 'better than'.

28. The history of *all but* is here described on the basis of the data set used by De Smet (2012), drawn from COHA (Davies 2011). COHA is at present the richest data source for nineteenth- and twentieth-century English, but only poorly represents the very first decades of the nineteenth century and contains no data predating 1810. This makes it difficult to establish the exact order of events before 1830. Some early examples from the Old Bailey Corpus, however, support the assumption that *all but* developed into a degree modifier with noun phrases and then first spread to predicative contexts. Early examples of the degree modifier use show *all but* modifying nouns (as in *he was not half a yard from me; I had* all but *hold of him* (1789, OBC)) or modifying predicates introduced by copular *be* (as in *The windows and shutters were* all but *to pieces* (1794, OBC) or in *Martha Green was* all but *dead in the kitchen; she was speechless* (1817, OBC)).

29. For *as good as* the trajectory in Figure 11.1 is based on first attestations (as provided above). For *all but*, whose earliest history is less well documented, the trajectory is partly based on first attestations and partly inferred from the timing and pace of subsequent increases in usage frequencies (see De Smet 2012).

30. The history of *zo goed als* is here described on the basis of the WNT quotation database, the self-compiled CHK (a newspaper corpus of eighteenth- and nineteenth-century Dutch based on the *Historische Kranten Online* archive), and the TNC (another large newspaper corpus covering Present-Day Dutch).

PART VI

Ambiguity

CHAPTER 12

Syntactic Ambiguity in Real-Time Language Processing and Diachronic Change

Claudia Felser

12.1 Introduction

Ambiguity is ubiquitous in human language and presents a potential obstacle to successful comprehension. Ambiguity can be found at all linguistic levels: strings of human speech sounds (or strings of graphemes) may be compatible – at least, temporarily – with more than one possible phonological, morphological, syntactic, semantic or pragmatic representation. From the perspective of left-to-right, incremental language processing, virtually every utterance starts out as multiply ambiguous. English sentences, for example, frequently begin with the determiner *the*, which usually signals the start of a definite determiner phrase but lacks overt specifications for grammatical features such as number or case. In the absence of any further cues as to the predicted noun phrase's properties or function, a sentence-initial determiner could potentially introduce a variety of different types of constituent. These include an unmodified subject noun phrase, a modifying possessor phrase (e.g. *The neighbor's new car*), a topicalised object (e.g. *The person on the far right, John did not recognise*), an adverbial expression (e.g. *The last time I visited Paris . . .*) or a comparative correlative structure (e.g. *The sooner you leave, the better*), among others.

   An incoming new word or phrase gives rise to structural ambiguity if there is more than one possibility of integrating it into the emerging phrase structure representation, as in *Sarah watched the film with the famous actor*, which contains an ambiguous prepositional phrase. Ambiguity also arises if a word's categorial status is unclear, as illustrated by humorous newspaper headlines such as *Eye drops off shelf* or *British left waffles on Falkland Islands*.[1] Most of the time, however, subsequent words and/or higher-level contextual information will quickly help reduce, and ultimately eliminate, any initial ambiguity. Another type of sentence-level ambiguity, which how-ever does not give rise to any structural ambiguity, involves lexical homo-nyms as in *The visitors liked the port*. Utterances containing lexical or structural ambiguities that are not ultimately resolved are called globally ambiguous.

Despite its potential for impeding comprehension, ambiguity is not necessarily a bad thing. Piantadosi, Tily and Gibson (2012) suggest that ambiguity increases a linguistic system's communicative efficiency. Ambiguity has also been implicated in syntactic change (e.g. Harris and Campbell 1995), something which will be discussed in more detail below. The question of how the human sentence processor handles temporarily or globally ambiguous input has been investigated extensively in experimental psycholinguistics (for review and discussion, see Altmann 1998; Clifton and Staub 2008). Time-course sensitive techniques such as eye-movement monitoring or EEG recording allow psycholinguists to investigate ambi-guity resolution at the micro-scale by examining the millisecond-by-millisecond mental processes involved in analysing ambiguous words or sentences during listening or reading.

This chapter provides a selective overview of psycholinguistic approaches to ambiguity resolution and relevant empirical findings, focusing on (morpho-)syntactic ambiguity. I then go on to explore how misanalysis of syntactically ambiguous or underspecified input at the micro-scale might be linked to grammatical reanalysis at the macro-scale, that is, during diachro-nic change. For a discussion of the role of ambiguity in lexical-semantic change, see Denison (Chapter 13 in this volume).

12.2 Psycholinguistic Evidence for Misanalysis

Most of the time we remain blissfully unaware of any temporary ambiguity in the input. This indicates that the human sentence processor assigns an analysis (and corresponding interpretation) to incoming strings of words largely automatically. Misanalysis does occur, however, and cannot always be corrected without conscious effort. In order to investigate how the language processing system deals with ambiguous input, and to examine how different types of information interact during ambiguity resolution, experimental psycholinguists typically carry out group studies in con-trolled laboratory settings. Popular experimental methods include offline judgment or comprehension tasks, priming tasks and the use of time-course-sensitive online methods such as self-paced reading or listening, eye-movement monitoring or EEG recording during listening or reading (see, e.g., Carreiras and Clifton 2004). Most sentence processing research has focused on comprehension rather than production, mainly because in comprehension studies researchers can systematically manipulate the experimental stimuli, allowing them to selectively investigate a variety of linguistic factors that might affect processing. In language production, by contrast, the structural processor's input is the conceptual message devised in a speaker's mind, which is difficult for researchers to manipulate in a controlled and systematic fashion. It is also worth noting that, even though a given sentence or utterance may seem structurally (or otherwise) ambiguous to comprehenders, the message being conveyed is always unambiguous to the speaker or writer himself or herself. For these reasons, the following discussion will focus mainly on ambiguity resolution in comprehension.

Online processing studies often make use of temporarily ambiguous sentences, deliberately designed to initially mislead the processor. Such sentences are known as 'garden-path' sentences, like the famous example *The horse raced past the barn fell* (which is usually attributed to Tom Bever). At first, in the absence of any biasing contextual information, readers or listeners will almost inevitably misanalyse the participle *raced* as a finite main verb. It is only when the addressee gets to the final word (the verb *fell*) that she or he is in a position to disambiguate toward a reduced relative clause structure. The degree of processing difficulty experienced at this point may be so severe that participants (wrongly) consider the sentence to be ungrammatical.

Category ambiguities, including ambiguous verb forms such as *raced* in the example above, are rather frequent, especially in morphologically impoverished languages such as Modern English. Some examples are shown in (1a–c), with the critical ambiguous word(s) italicised.

(1)   a. The *rich cook* {only on Sundays / is a vegetarian}
       b. Sally replied *to* {the email / set the matter straight}
       c. The old man was hoping *for* {some attention / his daughter to visit him}

In (1a), *rich* is ambiguous since it can be either a prenominal or a nominalised adjective, while *cook* can be either a noun or a verb. In (1b, c), *to* and *for* can be either prepositions or clause-introducing elements. If, due to categorial indeterminacy, the wrong analysis is initially chosen, this may result in misinterpretation or lead to enhanced processing or comprehension difficulty at or following the point of disambiguation.

Other types of ambiguity that have featured prominently in experimental sentence processing research include, but are not limited to, those illustrated by (2a–e) (see Frazier and Clifton 1996: 12 for a more comprehensive list).

(2)   a. OBJECT VS. SUBJECT AMBIGUITY
          While the customers were drinking the beer turned stale.
       b. DP VS. CLAUSAL COORDINATION AMBIGUITY
          Lily smiled at Bill and his mother frowned.
       c. PP ATTACHMENT AMBIGUITY
          The policeman hit the robber with the stick.
       d. THEMATIC AMBIGUITY
          The submarine sank the fishing boat.
       e. LEFT- VS. RIGHT-BRANCHING COMPOUNDS
          the race horse stables/the brick horse stables

In sentences like (2a), for example, the determiner phrase (DP)[2] *the beer* will normally be taken to be the direct object of the verb *drinking* at first, which then leads to measurable processing difficulty at the point of disambiguation (i.e. the verb *turned*). In coordination ambiguities such as (2b), the parser's initial preference upon receiving the second DP *his mother* will normally be for interpreting the initial DP-*and*-DP string as an instance of DP conjunction. The final verb *frowned* is incompatible with this analysis, however. Ambiguous prepositional phrases (PPs) such as *with the stick* in (2c) will, in the absence of any information that biases toward a DP modification reading, usually be interpreted as modifying the verb phrase (VP) headed by *hit* rather than the verb's object DP *the robber*. For thematic ambiguities as in (2d), an initial preference for interpreting the verb *sank* intransitively, and the initial DP as a Theme rather than an agentive subject, may be observed depending on the strength of the verb's argument structure biases. Presenting participants with structurally ambiguous compounds as in (2e) can help us gauge whether readers or listeners prefer building left- or right-branching structures.

In reading- or listening-time experiments, increased processing difficulty at or following an unexpected disambiguation will be reflected in longer reading or listening times in comparison to an unambiguous control condition. Sentences containing temporary subject/object ambiguities such as (2a), for example, can be disambiguated by adding a comma as in (3).

(3)   While the customers were drinking(,) the beer turned stale.

Readers encountering the disambiguating verb *turned* in (3) will typically need longer to read the remainder of the sentence when the comma is absent than when it is present (e.g. Pickering and Traxler 1998), which provides indirect evidence that readers initially mistake the postverbal DP *the beer* for a direct object in the comma-absent condition. The relatively longer reading times are thought to reflect the additional processing effort associated with identifying and correcting the earlier error.[3]

Experimental evidence for an initial misanalysis can also be more direct. Roberts and Felser (2011), for example, manipulated an ambiguous DP's semantic fit as a direct object of the preceding verb in sentences such as (4a,b).

(4)   a. The journalist wrote the book had amazed all the judges.
        b. The journalist wrote the girl had amazed all the judges.

In (4a), the postverbal DP *the book* is a plausible direct object of the verb *write*, although this analysis turns out to be wrong later on. Attempting to integrate an implausible potential object DP such as *the girl* in (4b) with the preceding verb, however, involves violating the verb's selectional restrictions, causing a disruption in processing. In Roberts and Felser's study, this disruption was reflected in elevated reading times at the word following implausible compared to plausible object DPs in English native speakers, and at the manipulated noun itself in non-native speakers.[4]

Real-time sentence processing also involves making structural and semantic predictions (compare e.g. Gibson 1998). Encountering a determiner will trigger the prediction of a noun, for instance, and encountering a transitive verb the prediction of an object noun phrase. Evidence for predictive processing is provided by listeners' anticipatory eye movements toward objects capable of fulfilling thematic role or selectional requirements of the verbs preceding them (see, e.g., Altmann and Kamide 1999). In EEG data, participants' degree of surprise when encountering an unexpected sentence continuation is indicated by certain characteristic brain responses observable from about 300 milliseconds after the critical word's onset (van Petten and Luka 2012).

Syntactic misanalysis during processing typically involves (initially) misplacing constituent boundaries or attachment of an ambiguous phrase to the wrong node in the emerging phrase structure representation.[5] For illustration, consider the examples in (5) and (6) below.

(5)   a. Emma gave her flowers to Tom.
        b. Emma gave [her] [flowers]
        c. Emma gave [her flowers] [to Tom]

When encountering the beginning of a sentence like (5a), the parser's attempt to saturate the argument structure grid of *give* as soon as possible may result in *her* and *flowers* being analysed as the verb's indirect and direct objects respectively (5b). This analysis must later be corrected so as to allow for the real Goal argument, the PP *to Tom*, to be properly integrated into the verb phrase (5c).

In (6a) (= 2b), *Bill and his mother* are likely to be analysed as a single conjoined noun phrase initially (6b), with the arrival of a second verb, *frowned*, signaling that *his mother* is actually the subject of a clausal conjunct (6c).

(6)   a. Lily smiled at Bill and his mother frowned.
        b. Lily smiled at [Bill and his mother]
        c. [Lily smiled at Bill] and [his mother frowned]

Psycholinguistic evidence for initial misanalysis shows that the input is processed incrementally (Bader and Lasser 1994; Frazier and Rayner 1982; Kamide and Mitchell 1999; Trueswell, Tanenhaus and Garnsey 1994; among many others). That is, each new incoming word or phrase is integrated into the current partial sentence representation immediately, even where there is a high degree of indeterminacy (compare also Crocker 1996; Marslen-Wilson 1973). If an initially favored analysis is proven wrong by subsequent input, then the processing system will normally strive to correct the error. If recovery fails, as might sometimes happen during the processing of difficult garden-path sentences such as *The horse raced past the barn fell*, a sentence may be deemed ungrammatical and/or incomprehensible.

Processing models differ with regard to their assumptions about the mental mechanisms involved in recovery from misanalysis. In the next section, I will briefly outline some theoretical approaches to structural misanalysis and revision during real-time processing.

12.3   Psycholinguistic Models and Mechanisms of Ambiguity Resolution

12.3.1   Serial vs. Interactionist Processing Models

Psycholinguistic models of sentence processing fall, roughly, into two types. One type assumes that a syntactic analysis is initially performed on the basis of bottom-up (i.e. syntactic category) information only. According to serial or *syntax-first* processing models (Frazier 1979; Frazier and Clifton 1996; Friederici 2002), the syntactic analysis computed initially is not influenced by higher-level information such as semantic plausibility or contextual biases. Ambiguous words or phrases are integrated into the emerging structural representation in accordance with a narrow set of structure-based minimal effort principles. Many cases of syntactic misanalysis can be attributed to a general preference for the simplest possible analysis compatible with the current input, and for integrating new incoming words or phrases into the constituent currently being processed. These two structure-based economy constraints are known as *Minimal Attachment* and *Late Closure*, respectively (Frazier 1979; Frazier and Clifton 1996).

This hypothesized preference for the simplest syntactic analysis provides a plausible account for many types of garden-path phenomena. For garden-path ambiguities as in *The horse raced past the barn fell*, for example, analysing the verb *raced* as a main verb (7a) requires a less complex representation than analysing it as a relative clause-introducing participle (7b), an analysis that requires postulating an embedded clausal constituent which separates the head of the subject phrase (*the horse*) from the predicted main clause predicate.

(7)   a. [$_{DP}$ The horse] [$_{VP}$ raced [$_{PP}$ past the barn]]
      b. [$_{DP}$ The horse [$_{RC}$ raced [$_{PP}$ past the barn]]] [$_{VP}$ fell]

Another well-attested processing preference is for new incoming words or phrases to be integrated into the most recently processed constituent. This Late Closure (or local attachment) preference can, for example, account for the parser's initial preference for analysing the postverbal DP *the beer* in (2a) as a direct object of the preceding verb *drinking* rather than as the subject of the (predicted) main clause. The alleged universality of the Late Closure principle has been called into question, however, by findings suggesting that it is not necessarily applied consistently across different languages (see, e.g., Brysbaert and Mitchell 1996; Carreiras and Clifton 1993; Cuetos and Mitchell 1988; Frenck-Mestre and Pynte 1997; Papadopoulou and Clahsen 2003).

Information other than structural economy constraints which can affect the likelihood of misanalysis includes probabilistic information such as verb subcategorisation biases, semantic information such as noun phrase (in-)definiteness, and referential information provided by the situational or discourse context. Experimental findings which suggest that these factors are able to affect the processing system's initial analysis of ambiguous input (e.g. Altmann and Steedman 1988; Britt 1994; Garnsey, Pearlmutter, Myers and Lotocky 1997; Trueswell, Tanenhaus and Kello 1993; Trueswell et al. 1994) are problematic for strictly serial (i.e. syntax-first) processing models.

Interactionist models, by contrast, assume that sentence processing is influenced by a range of simultaneously interacting linguistic (and,

possibly, non-linguistic) constraints, with semantic and pragmatic interpretation cues potentially affecting the initial analysis (for review, see
McRae and Matsuki 2013). These models differ from syntax-first models
in that they do not assume syntactic or category information to be in any
way privileged. Under this view, the way ambiguous input is first integrated into the current representation will be influenced by lexical-
semantic, pragmatic and probabilistic biases (e.g. MacDonald 1994).
Interactionist models are supported by the observation that garden-path
effects can often be ameliorated, or even prevented, by semantic or pragmatic information. In (8) below, for instance, the sentence-initial animate
DP *the defendant* in (8a) is a much better potential Agent argument of the
verb *examine* than the inanimate DP *the evidence* in (8b). This makes
comprehenders more likely to initially adopt an erroneous main verb
analysis for *examine* in (8a) than in (8b) (Trueswell et al. 1994 – but cf.
Ferreira and Clifton 1986 for different findings).

(8)   a. The defendant examined by the lawyer turned out to be unreliable.
        b. The evidence examined by the lawyer turned out to be unreliable.

Many interactionist models assume that all possible analyses are computed in parallel, ranked either according to preference or likelihood (e.g.
Gibson 1991) or with respect to their relative activation levels (e.g. McRae,
Spivey-Knowlton and Tanenhaus 1998) and continuously evaluated as
processing proceeds. Analyses that prove incompatible with the current
input will be discarded or their activation level will be reduced.

While there is broad agreement that structural ambiguity resolution is
influenced by a variety of different types of constraints (Altmann 1998;
Gibson and Pearlmutter 1998), psycholinguists still disagree as to (a) whether
processing is serial or proceeds in parallel, (b) whether one or more information sources are privileged in some way and (c) the point in time at which
different types of information begin to affect processing. Other controversial
issues concern the separability of grammar and parser and the way grammatical knowledge interacts with least-effort processing constraints such as the
hypothesized preferences for local attachment and for the smallest possible
structural representations. An in-depth discussion of these issues is beyond
the scope of this chapter, however.[6]

12.3.2 Recovering from Misanalysis

In sentence processing research, the term *reanalysis* is used to refer to the
mental processes involved in correcting an erroneous first analysis of

the input. Successful reanalysis during processing will help ensure that the listener or reader arrives at exactly the interpretation that the speaker or writer intended, after initially being side-tracked by ambiguous or under-specified input. The psycholinguistic use of the term thus differs from its use in historical linguistics, where reanalysis refers to the re-structuring of (ambiguous) surface strings in the course of language change (Langacker 1977). To avoid any unnecessary confusion, in the following, I will use the term *neoanalysis* (Andersen 2001a; Traugott and Trousdale 2013) to refer to reanalysis in the historical linguistics sense.

Serial and interactionist processing models make different assumptions about how the parser goes about recovering from initial misanalysis. From the point of view of parallel or interactionist models, corrections made in the face of incompatible or disambiguating input may, for example, involve a re-ranking of options (e.g. Gibson 1991) or a change to the relative activation levels of competing analyses (e.g. McRae et al. 1998). Serial models, on the other hand, typically assume that an erroneous structural representation needs to be repaired, following backtracking and error identification (see, e.g., Fodor and Inoue 1994; Sturt, Pickering and Crocker 1999). Individual proposals differ with regard to the technical details of how repairs might be accomplished, but there is evidence showing that some types of error are easier to undo than others.

Consider sentences containing temporary subject/object ambiguities such as (9a,b), for example. Sentences such as (9a), which involve an adjunct clause that precedes the main clause, often give rise to stronger garden-path effects than sentences such as (9b), in which the main clause verb takes a clausal complement, following the point of disambiguation, the auxiliary *was* (e.g. Sturt, Pickering and Crocker 1999).

(9)   a. While Peter was baking the cake was sold to a young woman.
        b. Mary reported the crime was extremely serious.

This indicates that detaching the ambiguous DP (*the cake* in 9a, and *the crime* in 9b) from the preceding verb and reanalysing it as the subject of the following predicate incurs greater processing cost in (9a) than in (9b). From the point of view of repair-based approaches to reanalysis, this observation has been argued to suggest that reanalysis which involves elevating a misanalysed constituent to a hierarchically higher position (such as the main clause subject position in 9a) is more difficult than reanalysis that does not change the original dominance relations (e.g. Pritchett 1992). Parallel-interactionist models, on the other hand, would assume that a higher processing cost is associated with changing the relative ranking or activation levels of the two competing analyses in (9a) compared to (9b), possibly because a verb such as *report* in (9b) admits clausal complements quite readily (compare e.g. Garnsey et al. 1997).

A wrong analysis may also be harder to undo if it can be maintained for a long time (e.g. Ferreira and Henderson 1991), as in example (7) above, and an initially highly plausible misanalysis is more difficult to correct than an initially implausible one (e.g. Pickering and Traxler 1998). Contextual or discourse biases may also affect the way structural ambiguities are resolved (e.g. Altmann and Steedman 1988). Our processing system is able to correct many types of initial misanalysis automatically, that is, without our conscious awareness. Some types of misanalysis, for instance that involved in the processing of difficult garden-path sentences such as (7), may require some conscious effort to be resolved or can lead to processing breakdown. Other cases of reanalysis failure may go unnoticed rather than leading to processing breakdown, with the resulting misinterpretation being maintained (Christianson, Hollingworth, Halliwell and Ferreira 2001; Ferreira 2003).

12.3.3   'Good Enough' Processing

As we saw earlier, for temporarily ambiguous sentences that are strongly biased toward a specific analysis, the parser normally commits to this analysis very quickly. Psycholinguistic experiments have shown that the resulting incorrect interpretation is sometimes carried forward even after a sentence has been grammatically (or otherwise) disambiguated. Christianson et al. (2001), for example, found that readers would often misunderstand sentences such as (10) below, in which the postverbal NP *the deer* is a highly plausible direct object of the verb *hunted*, despite the fact that the following verb *ran* clearly signals that the direct object analysis is incorrect.

(10)   While the man hunted the deer ran into the woods.

When asked whether the man hunted the deer, comprehenders would frequently respond with 'yes' even though sentence (10) does not in fact provide any information at all as to what the man was actually hunting. Such cases of semantic persistence could, in principle, result from failed or incomplete reanalysis (Christianson et al. 2001), from a failure to erase incorrect representations completely from memory (Slattery, Sturt, Christianson, Yoshida and Ferreira 2013) or from comprehenders computing underspecified syntactic analyses in the first place. According to

Ferreira (2003), comprehenders may sometimes compute syntactically shallow, semantics-based representations of the input that are just 'good enough' for recovering basic sentence meaning. Another way to account for Christianson, Ferreira and colleagues' findings is to assume a dual-pathways model of sentence processing, according to which syntactic and semantic analyses can proceed in parallel but largely independently (e.g. Townsend and Bever 2001), and with the semantically driven or 'good enough' route to comprehension sometimes winning out over the syntactic one (for review and discussion, see Ferreira and Patson 2007).

Effects of semantic persistence have also been observed in studies using time-course sensitive experimental methods such as eye-movement monitoring (Jacob and Felser 2015; Sturt 2007). Jacob and Felser had participants read sentences containing temporary subject/object ambiguities such as (11). These sentences were disambiguated twice: first by a finite auxiliary (e.g. *were*) in need of a subject, and later on by a verb phrase that was pragmatically inconsistent with a direct object analysis (e.g. *being arranged for the party*).

(11)   While the young girl was drawing the flowers were carefully being arranged for the party.

Despite receiving two consecutive disambiguation cues, native English readers retained the incorrect direct object reading of *the flowers* in around one in three cases.

Taken together, these findings suggest that encountering disambiguating input does not always lead to successful structural revision or repair. Understanding how syntactic misanalysis comes about – and why it sometimes persists – in real-time language processing might also contribute to a better understanding of syntactic neoanalysis.

Recall that for the kind of garden-path sentences and attachment ambiguities considered thus far, an initial misanalysis will also give rise to an erroneous interpretation. Computing a fully detailed, accurate grammatical representation is not always necessary for recovering the intended meaning, however. For illustration, consider complements of perception verbs such as *see* in *I saw the neighbor painting the fence*. These can be shown to be three-ways structurally ambiguous (e.g. Declerck 1982; Felser 1999). The different analysis options are shown, in simplified form, in (12a–c).

(12)   a. REDUCED RELATIVE CLAUSE ANALYSIS
        I saw [$_{DP}$ the neighbour [$_{RC}$ painting the fence]]
        "I saw the neighbour who was painting the fence"

b. PARTICIPIAL ADJUNCT ANALYSIS
   I saw [$_{DP}$ the neighbour] [$_{CP}$ painting the fence]
   "I saw the neighbour as she was painting the fence"
c. CLAUSAL COMPLEMENT ANALYSIS
   I saw [$_{AspP}$ [$_{DP}$ the neighbour] [$_{VP}$ painting the fence]]
   "I saw the event of the neighbour's painting the fence"

Example (12a) shows the reduced relative clause analysis, with *painting the fence* functioning as a non-finite clausal modifier of the DP *the neighbour*. In (12b), *painting the fence* functions as an adverbial rather than as a postnominal modifier. Whilst in (12a) and (12b), *the neighbour* is the direct object of *see*, the complement of *see* in (10c) is a non-finite clausal constituent (an Aspect Phrase, in Felser's 1999 analysis), with *the neighbour* functioning as the embedded clause's subject. As the paraphrases in (12a–c) indicate, the three structural options each correspond to slightly different semantic interpretations. Nothing crucial hinges on the specific choice of analysis, though, as all three options essentially describe the same thing being witnessed: the neighbor in the process of painting the fence. Comprehenders who compute a different analysis from the one intended by the speaker or writer would thus not miss out on any key information. Provided that contextual information does not somehow disambiguate the sentence, this gives rise to two possibilities: comprehenders will either compute one of the three possible analyses in (12a–c) at random (or probabilistically, based on their relative occurrence frequencies) or compute a syntactically underspecified analysis.

There is processing evidence to suggest that comprehenders do indeed sometimes compute underspecified grammatical representations. Swets, Desmet, Clifton and Ferreira (2008), for example, report reading-time evidence showing that readers do not necessarily commit to a specific attachment choice for ambiguous relative clauses in sentences such as (13a), unless they expect to be asked detailed questions about the sentence's content. That is, comprehenders will understand that somebody has burned herself but may not immediately decide whether the person in question was the schoolgirl (13b) or the schoolgirl's sister (13c).

(13)   a. The sister of the schoolgirl who burned herself was usually very careful.
       b. The sister of [$_{DP}$ the schoolgirl who burned herself]
       c. [$_{DP}$ The sister [$_{PP}$ of the schoolgirl] who burned herself]

Evidence for morphosyntactic underspecification comes from a reading-time study by Pickering, McElree, Frisson, Chen and Traxler (2006), who found that readers may leave a verb phrase's aspectual (telic vs. atelic) value unspecified initially when encountering aspectually ambiguous sentence fragments such as *The insect hopped*. Not committing to a specific analysis of ambiguous input may save comprehenders time and/or processing resources, and helps avoid the need for a potentially costly reanalysis later on (see also Sturt, Pickering, Scheepers and Crocker 2001).

In short, the examples in (12) and (13) illustrate cases of ambiguity where recovering the intended structural analysis is not crucial for gist comprehension, in communicative situations which involve what Denison (Chapter 13 in this volume) describes as 'vagueness'.

12.4 Real-Time Syntactic Misanalysis and Diachronic Change

The role of processing constraints in language change has not received a great deal of attention in the past, and possible links between real-time structural misanalysis and syntactic change have not yet been systematically explored (but see Hawkins 2012 for some relevant discussion). As noted above, sentences or utterances are not ambiguous to those generating them, but will usually appear at least temporarily ambiguous to comprehenders, who face the task of having to recover the underlying hierarchical representation (and corresponding compositional meaning) from a linearly presented string of words. This production/comprehension asymmetry provides ample opportunities for readers or listeners to misanalyse the input.

Harris and Campbell's (1995: 61) definition of reanalysis in language change (what we are calling 'neoanalysis') as 'a mechanism which changes the underlying structure of a syntactic pattern and which does not involve any immediate or intrinsic modification of its surface manifestation' also applies to syntactic misanalysis. The most obvious difference between them concerns their relative time scales. Language change is typically slow and gradient (but cf. Lightfoot 1997), whereas misanalysis during language processing occurs within a couple of hundred milliseconds after the onset of an ambiguity in the mind of an individual comprehender. Whilst the syntactic representations built during real-time misanalysis will normally be constrained by existing grammatical rules (that is, they will be at least locally grammatical), neoanalysis yields representations that alter or extend the range of grammatical possibilities in a language. As Traugott and Trousdale (2010a: 38) point out, we should therefore 'distinguish between parsing and interpretation as a precondition and potential for change, and reanalysis as a mechanism'.

Real-time misanalysis during parsing and neoanalysis (as a presumed starting point of language change) nevertheless have several things in common. Both processes are discrete; that is, in both cases an erroneous or novel analysis is computed in an individual's mind. Trousdale (2013: 32), for example, points out that '[e]ach constructional change is a neoanalysis, i.e. a new analysis on the part of a given speaker/hearer'. From a psycholinguistic perspective, neoanalysis can be viewed as an innovative misanalysis which then persists and gradually spreads in a given speaker community, rather than being corrected or rejected, and which eventually becomes part of that speaker community's grammar.

It is often assumed that neoanalysis requires ambiguity. Hawkins (2012), for example, explores possible links between increasing surface structure ambiguity in Middle and Early Modern English and the shift from SOV to SVO word order. However, as noted by De Smet (2009), ambiguity is normally the result of neoanalysis and structural change rather than its trigger. From the perspective of real-time language comprehension, ambiguity is actually a kind of underspecification, in the sense that the information available at a particular point in time is insufficient for allowing the comprehension system to decide between two or more alternative analyses. As we shall see below, underspecification may indeed also be a prerequisite for neoanalysis.

Both misanalysis during processing and historical neoanalysis may be facilitated by factors from other linguistic domains. These can be phonological, morphological, semantic or pragmatic in nature. In language processing, noisy input may make phonologically less salient elements, including morphological affixes, difficult to perceive, making it harder for comprehenders to identify word or constituent boundaries (see also Ellis, Chapter 4 in this volume). At historical time-scales, phonological weakening and the loss of morphological distinctions have often been implicated in syntactic change (compare e.g. Traugott, Chapter 5 in this volume). The disappearance of the Old English dative case may have helped facilitate the rise of clausal *for*-NP-*to* infinitives, for example, together with other factors such as word order change (Fischer, van Kemenade, Koopman and van der Wurff 2000). Conceivably, neoanalysis might also be facilitated by semantic or pragmatically triggered expectations, both of which are known to affect ambiguity resolution in real-time language processing. Last but not least, there may also be cross-linguistic influence during or arising from language contact situations.

A less obvious potential similarity between processing misanalysis and neoanalysis concerns directionality in language change, such as the development of modals from lexical verbs, rather than the other way around. As we saw above, misanalysis during comprehension also often happens in a predictable way (although psycholinguists do not normally refer to these patterns as 'directional'), with many logically possible structural misanalyses being systematically avoided. In the following, I will discuss some well-known examples of grammatical change in the history of English from the perspective of incremental, left-to-right syntactic processing. As we shall see, least-effort principles of the kind that have been proposed in the sentence processing literature may also be involved in neoanalysis. For expository reasons, I will focus on structural factors and deliberately ignore semantic and pragmatic factors here, even though these are likely to play an important role in language change or neonalysis (see, e.g., Bybee, Chapter 7 in this volume).

12.4.1 Category Change: Conversion

Many English words belong to more than one syntactic category, with N-to-V conversion (e.g. *to send an email – to email*) being a particularly productive example. Denison (2010a) distinguishes between category change with and without structural change. Examples of recategorisation that does not require any restructuring include cases of N-to-A conversion as in *It was a fun event* or *He is a rubbish footballer*. This kind of change might have been facilitated by examples like (14) in which the categorical status of *fun* is not unambiguously determined by the syntactic context, and given that nouns and adjectives show some overlap in their defining features (see, e.g., Denison 2013, Chapter 13 in this volume).

(14)   a. The party was [$_{A / N}$ fun]
       b. Last night's film was [$_{A / N}$ rubbish]

From a processing perspective, there are several theoretical possibilities as to how comprehenders may deal with contextually underspecified words such as *fun* or *rubbish* in bridging contexts such as (14a, b). Normally the processor would retrieve the word's categorical features from its lexical entry and then create a corresponding syntactic head node. Miscategorisations may occur if the processor determines an incoming word's category label on the basis of the syntactic context (and/or probabilistic biases) alone, either failing to check or simply overriding the word's categorial specification. Note that the interpretive consequences of choosing one contextually licensed analysis over the other seem to be fairly minimal here. An alternative possibility would be for the processor to leave the post-copular node underspecified. Whilst in cases such as (14) above, computing an underspecified or 'good enough' analysis seems perfectly sufficient for comprehension, underspecification at the phrase structure level would not by itself account for lexical recategorisation.

During incremental language processing, the immediate assignment of category labels to new incoming words is thought to be a prerequisite for efficient syntactic structure-building. Rapid syntactic categorisation aids processing in at least two ways: (a) by allowing for new words to be integrated into the emerging structural representation immediately, thus helping to speed up processing, and (b) by enabling the parser to make predictions about the constituents yet to come, or which are required to complete the sentence in a grammatically appropriate way. With these two points in mind, let us consider the following (largely speculative) scenario in relation to (14) above. Having encountered the auxiliary or copula *be*, the processor may predict that *be* is most likely going to be followed by an adjective here, thus generating an adjectival node in anticipation. The absence of a determiner before *fun* or *rubbish* is fully consistent with this prediction, making the anticipated analysis more likely to be maintained. If the word's lexically specified categorical features then turn out not to match after all, the processor has two choices: either to correct the analysis by analyzing *fun* and *rubbish* as nouns instead, or to 'attach anyway' (to borrow a term from Fodor and Inoue 2000), that is, to force these words into the predicted adjectival slot. As a result of such a forced match, the word's categorial features may be altered or overwritten, ultimately leading to the creation of a homophonic lexical entry with different categorial specifications.

Let us briefly switch perspective from language comprehension to language production. This is thought to involve, among other things, the creation of a syntactic frame for the intended utterance, with lexical items that match in terms of their categorical specification then being inserted into appropriate syntactic slots (e.g. Bock and Levelt 1994). Speakers who have successfully recategorised a particular noun as an adjective should then be able to slot this word into adjectival positions other than contextually underspecified ones as in (14), as well as into nominal positions. The comprehension-based scenario outlined above does not preclude the possibility that innovative recategorisations may originate in individual speakers' or writers' minds, of course, as witnessed by the fact that conversion is a popular linguistic device in poetry.[7] Consider the following examples (15a–c) from Shakespeare (cited by Crystal 2004: 332–33) for illustration:

(15)   a. Thank me no thankings, and proud me no prouds
           (*Romeo and Juliet*, 3.5.125)
        b. a hand that kings have lipped (*Anthony and Cleopatra*, 2.5.30)
        c. Thou losest here, a better where to find (*King Lear*, 1.1.261)

Many cases of diachronic category change, including the examples in (14) above, show signs of gradience. This raises important questions about the nature and mental representation of syntactic categories, which the results from real-time sentence processing or ambiguity resolution studies cannot currently answer. For a fuller discussion, see, e.g., Denison (2010a, 2013, Chapter 13 in this volume) and Trousdale (2013). Some examples of category change with accompanying structural change will be discussed below.

12.4.2   Constituent Boundary Shift

As constituent boundaries are not always indicated clearly by prosody or punctuation marks, they can easily be misplaced during listening or reading. A shift of constituent boundaries is also sometimes seen in language change. The recategorisation of the preposition *for* as a complementiser during the change from Middle to Modern English, for example, presumably involved constituent rebracketing as illustrated in (16), below (compare e.g. Fischer 1988; Harris and Campbell 1995: 62).[8]

(16)   a. It is better [$_{PP}$ for me] [$_{CP}$ PRO to slay myself] than to be violated thus
        b. It is better [$_{CP}$ for me to slay myself] than to be violated thus

From a processing perspective, the bracketing in (16b) is more attractive because it yields a structurally less complex sentence representation than (16a), which contains a prepositional phrase plus an infinitival clause lacking an overt subject. Covert or 'understood' subjects (indicated by *PRO* in 16a) are, by definition, not visible or audible, but once their existence has been inferred they must be linked to a suitable antecedent for the sentence to be fully interpretable. The need for establishing this referential dependency further increases the computational cost associated with building the representation in (16a) compared to that in (16b).

Cases of grammaticalisation such as the formation of the *be-going-to* future, illustrated in (17), also involve constituent boundary shifts (e.g. Hopper and Traugott 2003).

(17)   a. Mary$_i$ [$_{TP}$ [$_{TP}$ is [$_{VP}$ going]] [$_{CP}$ PRO$_i$ to buy some bread]]
        b. Mary [$_{TP}$ [$_T$ is going to] [$_{VP}$ buy some bread]]

Analysing *going* as part of a modal (17b) rather than as a lexical verb (17a) again involves structural simplifications. As in (17a) above, the purpose clause's understood subject is inaudible, thus facilitating its omission from the syntactic representation generated by comprehenders and corresponding rebracketting. The observation that lexical verbs can become auxiliaries or modals (but not the other way around) is consistent with comprehenders' preference for delaying the closing off of the constituent currently being processed for as long as possible. During left-to-right processing, T(ense) and/or M(odality) nodes will be generated earlier than VP nodes in English, providing a potential home for any verb-like elements that can express tense or modality. Since the processor is keen to slot new incoming words into corresponding phrase structure positions as soon as possible, and assuming that in root clauses T and/or M nodes are created automatically, it is unlikely that the integration of a modal should be delayed and the modal slotted into a verbal head position further downstream instead.[9]

Other cases of rebracketting include the formation of complex determiners involving *kind of* or *sort of* (e.g. Brems and Davidse 2010; Denison 2002, 2006, Chapter 13 in this volume). Here a noun and the head of a following prepositional phrase (18a) fuse and form a complex determiner with a preceding article (18b).

(18)   a. a rare [$_{NP}$ [$_N$ kind] [$_{PP}$ of bird]]
       b. [$_{DP}$ [$_D$ these kind of] jokes]

In (18b), the lack of number agreement between *kind* and the preceding determiner indicates that *kind* is not a head noun here. Note that during speech perception, the original constituent boundary between *kind* and *of* may not be easy for comprehenders to discern; example (18b) is in fact reminiscent of a fairly common type of 'slip of the ear' error involving missing or misplaced word boundaries (Bond 1999). Complex determiner formation, whilst creating new multi-word lexical entries (or 'prefabs', see Denison, Chapter 13 in this volume), again yields simpler phrase structures.

Complex prepositions such as *on behalf of* in (19b), which are discussed in some depth by Denison (2010a), appear to provide a similar example of fusion:

(19)   a. [$_{PP}$ on [$_N$ behalf] [$_{PP}$ of DP]]
       b. [$_{PP}$ [$_P$ on behalf of] DP]

Besides resulting in less complex phrase structure representations, the changes illustrated by (16)–(19) above are all consistent with some form of the Late Closure processing principle. In (16), rather than closing off the constituent headed by *for* after the pronoun *me*, the following string *to slay myself* is incorporated into it. In (17), *going to* is incorporated into the functional head expressing tense/modality, whilst in (18) and (19), *kind of* and *behalf of* fuse with a preceding determiner or prepositional head, respectively.

12.4.3   Summary

Examining some well-known examples of syntactic change from the point of view of left-to-right incremental processing served to illustrate the potential role of underspecification and structural least-effort principles in facilitating neoanalysis. The observation that syntactic change leads to structural simplifications is by no means new (see, e.g., Roberts 1993; Roberts and Roussou 2003), but few scholars have previously considered neoanalysis from a strictly left-to-right processing perspective (but see Lightfoot 2006 for some useful discussion). By ignoring semantic and other potentially relevant factors, we obviously get a rather one-dimensional view of neoanalysis, however. The precise extent to which misanalysis during processing and neoanalysis really do resemble one another remains to be determined. There may be cases of constituent boundary shift that do not lead to structural simplifications, and cases where semantic change demonstrably precedes structural change, both of which would require us to refine or rethink the processing-based scenarios outlined above.

12.5   Concluding Remarks

The primary purpose of this chapter was to illustrate how ambiguity or underspecification can give rise to misanalysis during real-time processing, and to explore possible parallels with diachronic reanalysis (or 'neoanaly-sis'). Given that, from a processing point of view, ambiguity is in the mind of the reader or hearer – rather than in the mind of the writer or speaker – the discussion focused on language comprehension rather than produc-tion. Both misanalysis during language processing and neoanalysis in language change always happen instantaneously in individual people's minds. We saw that misanalysis during processing tends to involve struc-tural simplifications consistent with processing economy constraints, which is also true for many cases of neoanalysis. In future, researchers may want to explore the extent to which processing factors are implicated in language change more systematically, and possibly experimentally. For patterns of synchronic variation, preferred disambiguations or word order variants should, other things being equal, elicit faster processing times compared to dispreferred ones. Systematically collected acceptability judgments can provide useful information about the extent to which innovations have become acceptable in Present-Day English, with the use of speeded or timed judgments likely to reduce the influence of prescriptive norms and also potentially provide a measure of relative processing difficulty (compare e.g., Schütze 1996).

A number of important questions have remained unanswered. One question which current psycholinguistic research on human language processing cannot answer concerns gradience, and another the mechanisms by which recategorisations and new structural patterns spread across speaker communities. Others concern the role of probabilistic, semantic or pragmatic factors in giving rise to neoanalysis. Another issue that I have not considered here is the possible role of mono- or multilingual acquisition settings in facilitating neoanalysis. Within the generative tradition, child language learners are sometimes considered to be the primary drivers of diachronic change (e.g. Lightfoot 1979, 2006 – but cf. Lieven, Chapter 14 in this volume). Other scholars have drawn attention to the role of language contact and bilingualism in language change (e.g. Meisel 2011). Although there is evidence that language learners are especially prone to misanalysing ambiguous input (e.g. Jacob and Felser 2015; Trueswell, Sekerina, Hill and Logrip 1999; Traxler 2002), the role of language acquisition and contact in giving rise to successful neoanalyses clearly needs to be investigated further.

Acknowledgments

My work on this chapter was supported by an Alexander-von-Humboldt professorship to Harald Clahsen, which is gratefully acknowledged. I thank David Denison, Marianne Hundt, Cheryl Frenck-Mestre, Sandra Mollin and Georgina Wood for their helpful and constructive comments on an earlier draft.

Notes

1. See, e.g., www.alta.asn.au/events/altss_w2003_proc/altss/courses/somers/head lines.htm (accessed on 23 October 2015).
2. Determiner phrases (Abney 1987) are more commonly referred to as noun phrases (NPs), especially where a distinction between them is deemed irrelevant.
3. Hill and Murray (2000) showed that punctuation does not always serve as an effective disambiguation cue, however (see also Jacob and Felser 2015).

4. This between-group difference suggests that non-native comprehenders are potentially more strongly guided by plausibility or semantic fit than native ones. Roberts and Felser (2011) also report evidence that their non-native participants had more difficulty recovering from an initially plausible misanalysis than their native participants. In the monolingual processing literature, subject-object ambiguities sometimes fail to trigger garden-path effects altogether under certain conditions (Holmes, Stowe and Cupples 1989).

5. Compare also Ellis's (Chapter 6 in this volume) discussion of the role of 'chunking' in language processing and acquisition.

6. For a fuller discussion of the grammar-parser relationship, see, e.g., Berwick and Weinberg (1984), Hawkins (1994, 2004, 2014) and Phillips (2013).

7. Consider also Lewis Carroll's famous *Jabberwocky* poem, in which nonce words 'inherit' their word class from the context only.

8. Garrett (2012: 62), however, argues instead that 'the *for* NP *to* VP pattern was always clausal [. . .] but that nevertheless, until the sixteenth and later centuries, it was mainly used in contexts where it seemed ambiguous syntactically'.

9. This idea might be seen as a left-to-right processing equivalent of Van Gelderen's (2004) *Late Merge* hypothesis.

CHAPTER 13

Ambiguity and Vagueness in Historical Change

David Denison*

13.1 Introduction: Incomplete Knowledge

13.1.1 Participants

This chapter concerns the role of incomplete knowledge in linguistic change, particularly on the part of an addressee/reader (AD/R). I will argue that the speaker/writer (SP/W) may sometimes lack complete knowledge, too. In addition, of course, the linguist rarely has complete knowledge either. What is **not** known may have a bearing on appropriate theories of language. I begin with a brief look at the difference between the (un)knowns of historical linguists and psycholinguists as observer-participants in acts of linguistic communication.

In historical linguistics, where written data is still the norm, a linguist R is a little different from the original readership envisaged by W: potentially more knowledgeable in some ways, whether by virtue of hindsight or specialist knowledge, but then again perhaps ignorant of cultural and pragmatic facts obvious to a contemporary reader. For recent audio broadcast or telephone data, the historical linguist is much like a normal AD, except that she or he can listen repeatedly to a sound clip. With spoken conversational data, non-verbal cues are usually lacking. In broad terms, however, the historical linguist is simulating being AD/R of an individual act of linguistic communication and – in corpus linguistics – generalising across many such acts.

A psycholinguist, on the other hand, does not resemble AD/R but is rather an intimate, external observer of the SP/W–AD/R dyad. Linguistic situations are contrived experimentally in order to get data which might not occur in normal life, or at least not with sufficient control or sufficient frequency for good statistics. Psycholinguists also look in detail at the processes involved in AD/R's reception and sometimes SP's (rarely W's) production.

13.1.2   *Ambiguity vs. Vagueness*

I distinguish two kinds of incomplete knowledge. Ambiguity is where AD/R (and linguist) cannot be sure which of two or more linguistic possibilities was intended by SP/W, and something hangs on the choice. Vagueness is where a linguistic analysis is in some relevant respect underdetermined, at least for AD/R (perhaps for SP/W, too), but no further information is needed for interpretation. The distinction is a familiar one in lexical semantics, and, later in this chapter, I will extend it to other linguistic domains such as syntactic structure and lexeme boundaries.

What differentiates ambiguity from vagueness is whether or not SP/W could have made a choice, and furthermore, whether such a choice would have mattered. Since neither the existence nor the importance of a choice is a wholly clear-cut notion, there could in principle be some middle ground between ambiguity and vagueness; one such case is noted in Section 13.2.1.

Lexical ambiguity is easy to illustrate. It can be the outcome of divergence between senses of a polysemous word, or it may be due to accidental homonymy, as with *bank* 'financial institution' vs. 'ground bordering a river' (see here *OED* s.vv. *bank* n.[1] and n.[3]). The word *bank* in the second clause of (1), which directly follows a sentence mentioning the River Nile, is in principle ambiguous:

(1)   When Ethiopia sought World Bank financing for this dam more than 20 years ago, the U.S. leaned on the bank to say no. (2013, via WebCorp)

Of course, in practice there is no real doubt in this case. Although lexical ambiguity can be striking and may sometimes be implicated in semantic change, it is not a prerequisite, whereas vagueness often is, as we will see in Section 13.2.

Vagueness is a trickier concept. It is difficult to restrict in a systematic way what is underdetermined in a given instance of vagueness. Traugott and Trousdale (2013: 199) use a more practical definition of vagueness in lexical semantics: 'blended, simultaneously present subcases of a more general meaning', which can be extended to other domains.

With ambiguity there is a risk of choosing the 'wrong' reading. A mistake may subsequently become apparent to AD/R; for example, 'garden-path' sentences suggest a reading that comes to a dead end as more of the utterance is processed, in principle forcing AD/R to backtrack and explore an alternative analysis. *A priori*, vagueness should be less costly than ambiguity, as there is no need for AD/R to backtrack and try again. However, there is some evidence from psycholinguistics that, in practice, AD/Rs are reluctant to backtrack and may stick with the wrong reading, even at the cost of contradiction (Felser, Chapter 12 in this volume). With vagueness, there is no 'wrong' reading (though of course an AD can choose to ask SP to be more specific).

In subsequent sections we look at how ambiguity and vagueness play out diachronically in a number of different linguistic domains. I will argue that, in many cases, greater weight should be given to vagueness than to ambiguity as a driver of change, and consequently that tolerance of vagueness is necessary for realistic linguistic analyses.

13.2 Semantic Change

A particular context may invite a reinterpretation of the meaning of a word or expression. Numerous accounts of semantic change invoke such a starting-point, generally locating the novel contextual meaning in the pragmatics of the utterance rather than the semantics of the individual expression. The idea is that repeated association with that context may lead to the new sense becoming part of the semantics, no longer dependent on the particular context. The old sense remains – at least to begin with – beside the new, and the resulting polysemy often persists.

Details and emphasis vary between scholars. One approach looks for a mismatch between SP/W's and AD/R's interpretation in a so-called 'bridging context' (Evans and Wilkins 2000: 549–50; Diewald 2002; Heine 2002), one where either sense would fit and neither participant need be aware of any discrepancy. Vagueness in the semantics is crucial to such a process, whereas ambiguity is unlikely to recur often enough to affect the entrenchment or spread of an innovation, except as suggested in Section 13.2.2.

More elaborated is the 'Invited Inferencing Theory of Semantic Change' (Traugott 1999; Traugott and Dasher 2002; see also Hansen and Waltereit 2006), an interaction of pragmatics and semantics that is applied to various expressions with an element of subjectivity. It can be summarised as follows. SP/Ws may exploit an invited inference (IIN) to add meaning to an utterance that is not, strictly speaking, derivable from the semantics of an expression. Such a one-off inference may be context-dependent, for example *It's raining!* as a request to bring the washing in, or dependent on encyclopaedic knowledge, for example, the name of a country's capital city as journalistic shorthand for the national government. If such an IIN becomes conventionalised through repetition, it becomes a Generalized Invited Inference (GIIN). At this stage it is still part of pragmatics and is cancellable, but a further step may semanticise the GIIN so that it moves from pragmatics to become part of the (en)coded meaning of the expression. Thus the process as envisaged here is speaker-led, or at least intersubjective – a sort of implicit conspiracy between SP/W and AD/R. Vagueness is crucial, because only inferences that are underdetermined by the semantics can be added pragmatically.

The case studies below illustrate with dictionary and corpus evidence the development of new senses and the loss of old ones. Note that historical lexicography has tended to emphasise first and last attestations, whereas corpus linguistics sets greater store by frequency.

13.2.1 Semantic Vagueness and Ambiguity

The etymology of *holiday* in British English is transparent. The *OED* senses that are relevant for our purposes are shown in Table 13.1. The difference between senses 1 and 2a can be stated in terms of inherent and inferential features (Lipka 1985), with sense 1 inherently (i.e. semantically) about religion, and 'no work' an inferential feature (= contextual pragmatic inference). In sense 2a the 'no work' component has become inherent (has been semanticised) and the 'religious festival' component has been lost, while in sense 2b the 'duration of one day' component has been lost as well (Leech 1981). The dictionary's comment on sense 2a, '[i]n early use not separable from sense 1', implies that in late Middle English there were many bridging contexts where the defining characteristic of the semantics could be either the religious festival or the time off work, or both: the features were pragmatically equivalent. It is difficult in such a case to distinguish between ambiguity and vagueness.

Consider now *passenger*. We concentrate on the two senses surviving into Modern English, both probably borrowed from Anglo-Norman in the

Table 13.1 *Some senses of* holiday

Sense	Currency	OED definition
1	OE–	A consecrated day, a religious festival; now usually written *holy-day*
2a	a1400(a1325)–	[. . .] a day of exemption or cessation from work; a day of festivity, recreation or amusement
2b	c1400–	*collect. pl. or sing.* A time or period of cessation from work, or of festivity or recreation; a vacation

Middle English period. One is '[a] person who passes by or through a place; a traveller, esp. a traveller on foot'. It is marked by *OED* as obsolete and chiefly Scottish in later use (s.v., 3a, a1450-1886). In fact it survives into the twentieth century, as (2) attests:

(2)   a. But other passengers were approaching Lincoln meanwhile by other roads on foot. (1919 Woolf, *Night & Day*)
       b. ... his quick walk along the streets and in and out of traffic and foot-passengers (1919 Woolf, *Night & Day*)

The other is what the *OED* calls 'now the usual sense', defined as '[a] person in or on a conveyance other than its driver, pilot or crew' (s.v., 4, 1511–).[1] Both senses refer to travelers other than those driving or directing some form of conveyance (horse, carriage, bicycle, boat, etc.). In early use it was possible to have vague contexts which did not require the senses to be distinguished:

(3)   'It is the Watermen that cals for passengers to goe Westward now.' (1595, *OED* s.v. *ho*, int.[1])

There are 15 instances of *passenger(s)* in PPCMBE (948,895 words, 1700–1914), of which 14 concern people aboard ships, a context which virtually guarantees the 'conveyee' sense (though cf. (3)). The sole exception, from the play *She Stoops to Conquer*, is

(4)   a. As you say, we passengers are to be taxed to pay all these fineries. (1773, PPCMBE)

The context is (so the speaker believes) an inn to which he and his companion in a post-chaise have been directed, so either sense of *passenger* will fit, though contextually 'passing traveller' (sense 3a) is more likely, and indeed the companion responds:

(4)   b. Travellers, George, must pay in all places ...

The 'passing traveller' (increasingly, 'traveller on foot') and 'conveyee' senses move far enough apart to permit at least theoretical ambiguity:

(5)   The police believe they have a clue to the man who placed the nitro-glycerine which last night blew up a Euclid Avenue car and injured four passengers. (1899, COHA)

Four people in the car or four passers-by? The difference matters. The 'conveyee' sense is a relationship word, implicating the existence of a conveyance. Conversely, the word *passenger(s)* in the context of a conveyance (ship, train, car, etc.) tends to implicate the 'conveyee' sense, as in (5), and even more strongly when used with the definite article. The 'passing traveller' sense increasingly needs contextual support.

The *OED*, as updated in 2005, has the following note against sense 4 of *passenger*:

> *N.E.D.* (1904) notes 'now always with the implication of a public convey-ance entered by fare or contract'. After motor vehicles, other than buses and coaches, became widespread this implication ceased to be felt.

One could speculate that extralinguistic factors – the enormous growth first of public (paid-for) transport and later also of private cars – might have strengthened the 'conveyee' sense. Can its dominance be linked to the loss of 'passing traveller (on foot)'? – a sense whose obsolescence by 1919 is suggested by the more explicit compound *foot-passenger* in (2)b. Perhaps potential ambiguity hastened the loss. Compare how the 'homosexual' sense of *gay* has made earlier senses almost unusable.

13.2.2 Hidden Ambiguity

Ambiguity need not involve senses known to both SP/W and AD/R – a choice easily resolved if noticed. My definition of ambiguity encompasses the situation where AD/R encounters an unfamiliar term and in effect makes a guess as to the meaning. AD/R's approximation to the original sense may later enter more general usage. Strictly speaking, there is no ambiguity within the individual grammars of either SP/W or AD/R, since their patterns of usage barely overlap: ambiguity here is essentially a contact phenomenon, at least at first.

One obvious context is when a term from a technical jargon is recruited for more general use. Thus *parameter* is a term with exact meanings in various fields. Its sense in mathematics, illustrated in (6) below, is probably too subtle for most non-mathematicians:

> A quantity which is fixed (as distinct from the ordinary variables) in a particular case considered, but which may vary in different cases. (OED, s.v., 3.a)

In more general discourse *parameter* has widened to '[a]ny distinguish-ing or defining characteristic or feature, esp. one that may be measured or quantified; an element or aspect of something', see (7), and for many speakers it has become merely a high-flown alternative to *boundary* or *limit*, as in (8) (both developments recorded in *OED* s.v., 8), the latter no doubt with some contamination from *perimeter*.

(6)   This technique determines a new solution with one extra parameter α.
       (BNC, B2K 727)

(7)   It is their responsibility to decide what new equipments [*sic*] are needed, and
       to specify their performance and other critical parameters. (BNC, ABA 205)

(8)   This sense of collaborative work [in a drama lesson] – within agreed
       parameters – is a key to good control and good drama. (BNC, HYA 944)

Vagueness may play a part in the spread of the innovation in examples
which blur the distinction between a technical and a more general sense:

(9)   The precise scale you can't quantify, but I can give you the parameters.
       (BNC, A44 371)

Other technical terms which have entered general usage with rather
different meanings include *at fault* (originally of hounds which have lost
the scent), *crisis* (moment when illness turns towards either recovery or
death), *quantum leap* (the smallest possible change in energy level of an
electron) and psychological terms like *schizophrenic*.

13.2.3   *Pragmatic Vagueness*

The closely related seventeenth-century Latin borrowings *discriminate*
v. and *discrimination* n. exemplify the development of new senses in
interaction between pragmatics and semantics. They have by and large
kept in step with each other through later semantic changes, which I label
as stages A–D in Table 13.2. The next two columns of the table have
a synopsis of the relevant senses in the respective *OED* entries, together
with the date range over which each numbered sense is recorded. (Only
sense 3 of the noun is marked as obsolete.) The last column notes whether
there is an element of evaluation in the connotation.

    Some examples follow:

(10)   an instance of the judgment of the ancient Sculptors in their nice
       discrimination of character. (1821–2, CLMET3.0) [stage A]

(11)   Man would cease to be Man: on the one side he would lose his
       discrimination from God, and on the other from Nature. (1867, *OED*)
       [stage A']

(12)   and ridiculing the public for their want of taste and discrimination in not
       admiring it. (1838, CLMET3.0 [stage B]

(13)   They do not discriminate against ships belonging to the other states. (1786,
       OED) [stage C]

Table 13.2 *Some senses of* discriminate/ion

Stage	*discriminate* v.	*discrimination* n.	Evaluation
A	2a. tr. 'distinguish X (from Y)' 1615–	1a. 'action of noting/making a distinction (of X)' 1621–	neutral
A	2b. intr. 'distinguish (among Xs; between X and Y)' 1645–	1a. 'action of noting/making a distinction (between X and Y)' 1621–	neutral
A'		3. 'fact/condition of being differentiated' 1666–1867	neutral
B		4. 'power/faculty of making exact distinctions,; discernment' 1764–	usually positive
C	3. econ., orig. U.S., intr. '(against X), treat X (less) favourably' 1786–	5. econ., orig. U.S. '(un)favourable treatment' 1789–	neutral
D	4. intr. '(against X), treat unjustly' 1857–	6. orig. U.S. 'unjust/prejudicial treatment (against X)' 1819–	negative

(14)   a. More American women than ever before are filing charges that they're being discriminated against in employment. (1970, COHA) [stage D]
   b. The discrimination of Arab-Americans since 9/11 has been vastly overlooked in society. (2005, COCA) [stage D, usage not yet in *OED*]

The earliest stage for both verb and noun, A, illustrated in (10), carries no value judgment, nor the stage A' of (11), which is merely a statal result use of *discrimination* – an easy kind of sense extension for action nouns, found also in *commitment, extension, finding* and many others.

In the eighteenth century the focus with the noun switches to the discriminator, stage B: *discrimination* regarded as a human faculty. This is a metonymy, or arguably an inference/implicature: the act or fact of discrimination implies the existence of a human mind endowed with the ability to make fine distinctions. Possession of that ability need not evoke a subjective evaluation, but one can easily arise through inference/implicature, in principle either positive (e.g. the faculty of a good judge) or negative (e.g. of a fusspot). Evidently it was positive connotations that stuck, perhaps through contextual association and repeated collocation with particular items, for example premodifiers like *nice* or coordination with *taste* or *delicacy*; cf. (12).

A separate semantic development, stage C, focuses on the discriminatee, at first with a specialised use in trade and economics for the favoring or disfavoring of particular products or countries, as in (13). In this factual, technical usage there need be little or no subjective speaker evaluation – the sense is vague in that respect. However, an extension to human discriminatees in the nineteenth century facilitates the addition to both verb and noun of an inference/implicature 'unjust' or 'unjustified', a negative subjective evaluation, perhaps because (economic) discrimination *against* is much commoner than discrimination *in favour of*, both in practice (imposition of tariffs, or import bans, for example) and in language use. The addition of an 'unjust' element is favored culturally or politically through changes in mainstream social attitudes, and linguistically through repeated premodification by *racial* or *sex* or by coordination with *prejudice*. If 'unjust' becomes part of the semantics, we have reached stage D, as in (14). Collocation with immediately following *against* is a convenient test to distinguish stages C and D from A, A' and B. We can see the growth of *discriminat* against* in COHA (400 million words, 1810–2009):

Figure 13.2 shows the growth in frequency of such premodifiers as *race* or *sex*,[2] essentially from the 1920s onward after sporadic attestations beginning in 1885.

Although nearly all the senses mentioned here remain available, stage D is probably dominant in present-day use of both noun and verb, with older meanings needing more contextual support. Notice by contrast that the adjective *discriminating* seems to retain as its default a positive connotation similar to stage B. Other factors must determine the direction of semantic change and whether it takes place at all; pragmatic vagueness is merely a prerequisite.

A more recent example is *sketchy*, a denominal adjective used transparently from 1805 of writings or drawings in the sense 'giving only a sketch or outline' (my précis of *OED* s.v., 1 and 2). By 1878 a colloquial sense '[o]f a light, flimsy, unsubstantial or imperfect nature' (s.v., 3) is recorded, which I take to be a metaphorical extension: different domain, senses related by similarity. A further shift turns 'flimsy, imperfect' into 'unsafe, disreputable, dishonest', presumably when applied to such concrete or abstract referents as buildings or legality. Dubiousness and illegality are not yet recognised for *sketchy* by the *OED* but are current in the US (OxfordDictionaries.com: 'dishonest or disreputable'; Merriam-Webster: 'likely to be bad or dangerous'; Urban Dictionary: 'gives off a bad feeling; unsafe'), even allowing a human referent:

(15)   it pays to be suspicious of large, seemingly useless gifts from one's sworn enemy. And that includes your aunt's sketchy second husband. (2011 COCA, Caprice Crane, *With a little luck: a novel*)

SECTION	1810	1820	1830	1840	1850	1860	1870	1880	1890	1900	1910	1920	1930	1940	1950	1960	1970	1980	1990	2000
FREQ	0	1	0	0	1	5	7	43	37	39	78	62	100	105	117	99	148	109	72	96
PER MIL	0.00	0.14	0.00	0.00	0.06	0.29	0.38	2.12	1.80	1.76	3.44	2.42	4.06	4.31	4.77	4.13	6.21	4.31	2.58	3.25

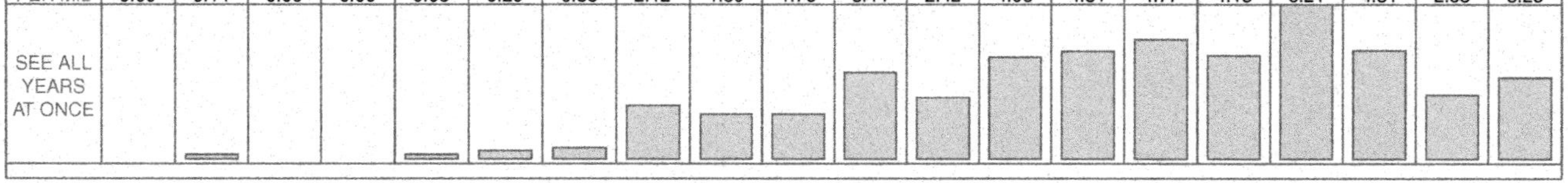

SEE ALL YEARS AT ONCE

Figure 13.1 *Discriminat* against* in COHA.

SECTION	1810	1820	1830	1840	1850	1860	1870	1880	1890	1900	1910	1920	1930	1940	1950	1960	1970	1980	1990	2000
FREQ	0	0	0	0	0	0	0	1	1	2	2	8	9	32	46	99	87	94	52	81
PER MIL	0.00	0.00	0.00	0.00	0.00	0.00	0.00	0.05	0.05	0.09	0.09	0.31	0.37	1.31	1.87	4.13	3.65	3.71	1.86	2.74

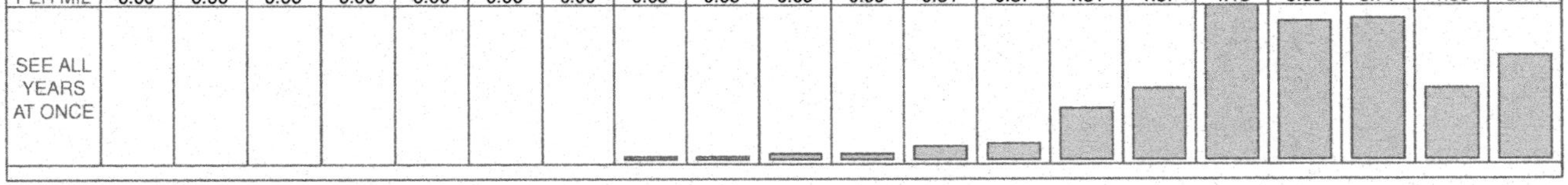

SEE ALL YEARS AT ONCE

Figure 13.2 Selected premodifiers of *discriminat** in COHA.

These latest shifts in semantics are enabled by the source sense being pragmatically vague as to evaluation.

In the examples discussed it is mostly vagueness that promotes the change. Ambiguity can play a part in the aftermath, but may be more centrally involved in language contact.

No attempt has been made to offer a complete typology of semantic change.

13.3 Word Class Change

Normal word class change is immediate and complete. There is no vagueness or ambiguity in derivations like *funny* adj. < *fun* n., *hammer* v. < *hammer* n., *peddle* v. < *pedlar* n. One can, however, imagine a period of vagueness in developments of the *bitter* n. < *bitter beer* type, as mere ellipsis of a head noun after the adjective gives way to a new self-standing noun.

I have studied yet another kind of word class change, an incremental process which in the early stages requires an underdetermined word class – essentially an analytic vagueness. Such stepwise developments in English include determiner < adjective, adjective < verb, pronoun < adverb, and adjective < noun. The old word class is not lost (cf. Section 13.2 on semantic change). We will look in detail at adjective < noun, particularly evident in recent decades in such words as

(16)   *ace, amateur, apricot, bandaid, cardboard, champion, core, corker, cowboy, designer, dinosaur, draft, freak, fun, genius, key, killer, landmark, luxury, niche, pants, powerhouse, rubbish, surprise, toy, Velcro*

13.3.1   Stepwise Adjective < Noun

Noun and adjective are distinct word classes in English, but crucially they have some distributional properties in common. Both can occur as pre-modifier of a head noun, thus *real* adj. in (17) and *inflation* n. in (18):

(17)   Gold is real money and paper is pretend money. (1974, *OED*)
(18)   That's why inflation money is false purchasing power. (1946, WebCorp)

The word class membership of these two items is securely known from behavior elsewhere. (More problematic is *pretend* in (17), which in other slots is more familiar as a verb.)

Nouns and adjectives also share the possibility of occurring as predicative complement, thus *beautiful* adj. and *fakes* n. in (19), and *fake* adj. in

(20). (The latter must be an adjective, since *fake* does not occur as a mass noun, and only mass nouns and plurals can form a grammatical NP without determiner.)

(19)   . . . a third of the pictures are beautiful, but I think two-thirds of the pictures are fakes. (BNC, EBX 1777)

(20)   His gentleness was fake, ... (BNC, BP7 1362)

The premodifier and sometimes the predicative complement contexts can leave the word class of their filler underdetermined if that word exists both as noun and adjective. Consider *expert* in these examples, uncontroversially an adjective in (21) and a noun in (22):

(21)   Naihe from Ka'u on the Big Island was so expert a surfer that his fellow chiefs grew jealous . . .. (BNC, ASV 62)

(22)   An expert's decision is usually final and binding. (BNC, J6Y 2079)

Note that the adjective goes back to Middle English, whereas the noun use can only be traced back to 1825, probably by re-borrowing from French (*OED* s.v.): I am not citing this as an example of historical change, merely as a clear-cut case of synchronic homonymy for which Present-Day English (PDE) speakers need lexical entries both as noun and adjective. What then is the word class of *expert* in (23)?

(23)   You could do it yourself or get expert help. (BNC, A0 G 1488)

AD/R cannot know whether *expert* is noun or adjective here. This is vagueness, not ambiguity, since the choice makes no difference to interpretation and no difference to constituent structure. Psycholinguists might invoke the concept of 'good enough' processing here (Felser, Chapter 12 in this volume).

I would argue further that the SP/W of (23) need not have decided between two lexical entries for *expert*, although such a claim would pose difficulties for some models of language production. In the same vein, it seems to me arbitrary for a linguist to privilege one classification or the other by assigning either Adj or N to *expert* in (23) (and concomitantly AP or NP to its projection). If a decision is demanded by a linguistic theory which takes unique word class to be universal and basic, maybe the theory should be questioned.

Be that as it may, the kind of analytic vagueness seen in (23) is crucial in the histories of words (unlike *expert*) that start out as nouns but which come to show adjectival behavior as well. The premodifier and predicative slots are what we might call syntactic bridging contexts. When such a word appears there, AD/R may be prompted to regard it as an adjective even if SP/W only has a lexical entry as noun, especially with a referent that is semantically gradable.[3] I consider some evidence of stepwise progression toward full adjective behavior, with examples taken from the list of words in (16).

13.3.1.1   Vague N ‒ Adj Contexts

Frequent use of a noun as an attributive modifier of other nouns may suggest that it is in some way adjectival:

(24)   . . . he reeled through four savage rounds before he got the killer punch . . .
       (1982, COHA)

And indeed the noun *killer* has developed a sense '[v]ery effective; excellent, "sensational"' (*OED* s.v., 7b, 1979–), with later examples than those in the *OED* showing other and better evidence of true adjectival status; see (31), (35), below.

Neutralisation in predicative complement position is possible when NP and AP take the same form, i.e. if the noun is non-count:

(25)   Oh! it was fun! (1872, COHA)

At that date *fun* was most probably a noun, but after the 1960s, when for some speakers *fun* had developed full adjectival behavior alongside its noun use, examples like (25) are syntactically underdetermined – at least for such speakers.

If the word in question is coordinated with a true adjective, as *fun* is with *safe* in (26), then AD/R may well take it to be an adjective too:

(26)   . . . so that the hobby, which often proved fatal, would be safe as well as fun.
       (1966, TIME)

However, coordination is not a knockdown test of category status, as in the right context, different phrasal categories can be successfully coordinated (Huddleston and Pullum 2002: 1326–9):

(27)   a. She was old and a snob. (BNC, CDY 1516)
       b. . . . her father, who is now elderly and in poor health. (2011, COCA)

13.3.1.2   Contexts Weighted toward Adj

Premodifiers are subject to constraints on their relative order: determiners generally precede adjectives (for a systematic exception see (21)), certain types of adjective typically precede others (*a tall friendly old man* vs. ?*a tall *old friendly man, ?an old tall friendly man*, etc.) and modifying adjectives typically precede modifying nouns (*an expensive visitor experience* vs. **a visitor expensive experience*). This last claim gives us a test of adjective status, since if an attributive modifier like *powerhouse* occurs to the left of a clear adjective like *new*, it should be an adjective itself rather than an attributive noun:

(28)   The powerhouse new bestseller from ELIZABETH GEORGE (1996 Bantam Press advertisement, *The Guardian* p. 1 (3 Feb.))

However, once again there are exceptions which suggest that the order-ing 'rule' is merely a strong tendency, since there is no reason to think that *emergency* or *deathbed* are in any way adjectival:

(29)   In the case of an emergency premature delivery . . .. (2008, WebCorp)

(30)   I just got a different feel from the movie/novel – that Padme's deathbed final words were to be understood as more than a mere guess. (2009, WebCorp)

Although N-Adj orderings for premodifiers are much less common than Adj-N, relative order cannot be a sufficient condition for distinguishing adjective from noun.

Modification by *very* provides an indication of *killer*'s adjective status in (31):

(31)   WOOOOOOOW sexy mistress posing in very killer stainless steel custom made 9inch high heels! (2013, via WebCorp)

Inconveniently, the same sorts of modifier – *so, very, too*, etc. – go with proper names (usually taken to be NPs) when the person or place has well-known identifying characteristics, as in (32), though not with common nouns. This weakens the test without vitiating it.

(32)   It's very silly, it's very odd, it's very Woody Allen. Love it. (2008,

www.sofacinema.co.uk/visitor/product/2584-Everything-You-Always-Wanted-To-Know-About-Sex-But-Were-Afraid-To-Ask.html)

13.3.1.3   *Clearly Adjectival Contexts*
Comparison is a property of prototypical adjectives that nouns lack. When a form in transition from noun to adjective develops a comparative or superlative, it has reached its destination. The syntactic comparison of *key* in (33) is arguably a variant of the use of intensifiers discussed just above, while morphological comparison, as in (34), is even more telling:

(33)   So therefore that was more key to you than [. . .]? That was more important to you? (1995, COCA)

(34)   Mirror, mirror on the wall, who's the keyest of them all . . . (2001 www .purplehunt.com/usedclues.htm (31 Jan.))

Some examples raise questions about linguistic playfulness vs. genuine grammaticality, but the more pertinent point is that during a transition, some speakers will be more advanced, others more conservative; see Section 13.3.2.

Given that the distributions of AP and NP overlap in the role of pre-head modification, Huddleston uses the criterion of post-head modification to help distinguish APs (see, e.g., Huddleston and Pullum 2002: 528–9, 552–3, 559–61; Matthews 2014: 10–13). Postmodification is possible after indefinite pronouns and sometimes when the adjective is coordinated or has its own dependents:

(35)   Each track has something killer on offer. (2013, via WebCorp)

(36)   A really lovely tea towel for your husband, wife, girlfriend, boyfriend, best friend, or anyone ace in your world! (2015, via WebCorp)

(37)   Adler believes in filling your surroundings with all things fun and [j]oyful, . . . (2005, COCA)

Certain derivational processes typically build on adjectival rather than nominal stems, for example addition of *–ly* to form an adverb, and hence may serve as a test:[4]

(38)   The concept of his art is inherently hard to put into words. But most commonly (and amateurly put), Turrell's Skyspaces can be described as . . . (2013, via WebCorp)

(39)   Trying to explain the ferry system very draftly. (2015, via WebCorp)

13.3.2   *Partial Word Class Change*

If such words as those listed in (16) simply developed a new adjective use by conversion, and if word classes were Aristotelian categories, then all the adjectival properties mentioned in Section 13.3.1 should arrive simultaneously. But they do not: acquisition of adjective behavior is generally stepwise rather than all at once. We see this both in corpus data and in informant testing, with speakers considering some but not all adjectival properties acceptable. In Denison (2010a: 110–11) I cited some examples of the word *rubbish* that were indeterminately noun or adjective, plus others that should have been impossible for a noun. What was striking was the acceptability judgments the data evoked in a group of students. The more obviously adjectival contexts (comparative and superlative forms, modification by *very*) scored poorly, averaging in the range 1.95–2.55 out of a maximum 5, as against 4.70–4.75 for the vague ones. This was not unexpected for a recent innovation. Yet the use of *rubbish* to postmodify an indefinite pronoun scored 4.6 – in other words, was found to be almost wholly acceptable. This remains to be confirmed by a proper psycholinguistic study, but I have little doubt that the result is robust and is largely independent of prescriptivist influence.

For another, similar case, the following attested examples support the categorisation of *fun* as adjective, but with differing acceptability:

(40) Doing something fun like redecorating your room ... is really interesting biz for a teen who loves being busy. (1951, *OED* s.v. *teen* n.2)

(41) And they are so fun to eat! (1979, COHA)

(42) Walking and looking is boring. Touching is funner. (1990, COCA)

Most speakers I have consulted accept the postmodification of (40) but reject the comparative of (42), while the acceptability of *so fun* in (41) (as opposed to *such fun*) is intermediate and more or less inversely correlated with age. Denison (2013) argues that differential acceptability of new patterns and the stepwise nature of change point to grammatical variation within a population, and that corpus techniques which rely on pooled data can only give limited insight; furthermore, a writer's date of birth may be as pertinent as date of publication. Informant testing with psycholinguistic techniques would be a better way of getting a snapshot of change in progress and teasing out the diachronic significance of word class vagueness. But of course the view of word classes espoused here has synchronic consequences for linguistic theory too.

13.4   Prefabs and Chunking

I use 'prefab' as a pretheoretical cover-term for a ready-made multiword unit. Recall the apparently anomalous word order of *emergency premature delivery* in (29) and *deathbed final words* in (30). The predictable orders might have been *premature emergency delivery* and *final deathbed words*, respectively (and both of these sequences are attested elsewhere), but syntax can apparently be overridden by a conflicting tendency to keep *premature delivery* and *final words* – incipiently lexicalising – as uninterrupted prefabs. Frequently recurring strings are liable to coalesce into prefabs.

The term 'chunking' is sometimes adopted from psychology (see for instance Beckner and Bybee 2009: 30–31 and references there; Ellis, Chapter 6 in this volume). Does a potential prefab behave as a single chunk, or can it be seen as a string of separate words, some of which have individual morphosyntax or recognisable semantics? Or indeed as both?

> We take the view that it is altogether common even for an individual speaker to have nondiscrete syntactic representations for the same word sequence. [. . .] Specifically, syntactic constituents are subject to ongoing influence from general, abstract patterns in language, in addition to more localized, item-specific usage patterns. The foregoing perspective makes it possible that the same word sequence may be characterized by multiple constituent structures and that these structures have gradient strengths rather than discrete boundaries. Our position in this article is thus that constituency may change in a gradual fashion via usage, rather than via acquisition, and that structural reanalysis need not be abrupt. (Beckner and Bybee 2009: 28–9)

Adoption of this position implies the presence of structural ambiguity or vagueness.

The formation of units from a recurrent sequence of free-standing elements plays an important part in both grammaticalisation and lexicalisation, whether the endpoint is a multiword unit or a word or morpheme. Historical change often involves a gradual shift from the component analysis to the prefab analysis (Bybee and Moder, Chapter 7 in this volume). Synchronically, too, there are many cases where language users can switch between the two.

A classic example is the analysis of strings like *in front of, on behalf of*. Quirk et al. (1985: 669–73) and Hoffmann (2005), among others, compare the merits of a prefab analysis as complex preposition with a component analysis where each word is assigned an individual word class. Beckner and Bybee (2009) trace the semantic development of *in spite of* from *OED* data, showing how it diverges from that of the noun *spite* ('grudge, rancorous malice', etc.) and moves toward a concessive sense, with some examples showing 'ambiguity' (in my terms, more like vagueness) between the sense of the noun in isolation and the new counter-expectation sense of the prefab:

(43) In spite of this aimlessness the wealth and empire of England are constantly increasing. (1859, *OED*)

They argue that it is valid and indeed necessary to adduce semantics as well as syntax in working out constituency.

Formalist and structuralist approaches, by contrast, usually insist on the linguist identifying *the* unique/correct/best analysis of a given sentence after weighing up the (non-semantic) evidence. The consequence is likely to be rejection of a prefab analysis if there is any sign whatsoever of autonomy in one or more of the component words, as for example in Huddleston and Pullum (2002: 618–23), where consideration is given only to structural analyses in which the putative complex preposition is not a constituent; any possible unit status for the whole string belongs to semantics or to the lexicon. Historical, psychological and corpus linguistic evidence suggests that such rigidity misses an essential truth about variation and change.

Below I identify ambiguity and vagueness in two different kinds of prefab.

13.4.1   Sort of/Kind of/Type of

Phrases consisting of the so-called SKT nouns with *of* are highly frequent strings: *sort/kind/type* + *of* occurs 46,064 times in the BNC at a rate of 468.54 per million words, equivalent to being among the 200 most frequent word tokens in the corpus.

The broad outlines of the history of SKT were sketched in Denison (2002), though subsequent work has refined certain parts of the picture and more data are available, while the fullest published examination of their syntax in PDE – within the NP at least – has been by Keizer (2007), and of their diachronic semantics by Brems and Davidse (2010).[5] Among the uses which have been identified are

(44) . . . the Canadians had one sort of sovereign, and the British had another sort. (BNC, A69 1471) [referential/binominal]

(45) There was a kind of inevitability about the whole proposal which appalled Alexei. (BNC, G17 1172) [qualifying]

(46) It kind of built his confidence with each successive flask. (BNC, A14 937) [adverbial]

(47) . . . but she should keep those sort of remarks to herself. (BNC, CDY 1447) [postdeterminer/complex determiner]

(48) They are used to all sorts of emergencies, . . . (BNC A2X 404) [quantifying]

(49) It was a grim sort of place, . . . (BNC, A2J 4) [descriptive modifier]

Now, even Huddleston and Pullum (2002: 621) recognise reanalysis in the adverbial (46) type, where *of* can hardly be called a preposition any more. As shown in Denison (2002), modified by Brems and Davidse (2010), it is possible to reconstruct the developmental paths of the various idiomatic uses of *sort of* and *kind of*, and in each case there are intermediate examples which are either vague or ambiguous. Here I give just three, the last involving not just the prefab *kind of* but also the newer prefab *kind of thing*, which has been developing into a discourse particle:

(50) 'Don't worry, a bit of body-popping won't kill me.'
'What on earth is body-popping?'
'It's a sort of dancing. Why, what did you think it was?' (BNC, A0 F 2702–5)

(51) I Answered, That Religion being a design to recover and save Mankind, was to be so opened as to awaken and work upon all sorts of people, and generally men of a simplicity of Mind, were those that were the fittest Objects. (PPCEME, Burnet 1680)

(52) It created this mushroom kind of thing that people stared at. (BNC, AB5 1270)

In (50), *sort* can be head in the binominal construction ('one variety of dancing'), or *dancing* is head in the qualifying construction ('something roughly answering to dancing'). The semantic difference is slight but identifiable, so this is probably best viewed as ambiguity. Example (51) is taken from Brems and Davidse (2010: 188), where it is suggested that a binominal use of *sort* quantified by *all* offers an invited inference of a great number, which can then be semanticised in later examples as the quantifying meaning of *all sorts of*. In (52), either *mushroom* is a modifier and *kind of thing* is nominal, or *mushroom* closes the NP, in which case *kind of thing* becomes an adverbial hedge. Structurally this must be a case of ambiguity, though pragmatically it makes little difference.

13.4.2   Piece of Work

A famous line in *Hamlet* is probably indirectly responsible for a modern application of the phrase *piece of work* to human referents:

(53) What a piece of worke is a man! (1623, *Hamlet* First Folio II.ii)

The definition the *OED* gives (s.v. *piece* n. P4, c.) is:

colloq. (freq. *derogatory*). A person, *esp.* one notable for having a strong (usually unpleasant) character. Usu. with modifying word; cf. NASTY *adj.* 2 c.

In the BNC, 12 out of 190 examples of the string *piece of work* have a human referent. One is the Shakespearean quotation of (53) in modern spelling, one is (54), and the remaining 10 are all preceded by the adjective *nasty*, as in (55):

(54)   'You're some piece of work, Mrs Sutherland, you know that?' (BNC, FPF 1142)

(55)   a. You'd best steer clear of him, Manderley, he's a nasty piece of work. (BNC, HJC 1764)
        b. He was also a member of the Mafia, and he was up to his eyeballs in drugs. Altogether a very nasty piece of work. (BNC, GV6 3045)

(56)   It was a nasty piece of work, done with thoroughly malicious intent. (BNC, K4W 477)

(Example (56) is the only time *nasty piece of work* is used of a non-human referent.)

Clearly, then, we have a prefab, somewhat lexically and semantically restricted, which plays its part in production and reception. However, the precise extent of the prefab is vague. It might, for example, be any of:

(57)   a. *piece of work*
        b. *a piece of work*
        c. *a* ([optional intensifier]) [pejorative adjective] *piece of work*
        d. *a* (. . .) *nasty piece of work*

Any decision is going to be somewhat arbitrary. Such vagueness as to the boundaries and the fixedness of an idiom, though no hindrance to communication, is problematic for purely algorithmic theories of language use where a specific lexical item has to be mapped against an interpretive component.

13.4.3   The Process of Chunking

What we see here is prefabs of different degrees of schematicity, whose parts may be inflected or interrupted (Bybee 2013: 54) – and interrupting elements are freely chosen in some cases, but in others tend to come from a restricted set (as in Section 13.4.2). This supports a usage-based model of language involving emergent grammar, where both prefab and word-by-word analyses play a part, but to different degrees, and the proportions change over time. That, however, is a statistical overview. What of the individual utterance? As soon as we turn our conscious attention to the wording, we are pushed toward recognising syntactic ambiguity, as however potentially present the two (or more) analyses may be, it is hard to conceive of them as **simultaneously** active (cf. non-linguistic perceptual ambiguities like Rubin's vase or the Boring figure). What actually happens in the routine, unthinking speech situation is a question for psycholinguists to resolve. Hilpert (Chapter 3 in this volume: Section 3.6) notes that 'the linguistic competence of speakers must include probabilistic knowledge of variation'. Speakers are certainly (unconsciously) aware of alternative analyses of a potential prefab, and a speculative extension of Hilpert's observation would suggest that the relative strengths of the variant analyses of a given string might also form part of speakers' competence.

Structural ambiguity is not incompatible with semantic or pragmatic vagueness. Such vagueness can contribute to the ill-definedness of chunking in a given utterance and promote the gradual formation of prefabs.

13.5   Structural Change

While chunking is the accretion of two or more separate words or morphemes into a larger whole, schematically A B > [A B] or AB, with concomitant semantic and phonological changes, the topic of this section is the related one of reassignment of constituency, A [B C] > [A B] C, often called rebracketing or reanalysis or, more recently, neoanalysis (Traugott and Trousdale 2013). Here there is a **dis**sociation of B and C. Chunking is involved if [A B] is a recurrent string, though purely syntactic reorganisation is possible too. Reanalysis has been taken to be a central mechanism of syntactic change (Langacker 1977: 57; Harris and Campbell 1995: 61), though Haspelmath (1998) – in a discussion of grammaticalisation – relegates it to a minor role, and Traugott and Trousdale (2013) suggest that it typically applies to 'micro-steps' rather than bringing about wholesale reorganisation.

The consensus among proponents of reanalysis is that structural ambiguity is a necessary precondition. Paradoxically, however, reanalysis may go ahead even if only a few subtypes of the pattern in question are actually ambiguous (Timberlake 1977: 148–50). For example, a change of grammatical relations such as indirect object to subject may apparently need the NP in a particular surface pattern to have no case marking, or at most a neutralised dative-or-nominative inflection, yet in practice it may be that only a minority of NPs in that pattern have an appropriate (lack of) case marking; such a subset of contexts is called the 'basis of reanalysis' by Harris and Campbell (1995: 72).

An alternative to structural change is promoted by Whitman (2001), Garrett (2012) and Whitman (2012), with the claim that most or all alleged examples of reanalysis involve processes other than reassignment of constituent structure: grammaticalisation, analogy, the relabeling of nodes; see also Fischer (2007), De Smet (2009), Kiparsky (2014). Rather than ambiguity of structure, it is vagueness that allows change to take place.

To begin with, however, I couch both my examples in terms of reanalysis.

13.5.1   Prepositional Passive by Reanalysis

The prepositional passive begins to appear around 1200 (Denison 1985, 124–7, 1993: 140–43). Fischer and van der Wurff (2006: 196–7) explain its advent as follows. A general change in word order culminating in Middle English turned English from a V-2/V-final language into what is sometimes called a V-3 or SVO language, after which a PP collocated with an intransitive verb would almost always follow the verb directly, with verb and preposition adjacent.[6] This routine adjacency enabled a reanalysis to take place:

(58)   V [$_{PP}$ P NP] > [$_V$ V + P] NP

Thus, for example, probably through frequent euphemistic use, *lie by* 'lie beside' can develop the meaning 'have sexual intercourse with', (59). The semantic change and concomitant chunking of verb and preposition allows reanalysis (58) to go ahead, weakening or destroying the unity of the PP. Now the string *lie by* behaves as if the following NP is complement not of the preposition alone but of the new transitive composite verb, and so a passive can be formed (60).

(59)   Vulcanus..foond thee lyggyng by his wyf allas. (c1385, *MED*)
       Vulcan . . . found you 'lying by' his wife alas

(60)   Þis maiden..feled al so bi her þi Þat sche was yleyen bi. (c1330(?a1300), *MED*)[7]
       this maiden . . . felt also by her thigh that she had-been 'lain by'

A similar process explains the early advent of passives of such prepositional verbs as *fare with* 'deal with, treat', *send after* 'summon', *speak of* 'mention' and so on.

I have made a case for the new construction to have spread at first by lexical diffusion among closely related verb-preposition combinations (Denison 1993: 141). More generally, Fischer and van der Wurff (2006: 197) observe that the semantics of prepositional verb combinations has to allow an 'object interpretation' of the complement NP. Typical semantic roles for such NPs are Stimulus or Cause with experiential verbs and Patient or Goal with others (Denison 1993: 140–1). Dreschler (2015: 120–25) advocates syntactic reanalysis but makes a case for its acceptability passing almost unnoticed via minimal alteration of several existing structures.

13.5.2   Prepositional > Phrasal Verb by Reanalysis

In one context the polysemous prepositional verb *run over* undergoes an interesting semantic and syntactic change in late Modern English. There are numerous examples in the Old Bailey Corpus (14 million words, 1720–1913) where the literal sense of intransitive *run* involving rapid movement of a person or (part of) a vehicle collocates with an *over*-phrase to indicate path (61), and for quite a few of these the context is a (potential) collision (62):

(61)   . . . we pursue'd him over the Downs, and towards a Wooden Bridge at the Bottom of the Downs . . .. He ran over the Bridge. (The Old Bailey Corpus 1720–1913 (version 1.0, 2013–06–04), 1739, t17390718-10)

(62)   a. it was bent, and look'd as if a Coach-wheel had ran over it. (OBC, 1732, t17320114-38)
       b. I saw a Hansom cab standing at No. 21; I saw it go past our door; the prisoner was driving it – it was going very fast – it knocked the men down and ran over them. (OBC, 1878, t-18780311–341)

Now consider a collision example like (62) made passive – also frequent:

(63)   the man was run over on the legs [. . .] it was through the furious driving – he was knocked down by either the bar or the van, I could not take my oath which. (OBC, 1861, t-18610408–325)

(64)   a. a young woman with a child in her arms endeavour'd to stop the horses; I called to her to let them go, as I saw she would be run over else. (OBC, 1770, t17700711-39)
       b. the prisoner came up and told me I was not to go too fast, for if I did I should get run over – she told me to wait till all the carriages and horses were gone by. (OBC, 1849, t-18490226–699)

There is a potential structural and semantic ambiguity in (64) (but not (63)): either *over* is a preposition referring to the trajectory of the moving vehicle across and above an obstacle, or it is a resultative adverbial particle describing the trajectory of the victim out of upright position, part of a transitive phrasal verb *run over* 'injure with a vehicle', like *knock down*.

In general, Patient or Goal is a typical semantic role for the subject of a prepositional passive (Section 13.5.1), and that association would encourage the innovative reading of (64), where the Patient role is even more marked. Note that another potential source of ambiguity does not seem to be much in evidence in the period of reanalysis, namely active VPs with a non-pronominal NP: active *run over* NP could in principle be ambiguous between prepositional and phrasal verb, but I have found no convincing examples in OBC, only in later corpora.

After reanalysis of the passive to the phrasal verb structure, new patterns become possible:

(65)   a. She [...] got on her bike and roared off. My father tried to stop her by
           standing in her way, so she ran him over and broke his leg quite badly.
           (BNC, HWC 2340)
        b. Someone's going to run a little child over soon because the lollipop lady
           is busy asking drivers to move on. (BNC, K55 9072)

Since *over* follows the object NP in (65), it must be an adverbial particle rather than a preposition.

The period of transition seems to be largely in the second half of the twentieth century. I could not find any clear examples of active *run over* in the required sense as a phrasal verb in COHA until 1949, 1955 and later.[8] Interestingly, the linguistic change is observed around then by Wood (1955–6: 22; see also Parker 1976: 451–2). However, the *OED* has managed to trace the pattern as far back as 1860 (s.v. *run* v. PVi, i). A similar ambivalence between prepositional and phrasal verb analysis, but often with unclear semantic difference or directionality of change, is seen in verbs like *pass, read* in combination with path particles like *by, over, through* and (less often) *about, round*.

13.5.3   *Reformulation without Reanalysis*

Is reanalysis important in language change? Indeed, is it real? To some extent the questions are terminological, but only to some extent. If most reanalysis scenarios can be repackaged convincingly as examples, say, of analogy, there are real consequences. Directionality and context of change may be better explained. SP/W becomes as important as AD/R in such changes – or more important, even. And change is not so limited to the life stage of language acquisition; see here Lieven's argument (Chapter 14 in this volume) against child errors as a source of change, and also López Couso (Chapter 15 in this volume).

Consider the examples discussed above. For the prepositional passive, two crucial ingredients of the new structure are already in place before it appears, namely passive verb participles and stranded prepositions (the latter in relative and infinitive clauses, for instance). Furthermore, some of the actual lexical verbs that appear in the prepositional passive early on are (more) often used transitively and therefore already have conventional passives: *do, let, send, set, tell,* perhaps *tend.* Therefore, the new kind of passive could have been formed analogically rather than – or as well as – by reanalysis in the active. Its structure is vague, related as it is at one and the same time to its equivalent in the active voice, to other kinds of stranding pattern and to other kinds of passive; cf. here the notion of 'serial relationship' (Quirk 1965), and now also Dreschler's (2015) rather different take on multiple resemblances to existing structures.

Turning to the replacement of the prepositional verb *run over* by a phrasal verb, the new structure is well established in the language for other phrasal verbs (including many with *over*) long before the change in question. In the context of vehicle collisions with pedestrians, it is not clear how much of a semantic difference there is between the two passive structures, so that there is at least a case to be made for semantic vagueness rather than ambiguity in the construction as a whole (though not for the semantics and syntax of *over*).

It looks as if the apparently reanalysed structures, or something closely similar, had a prior existence with other exponents or in other contexts. Such extension of an existing structure to new material shows innovation 'sneaking in' where least salient. In my case studies there is a clear semantic or pragmatic component. If this is a precursor of the structural change, then the structural change (or changes, if analysed in terms of micro-steps) would seem to arise from vagueness rather than ambiguity.

13.6 Closing Remarks

I have presented a varied sample of historical phenomena that involve the notions of ambiguity and/or vagueness. A fuller survey could bring in examples from phonology, language (and dialect) contact, grammaticalisation and discourse, to name some obvious gaps, as well as finding space for a more nuanced discussion of grammaticality and grammaticality judgments. Even within the limitations of the sample, however, we see how often it is necessary to consider related changes in different domains – syntax, semantics, pragmatics, chunking, etc. Whether this is an argument for a cascade of effects across self-contained linguistic modules or an argument against modularity is beyond the scope of this chapter.

Change often has a beginning in vague contexts where the old analysis remains viable. This is consonant with the general proposition that less-salient contexts lead change; see here Traugott (Chapter 5 in this volume, Section 5.3), particularly in relation to morphosyntactic change, and De Smet (2012: 605) ('language change is "sneaky"'). If Ellis (Chapter 4 in this volume, Sections 4.1.3.1 and 4.1.3.2), by contrast, associates change with high salience, that may indicate that the kinds of change discussed here are not, or not exclusively, associated with early L1 acquisition.

As for ambiguity vs. vagueness, vagueness is typically an enabler of change 'from below' (in the sense of unconscious change), though other factors determine whether and how the change proceeds. Ambiguity seems to be more peripheral and is often the *result* of change – though it may then prompt further, prophylactic change from above. Change via micro-steps would fit well with a variation-space that is closer to vagueness than to ambiguity. Ambiguity and vagueness represent two extremes of incomplete knowledge for language users, but linguists should engage with them as 'known unknowns'.

Notes

* I am particularly grateful to Anne Curzan as well as to the editors for helpful comments on a first draft.

1. A later, figurative connotation of laziness or freeloading is not explored here.

2. The search string age|race|racial|racially|racist|sex|sexual|sexist|ethnic discriminat* used for Figure 13.2 picks up *racial discrimination* and *race discrimination*, but also a few examples of *racially discriminatory*, etc.

3. On possible semantic gradability in nouns, see Gnutzmann (1975), Huddleston and Pullum (2002: 532).

4. *OED* cites as solitary exception the denominal adverb *partly* (s.v. -*ly* suffix²).

5. Other work on SKT nouns includes Aijmer (1984), Meyerhoff (1992), Tabor (1993), Kay (1997a), De Smedt (2005), De Smedt, Gries and David (2007), Davidse (2009), Denison (2010b).

6. Mentioned also as a factor in Denison (1993: 143). Notice, though, that some early prepositional passives are verb-final, albeit usually in verse.

7. Dreschler (2015: 111–12) is troubled by the fact that (60) is a verse example.

8. Search strings in COHA were '[run] me|you|him|her|us|them over' and '[run] a|the *.[N*] over'.

PART VII

Acquisition and Transmission

CHAPTER 14

Developing Language from Usage: Explaining Errors

Elena V. M. Lieven

14.1 Introduction

In the course of learning language, children make a number of systematic errors. Explaining these errors provides challenges for all theoretical approaches. From the perspective of an innate universal grammar (UG), explanations centre on the problems of mapping between UG and specific features of the language that children are learning. From a usage-based (UB) approach, explanations centre on interactions between learning processes and features of the input, including, importantly, the relative frequencies of different strings (see Chapter 2 by Baayen et al. and Chapter 3 by Hilpert, this volume).

Since diachronic language change involves variability, language-learning children and the systematic errors that they make have been seen by some researchers as the source of that variability. This is particularly the case from a UG perspective, partly because of the idea that the core UG cannot change and partly because of the idea of a critical period for language acquisition after which the parameters of UG are set. However, UG approaches to diachronic change encompass a wide range of different positions. In some, different children may entertain different parameter settings in their grammars, and over time, as the number of children with the changed parameter setting increases, so the language changes (see, e.g., Lightfoot 2006). In others, while children are the source of language change, this occurs in situations of second language learning and multi-lingual contact (see Meisel, Elsig and Rink 2013; Kroch 2001,) rather than with children who are growing up in monolingual environments (for an evaluation of both views see Thomason 2013 and for other approaches that come to a similar conclusion see Hickey 2013; Cheshire, Kerswill, Fox and Torgesen 2013).

Usage-based accounts start from the position that children learn language from re-using what they hear, in smaller or larger chunks. In the UB approach, linguistic categories such as noun, verb, noun phrase, subject and object are not pre-given but emerge as the child constructs language. Early on, children's constructions will consist not only of single words but also of 'big words', i.e. rote-learned, unanalyzed strings of words (e.g. *Whassis?*, *Whatchadoing?*, Dąbrowksa 2000; see also Peters 1983; Lieven, Pine and Dresner Barnes 1992; Bannard and Matthews 2008; Arnon and Snider 2010; McCauley and Christiansen 2014) or of stems with a specific array of morphemes. The development of lexical categories is tied to children starting to develop low-scope, slot-and-frames patterns based on the frequencies in the input. Examples from English are *What's X do-ing?*, *It's X-ing*, *I want a Y*, *That's a Z*. The slots in these patterns are the basis of emergent categories, initially of low-semantic scope such as 'THING' or 'ACTION', but showing increasing evidence of abstraction. In principle, morphological learning could follow the same pattern, with children first developing slot-and-frame templates from which morphological categories emerge. Thus, grammar is learned through a continuous process of abstraction. Constituency and more complex syntax emerge through this process. Frequency at different levels (for instance the effects of type and token frequency) is critical in driving this process, and large numbers of studies, not only for English, have found that frequency in the input is closely associated with what children learn (Ambridge, Kidd, Rowland and Theakston 2015).

A second important thrust of the UB approach is that most or all of early language learning can be explained by general cognitive processes (e.g. working memory, processing speed, the development of prototypes) rather than by any syntactically dedicated (innate) factors. Thus the roles of frequency, salience, processing speed and memory are crucial to UB explanations of language learning and development. In what follows I will demonstrate how these factors interact to generate the systematic errors we see in children's language development.

From a usage-based perspective, errors either arise from the use of a rote-learned string or a low-scope schema in an inappropriate context (e.g. errors such as *Why does he doesn't like peas?* which are suggested to arise from combining a *Why does X* schema with a declarative statement of what the child wishes to question: *He doesn't like peas*), or from the use of an item in a schema with which it is less than optimally compatible (e.g. generalising an intransitive into a transitive schema: *You cried her* for 'You made her cry', for details see Ambridge and Lieven 2015: sections 6.3 and 7.1.2).

During development, there is competition in a network of form-meaning mappings, some target-like and others not. The non-target-like errors are eventually out-competed. Below, I give a number of examples of research illustrating these processes. I will deal with the evidence for variability in early syntactic development in terms of the errors or departures from the adult system that children make. The question is whether these errors could be the source of diachronic change. I will argue, along with many researchers of all theoretical persuasions, that young, monolingual, language-learning children recover from these errors and that, therefore, they are highly unlikely to be the source of diachronic change. I will examine a number of systematic errors made by children and consider the explanations provided for them before returning to the issue of any relationship between errors in language development and diachronic change.

14.2 Errors

When deciding whether or not an error is systematic or, alternatively, can just be attributed to online processing glitches or 'noise', it is important to realise that this depends crucially on the level of granularity at which the error is counted. To give a telling example, Aguado Orea and Pine (2015) analysed two Spanish children's early development of verbal morphology. The study found that, although the overall error rate of person-marking in present tense was low at around 4.5 per cent, there were pockets of very high error rates (for instance, the marking of third-person plural was wrong 31 per cent of the time for one child and 67 per cent for the other). When the data were analysed verb by verb, the error rate went up inversely with the relative frequency of each verb form. Thus the overall error rate for the 58 verbs requiring first-person singular was 4.9 per cent. However, *quiero* (*want*-1st-SING) and *puedo* (*can*-1st-SING) accounted for around 60 per cent of the children's correct first-person usage. Once these two correctly marked (and likely rote-learned) verb forms were taken out, the error rate climbed to 10.4 per cent and largely involved the use of the third-person singular inflection instead of the correct first- or second-person singular inflection. The third-person singular inflection was the most frequent form in the speech addressed to the children and thus, in these early stages, the children were incorrectly using this inflection when they did not know the correct form. Two important implications follow from these results. First, despite an overall low error rate, agreement morphology is actually being learned gradually, with pockets of high error which are related to input frequencies. Second, the level of abstraction at which one counts the frequency of a form is important: Errors are low if one treats AGREEMENT as a category, but much higher when one looks at the system in terms of either marking for PERSON or at individual forms.

14.3 'Optional Infinitive' Errors

An area that has been a focus for both sides of the generativist versus usage-based debate is that of so-called 'optional infinitive' (OI) errors – utterances that lack finiteness marking (e.g. *He going, He do that*). In probably the most influential generativist approach to this issue, the Agreement-Tense Omission Model (ATOM), Wexler (1998) suggested that while children have correctly set the tense and agreement parameters of their language from a very early stage, they are subject to a unique checking constraint in early development, which means that one of these features may be optionally underspecified. This theory makes the prediction that, in languages in which subjects can be dropped ('prodrop' languages), the rate of OI errors will be very low because children do not have to deal with checking the agreement feature on the subject. In support of this, young Spanish-speaking children make few OI errors while German- and Dutch-speaking children, who are learning non-prodrop languages, show very high rates, with rates in Dutch-learning children even higher than in German-learning children. However, Freudenthal, Pine, Aguado-Orea and Gobet (2007) have shown that differential rates in OI errors can be accounted for by the relative frequency of utterance-final, non-finite verbs (Dutch 87 per cent, German 66 per cent, Spanish 26 per cent), which results from the verb-second rule in Dutch and German (see also Wijnen, Kempen and Gillis 2001). The suggestion is that the child's processing mechanism may be differentially picking up forms at the ends of utterances and it is this that gives rise to the different rates of OI errors.

A more recent study by Freudenthal, Pine and Gobet (2010) compared the UB position on the quantitative variation in rates of OI errors in different languages with the 'Variable learning model' (VLM) of Legate and Yang (2007). In this model, the child's system is seen as composed of a number of different grammars or parameter settings, each associated with a particular probability. Relevant data from the input is seen as increasing or decreasing the probability of these competing grammars. The time taken to fix on a +-tense-marking or –tense-marking grammar (e.g. Mandarin Chinese) will depend on the quantitative extent of tense marking in the input. Both the Freudenthal et al. (2010) model and the VLM model account reasonably well for the quantitative differences in OI errors between languages. However, Freudenthal et al. (2010) also found that the particular verbs with which children were more likely to make OI errors were those that occurred more frequently in complex verb phrases in the input, suggesting a specific lexical effect on learning. This cannot be explained in the Legate and Yang (2007) model, which has no role for lexical effects since the model operates at the abstract level of a TENSE parameter.

Theakston, Lieven and Tomasello (2003) showed a similar effect of input in an experimental study in which children who only ever heard novel verbs in complex verb phrases (i.e. without tense marking) were significantly more likely to produce them as OI errors. However, in support of the idea that children are engaged in gradual abstraction, the results indicated that these children's learning of finiteness marking was developing: if they heard the novel verb in the finite form, they never incorrectly produced it as non-finite. Thus, development is gradual and piecemeal: children are not leaping from rote-learned utterances to a fully abstract adult grammar.

14.4   Pronoun Case Errors

In a study with a somewhat similar logic to the Freudenthal et al. (2007) study on OI errors, Kirjavainen, Theakston and Lieven (2009) investigated whether complex utterances in the input (e.g. *Let me do it*) might explain the origin of English-speaking children's first person pronoun case errors, where accusative pronouns are used in nominative contexts (*me do it*). Naturalistic data from 17 two- to four-year-olds were searched for first-person singular, accusative-for-nominative, case errors and for all first-person singular, preverbal, pronominal contexts. Their caregivers' data was also searched for first-person singular, preverbal, pronominal contexts. The data show that the proportion of children's *me*-for-*I* errors was correlated with their caregivers' proportional use of *me* in first person singular, preverbal contexts. Furthermore, the particular verbs that children produced in *me*-error utterances appeared in complex sentences containing *me* in the input more often than the verbs that did not appear in the children's errors.

Of course, there is no direct mapping from *me* used as a subject in the input (which never happens), but children are learning and using lexical strings from the input in which *me* appears before the verb. For at least one of the children, this becomes a productive pattern: she uses the *me* +*V* pattern very often, using verbs with which *me* has not appeared in her input, including some which are tense-marked and would never appear after *me* in adult speech (e.g. *me got, me goes, me can't*). This is interesting since it indicates a process of schema formation in which children initially learn a string from the input and then generalise it to produce utterances which they will never have heard (which will, of course, eventually become of very low or non-existent frequency as the frequency of competing correct constructions builds up).

Pronoun case-marking errors in German are reported as being rare, but this may well be the result of thin sampling. Stumper and Lieven (2011) investigated the acquisition of case on first- and second-singular German personal pronouns (nominative: *ich* 'I', *du* 'you'; accusative/dative: *mich/mir* 'me', *dich/dir* 'you') by one German-speaking child, Leo, on the basis of extensive longitudinal data from spontaneous speech (Behrens 2006). Contrary to earlier results, pronoun case errors in this corpus range from 2 per cent to 24 per cent, depending on the particular error, and show a systematic pattern. On the one hand, Leo has a clear-cut preference for erroneous use of ACC pronouns in reflexive events. Between the ages of 2;7 and 3;0, he repeatedly chooses ACC instead of DAT when referring to himself reflexively (e.g. *Du reibst *dich/dir die Augen* 'You rub yourself*ACC/DAT the eyes.'; 2;7.2). The 'you_yourself*ACC/DAT' error, which comprises both a case and a reversal error, was recorded first followed by a two-month period of 'I_myself*ACC/DAT' errors. On the other hand, between the ages of 2;4 and 3;1, there was a clear-cut preference for erroneous use of DAT pronouns in two-participant events that involve a preposition (e.g. *Ich habe für *dir/dich Getränke.* 'I have for you*DAT/ACC something to drink'). Eisenbeiss, Bartke and Clahsen (2006) explained German children's case-marking errors as being mainly due to having to learn verbs that exceptionally require DAT on the direct object or ACC on the indirect object (termed 'lexical case marking') rather than errors arising from the mis-assignment of the case of a particular phrase structure position: ACC for direct objects and DAT for indirect objects. This is known as 'structural case marking', and children were expected to have hardly any problems with this (e.g. *Ich wasche dich*ACC 'I'm washing you' vs. *Ich wasche dir*DAT *die Haare* 'I'm washing your hair'). However, Leo's errors do not fit this account. In contrast, in his ACC for DAT errors, he is mostly struggling with DAT for recipients in ditransitive events. His errors with DAT for ACC, mostly following the preposition *für*, which never assigns DAT, also suggest these errors do indeed involve structural case. Again, the errors seem to be due to schemas that the child has constructed, in this case possibly on the basis of semantics, which will eventually be out-competed by the correct constructions.

14.5 Competition between Constructions

The idea that constructions might compete and give rise to errors was directly addressed in a recent experimental study. In two corpus analyses, Kirjavainen, Theakston, Lieven and Tomasello (2009) and Kirjavainen and Theakston (2011) showed that the omission of infinitival *to* might result from competition between two constructions involving the verb WANT: *want to + [verb]* and *want + [X]* giving rise to errors of the type *want + [verb]* (e.g. *want go, want eat cookie*) in which the infinitival marker is omitted. Following this, Kirjavainen, Lieven and Theakston (2016) tested this idea experimentally. In a within-subjects design1, they primed 2- and 3-year-old children with *want + X* (e.g. *I want my big bike now*) and *want to + verb* (e.g. *I want to get my bike*) constructions. After each priming episode, the children were asked to produce a sentence starting with *I want* in an obligatory infinitival-*to* context, and the rate of *to*-omission as a function of the preceding prime was measured. Both age groups showed priming effects, but these differed: the two-year-olds provided more correct *want to + verb* constructions after a *want-to* prime. The older children showed a reduction in the provision of *to* after priming with *want + X* constructions and also produced correct infinitival *to* after a *want-to* construction, provided they had both heard and repeated the prime.

14.6 Non-Inversion Errors

One approach to children's systematic errors is to see them as a reflection of an initially abstract linguistic system in which a parameter is not yet, or wrongly, set. The alternative view assumes that many errors arise from the entrenchment of high-frequency strings, which then compete with differential rates of semantic and syntactic generalisation in related parts of the network. An example are the well-attested non-inversion errors that English-speaking children make with the syntax of questions (e.g. *Why she can't do it?*, Dąbrowska 2000). These have been explained in terms of relatively abstract structures. So, for instance, Stromswold (1990) suggests that the *wh*-word is mis-analysed as unmoved and generated in place, and Santelmann, Berk, Austin, Somashekar and Lust (2002) argue that errors can be explained by specific features of English syntax (the main verb inversion of copula BE and DO-support). However, children are significantly less likely to make errors with question frames that are frequent in the input (Rowland and Pine 2000; Rowland 2007). Non-inversion errors occur on low-frequency strings and, crucially, children can show patterns of alternation between correct and incorrect inversion while the system is developing. In an experimental study in which children had to produce questions using combinations of *wh*-words and auxiliaries, Ambridge, Rowland, Theakston and Tomasello (2006) showed that lexically specific strings of particular *wh*-words and particular auxiliary forms could account better for the pattern of errors than either the *wh*-word or the auxiliary type alone (i.e. more non-inversion errors for *who do . . . ?* and *what do . . . ?* than for *what does . . . ?* and *who does . . . ?*).

On the other hand, entrenched high-frequency strings can also lead to errors. Ambridge and Rowland (2009) found that if the children had an entrenched positive question frame such as *What does X?*, they were significantly more likely to make auxiliary doubling errors when the related negative question was elicited (i.e. to say *What does* (+) *she doesn't like?* instead of *What doesn't she like?*). In addition, when a declarative chunk (e.g. *She can't X*) was highly frequent, relative to a question frame (e.g. *what can't*), the children were more likely to use the declarative chunk and put a question word on the front (e.g. *what + she can't X*), giving an error. However, when the declarative string was of low frequency (e.g. *She does X*), this did not happen.

14.7   Recovery from Over-Generalisation Errors

A problem that has received continuous attention over the last 40 years is how children recover from over-generalisation errors (Bowerman, 1988; see Ambridge and Lieven 2011 for a detailed discussion). This is a particularly hard problem because, on the one hand, children must be able to form generalisations in order to use language productively. On the other, they are unlikely to be able to retreat from incorrect generalisations purely on the basis of corrective evidence in the input, particularly since there is often no clear competition between different forms – unlike the case with the *me*-for-*I* errors discussed above. For instance, what would be the competitors with the generalisations produced by Eva Bowerman, *How do you unsqueeze it?* (aged 3;11, coming to her mother with a clip earring on and wanting it removed). Much of the discussion of this type of pre-emption concerns how to determine the distance between the error and the potential pre-empting form which could act as a competitor and replace it (e.g. is '*the man who is/was afraid* a pre-empting form for '*the afraid man*'?, Boyd and Goldberg 2011). Pinker's (1989) solution to the problem of verb argument structure overgeneralisations was based on the interaction of verb meaning with syntax. He suggested that children start with broad-range rules that allow a wide range of verbs to appear in a particular syntactic structure (e.g. action verbs in a causative transitive), thus giving rise to these types of errors. Subsequently, children start to form narrow-range semantic verb classes that define which verbs can alternate and which cannot, and this eliminates the errors. An alternative, though, as it turns out, not conflicting line of research, is based on the finding that frequency is very important in determining which verbs children are likely to over-generalise, with consistent results showing that low-frequency verbs are much more vulnerable (Brooks, Tomasello, Lewis and Dodson 1999; Theakston 2004). Recent research has shown that both frequency and semantics are independently important and that, rather than narrow and discontinuous verb classes, the issue in semantics is the degree of fit with the construction as a function of what the child already has learned, i.e. there is a semantic continuum. Thus, Blything, Ambridge and Lieven (2014) primed children as young as 4;0 to produce verbs of different frequencies with *un*-prefixes. They found the production probability of verbs in *un*-form was negatively related to the frequency of the target verb in bare form (e.g. *squeez/e/ed/es/ing*), as well as being independently, negatively predicted by the frequency of synonyms to a verb's *un*-form (e.g. *release/*unsqueeze*). Ambridge, Pine, Rowland, Chang and Bigood (2013) provide a recent review of this debate.

14.8   Conclusions

Children do indeed make errors in the course of language development. In fact, when analysed at the level of form rather than abstract linguistic category, there are pockets of systematic errors which can be quite substantial. Many of these errors can be analysed as the result of the learning of strings from the input and the abstraction of low-scope schemas from these strings (e.g. some OI errors). Others result from relative frequencies in the input, which means that the child learns some forms much faster than others and defaults to the more frequent form (e.g. third person in Spanish present tense in place of other person markers on less-frequent verbs). Still others result from the blending of two schemas (e.g. some non-inversion errors). These errors co-exist with correct forms and gradually reduce as the correct forms out-compete the errors and as the child learns the more subtle distinctions that assign words to constructions.

This chapter has thus illustrated the role of errors in children's language acquisition. However, addressing the main question of this volume, can these errors be assumed to lead to or be otherwise connected to language change? Many of these errors/innovations/over-generalisations reduce fairly early in development and are all but gone by school age. Kerswill's (1996) survey of three groups (children aged 0–6, preadolescents aged 6–12 and adolescents aged 12–17) suggests that, indeed, younger children are developing toward the norms of the adult population and that it is the older preadolescents and adolescents who are the youngest sources of change, as argued by Labov (1982; see also Cheshire et al. 2013). Bowerman (1988) reports many fewer errors after the age of five, although 'sporadic' errors do still occur up to the age of 12 (see Croft 2000: 49). Also on past tense, Bybee and Slobin (1982) argue that there is a major difference between the ways in which pre-schoolers deal with some aspects of past tense and the ways that school-age children and adults do. They conclude,

> These differences between children and adults have important implications for the relation between child language and historical change. It has often been suggested that children's innovations in the morphological system are the source of diachronic changes in this system; but this could be true only if children's creations survived with them into adulthood. Our data show that, in some areas of English verb morphology (e.g. the treatment of no-change verbs), children's and adults' strategies are somewhat different, and that a real change in approach takes place before age eight. (Bybee and Slobin 1982: 287)

In the most detailed study of one child's past tense and plural over-generalisations between the ages of two to four, Maslen, Theakston, Lieven and Tomasello (2004) show that the over-generalisation rate for past tense shows a major peak between 2;11 and 3;0 and then reduces to zero at 3;11. Interestingly, in this study, there were a small number of errors that, despite massive amounts of evidence in the input as to the correct form, seem to be highly resistant to the exclusive production of the correct form. Although *goed* was only produced for less than a month, this was in the face of very high input frequencies of the correct form, so why did the child persist in this over-generalisation? The explanation given by the authors (as well as by Bybee and Slobin 1982 who found a similar result) is that the present and past tenses of this verb are very far apart and, if the child does not yet realise that all forms of *go* are related, this may account for the error. Over-generalisations of *come* (*comed*) lasted much longer – at least 13 months. *Come* only undergoes vowel change in the past tense and the present tense ends in a consonant that does not carry 'high past-tense salience' (Maslen et al. 2004: 1,327). Note that in both cases, the child has produced a number of examples of the correct form before the errors start to occur. So these are examples where the child has formed a schema which, perhaps partially through self-reinforcement, becomes, for longer or shorter intervals, resistant to highly frequent evidence in the input of the correct form. These errors and the process of schema formation that underlies them may also be characteristic of some adults and second language learners. However, Bybee and Slobin (1982) argue that although some innovations that are found in both child and adult speech can be related to language change, children are unlikely to be the source of these changes. It is more likely that adolescents, adults and second language learners are the source: a conclusion that the majority of authors in this field, whatever their theoretical approach, appear to agree with (Aitchison 1991; Kroch 2002; Labov 1982; Meisel, Elsig and Rink 2013; Kerswill 1996; Ravid 1995).

Young children conform remarkably closely to the language of their environment. Thus, their errors are not maintained into adulthood and therefore cannot become part of the changed language of the next generation (Croft 2000). Language-learning children will, of course, have to be the ultimate propagators of change if they learn innovations made by others in adolescence or adulthood and then maintain them and pass them on to the next generation, but there seems to be widespread agreement by many researchers that there is little evidence that they are the innovators.

Yet may it be possible that language change and language acquisition are related beyond the influence of errors? If we are looking for commonalities between child language development and historical language change, my guess is that these lie much more in the processes involved (i.e. for instance the roles of frequency, salience, entrenchment, schema formation, semantics and expressive need) in driving the ways in which children, adolescents, adults and second language learners innovate in their communicative exchanges (also see the chapters on frequency and salience in this volume). The study of how these processes operate as children build their language may well help to inform how the same processes operate in language change.

Note

1. A design in which the same children are primed with both constructions.

CHAPTER 15

Transferring Insights from Child Language Acquisition to Diachronic Change (and Vice Versa)

María José López-Couso*

15.1 Introduction

For some time now, research has identified remarkable similarities in developmental patterns between diachronic change and first language acquisition in various domains. The existence of such parallels can be interpreted as lending support to the generativist idea that grammar change (as opposed to shifts in language use) is located in the L1 acquisition process (see, e.g., Kiparsky 1968; Lightfoot 2006). For others, by contrast, the child learner does not play such a causal role in change; rather, the attested cases of sequential isomorphism between historical development and child language acquisition result from the operation of similar psychological mechanisms, such as analogy and entrenchment, in both diachrony and ontogeny (see Diessel 2012).

The aim of this chapter is to contribute further to this ongoing debate by examining a number of potential parallels between diachrony and ontogeny in English. Section 15.2 sets the scene for the discussion, introducing recapitulationist views on the relation between ontogeny and phylogeny. Section 15.3 adds diachrony in the picture, presenting some attested developmental parallels between L1 acquisition and historical change (Section 15.3.1) and paying special attention to whether similar or different dynamics are involved in such parallels (Section 15.3.2) and to whether child language acquisition can safely be taken as the locus of change (Section 15.3.3). A comparison of the historical and ontogenetic developments of the *going to*-future is the focus of Section 15.3.4, which highlights the most significant similarities and differences between the two types of processes. The concluding remarks question the validity of a child-centred theory of language change, while admitting that '[w]e can understand certain kinds of change by understanding how acquisition happens, and, vice versa, we can learn much about acquisition by understanding how structural shifts take place' (Lightfoot 2006: 6).

15.2   Setting the Scene: Recapitulation and the Relation between Ontogeny and Phylogeny

Under different formulations, recapitulation has been a recurrent notion in a wide variety of fields, from evolutionary biology to developmental psychology and anthropology. Analogical relations between human development and organic history are already found in Aristotle's *De generatione animalium* and his epigenetic views. However, recapitulationism became a contentious issue particularly with the nineteenth-century German biologist Ernst Haeckel and his biogenetic law. According to Haeckel's recapitulation theory, succinctly summarized as 'ontogeny recapitulates phylogeny', the development of every individual organism (ontogeny) repeats the same sequence of developmental stages as have occurred in the evolutionary history of its species (phylogeny). Though largely discredited during the first decades of the twentieth century (see Rasmussen 1991), the Haeckelian view of recapitulation and adaptations of it were taken up by various scientists in the latter part of the century, particularly by the paleontologist and evolutionary biologist Stephen Jay Gould. Making use of a modified version of Haeckel's biogenetic doctrine and focusing on a number of parallels between ontogeny and phylogeny, Gould (1977) maintains that the relationship between the two developments cannot be denied in biological theory and that '[e]volutionary changes must be expressed in ontogeny and phyletic information must therefore reside in the development of individuals' (1977: 2). Recent evolutionary research has shown, however, that a strict interpretation of the biogenetic law, with its strong Darwinist character, is no longer tenable. A critical appraisal of recapitulation is found in, for example, Langer's (2000) constructivist theory of the evolution of cognition in primates. His findings suggest that the ontogeny of human cognition does not simply recapitulate its primate phylogeny, as testified by the development of specific cognitive specializations in certain species of primates, as opposed to others.

From a rather different perspective, parallels between ontogeny and phylogeny have also been recognized in the field of developmental psychology. Thus, for example, one of the tenets of Piaget's genetic epistemology is that the development of thought in children resembles the evolution of consciousness in humans, so that studies of the former can definitely contribute to a more complete understanding of the latter. In Piaget's words,

> The fundamental hypothesis of genetic epistemology is that there is a parallelism between the progress made in the logical and rational organization of knowledge and the corresponding formative psychological processes. With this hypothesis, the most fruitful, most obvious field of study would be the reconstituting of human history – the history of human thinking in prehistoric man. Unfortunately, we are not very well informed in the psychology of primitive man, but there are children all around us, and it is in studying children that we have the best chance of studying the development of logical knowledge, mathematical knowledge, physical knowledge, and so forth. (Piaget 1969: 4)

Nevertheless, Piaget explicitly rejects recapitulation as the mechanism behind such parallels; rather, in his view ontogeny and phylogeny follow comparable paths of development under the influence of similar external constraints.

Over the last few decades, recapitulationist and analogical arguments have also been adduced by various linguists. Lamendella (1976) and Bickerton (1981, 1990), among others, explicitly defend the existence of parallels between L1 acquisition and the historical development of language. In fact, some of Lamendella's statements are strongly reminiscent of strict recapitulation as described above: 'Most recently encoded genetic information tends to unfold later in ontogeny so as to preserve the temporal sequence in which the new components of the genetic information code were laid down' (Lamendella 1976: 398). Bickerton is slightly more cautious when he maintains that '[t]he evidence of children's speech could thus be treated as consistent with the hypothesis that the ontogenetic development of language *partially* replicates its phylogenetic development' (Bickerton 1990: 115; emphasis mine). A similar perspective is taken by Givón (1979, 1998, 2002, 2009), who presents a number of arguments for a neo-recapitulationist view (1979: 273 ff.), proposing proto-grammars for both children and phylogeny (1998: 93 ff.)[1] and maintaining that 'an analogical, recapitulationist perspective on language evolution is both useful and legitimate' (2002: 35). Interestingly, Givón also incorporates diachrony into the recapitulationist picture, when he affirms that '[i]n each of the three developmental processes pertaining to human language, evolution, acquisition, diachrony – the very same sequence seems to have been involved' (Givón 1998: 102).

15.3   On the Parallels between Diachronic and Acquisitional Developmental Pathways

In Givón's neo-recapitulationist scenario, developmental shared trends between the domains of evolution, acquisition and diachrony can be identified in, for example, the emergence of syntactic complexity. Summarizing the development as 'simple clauses before complex clauses' (2002: 38), Givón explains how simple clauses overwhelmingly predominate both in spontaneous primate communication (see Tomasello and Call 1997) and in early child syntax (see Bowerman 1973). Moreover, in both language acquisition and language history, complex sentences typically arise from the merging of simple clauses. The development of complex sentences from earlier paratactic structures in both ontogeny and diachrony is precisely one of the central arguments of Givón's *The genesis of syntactic complexity* (2009), where the author contends that functional motivations underlie the development of syntax in both L1 acquisition and language change.

Regardless of whether or not some sort of recapitulatory relationship is considered to exist between diachrony and ontogeny, and regardless of whether it is believed that the same or similar cognitive processes lie behind both the diachronic and the ontogenetic development of language (cf. Section 15.3.2, below), the existence of striking parallels between the way in which language develops in L1 acquisition and how languages develop over time can certainly not be denied.

15.3.1   Some Attested Parallels

The literature provides numerous examples of such parallels for a wide range of linguistic domains in various languages. For example, comparable ontogenetic and diachronic tendencies have been attested between the sequence of acquisition of the Brazilian Portuguese verbal endings by children and the historical development of such inflections (see Hooper 1980). Similarly, frequency effects have been shown to operate in a large number of developments both in early child speech and in the history of languages. Thus, for example, high-frequency irregular forms in morphology are more resistant to analogical pressures than low-frequency items, both in child language acquisition (see Hooper 1980: 178) and in processes of language change (see, among others, Hooper 1976; Bybee and Slobin 1982; Bybee 1985; López-Couso 2007; Hilpert, Chapter 3 in this volume).[2]

Modality constitutes a good testing ground for the identification of potential parallels between ontogeny and diachrony. In an analysis of the acquisition of deontic and epistemic modality in Greek and English, Stephany (1986) demonstrates that children express the deontic modal meanings of obligation and permission earlier than the epistemic meanings of possibility and necessity.[3] This ontogenetic pathway agrees nicely with the development of deontic and epistemic uses of the modals in the history of English, as described in, for example, Goossens (1982), Traugott (1989), van der Auwera and Plungian (1998) and Traugott and Dasher (2002: 105 ff.).

One of the most-often cited examples of possible parallels between ontogeny and diachrony is that of the development of the present perfect construction. Slobin (1994; see also 2002: 383–4) shows that the present perfect is first used by English-speaking children in resultative contexts (e.g. *She has caught a cold*), much earlier than in other contexts, such as the perfect of experience (e.g. *She has been to Hong Kong a couple of times*) and the continuative perfect (e.g. *She has known him for five years now*). Significantly, as is the case in Child English, the resultative perfect represents the core meaning of the emerging perfect construction in the Old English period (see Carey 1990), while the other types of perfect constructions develop later in the history of English.[4]

Examples of further resemblances between the ontogenetic and the historical development of grammatical markers and constructions are not difficult to find, both for English and for other languages. Slobin (2002: 381–2), for instance, notes the parallel between the acquisition of the Mandarin Chinese accusative marker *bǎ* in constructions of the type Subject + *bǎ* + Direct Object + Verb and its diachronic grammaticalization from the full verb *bǎ* meaning 'take hold of'. Erbaugh (1986) also observes interesting similarities between the acquisition of the Chinese noun classifier system and its diachronic pattern: in both language history and L1 acquisition, classifiers appear first with single prototypical nominal referents and then extend their scope to class reference.

Enlightening approaches to how first language acquisition can contribute to a better understanding of diachronic processes in the history of English are found in López-Couso (2011) and van Kemenade and Westergaard (2012). The former compares the diachronic grammaticalization of English existential *there* with the developmental relation between deictic and existential *there* identified for Child English by Johnson (1999, 2001, 2005), who explains the process with his theory of 'constructional grounding' or 'developmental reinterpretation'. In Johnson's approach, children use occurrences of one pattern (the 'source construction') as a model for the acquisition of a related structure (the 'target construction'), through 'overlap utterances' which exemplify formal and semantic-pragmatic properties of both patterns (Johnson 2001: 124).[5] Taking Johnson's longitudinal evidence from the CHILDES database (MacWhinney 2000) as a point of departure and drawing on data from the Old and Middle English sections of the Helsinki Corpus, López-Couso (2011) concludes that, as is the case in ontogenetic development, in diachronic terms, *there* is originally a distal deictic adverb, which comes over time to be used in overlap (bridging) contexts, where it performs both a deictic and an existence-informing function; at a later stage, *there* starts occurring in contexts which are incompatible with the deictic reading (e.g. negative clauses), thus testifying to the split between locative *there* and existential *there*. Similarly, van Kemenade and Westergaard (2012) look into the variation between verb-second and non-verb-second word order in declarative clauses in Early English and the decline of the former pattern in the medieval period by using developmental data from varieties of Present-Day Norwegian with variable verb-second orders similar to those attested in the history of English. Their findings show that syntactic factors and information structure factors closely interact in both language acquisition and language history (e.g. in developments affecting rather infrequent word order patterns where inversion is triggered by information structure factors). Their analysis proves that valuable insights can be gained by looking at historical changes from the perspective of attested processes and preferences in L1 acquisition.

15.3.2   Similar Principles behind the Parallels?

Recognizing the existence of these and similar parallels between acquisitional and diachronic developmental routes could be taken as a strong indication that diachrony recapitulates ontogeny. Yet, even though it is certainly tempting to look at some of the developments outlined in Section 15.3.1 as true cases of sequential isomorphism in ontogeny and diachrony, it may well be the case that the contexts in which these developments take place in child language acquisition differ from those found in the history of language and that, in fact, different psychological processes are at work in the two types of superficially similar development.

Slobin (1994, 2002), for example, argues that the L1 learner acquires the resultative perfect first (cf. Section 15.3.1) because it is more salient,[6] more accessible and less complex than other uses of the perfect construction.[7]

This explains why the English resultative perfect is already part of the inventory of two-year-old children, while the perfect of experience or the continuative perfect, being cognitively more complex, normally develop only after age four. By contrast, processes of pragmatic extension and reanalysis, rather than degrees of cognitive complexity, seem to lie behind the diachronic development of the different types of perfect in English. This leads Slobin to conclude that the parallel between ontogeny and diachrony is simply 'illusory' (Slobin 1994: 128) and that 'the dynamics of early grammar formation and the dynamics of adult grammaticization are quite different' (Slobin 2002: 382). In other words, Slobin suggests that the same mappings between conceptual domains are involved in ontogenetic and diachronic grammaticalization, while denying that children simply recapitulate the pragmatic inferences that give rise to the development of grammatical markers historically. Slobin's characterization of the parallels between ontogenesis and diachrony as illusory is certainly appealing, though probably as difficult to sustain empirically as claims in favor of the existence of genuine parallels between the two domains. The lack of direct evidence to actual data from earlier stages of the language, which can only be approached by means of corpus material, represents a serious methodological problem here.

Ziegeler (1997) takes a somewhat different perspective to that of Slobin (2002). For her, the attested correlations between developmental patterns in ontogenetic and diachronic grammaticalization can be attributed to the existence of a common 'semantic space': in both child language acquisition and historical change, grammaticalization makes use of a limited number of basic source concepts (with relatively concrete meanings) for the development of more complex (abstract) and semantically underspecified concepts (see also Bowerman 1985). It is probably not coincidental, therefore, that verbs which children acquire very early across different languages and which are frequently used in the early stages of L1 development (see Clark 1978), such as those meaning 'have', 'go', 'finish', 'want', etc., also represent the most common input for the grammaticalization of tense, aspect and modality markers cross-linguistically (see, e.g., Bybee et al. 1994: 10). An explanation based on shared general cognitive principles is also given by Diessel (2012), who maintains that ontogenetic and diachronic developments are often parallel because child language acquisition and historical language change are driven by similar psychological mechanisms, such as analogy,[8] entrenchment and categorization (2012: 1,601, 1,609–10).

15.3.3   The Controversial Role of Child Language Acquisition
in Diachronic Change

The existence of parallels between child language acquisition and diachronic change such as those outlined in the preceding sections has led some linguists to attribute to children a causal role in the historical development of languages. Though the child-centred theory of language change is most readily associated with generative linguistics (see below), the idea that the child plays a major role in diachronic change has been around since at least the late nineteenth century. Paul (1960 [1880]: 34), for instance, maintains that the process of L1 acquisition is the most important cause for changes in language use. A more explicit defense of the relevance of language acquisition for linguistic change and of the transmission of a language from one generation to the next is found in Sweet (1888: 15), for whom children's imperfect or defective imitation of the speech of their elders is the primary cause of sound change.[9] Similarly, Müller (1890: 75) suggests that the gradual regularization of irregular nominal, adjectival and verbal morphology results from the influence of the 'dialect of children'.

The role that imperfect learning plays in triggering diachronic change has also come to the fore in more recent non-generative linguistics. Andersen (1973), for example, proposes a model of phonological change which distinguishes between two modes of change, abduction and deduction, which apply cyclically in the process of L1 acquisition. In Andersen's model, in the learning process children observe the speech of their models and postulate hypotheses about the laws that govern language, inferring that something may be the case (abductive change) (Andersen 1973: 775); then, they evaluate those abductive inferences by producing new data in conformity with the rules of language (deductive change) (Andersen 1973: 777). It seems, however, that the application of abduction and deduction on the part of children in the process of language acquisition does not always yield the expected output.[10] It is precisely in the production of such deviations from the norms of their elders that, in Andersen's view, diachronic change takes place. Croft (2000: 119) also recognizes the relevance of abduction in processes of form-function reanalysis. In contrast to Andersen (1973), however, he maintains that abductive changes occur in language use, not in language acquisition.

As mentioned above, it is in generative linguistics that child language acquisition is given a more prominent position in explanations of language change. Starting from the assumption that all humans are genetically equipped with a knowledge of universal aspects of core grammar (see

Chomsky's (1981) Universal Grammar),[11] L1 acquisition is considered the locus of grammar change. Halle (1962), Kiparsky (1968) and Lightfoot (1991, 1999, 2006), among many others, stress the relevance of the transmission of grammatical knowledge from generation to generation and of children as the vehicles for structural change. A crucial distinction here is that between Internal or I-languages, i.e. those that 'exist in people's brains', and external or E-languages, which are 'part of the outside world' (Lightfoot 2006: 12). Lightfoot argues that I-languages 'are formed within a critical period, the first few years of a person's life' (2006: 162), when elements of sound structure and properties of basic phrase structure are determined and fixed.

It has been shown, however, that many of the assumptions of the child-based theory of language change are untenable. Serious doubts have been cast on the innateness hypothesis by Sampson (1997), Croft (2001), Dąbrowska (2004) and Christiansen and Chater (2008). Moreover, Tomasello (1999: 41–5), Croft (2000: 44–59) and Bybee (2010: 114–9), among others, have provided convincing arguments in favor of a usage-based approach to language change, which contrasts with the aforementioned generative view of I-language vs. E-language. In usage-based approaches, language use itself, governed by different cognitive and social principles, is the primary cause for language change.[12] This is also the view adhered to here. As Tomasello (2008: 300) puts it, '[l]anguage creation and change result from the fact that human communication is open and dynamic, with interlocutors constantly adjusting to one another in order to communicate effectively and accomplish other social goals'.

In this context, an interesting prediction of the usage-based approach to early language development is the existence of considerable variation across children. This is in stark contrast with the idea prevalent within the generative approach that children's acquisition of grammatical competence follows homogeneous developmental pathways, as predicted by the notion of Universal Grammar. In a comprehensive analysis of the acquisition of auxiliaries, Richards (1990) effectively demonstrates that there exist important inter-individual differences in the process of language learning as regards both the age at which auxiliary verbs emerge and the rate of development. Crucially, Richards's study proves that such variation is closely linked with the input received by children in conversational interaction. Differential developmental patterns across children have also been identified by Schmidtke-Bode (2009) in his analysis of the acquisition of the related patterns *going-to-V* and *gonna-V*, where the relevance of the nature and frequency of the input in the process of L1 acquisition is also stressed.

15.3.4   Probing the Parallel(s) between the Diachronic and Ontogenetic Developments of the Going to-*Future*

In the grammaticalization literature, the historical development of the *going to*-future is considered one of the paradigm cases of grammaticalization,[13] which makes it a suitable testing ground for probing the apparent parallels between child language acquisition and diachronic change.

In diachronic terms, the *going to*-future construction is taken to originate in a biclausal structure involving the main verb *go* in its motion sense, combined with a non-finite purpose clause, as in (1a). At a later stage, this motion-with-purpose pattern is syntactically reanalysed, as shown in (1b), a change which is made possible by the metaphoric and metonymic inference of futurity from purposive directional constructions (i.e. 'he is moving in order to get a beer' > 'he will get a beer in the near future').[14] Reanalysis is made manifest in cases which are incompatible with a purpose reading, such as those where *going to* is followed by state verbs, such as *like* in (1c), as well as instances with inanimate subjects, as in (1d). Once reinterpretation takes place and the construction generalizes to a wider range of contexts, *going to* can be subject to processes of phonological reduction and word boundary loss, resulting in the form *gonna*, as in (1e). Here frequency effects (cf. Bybee and Thompson 1997; Krug 1998; Bybee and Scheibman 1999; Scheibman 2000; Hilpert, Chapter 3 in this volume) and automatization (cf. Haiman 1994) clearly played a decisive role.

(1)   a. [*He is going*] [*to get a beer*]
        b. [*He is going to*] [*get a beer*]
        c. *He is going to like that beer*
        d. *The stock market is going to collapse*
        e. *He's gonna like that beer*

An often-cited early example of the *going to*-future in the history of English is the late fifteenth-century instance in (2) below. Both Hopper and Traugott (2003: 89) and Eckardt (2006: 93), however, rightly acknowledge that the motion interpretation cannot be completely discarded here, since the sequence can also be understood metaphorically as referring to the soul's journey after death.

(2)   *Thys onhappy sowle ... was goyng to be broughte into helle for the synne and onleful lustys of her body.*
                            (1482; Monk of Evesham; quoted from Hopper and
                                                      Traugott 2003: 89)

Similar indeterminate examples of the use of the *be going to*-construction are rather common throughout the Early Modern English period, though unambiguous uses also occur at this time and become fairly common by the end of the seventeenth century (see Rissanen 1999: 223). An example is given in (3).

(3) *he is fumbling with his purse-strings, as a Schoole-boy with his points, when hee is going to be whipt.*

(1628, Earle; quoted from Eckardt 2006: 93)

Interestingly, the construction is already acknowledged as a marker of the imminent future in Joshua Poole's grammar book *The English Accidence* (1646):

> About to, going to, is the signe of the Participle of the future . . .: as *my father when he was about [to] die, gave me this counsell: I am [about; or going to] read.*   (quoted from Danchev and Kytö 1994: 67)

As to the reduced form *gonna*, occasional occurrences are found in the course of the nineteenth century,[15] as shown in (4a, b), though its actual expansion is mostly a twentieth-century development.

(4) a. *Now, Willie lad, I'm ganna gie You twa or three directions.*
(1806, A. Douglas Poems 70; OED s.v. gonna v.1)
   b. *'The Heart o' Mid-Lothian' is gaunna be acted.*
(1856, D. Pae Jessie Melville vii. 76; OED s.v. gonna v.1)

Since the different layers of the construction shown in (1) above are still available in Present-Day English, Schmidtke-Bode (2009) examines in detail the interplay of such layers in ontogenetic development, using longitudinal data of two monolingual American children from the CHILDES archive and taking into account not only the children's production, but also their respective input. Applying explorative Configurational Frequency Analysis (von Eye 1990) and the notion of constructional networks from construction grammar, Schmidtke-Bode (2009) is able to look into the formal and structural similarities between the different production types of *going-to-V* and *gonna-V* in the corpus[16] as well as the developmental routes followed by the various types. For one of the children (Adam), the development can be summarized as follows (Schmidtke-Bode 2009: 520–6):[17]

(a) The earliest type in the child's production is $Gon_{(aux)}$ *to V* (attested at about 2;3), which forms a cluster with two other types, $Gon_{(aux)}$ *V* and $Gon_{(ambig)}$ *V*.

(b) The next cluster to emerge is that containing the first *going* forms (e.g. *I going V, We going V*) either with literal (motion) meaning or in auxiliary function. Within this cluster, the most highly entrenched type is *I going(aux) V*.

(c) The data reveal that at the age of 3;0 the *going*-types of the previous stage increase in complexity in Adam's production by means of the introduction of an inflected form of *be*, the insertion of *to* and the expansion to a non-declarative sentence-type (e.g. *You going V?*; *They going to V*).

(d) Also at around 3;0, Adam starts using the construction with inanimate subjects in the types *It's going V* and *It's going to V*, the latter winning out from 4;2 onwards. These two types, which show the reduced form of the auxiliary *be* (*'s*), belong in a rather large cluster in the network which also comprises the first *gonna* forms in the child's production (also at about 3;0). Unexpectedly, *gonna* occurs with third-person subjects (e.g. *It's gonna V*; *NP's gonna V*, etc.) about 18 months earlier than with the first-person subject (*I'm gonna V*). The latest type to emerge within the *gonna* cluster (at around 4;3) is that involving subordinate clauses (e.g. *(that/if) it's gonna V*; *(that/if) I'm gonna V*).

A comparison of the history of the *going to*-future outlined above with Schmidtke-Bode's (2009) results for Child English reveals a number of striking similarities between the diachronic and the ontogenetic developments. For example, the earliest occurrences of the *going-to-V* pattern in the children's production correspond to cases in which the construction is used with its literal motion-with-purpose meaning, in contexts similar to that in (1a, b) above. Illustrative examples are given in (5a, b) below (quoted from Schmidtke-Bode 2009: 526), where the conversational context suggests the meaning of literal motion in order to achieve a goal. Ambiguous instances of this kind clearly invite a reinterpretation of *going to* as a marker of futurity, before the construction is extended to non-ambiguous grammaticalized contexts such as those in (6a, b), which feature third-person inanimate subjects (cf. (1d) above).

(5) a. *going wash a hands* (Adam 2;8.01)
     b. *I goin(g) wash em* (Sarah 3;0.18)

(6) a. *This going be a dog* (Sarah 3;4.09)
     b. *It's going to fall* (Sarah 3;5.20)

Data from L1 acquisition research therefore shows that ontogeny follows a parallel path to that suggested by diachronic evidence, at least as regards the early stages of development of the *going to*-future, with literal motion meanings preceding grammaticalized meanings. The obvious question which arises here is whether the same mechanisms lie behind the grammaticalization of the *going to*-future in child language acquisition and in historical change (see Section 15.3.2). The answer seems to be in the negative. To begin with, the circumstances in which the two 'parallel' processes of grammaticalization take place are noticeably different. Historically, the *going to*-future emerged as a result of the conventionalization of pragmatic inferences in specific contexts, giving rise chronologically to different layers of the construction. By contrast, in the process of L1 acquisition, children are exposed to the various layers of the construction simultaneously and acquire less-complex meanings (here the literal motion-with-purpose meaning) earlier than extended metaphorical meanings (in this case, the meaning of futurity), which show a higher degree of cognitive complexity.

Be that as it may, certain similarities between historical change and child language acquisition can also be recognized in the later stages of development of the *going to*-construction. Thus, Schmidtke-Bode's (2009) data for the emergence of the reduced form *gonna* in Adam's speech appear to be consistent with the diachronic facts summarized above (cf. (1e)): *gonna* occurs only after the earlier *going to*-type is firmly consolidated in the child's production. The trends identified in Adam's speech cannot, however, be directly extrapolated to Child English as a whole. As shown by Schmidtke-Bode (2009: 529–30), in Sarah's output *gonna* is attested very early, side by side with the *going-to* pattern, certain types of the former cluster even occurring earlier than some types of the latter. It seems therefore that the existence of some kind of recapitulatory relationship between the ontogenetic and diachronic processes of grammaticalization of the *going to*-future has to be dismissed. A likely explanation for the differential developmental patterns in the linguistic production of the two children is found in the nature of their respective inputs: while Adam's input shows very low frequencies for the reduced form, Sarah's abounds with *gonna*'s, especially in the earliest transcripts from the CHILDES archive (Schmidtke-Bode 2009: 529). This seems to lend support to the predictions of usage-based approaches to language change discussed in Section 15.3.3, above, and especially to Richards's (1990) findings that the input frequency of a particular pattern plays a key role in the process of L1 acquisition. Lieven (Chapter 14 in this volume) also reports on the influence of input frequencies on the production of pronoun case errors made by English-speaking children, such as the use of accusative pronouns in nominative contexts (e.g. *me do it*).

15.4 Closing Remarks

The foregoing discussion has shown that the existence of remarkable parallels between ontogenetic and diachronic developments cannot be taken as definite evidence in favor of some sort of recapitulationist view between child language acquisition and historical change. Striking parallels can indeed be established in various domains, such as the resistance of high-frequency irregular formations in morphology to become regular (cf. Section 15.3.1), the emergence of epistemic modal meanings out of deontic ones (cf. Section 15.3.1), the development of the different meanings of the present perfect and that of the existential *there* from the locative *there* (cf. Section 15.3.1) and the directional change in the *going to*-pattern from motion to future meaning (cf. Section 15.3.4). Nevertheless, matching developmental pathways cannot be adduced for other types of change. Thus, while developmental parallels between ontogeny and diachrony are relatively common on the morphological and syntactic levels (as shown by the examples discussed in the preceding sections), it seems that sound change does not produce such good results. Although certain phonetic processes, e.g. the reduction of consonant clusters, bear strong similarities in child speech (Menn and Stoel-Gammon 1994) and in language history (Hock 1991: 80 ff.), other potential parallels are more questionable, and cast serious doubts on the idea that it is the child that causes historical sound change, especially by failure. Starting from Stampe's (1969) conjectures along these lines, Drachman (1978) compares a number of phonetic processes in language acquisition and historical change,[18] and concludes that '*some* kinds of sound change cannot be attributed to learning failures during primary acquisition, while other kinds must remain ambiguous in this respect' (Drachman 1978: 123) and that, therefore, 'the role of primary acquisition in language change seems to have been exaggerated' (Drachman 1978: 138).[19]

Even in cases where ontogeny and diachrony exhibit strong similarities, different processes and factors may lie behind the two types of development and, as a consequence, not all stages identified in the former can be recognized in the latter, and vice versa. Thus, whereas pragmatic inferencing plays a decisive role in diachronic grammaticalization, cognitive complexity seems to be a more relevant factor in ontogenetic grammaticalization. The acquisition of the *going to*-future discussed in Section 15.3.4 provides a paradigmatic example (Schmidtke-Bode 2009), to which those of the perfect construction (Slobin 1994, 2002) and of deontic and epistemic modal meanings (Stephany 1986) could be added (cf. Sections 15.3.1

and 15.3.2). In all likelihood, degrees of cognitive complexity also play a role in other L1 developments mentioned in this chapter, such as the emergence of the more abstract existential meaning in *there* out of its concrete spatial meaning (Johnson 1999; 2001, as referenced in Section 15.3.1). It seems therefore that some of the attested parallels between ontogeny and diachrony are likely to be just 'illusory', to use Slobin's (1994: 128) term.

Further arguments against the idea of recapitulation are provided by the existence of significant inter-individual differences in the process of L1 learning, as shown by Richards (1990) for the acquisition of auxiliaries (cf. Section 15.3.3) and Schmidtke-Bode (2009) for the development of the *going to-/gonna*-patterns (cf. Section 15.3.4). Such inter-individual differences are very likely caused by input differences, therefore dismissing the belief prevalent in generative linguistics that child language acquisition is the locus of diachronic change (cf. Section 15.3.3). Rejecting the idea that L1 learning plays a causal role in language change does not imply, however, ruling out the parallels between ontogenetic and diachronic developments. Although the cases discussed in this chapter question the validity of a child-centred theory of language change, it has to be admitted that ontogeny sometimes 'retraces' historical change and that certain diachronic developments can be more fully understood by observing how acquisition happens, and vice versa.

Notes

* I gratefully acknowledge the financial support of the European Regional Development Fund and the Spanish Ministry of Economy and Competitiveness (grants FFI2014-52188-P and FFI2014-51873-RED). I am also grateful to the editors of the volume and to an anonymous reviewer for their useful comments on an earlier version of this chapter.

1. For Givón, parallel pathways can also be identified in developmental processes in pidginization and creolization (see, e.g., Givón 1998, 2002, 2009).

2. On the relevance of frequency of occurrence in language acquisition, language production and comprehension, and diachronic change, see also Diessel (2007).

3. Similar developmental patterns have been observed also for other languages, including French, German, Polish, Korean and Mandarin Chinese (see Papafragou 2001: 173–4), as well as in creolization (see, e.g., Shepherd 1982 on Antiguan Creole).

4. As shown by Slobin and Aksu (1982), Aksu-Koç and Slobin (1986) and Aksu-Koç (1988), the L1 acquisition of the Turkish perfect and its historical development also follow similar paths.

5. See De Smet and Fischer (Chapter 11 in this volume), who also take structural mapping as a central process in language change.

6. On salience, see Chapters 4 and 5 by Ellis and Traugott in this volume.

7. Other parallels adduced in Section 15.3.1. have also been explained in this way. For example, Stephany (1986) attributes the emergence of deontic modal meanings earlier than epistemic ones in L1 acquisition to the higher degree of cognitive complexity of the latter meanings in comparison with the former.

8. The relevance of analogy in language acquisition and language processing is discussed at length in the chapter by Behrens in this volume, who also pays due attention to similarities and differences between acquisition and change.

9. Jespersen (1922: 162) notes that Sweet in fact showed an undecided attitude, which on other occasions led him to claim that the process of language learning is not the main cause of sound change.

10. On the relevance of errors in language learning and language change, see Lieven (Chapter 14 in this volume).

11. See Everett (2012) and Roberts (2015) for some recent claims against the existence of Universal Grammar.

12. Synchronic innovations through use by individual speakers are to be distinguished from diachronic changes, which involve the spread and conventionalization of innovations in the language community (see Traugott, Chapter 5 in this volume).

13. The grammaticalization of the *going to*-future is discussed in Bybee and Pagliuca (1987), Pérez (1990), Danchev and Kytö (1994), Traugott and Dasher (2002), Hopper and Traugott (2003: 2–3, 87–94), Eckardt (2006: 91–127) and Garrett (2011: 66–70), among many others.

14. According to Fischer (2007: 124), formal analogy with other structures of the type [Aux V] (e.g. *will* + infinitive) also played also a role in the process of reanalysis. On the relevance of analogy, see further the chapters by De Smet and Fischer (Chapter 11) and Behrens (Chapter 10) in this volume.

15. The reduced form was probably used in speech long before its first attestations in the written language.

16. The variables examined by Schmidtke-Bode (2009) include subject type, presence/absence and contraction of *be*, specific form of *go*, presence/absence of *to*, sentence type and meaning.

17. The more scarce data from the other child (Sarah) examined by Schmidtke-Bode (2009) yield a similar picture to Adam's, with the grammaticalized types of the construction emerging later than the literal and ambiguous types.

18. The sound changes examined by Drachman (1978) include weak syllable loss, consonantal distant assimilation, certain types of epenthesis, metathesis, contact assimilations and cluster simplification, among others.

19. On the differences in sound change between child language and language history, see also Vihman (1980) and Aitchison (1991: 174–8).

Bibliography

Abbot-Smith, Kirsten F., and Behrens, Heike 2006. 'How known constructions influence the acquisition of other constructions: The German passive and future constructions', *Cognitive Science* 30(6): 995–1026

Abney, Steven P. 1987. *The English noun phrase in its sentential aspect*. Doctoral dissertation. Massachusetts Institute of Technology

Abraham, Werner, and Århammar, Ritva (eds.) 1987. *Linguistik in Deutschland: Akten des 21. Linguistischen Kolloqiums, Groningen 1986*. Tübingen: Niemeyer

Adams, Michael, Brinton, Laurel J., and Fulk, Robert D. (eds.) 2015. *Studies in the history of the English language. VI: Evidence and method in histories of English*. Topics in English Linguistics 85. Berlin: Mouton de Gruyter

Adamson, Sylvia 1998. 'The literary language', in Romaine (ed.), pp. 589–692

Adelman, James, Brown, Gordon D. A., and Quesada, José F. 2006. 'Contextual diversity, not word frequency, determines word-naming and lexical decision times', *Psychological Science*, 17.9: 814–23

Aguado-Orea, Javier, and Pine, Julian 2015. 'Comparing different models of the development of verb inflection in early child Spanish', *PloS One* 10(3): e0119613

Ahlqvist, Anders (ed.) 1982. *Papers from the 5th International Conference on Historical Linguistics*. Amsterdam and Philadelphia: John Benjamins

Aijmer, Karin 1984. '"Sort of" and "kind of" in English conversation', *Studia Linguistica* 38: 118–28

Aijmer, Karin 1996a. *Conversational routines in English: Convention and creativity*. New York: Longman

Aijmer, Karin 1996b. 'I think – an English modal particle', in Swan and Westvik (eds.), pp. 1–47

Aitchison, Jean 1991. *Language change: Progress or decay?* Cambridge: Cambridge University Press

Aitchison, Jean. 2003. 'Psycholinguistic perspectives on language change', in Joseph and Janda (eds.), pp. 736–43

Akhtar, Nameera 1999. 'Acquiring basic word order: Evidence for data-driven learning of syntactic structure', *Journal of Child Language* 26(2): 339–56

Aksu-Koç, Ayhan 1988. *The acquisition of aspect and modality: The case of past perfect in Turkish*. Cambridge: Cambridge University Press

Aksu-Koç, Ayhan, and Slobin, Dan I. 1986. 'A psychological account of the development and use of evidentials in Turkish', in Chafe and Nichols (eds.), pp. 159–67

Allan, Keith, and Jaszczolt, Kasia M. (eds.) 2012. *The Cambridge handbook of pragmatics*. Cambridge: Cambridge University Press

Allan, Lorraine G. 1980. 'A note on measurement of contingency between two binary variables in judgment tasks', *Bulletin of the Psychonomic Society* 15(3): 147–49

Allerton, David J. 2009. 'Tag questions', in Rohdenburg and Schlüter (eds.), pp. 306–23

Altmann, Eduardo G., Pierrehumbert, Janet B., and Motter, Adilson E. 2009. 'Beyond word frequency: Bursts, lulls and scaling in the temporal distributions of words', *PLoS ONE* 4(11): e7678

Altmann, Gerry T. M. (ed.) 1990. *Cognitive models of speech processing: Psycholinguistic and computational perspectives*. Cambridge, MA: The MIT Press

Altmann, Gerry T. M. 1998. 'Ambiguity in sentence processing', *Trends in Cognitive Sciences* 2(4): 146–52

Altmann, Gerry T. M., and Kamide, Yuki 1999. 'Incremental interpretation at verbs: Restricting the domain of subsequent reference', *Cognition* 73(3): 247–64

Altmann, Gerry T. M., and Steedman, Mark 1988. 'Interaction with context during human sentence processing', *Cognition* 30(3): 191–238

Ambridge, Ben, Kidd, Evan J., Rowland, Caroline F., and Theakston, Anna L. 2015. 'The ubiquity of frequency effects in first language acquisition', *Journal of Child Language* 42(2): 239–73

Ambridge, Ben, and Lieven, Elena V. M. 2011. *Child language acquisition: Contrasting theoretical approaches*. Cambridge: Cambridge University Press

Ambridge, Ben, and Lieven, Elena V. M. 2015. 'A constructivist account of child language acquisition', in MacWhinney and O'Grady (eds.), pp. 478–510

Ambridge, Ben, Pine, Julian M., Rowland, Caroline F., Chang, Franklin, and Bidgood, Amy 2013. 'The retreat from overgeneralization in child language acquisition: Word learning, morphology and verb argument structure', *Wiley Interdisciplinary Reviews Cognitive Science* 4(1): 47–62

Ambridge, Ben, and Rowland, Caroline F. 2009. 'Predicting children's errors with negative questions: Testing a schema-combination account', *Cognitive Linguistics* 20(2): 225–66

Ambridge, Ben, Rowland, Caroline F., Theakston, Anna L., and Tomasello, Michael 2006. 'Comparing different accounts of inversion errors in children's non-subject *wh*-questions: "What experimental data can tell us?"', *Journal of Child Language* 33(3): 519–57

Andersen, Henning 1973. 'Abductive and deductive change', *Language* 49(4): 765–93

Andersen, Henning 2001a. 'Actualization and the (uni)directionality of change', in Andersen (ed.), pp. 225–48

Andersen, Henning (ed.) 2001b. *Actualization: Linguistic change in progress*. Amsterdam: John Benjamins

Andersen, Roger W. 1984. 'The one-to-one principle of interlanguage construction', *Language Learning* 34(4): 77–95

Anderson, John R. 1982. 'Acquisition of cognitive skill', *Psychological Review* 89(4): 369–406

Anderson, John R. 1983. *The architecture of cognition*. Cambridge, MA: Harvard University Press

Anderson, John R. 1990. *The adaptive character of thought*. Hillsdale, NJ: Lawrence Erlbaum

Anderson, John R. 1991. 'Is human cognition adaptive?', *Behavioral and Brain Sciences* 14(3): 471–517

Anderson, John R. 1992. 'Automaticity and the ACT theory', *American Journal of Psychology* 105(2): 165–80

Anderson, John R. 1996. 'ACT: A simple theory of complex cognition', *American Psychologist* 51(4): 355–65

Anderson, John R. 2000. *Cognitive psychology and its implications*. 5th edition. New York: W.H. Freeman

Anderson, John R. 2009. *Cognitive psychology and its implications*. 7th edition. New York: Worth Publishers

Andronis, Mary, Debenport, Erin, Pycha, Anne, and Yoshimura, Keiko (eds.) 2002. *Proceedings of the 38th Meeting of the Chicago Linguistics Society*. Chicago: Chicago Linguistic Society

Anshen, Frank, and Aronoff, Mark 1999. 'Using dictionaries to study the mental lexicon', *Brain and Language* 68(1): 16–26

Anttila, Raymond 2003. 'Analogy: The warp and woof of cognition', in Joseph and Janda (eds.), pp. 425–40

Arcodia, Giorgio Francesco 2007. 'Chinese: A language of compound words?', in Montermini, Boyé and Hathout (eds.), pp. 79–90

Ariel, Mira 1990. *Accessing noun-phrase antecedents*. London: Routledge

Arnon, Inbal, Casillas, Marisa, Kurumada, Chigusa, and Estigarribia, Bruno (eds.) 2014. *Language in interaction: Studies in honor of Eve V. Clark*. Amsterdam: Benjamins

Arnon, Inbal, and Snider, Neal 2010. 'More than words: Frequency effects for multi-word phrases', *Journal of Memory and Language* 62(1): 67–82

Aronoff, Mark 1976. *Word formation in generative grammar*. Cambridge, MA: The MIT Press

Aslin, Richard N., and Newport, Elissa L. 2012. 'Statistical learning: From acquiring specific items to forming general rules', *Current Directions in Psychological Science* 21(3): 170–76

Auer, Peter 2014. 'Anmerkungen zum Salienzbegriff in der Soziolinguistik', *Linguistik Online* 66(4). http://dx.doi.org/10.13092/lo.66.1569 [accessed April 14, 2016]

Auer, Peter, Hinskens, Frans, and Kerswill, Paul (eds.) 2005. *Dialect change: Convergence and divergence in European languages*. Cambridge: Cambridge University Press

Axmaker, Shelley, Jaisser, Annie, and Singmaster, Helen (eds.) 1988. *Berkeley Linguistics Society 14: General session and parasession on grammaticalization.* Berkeley, CA: Berkeley Linguistics Society

Aylett, Matthew, and Turk, Alice 2004. 'The smooth signal redundancy hypothesis: A functional explanation for relationships between redundancy, prosodic prominence and duration in spontaneous speech', *Language and Speech* 47(1): 31–56

Aylett, Matthew, and Turk, Alice 2006. 'Language redundancy predicts syllabic duration and the spectral characteristics of vocalic syllable nuclei', *The Journal of the Acoustical Society of America* 119(5): 3048–58

Baars, Bernard J. 1997. 'In the theatre of consciousness: Global workspace theory, a rigorous scientific theory of consciousness', *Journal of Consciousness Studies* 4(4): 292–309

Baayen, R. Harald 1993. 'On frequency, transparency and productivity', in Booij and van Marle (eds.), pp. 181–208

Baayen, R. Harald 1994. 'Productivity in language production', *Language and Cognitive Processes* 9(3): 447–69

Baayen, R. Harald 2005. 'Morphological productivity', in Köhler, Altmann and Piotrowski (eds.), pp. 243–56

Baayen, R. Harald 2011a. 'Corpus linguistics and naive discriminative learning', *Brazilian Journal of Applied Linguistics* 11(2): 295–328

Baayen, R. Harald 2011b. 'Demythologizing the word frequency effect: A discriminative learning perspective', *The Mental Lexicon* 5(3): 436–61

Baayen, R. Harald 2014. 'Multivariate statistics', in Podesva and Sharma (eds.), pp. 337–72

Baayen, R. Harald, Hendrix, Peter, and Ramscar, Michael 2013. 'Sidestepping the combinatorial explosion: Towards a processing model based on discriminative learning', *Language and Speech* 56(3): 329–47

Baayen, R. Harald, Kuperman, Victor, and Bertram, Raymond 2010. 'Frequency effects in compound processing', in Scalise and Vogel (eds.), pp. 257–270

Baayen, R. Harald, Milin, Petar, Durdević, Dusica Filipović, Hendrix, Peter, and Marelli, Marco 2011. 'An amorphous model for morphological processing in visual comprehension based on naive discriminative learning', *Psychological Review* 118(3): 438–81

Baayen, R. Harald, Milin, Petar, and Ramscar, Michael 2015. 'Frequency in lexical processing', *Aphasiology* 30(11): 1174–220

Baayen, R. Harald, and Ramscar, Michael 2015. 'Abstraction, storage and naive discriminative learning', in Dąbrowska and Divjak (eds.), pp. 99–120

Baayen, R. Harald, Shaoul, Cyrus, Willits, Jon, and Ramscar, Michael 2016. 'Comprehension without segmentation: A proof of concept with naive discriminative learning', *Language, Cognition, and Neuroscience* 31(1): 106–28

Baayen, R. Harald, van Halteren, Hans, and Tweedie, Fiona 1996. 'Outside the cave of shadows: Using syntactic annotation to enhance authorship attribution', *Literary and Linguistic Computing* 11(3): 121–31

Bach, Emmon, and Harms, Robert T. (eds.) 1968. *Universals in linguistic theory*. New York: Holt, Rinehart and Winston

Baddeley, Alan D. 1997. *Human memory: Theory and practice*. Hove: Psychology Press

Bader, Markus, and Lasser, Ingeborg 1994. 'German verb-final clauses and sentence processing: Evidence for immediate attachment', in Clifton, Frazier and Rayner (eds.), pp. 225–42

Bailey, Ashlee C., Moore, Kevin E., and Moxley, Jeri L. (eds.) 1997. *Proceedings of the 23rd Annual Meeting of the Berkeley Linguistics Society, February 14–17, 1997*. Berkeley, CA: Berkeley Linguistics Society

Bailey, Nathalie, Madden, Carolyn, and Krashen, Stephen D. 1974. 'Is there a "natural sequence" in adult second language learning?', *Language Learning* 24(2): 235–43

Baker, Carl L. 1995. 'Contrast, discourse prominence, and intensification, with special reference to locally free reflexives in British English', *Language* 71(1): 63–101

Balota, David A., and Chumbley, James I. 1984. 'Are lexical decisions a good measure of lexical access? The role of word frequency in the neglected decision stage', *Journal of Experimental Psychology: Human Perception and Performance* 10 (3): 340–57

Balota, David A., Yap, Melvin J., Cortese, Michael J., Hutchison, Keith I., Kessler, Brett, Loftis, Bjorn, Neely, James H., Nelson, Douglas L., Simpson, Greg B., and Treiman, Rebecca 2007. 'The English lexicon project', *Behavior Research Methods* 39(3): 445–59

Baltin, Mark, and Collins, Chris (eds.) 2001. *The handbook of contemporary syntactic theory*. Oxford: Blackwell

Bannard, Colin, and Matthews, Danielle 2008. 'Stored word sequences in language learning: The effect of familiarity on children's repetition of four-word combinations', *Psychological Science* 19(3): 241–48

Barabási, Albert-László 2005. 'The origin of bursts and heavy tails in human dynamics', *Nature Reviews Neuroscience* 435(7039): 207–11

Barabási, Albert-László 2010. *Bursts: The hidden patterns behind everything we do, from your e-mail to bloody crusades*. London: Penguin

Bardovi-Harlig, Kathleen 2000. *Tense and aspect in second language acquisition: Form, meaning and use*. Oxford: Blackwell

Barðdal, Jóhanna 2008. *Productivity: Evidence from case and argument structure in Icelandic*. Amsterdam: Benjamins

Barlow, Michael, and Kemmer, Suzanne (eds.) 2000. *Usage-based models of language*. Stanford, CA: CSLI Publications

Baron, Naomi S. 1977. *Language acquisition and historical change*. Amsterdam: North-Holland

Barry, Christopher, and Seymour, Philip H. 1988. 'Lexical priming and sound-to-spelling contingency effects in nonword spelling', *Quarterly Journal of Experimental Psychology* 40(1): 5–40

Barsalou, Lawrence W. 1999. 'Perceptual symbol systems', *Behavioral and Brain Sciences* 22(4): 577–660

Barsalou, Lawrence W. 2008. 'Grounded cognition', *Annual Review of Psychology* 59: 617–45

Barsalou, Lawrence W., Huttenlocher, Janellen, and Lamberts, Koen 1998. 'Basing categorization on individuals and events', *Cognitive Psychology* 36(3): 203–72

Bartlett, Frederic C. 1967. *Remembering: A study in experimental and social psychology*. Cambridge: Cambridge University Press [1st edition 1932]

Bates, Elizabeth, and Goodman, Judith C. 1997. 'On the inseparability of grammar and the lexicon: Evidence from acquisition, aphasia and real-time processing', *Language and Cognitive Processes* 12(5–6): 507–86

Bates, Elizabeth, and MacWhinney, Brian 1987. 'Competition, variation, and language learning', in MacWhinney (ed.), pp. 157–93

Bates, Elizabeth, MacWhinney, Brian, Caselli, Cristina, Devescovi, Antonella, Natale, Francesco, and Venza, Valeria 1984. 'A crosslinguistic study of the development of sentence interpretation strategies', *Child Development* 55(2): 341–54

Bauer, Laurie 2001. *Morphological productivity*. Cambridge: Cambridge University Press

Bavin, Edith L. 1995. 'The obligation modality in Western Nilotic languages', in Bybee and Fleischman (eds.), pp. 107–33

Bayley, Robert, Cameron, Richard, and Lucas, Ceil (eds.) 2013. *The Oxford handbook of sociolinguistics*. Oxford: Oxford University Press

Beals, Katharine (ed.) 1993. *Papers from the 29th regional meeting of the Chicago Linguistic Society*. Chicago: Chicago Linguistic Society

Becker, Angelika, and Veenstra, Tonjes 2003. 'Creole prototypes as basic varieties and inflectional morphology', in Dimroth and Starren (eds.), pp. 235–66

Beckett, Samuel 1954. *Waiting for Godot*. New York: Grove Press

Beckner, Clay, Blythe, Richard, Bybee, Joan L., Christiansen, Morten H., Croft, William, Ellis, Nick C., Holland, John, Ke, Jinyun, Larsen-Freeman, Diane, and Schoenemann, Tom 2009. 'Language is a complex adaptive system: Position paper', *Language Learning* 59(s1): 1–26

Beckner, Clay, and Bybee, Joan L. 2009. 'A usage-based account of constituency and reanalysis', *Language Learning* 59(s1): 27–46

Behaghel, Otto 1909. 'Beziehungen zwischen Umfang und Reihenfolge von Satzgliedern', *Indogermanische Forschungen* 25: 110–42

Behaghel, Otto 1923–1932. *Deutsche Syntax*. 4 vols. Heidelberg: Winter

Behrens, Heike 2002. 'Learning multiple regularities: Evidence from overgeneralization errors in the German plural', in Skarabela, Fish and Do (eds.), pp. 72–83

Behrens, Heike 2006. 'The input-output relationship in first language acquisition', *Language and Cognitive Processes* 21(1–3): 2–24

Behrens, Heike (ed.) 2008. *Corpora in language acquisition research: History, methods, perspectives*. Amsterdam: John Benjamins

Behrens, Heike 2009. 'Usage-based and emergentist approaches to language acquisition', *Linguistics [Special Issue: Current Approaches to Language Learning]* 47(2): 383–411

Behrens, Heike 2011. 'Cues to form and function in the acquisition of German number and case inflection', in Clark and Arnon (eds.), pp. 35–51

Behrens, Heike, and Pfänder, Stefan (eds.) 2016. *Experience counts: Frequency effects in language.* Berlin: Mouton de Gruyter

Bello, Paul, Guarini, Marcello, McShane, Marjorie, and Scassellati, Brian (eds.) 2014. *Proceedings of the 36th Annual Conference of the Cognitive Science Society.* Austin, TX: Cognitive Science Society

Benveniste, Émile 1968. 'Mutations of linguistic categories', in Lehmann and Malkiel (eds.), pp. 85–94

Bergen, Benjamin, and Chang, Nancy 2013. 'Embodied construction grammar', in Hoffmann and Trousdale (eds.), pp. 168–90

Bergs, Alex, and Pentrel, Maike 2015. 'Ælc þara þe þas min word gehierþ and þa wyrcþ . . .: Psycholinguistic perspectives on early Englishes', in Adams, Brinton and Fulk (eds.), pp. 249–76

Bergs, Alexander, and Brinton, Laurel J. (eds.) 2012. *English historical linguistics. An international handbook*, vol. 2. Berlin and New York: Mouton de Gruyter

Bergs, Alexander, and Diewald, Gabriele (eds.) 2008. *Constructions and language change.* Berlin and New York: Mouton de Gruyter

Bernolet, Sarah, and Hartsuiker, Robert J. 2010. 'Does verb bias modulate syntactic priming?', *Cognition* 114(3): 455–61

Bernolet, Sarah, Hartsuiker, Robert J., and Pickering, Martin J. 2007. 'Shared syntactic representations in bilinguals: Evidence for the role of word-order repetition', *Journal of Experimental Psychology: Learning, Memory, and Cognition* 33(5): 931–49

Bernolet, Sarah, Hartsuiker, Robert J., and Pickering, Martin J. 2009. 'Persistence of emphasis in language production: A cross-linguistic approach', *Cognition* 112 (2): 300–17

Bernolet, Sarah, Hartsuiker, Robert J., and Pickering, Martin J. 2012. 'Effects of phonological feedback on the selection of syntax: Evidence from between-language syntactic priming', *Bilingualism: Language and Cognition* 15(3): 503–16

Bernolet, Sarah, Hartsuiker, Robert J., and Pickering, Martin J. 2013. 'From language-specific to shared syntactic representations: The influence of second language proficiency on syntactic sharing in bilinguals', *Cognition* 127(3): 287–306

Berwick, Robert, and Weinberg, Amy 1984. *The grammatical basis of linguistic performance: Language use and acquisition.* Cambridge, MA: The MIT Press

Biber, Douglas, Johansson, Stig, Leech, Geoffrey, Conrad, Susan, and Finegan, Edward 1999. *Longman grammar of spoken and written English.* Harlow, UK: Pearson Education

Bickerton, Derek 1981. *Roots of language.* Ann Arbor: Karoma Publishers

Bickerton, Derek 1990. *Language and species.* Chicago: University of Chicago Press

Bien, Heidrun, Baayen, R. Harald, and Levelt, Willem J. M. 2011. 'Frequency effects in the production of Dutch deverbal adjectives and inflected verbs', *Language and Cognitive Processes* 27(4–6): 683–715

Bird, Steven 2006. 'NLTK: The natural language toolkit'. *Proceedings of the COLING/ACL 2006 Interactive Presentation Sessions, Sydney, July 2006.* Association for Computational Linguistics, pp. 69–72

Bird, Steven, Klein, Ewan, and Loper, Edward 2009. *Natural language processing with Python.* Sebastopol, CA: O'Reilly Media, Inc.

Bisang, Walter, Himmelmann, Nikolaus P., and Wiemer, Björn (eds.) 2004. *What makes grammaticalization – A look from its fringes and its components.* Berlin and New York: Mouton de Gruyter

Bittner, Dagmar, and Köpcke, Klaus-Michael 2001. 'Acquisition of the German plural markings: A case study in natural and cognitive morphology', in Schaner-Wolles, Rennison and Neubarth (eds.), pp. 47–58

Black, Abraham H., and Prokasy, William F. (eds.) 1972. *Classical conditioning II: Current theory and research.* New York: Appleton-Century-Crofts

Blumenthal-Dramé, Alice 2012. *Entrenchment in usage-based theories: What corpus data do and do not reveal about the mind.* Berlin and New York: Mouton de Gruyter

Blything, Ryan P., Ambridge, Ben, and Lieven, Elena V. M. 2014. 'Children use statistics and semantics in the retreat from overgeneralization', *PLoS One* 9.10: e110009

Bock, J. Kathryn 1986. 'Syntactic persistence in language production', *Cognitive Psychology* 18(3): 355–87

Bock, J. Kathryn, Dell, Gary S., Chang, Franklin, and Onishi, Kristine H. 2007. 'Persistent structural priming from language comprehension to language production', *Cognition* 104(3): 437–58

Bock, J. Kathryn, and Ferreira, Victor S. 2014. 'Syntactically speaking', in Goldrick, Ferreira and Miozzo (eds.), pp. 21–46

Bock, J. Kathryn, and Griffin, Zenzi M. 2000. 'The persistence of structural priming: Transient activation or implicit learning?', *Journal of Experimental Psychology: General* 129(2): 177–92

Bock, J. Kathryn, and Levelt, Willem J. M. 1994. 'Language production: Grammatical encoding', in Gernsbacher (ed.), pp. 741–79

Bod, Rens 2009. 'From exemplar to grammar: A probabilistic analogy-based model of language learning', *Cognitive Science* 33(5): 752–93

Bod, Rens, Hay, Jennifer, and Jannedy, Stefanie (eds.) 2003. *Probabilistic linguistics.* Cambridge, MA: The MIT Press

Bond, Zinny 1999. *Slips of the ear: Errors in the perception of casual conversation.* New York: Academic Press

Booij, Geert E., and van Marle, Jaap (eds.) 1993. *Yearbook of morphology.* Dordrecht: Kluwer Academic Publishers

Bornschein, Matthias, and Butt, Matthias 1987. 'Zum Status des -s- Plurals im gegenwärtigen Deutsch', in Abraham and Århammar (eds.), pp. 135–54

Bouma, Gerlof, Krämer, Irene, and Zwarts, Joost (eds.) 2007. *Cognitive foundations of interpretation.* Amsterdam: Royal Netherlands Academy of Science

Bowerman, Melissa 1973. *Early syntactic development.* Cambridge: Cambridge University Press

Bowerman, Melissa 1985. 'What shapes children's grammars?', in Slobin (ed.), pp. 1257–319

Bowerman, Melissa 1988. 'The "no negative evidence" problem: How do children avoid constructing an overgeneral grammar?', in Hawkins (ed.), pp. 73–101

Bowerman, Melissa, and Brown, Penelope 2006a. 'Introduction', in Bowerman and Brown (eds.), pp. 1–26

Bowerman, Melissa, and Brown, Penelope (eds.) 2006b. *Crosslinguistic perspectives on argument structure: Implications for language acquisition*. Mahwah, NJ: Erlbaum

Bowerman, Melissa, and Choi, Soonja 2003. 'Space under construction: Language specific spatial categorization in first language acquisition', in Gentner and Goldin-Meadow (eds.), pp. 387–427

Bowern, Claire, and Evans, Bethwyn (eds.) 2014. *The Routledge handbook of historical linguistics*. London and New York: Routledge

Boyd, Jeremy K., and Goldberg, Adele E. 2011. 'Learning what not to say: The role of statistical preemption and categorization in a-adjective production', *Language* 87(1): 55–83

Boye, Kasper, and Harder, Peter 2012. 'A usage-based theory of grammatical status and grammaticalization', *Language* 88(1): 1–44

Braine, Martin D. S., and Bowerman, Melissa 1976. 'Children's first word combinations', *Monographs of the Society for Research in Child Development* 41(1): 1–104

Brandt, Silke, Kidd, Evan, Lieven, Elena V. M., and Tomasello, Michael 2009. 'The discourse bases of relativization: An investigation of young German and English-speaking children's comprehension of relative clauses', *Cognitive Linguistics* 20(3): 539–70

Branigan, Holly P., Pickering, Martin J., and Cleland, Alexandra A. 2000. 'Syntactic co-ordination in dialogue', *Cognition* 75(2): B13–B25

Branigan, Holly P., Pickering, Martin J., McLean, Janet F., and Cleland, Alexandra A. 2007. 'Syntactic alignment and participant role in dialogue', *Cognition* 104(2): 163–97

Branigan, Holly P., Pickering, Martin J., Pearson, Jamie, McLean, Janet F., and Brown, Ash 2011. 'The role of beliefs in lexical alignment: Evidence from dialogues with humans and computers', *Cognition* 121(1): 41–57

Brems, Lieselotte 2003. 'Measure noun constructions: An instance of semantically-driven grammaticalization', *International Journal of Corpus Linguistics* 8(2): 238–312

Brems, Lieselotte 2011. *Layering of size and type noun constructions in English*. Berlin and New York: Mouton de Gruyter

Brems, Lieselotte, and Davidse, Kristin 2010. 'The grammaticalisation of nominal type noun constructions with *kind/sort of*: Chronology and paths of change', *English Studies* 91(2): 180–202

Brennan, Susan E., and Clark, Herbert H. 1996. 'Conceptual pacts and lexical choice in conversation', *Journal of Experimental Psychology: Learning, Memory, and Cognition* 22(6): 1482–93

Bresnan, Joan 2007. 'Is syntactic knowledge probabilistic? Experiments with the English dative alternation', in Featherston and Sternefeld (eds.), pp. 77–96

Bresnan, Joan, Cueni, Anna, Nikitina, Tatiana, and Baayen, R. Harald 2007. 'Predicting the dative alternation', in Bouma, Krämer and Zwarts (eds.), pp. 69–94

Brinton, Laurel J. 1991. 'The origin and development of quasimodal *have to* in English'. Paper presented to the 10th ICHL, Amsterdam 1991. Unpublished manuscript. http://faculty.arts.ubc.ca/lbrinton/HAVETO.pdf [accessed April 24, 2016]

Brinton, Laurel J. 1996. *Pragmatic markers in English: Grammaticalization and discourse functions.* Berlin and New York: Mouton de Gruyter

Brinton, Laurel J. 2008. *The comment clause in English: Syntactic origins and pragmatic development.* Cambridge: Cambridge University Press

Brinton, Laurel J., and Traugott, Elizabeth C. 2005. *Lexicalization and language change.* Cambridge: Cambridge University Press

Britt, M. Anne 1994. 'The interaction of referential ambiguity and argument structure', *Journal of Memory and Language* 33(2): 251–83

Broeder, Peter, and Murre, Jaap (eds.) 2000. *Models of language acquisition: Inductive and deductive approaches.* Oxford: Oxford University Press

Brooks, Patricia J., Tomasello, Michael, Lewis, Lawrence B., and Dodson, Kelly 1999. 'Children's overgeneralization of fixed transitivity verbs: The entrenchment hypothesis', *Child Development* 70(6): 1325–37

Brown, Roger 1973. *A first language: The early stages.* Cambridge, MA: Harvard University Press

Brysbaert, Marc, and Mitchell, Don 1996. 'Modifier attachment in sentence parsing: Evidence from Dutch', *Quarterly Journal of Experimental Psychology* 49(3): 664–95

Burrows, John F. 1992. 'Computers and the study of literature', in Butler (ed.), pp. 167–204

Butler, Christopher S. (ed.) 1992. *Computers and written texts.* Oxford: Blackwell

Bybee, Joan L. 1985. *Morphology: A study of the relation between meaning and form.* Amsterdam and Philadelphia: John Benjamins

Bybee, Joan L. 1998. 'A functionalist approach to grammar and its evolution', *Evolution of Communication* 2(2): 249–78

Bybee, Joan L. 2001. *Phonology and language use.* Cambridge: Cambridge University Press

Bybee, Joan L. 2002. 'Sequentiality as the basis of constituent structure', in Givón and Malle (eds.), pp. 109–34

Bybee, Joan L. 2003. 'Mechanisms of change in grammaticalization: The role of frequency', in Joseph and Janda (eds.), pp. 602–23

Bybee, Joan L. 2006. 'From usage to grammar: The mind's response to repetition', *Language* 82(4): 711–33.

Bybee, Joan. L. 2008a. 'Grammaticalization: Implications for a theory of language', in Guo, Lieven, Budwig, Ervin-Tripp, Nakamura and Özçalişkan (eds.), pp. 345–55

Bybee, Joan L. 2008b. 'Usage-based grammar and second language acquisition', in Robinson and Ellis (eds.), pp. 216–36

Bybee, Joan L. 2010. *Language, usage and cognition*. Cambridge: Cambridge University Press

Bybee, Joan L. 2013. 'Usage-based theory and exemplar representations of constructions', in Hoffmann and Trousdale (eds.), pp. 49–69

Bybee, Joan L. 2014. 'Analytic and holistic processing in the development of constructions', in Arnon, Casillas, Kurumada and Estigarribia (eds.), pp. 303–13

Bybee, Joan L., and Beckner, Clay 2014. 'Language use, cognitive processes and linguistic change', in Bowern and Evans (eds.), pp. 503–18

Bybee, Joan L., and Fleischman, Suzanne (eds.) 1995. *Modality in grammar and discourse*. Amsterdam: John Benjamins

Bybee, Joan L., and Hopper, Paul (eds.) 2001. *Frequency and the emergence of linguistic structure*. Typological Studies in Language 45. Amsterdam: John Benjamins

Bybee, Joan L., and Pagliuca, William 1987. 'The evolution of future meaning', in Giacalone Ramat, Carruba and Bernini (eds.), pp. 108–22

Bybee, Joan L., Perkins, Revere, and Pagliuca, William 1994. *The evolution of grammar: Tense, aspect, and modality in the languages of the world*. Chicago: University of Chicago Press

Bybee, Joan L., and Scheibman, Joanne 1999. 'The effect of usage on degrees of constituency: The reduction of *don't* in English', *Linguistics* 37(4): 575–96

Bybee, Joan L., and Slobin, Dan I. 1982. 'Rules and schemas in the development and use of the English past tense', *Language* 58(2): 265–89

Bybee, Joan L., and Thompson, Sandra 1997. 'Three frequency effects in syntax', in Bailey, Moore and Moxley (eds.), pp. 378–88

Cai, Zhenguang G., Pickering, Martin J., Yan, Hao, and Branigan, Holly P. 2011. 'Lexical and syntactic representations in closely related languages: Evidence from Mandarin and Cantonese', *Journal of Memory and Language* 65(4): 431–45

Cameron-Faulkner, Thea, Lieven, Elena V. M., and Tomasello, Michael 2003. 'A construction based analysis of child directed speech', *Cognitive Science* 27(6): 843–73

Campbell, Byron A., and Church, Russell M. (eds.) 1969. *Punishment and aversive behavior*. New York: Appleton-Century-Crofts

Carey, Kathleen 1990. 'The role of conversational implicature in the early grammaticalization of the English perfect', in Hall, Koenig, Meacham, Reinman, and Sutton (eds.), pp. 371–80

Carey, Kathleen 1994. 'The grammaticalization of the perfect in Old English: An account based on pragmatics and metaphor', in Pagliuca (ed.), pp. 103–17

Carreiras, Manuel, and Clifton, Charles 1993. 'Relative clause interpretation preferences in Spanish and English', *Language and Speech* 36(4): 353–72

Carreiras, Manuel, and Clifton, Charles (eds.) 2004. *The on-line study of sentence comprehension*. Hove: Psychology Press

Carroll, John B., and White, Margaret N. 1973. 'Word frequency and age of acquisition as determiners of picture-naming latency', *Quarterly Journal of Experimental Psychology* 25(1): 85–95

Chafe, Wallace, and Nichols, Johanna (eds.) 1986. *Evidentiality. The linguistic coding of epistemology*. Norwood, NJ: Ablex

Chalmers, David J., French, Robert M., and Hofstadter, Douglas R. 1992. 'High-level perception, representation, and analogy: A critique of artificial intelligence methodology', *Journal of Experimental and Theoretical Artificial Intelligence* 4(3): 185–211

Chambers, Jack K., Trudgill, Peter, and Schilling-Estes, Natalie (eds.) 2002. *The handbook of language variation and change*. Oxford: Blackwell

Chang, Franklin, Dell, Gary S., and Bock, J. Kathryn 2006. 'Becoming syntactic', *Psychological Review* 113(2): 234–72

Chapman, Carol 1995. 'Perceptual salience and analogical change: Evidence from vowel lengthening in modern Swiss German dialects', *Journal of Linguistics* 31(1): 1–13

Chater, Nick, and Manning, Christopher 2006. 'Probabilistic models of language processing and acquisition', *Trends in Cognitive Science* 10(7): 335–44

Cheshire, Jenny, Kerswill, Paul, Fox, Sue, and Torgersen, Eivind 2013. 'English as a contact language: The role of children and adolescents', in Schreier and Hundt (eds.), pp. 560–607

Chiarcos, Christian 2011. 'On the dimensions of discourse salience'. www.linguistics.ruhr-uni-bochum.de/bla/beyondsem2011/chiarcos_final.pdf [accessed April 19, 2016]

Chiarcos, Christian, Claus, Berry, and Grabski, Michael 2011a. 'Introduction', in Chiarcos, Claus and Grabski (eds.), pp. 1–28

Chiarcos, Christian, Claus, Berry, and Grabski, Michael (eds.) 2011b. *Salience: Multidisciplinary perspectives on its function in discourse*. Berlin and New York: Mouton de Gruyter

Childers, Jane B., and Tomasello, Michael 2001. 'The role of pronouns in young children's acquisition of the English transitive construction', *Child Development* 37(6): 739–48

Chomsky, Noam 1981. *Lectures on Government and Binding*. Dordrecht: Foris Publications

Christiansen, Morten H., and Chater, Nick (eds.) 2001. *Connectionist psycholinguistics*. Westport, CO: Ablex

Christiansen, Morten H., and Chater, Nick 2008. 'Language as shaped by the brain', *Behavioral and Brain Sciences [Target Article for Multiple Peer Commentary]* 31(5): 489–509

Christiansen, Morten H., and Chater, Nick 2016. *Creating language: Integrating evolution, acquisition, and processing*. Cambridge, MA: The MIT Press

Christiansen, Morten H., and Kirby, Simon (eds.) 2003. *Language evolution*. Oxford: Oxford University Press

Christianson, Kiel, Hollingworth, Andrew, Halliwell, John F., and Ferreira, Fernanda 2001. 'Thematic roles assigned along the garden path linger', *Cognitive Psychology* 42(2): 368–407

Christie, William (ed.) 1976. *Current progress in historical linguistics*. Amsterdam: North Holland

Cienki, Alan J., Luka, Barbara J., and Smith, Michael B. (eds.) 2001. *Conceptual and discourse factors in linguistic structure*. Stanford: CSLI Publications

Clahsen, Harald 1999. 'Lexical entries and rules of language: A multidisciplinary study of German inflection', *Behavioral and Brain Sciences* 22(6): 991–1060

Clahsen, Harald, Rothweiler, Monika, Woest, Andreas, and Marcus, Gary F. 1992. 'Regular and irregular inflection in the acquisition of German noun plurals', *Cognition* 45(3): 225–55

Claridge, Claudia, and Kytö, Merja 2014. '"You are a bit of a sneak": Exploring a degree modifier in the Old Bailey Corpus', in Hundt (ed.), pp. 239–68

Clark, Andy. 2013. 'Whatever next? Predictive brains, situated agents, and the future of cognitive science', *Behavioral and Brain Sciences* 36(3): 181–204

Clark, Eve V. 1978. 'Discovering what words can do', in Farkas, Jacobsen and Todrys (eds.), pp. 34–57

Clark, Eve V. 1982. 'Language change during language acquisition', in Lamb and Brown (eds.), pp. 171–95

Clark, Eve V., and Arnon, Inbal (eds.) 2011 *Experience, variation, and generalization: Learning a first language*. Amsterdam and Philadelphia: John Benjamins

Clark, Herbert H. 1992. *Arenas of language use*. Chicago: University of Chicago Press

Clark, Herbert H. 1996. *Using language*. Cambridge: Cambridge University Press

Clark, Herbert H., and Wilkes-Gibbs, Deanna 1986. 'Referring as a collaborative process', *Cognition* 22(1): 1–39

Cleeremans, Axel, and McClelland, James L. 1991. 'Learning the structure of event sequences', *Journal of Experimental Psychology: General* 120(3): 235–53

Cleland, Alexandra A., and Pickering, Martin J. 2003. 'The use of lexical and syntactic information in language production: Evidence from the priming of noun-phrase structure', *Journal of Memory and Language* 49(2): 214–30

Clifton, Charles, Frazier, Lyn, and Rayner, Keith (eds.) 1994. *Perspectives on sentence processing*. Hillsdale, NJ: Lawrence Erlbaum

Clifton, Charles, and Staub, Adrian 2008. 'Parallelism and competition in syntactic ambiguity resolution', *Language and Linguistics Compass* 2(2): 234–50

Coates, Jennifer 1983. *The semantics of the modal auxiliaries*. London: Croom Helm

Cole, Peter, and Sadock, Jerrold Murray (eds.) 1977. *Syntax and semantics, vol. 8: Grammatical relations*. New York: Academic Press

Coltheart, Max 1978. 'Lexical access in simple reading tasks', in Underwood (ed.), pp. 151–216

Coltheart, Max (ed.) 1987. *Attention and performance XII: The psychology of reading*. Mahwah, NJ: Lawrence Erlbaum Associates

Coltheart, Max, and Leahy, Judi 1996. 'Assessment of lexical and nonlexical reading abilities in children: Some normative data', *Australian Journal of Psychology* 48(3): 136–40

Comrie, Bernard 2003. 'Reconstruction, typology and reality', in Hickey (ed.), pp. 243–57

Corder, Stephen P. 1967. 'The significance of learners' errors', *International Review of Applied Linguistics* 5(1–4): 161–69

Corral, Alvaro, Boleda, Gemma, and Ferrer-i-Cancho, Ramon 2015. 'Zipf's law for word frequencies: Word forms versus lemmas in long texts', *PLoS ONE* 10(7): e0129031

Cottrell, Garrison W., and Plunkett, Kim 1994. 'Acquiring the mapping from meaning to sounds', *Connection Science* 6(4): 379–412

Craig, Colette G. (ed.) 1986. *Noun classes and categorization*. Amsterdam: John Benjamins

Crocker, Matthew W. 1996. *Computational psycholinguistics: An interdisciplinary approach to the study of language*. Dordrecht: Kluwer Academic

Croft, William A. 2000. *Explaining language change: An evolutionary approach*. Harlow, Essex: Longman

Croft, William A. 2001. *Radical construction grammar: Syntactic theory in typological perspective*. Oxford: Oxford University Press

Croft, William A. 2010. 'The origins of grammaticalization in the verbalization of experience', *Linguistics* 48(1): 1–48

Croft, William, and Cruse, Alan D. 2004. *Cognitive linguistics*. Cambridge: Cambridge University Press

Crystal, David 2004. *The stories of English*. New York: The Overlook Press

Cuetos, Fernando, and Mitchell, Don 1988. 'Cross-linguistic differences in parsing: Restrictions on the use of the late closure strategy in Spanish', *Cognition* 30(1): 73–105

Culpeper, Jonathan, and Kytö, Merja 2010. *Early Modern English dialogues: Spoken interaction as writing*. Cambridge: Cambridge University Press

Cutler, Anne, and Carter, David M. 1987. 'The predominance of strong initial syllables in the English vocabulary', *Computer Speech and Language* 2(3): 133–42

Cutting, J. Cooper, and Bock, J. Kathryn 1997. 'That's the way the cookie bounces: Syntactic and semantic components of experimentally elicited idiom blends', *Memory and Cognition* 25(1): 57–71

Dąbrowska, Ewa 2000. 'From formula to schema: The acquisition of English questions', *Cognitive Linguistics* 11(1–2): 83–102

Dąbrowska, Ewa 2001. 'Learning a morphological system without a default: The Polish genitive', *Journal of Child Language* 28(3): 545–74

Dąbrowska, Ewa 2004. *Language, mind and brain: Some psychological and neurological constraints on theories of grammar*. Edinburgh: Edinburgh University Press

Dąbrowska, Ewa 2012. 'Different speakers, different grammars: Individual differences in native language attainment', *Linguistic Approaches to Bilingualism* 2(3): 219–53

Dąbrowska, Ewa, and Divjak, Dagmar (eds.) 2015. *Handbook of cognitive linguistics*. Berlin and New York: Mouton de Gruyter

Danchev, Andrei, and Kytö, Merja 1994. 'The construction *be going to* + infinitive in Early Modern English', in Kastovsky (ed.), pp. 59–78

Danks, David 2003. 'Equilibria of the Rescorla-Wagner model', *Journal of Mathematical Psychology* 47(2): 109–21

Daugherty, Kim G., and Seidenberg, Mark S. 1994. 'Beyond rules and exceptions: A connectionist approach to inflectional morphology', in Lima, Corrigan and Iverson (eds.), pp. 353–88

Davidse, Kristin 2009. '*Complete* and *sort of*: From identifying to intensifying?', *Transactions of the Philological Society* 107(3): 262–92

Davies, Mark 2010. 'The corpus of contemporary American English as the first reliable monitor corpus of English', *Literary and Linguistic Computing* 25(4): 447–64

Dawkins, Richard 1985. *The blind watchmaker*. New York: Norton

Deacon, Terrence W. 1997. *The symbolic species: The co-evolution of language and the brain*. New York: W. W. Norton

Deacon, Terrence W. 2003. 'Universal grammar and semiotic constraints', in Christiansen and Kirby (eds.), pp. 111–39.

de Bot, Kees, Lowie, Wander, Thorne, Steven L., and Verspoor, Marjolijn 2013. 'Dynamic systems theory as a comprehensive theory of second language development', in García Mayo, Gutierrez Mangado, and Martínez Adrián (eds.), pp. 199–220

Declerck, Renaat 1982. 'The triple origin of participial perception verb complements', *Linguistic Analysis* 10: 1–26

Degand, Liesbeth, and Simon, Anne Catherine 2005. '"My brother, he drives like crazy": Contextual salience, linguistic marking and discourse organisation in spoken French', in Stede, Chiarcos, Grabski, and Lagerwerf (eds.), pp. 43–52

de Houwer, Annick 2007. 'Parental language input patterns and children's bilingual use', *Applied Psycholinguistics* 28(3): 411–24

de Jong, Nivia H., Schreuder, Rob, and Baayen, R. Harald 2000. 'The morphological family size effect and morphology', *Language and Cognitive Processes* 15(4–5): 329–65

DeKeyser, Robert M. 2001. 'Automaticity and automatization', in Robinson (ed.), pp. 125–51

Dell, Gary S., and Chang, Franklin 2014. 'The P-Chain: Relating sentence production and its disorders to comprehension and acquisition', *Philosophical Transactions of the Royal Society of London B: Biological Sciences* 369(1634): 20120394

Demberg, Vera, and Keller, Frank 2008. 'Data from eye-tracking corpora as evidence for theories of syntactic processing complexity', *Cognition* 109(2): 193–210

Denison, David 1985. 'Why Old English had no prepositional passive', *English Studies* 66: 189–204

Denison, David 1993. *English historical syntax: Verbal constructions*. London and New York: Longman

Denison, David 2002. 'History of the *sort of* construction family'. Paper presented at ICCG2: Second International Conference on Construction Grammar, Helsinki, September 2002

Denison, David 2006. 'Category change and gradience in the determiner system', in van Kemenade and Los (eds.), pp. 279–304

Denison, David 2010a. 'Category change in English with and without structural change', in Traugott and Trousdale (eds.), pp. 105–28

Denison, David 2010b. 'SKT-constructions: The relation between synchronic and diachronic analysis'. Paper presented at SLE 43, Vilnius

Denison, David 2012. 'On the history of English (and) word classes'. Paper presented at ICEHL17, Zurich

Denison, David 2013. 'Parts of speech: Solid citizens or slippery customers?', *Journal of the British Academy* 1: 151–85

Denison, David in preparation. *English word classes: Categories and their limits*. Cambridge: Cambridge University Press

de Smedt, Liesbeth 2005. *Functions of the T-nouns kind, sort and type: A comprehensive, data-based description*. MA thesis. University of Leuven

de Smedt, Liesbeth, Brems, Lieselotte, and Davidse, Kristin 2007. 'NP-internal functions and extended uses of the 'type' nouns *kind, sort,* and *type*: Towards a comprehensive, corpus-based description', in Facchinetti (ed.), pp. 227–57

de Smet, Hendrik 2009. 'Analysing reanalysis', *Lingua* 119(11): 1728–55

de Smet, Hendrik 2012. 'The course of actualization', *Language* 88(3): 601–33

des Rosiers, Gabriel, and Ivison, David 1986. 'Paired-associate learning: Normative data for differences between high and low associate word pairs', *Journal of Clinical Experimental Neuropsychology* 8(6): 637–42

de Vincenzi, Marica, and Lombardo, Vincenzo (eds.) 2000. *Proceedings of AMLaP-96*. Dordrecht: Kluwer Academic Press

Dewaele, Jean-Marc 2004. 'Retention or omission of the *ne* in advanced French interlanguage: The variable effect of extralinguistic factors', *Journal of Sociolinguistics* 8(3): 433–50

Diessel, Holger 1999. *Demonstratives: Form, function, and grammaticalization*. Amsterdam: Benjamins

Diessel, Holger 2004. *The acquisition of complex sentences*. Cambridge: Cambridge University Press

Diessel, Holger 2007. 'Frequency effects in language acquisition, language use, and diachronic change', *New Ideas in Psychology* 25(2): 108–27

Diessel, Holger 2011. 'Grammaticalization and language acquisition', in Heine and Narrog (eds.), pp. 130–41

Diessel, Holger 2012. 'Diachronic change and language acquisition', in Bergs and Brinton (eds.), pp. 1599–613

Diessel, Holger, and Tomasello, Michael 2001. 'The acquisition of finite complement clauses in English: A corpus-based analysis', *Cognitive Linguistics* 12(2): 97–141

Diewald, Gabriele 2002. 'A model for relevant types of contexts in grammaticalization', in Wischer and Diewald (eds.), pp. 103–20

Diewald, Gabriele 2006. 'Context types in grammaticalization as constructions', *Constructions* 1: 1–29. http://elanguage.net/journals/index.php/constructions/article/viewFile/24/29 [accessed June 6, 2013]

Dimroth, Christine, and Starren, Marianne (eds.) 2003. *Information structure and the dynamics of language acquisition.* Amsterdam: Benjamins

Drachman, Geberell 1978. 'Child language and language change: A conjecture and some refutations', in Fisiak (ed.), pp. 123–44

Dreschler, Gea 2015. *Passives and the loss of verb second: A study of syntactic and information-structural factors.* Utrecht: LOT

du Bois, John W. 1985. 'Competing motivations', in Haiman (ed.), pp. 343–65

Dufouil, Carole, Pereira, Ewige, Chêne, Geneviève, Glymour, M. Maria, Alpérovitch, Annick, Saubusse, Elodie, Risse-Fleury, Mathilde, Heuls, Brigitte, Salord, Jean-Claude, Brieu, Marie-Anne, and Forette, Françoise 2014. 'Older age at retirement is associated with decreased risk of dementia', *European Journal of Epidemiology* 29(5): 353–61

Durrant, Philip, and Doherty, Alice 2010. 'Are high-frequency collocations psychologically real? Investigating the thesis of collocational priming', *Corpus Linguistics and Linguistic Theory* 6(2): 125–55

Ebbinghaus, Hermann 1885. *Memory: A contribution to experimental psychology.* New York: Teachers College, Columbia [Trans. Henry A. Ruger and Clara E. Bussenius, 1913]

Eckardt, Regine 2006. *Meaning change in grammaticalization. An enquiry into semantic reanalysis.* Oxford: Oxford University Press

Edwards, Jonathan 1752. *Misrepresentations corrected, and truth vindicated. In a reply to the Rev. Mr. Solomon Williams's book, intitled, The True State of the Question Concerning the Qualifications Necessary to Lawful Communion in the Christian Sacraments.* Boston: S. Kneeland

Eisenbeiss, Sonja, Bartke, Sonja, and Clahsen, Harald 2006. 'Structural and lexical case in child German: Evidence from language-impaired and typically developing children', *HLAC* 13(1): 3–32

Ekwall, Eilert 1975. *A history of Modern English sounds and morphology.* Translated and edited by Alan Ward. Oxford: Blackwell

Ellis, Nick. C. 1994a. 'Vocabulary acquisition: The implicit ins and outs of explicit cognitive mediation', in Ellis (ed.), pp. 211–82

Ellis, Nick C. (ed.) 1994b. *Implicit and explicit learning of languages.* San Diego, CA: Academic Press

Ellis, Nick C. 1996. 'Sequencing in SLA: Phonological memory, chunking, and points of order', *Studies in Second Language Acquisition* 18(1): 91–126

Ellis, Nick C. 2002. 'Frequency effects in language processing: A review with implications for theories of implicit and explicit language acquisition', *Studies in Second Language Acquisition* 24(2): 143–88

Ellis, Nick C. 2005. 'At the interface: Dynamic interactions of explicit and implicit language knowledge', *Studies in Second Language Acquisition* 27(2): 305–52

Ellis, Nick C. 2006a. 'Language acquisition as rational contingency learning', *Applied Linguistics* 27(1): 1–24

Ellis, Nick C. 2006b. 'Selective attention and transfer phenomena in L2 acquisition: Contingency, cue competition, salience, interference, overshadowing, blocking, and perceptual learning', *Applied Linguistics* 27(2): 164–94

Ellis, Nick C. 2012. 'What can we count in language, and what counts in language acquisition, cognition, and use?', in Gries and Divjak (eds.), pp. 7–34

Ellis, Nick C. 2013. 'Construction grammar and second language acquisition', in Hoffmann and Trousdale (eds.), pp. 365–78

Ellis, Nick C. 2016. 'Frequency in language learning and language change: The contributions to this volume from a cognitive and psycholinguistic perspective', in Behrens and Pfänder (eds.), pp. 239–54

Ellis, Nick C., and Beaton, Alan 1993. 'Psycholinguistic determinants of foreign language vocabulary learning', *Language Learning* 43(4): 559–617

Ellis, Nick C., and Larsen-Freeman, Diane 2006. 'Language emergence: Implications for applied linguistics', *Applied Linguistics* 27(4): 558–589

Ellis, Nick. C., and Larsen-Freeman, Diane 2009. *Language as a complex adaptive system*. Oxford: Wiley-Blackwell

Ellis, Nick C., Römer, Ute, and O'Donnell, Matthew B. 2016. *Usage-based approaches to language acquisition and processing: Cognitive and corpus investigations of construction grammar*. Malden, MA: Wiley-Blackwell

Ellis, Nick C., and Sagarra, Nuria 2010. 'The bounds of adult language acquisition: Blocking and learned attention', *Studies in Second Language Acquisition* 32(4): 553–80

Ellis, Nick C., and Sagarra, Nuria 2011. 'Learned attention in adult language acquisition: A replication and generalization study and meta-analysis', *Studies in Second Language Acquisition* 33(4): 589–624

Ellis, Nick C., and Schmidt, Richard 1998. 'Rules or associations in the acquisition of morphology? The frequency by regularity interaction in human and PDP learning of morphosyntax', *Language and Cognitive Processes* 13(2–3): 307–36

Ellis, Nick C., and Simpson-Vlach, Rita 2009. 'Formulaic language in native speakers: Triangulating psycholinguistics, corpus linguistics, and education', *Corpus Linguistics and Linguistic Theory* 5(1): 61–78

Ellis, Nick C., Simpson-Vlach, Rita, and Maynard, Carson 2008. 'Formulaic language in native and second-language speakers: Psycholinguistics, corpus linguistics, and TESOL', *TESOL Quarterly* 42(3): 375–96

Elman, Jeffrey L. 1990. 'Finding structure in time', *Cognitive Science* 14(2): 179–211

Elman, Jeffrey L. 2003. 'Generalization from sparse input'. *Proceedings of the 38th Annual Meeting of the Chicago Linguistics Society*, pp. 175–200

Elman, Jeffrey L. 2004. 'An alternative view of the mental lexicon', *Trends in Cognitive Science* 8(7): 301–6

Elman, Jeffrey L., Bates, Elizabeth A., Johnson, Mark H., Karmiloff-Smith, Anette, Parisi, Domenico, and Plunkett, Kim 1996. *Rethinking innateness: A connectionist perspective on development*. Cambridge, MA: The MIT Press

Erbaugh, Mary S. 1986. 'Taking stock: The development of Chinese noun classi-fiers historically and in young children', in Craig (ed.), pp. 399–436

Erkelens, Maria A. 2009. 'Learning to categorize verbs and nouns: Studies on Dutch'. Leiden: LOT dissertation, Nr. 211

Erman, Britt, and Kotsinas, Ulla-Britt 1993. *Pragmaticalization: The case of 'ba' and 'you know', Studier i Modernspråkvetenskap* 10: 76–93.

Erman, Britt, and Warren, Beatrice 2000. 'The idiom principle and the open choice principle', *Text* 20(1): 29–62

Evans, Nicholas, and David Wilkins 2000. 'In the mind's ear: The Semantic extensions of perception verbs in Australian languages', *Language* 76(3): 546–92

Evans, Vyvyan, and Pourcel, Stephanie S. (eds.) 2009. *New directions in cognitive linguistics*. Amsterdam and Philadelphia: Benjamins

Everett, Daniel L. 2012. *Language: The cultural tool*. New York: Pantheon Books

Facchinetti, Roberta (ed.) 2007. *Corpus linguistics 25 years on. Language and Computers – Studies in Practical Linguistics 62*. Amsterdam and New York: Rodopi

Farkas, Donka, Jacobsen, Wesley M., and Todrys, Karol W. (eds.) 1978. *Papers from the parasession on the lexicon*. Chicago: Chicago Linguistic Society

Featherston, Sam, and Sternefeld, Wolfgang (eds.) 2007. *Roots: Linguistics in search of its evidential base*. Berlin and New York: Mouton de Gruyter

Felser, Claudia 1999. *Verbal complement clauses: A minimalist study of direct perception constructions*. Amsterdam: Benjamins

Ferguson, Charles A., and Slobin, Dan I. (eds.) 1973. *Studies of child language development*. New York: Holt, Reinhart, and Winston

Ferreira, Fernanda 2003. 'The misinterpretation of noncanonical sentences', *Cognitive Psychology* 47(2): 164–203

Ferreira, Fernanda, and Clifton, Charles 1986. 'The independence of syntactic processing', *Journal of Memory and Language* 25(3): 348–68

Ferreira, Fernanda, and Henderson, John M. 1991. 'Recovery from misanalyses of garden-path sentences', *Journal of Memory and Language* 30(6): 725–45

Ferreira, Fernanda, and Patson, Nikole D. 2007. 'The "good enough" approach to language comprehension', *Language and Linguistics Compass* 1(1–2): 71–83

Ferreira, Victor S., Bock, J. Kathryn, Wilson, Michael P., and Cohen, Neal J. 2008. 'Memory for syntax despite amnesia', *Psychological Science* 19(9): 940–46

Ferrer-i-Cancho, Ramon, Dębowski, Łukasz, and Moscoso del Prado Martín, Fermín 2013. 'Constant conditional entropy and related hypotheses', *Journal of Statistical Mechanics: Theory and Experiment* 07: L07001

Ferrer-i-Cancho, Ramon, and Solé, Richard V. 2003. 'Least effort and the origins of scaling in human language'. *Proceedings of the National Academy of Sciences* 100(3): 788–91

Field, John 2008. 'Bricks or mortar: Which parts of the input does a second language listener rely on?', *Tesol Quarterly* 42(3): 411–32

Fillmore, Charles J. 1977. 'The case for case reopened', in Cole and Sadock (eds.), pp. 59–81

Fine, Julian M., and Lieven, Elena V. M. 1993. 'Reanalyzing rote-learned phrases: Individual differences in the transition to multi-word speech', *Journal of Child Language* 20(3): 551–71

Firbas, Jan 1992. *Functional sentence perspective in written and spoken communication*. Cambridge: Cambridge University Press

Firth, John R. 1957. *A synopsis of linguistic theory, 1930–1955*. Oxford: Basil Blackwell

Fischer, Kirsten (ed.) 2006. *Approaches to discourse markers*. Oxford: Elsevier

Fischer, Olga 1988. 'The rise of the "for NP to V" construction: An explanation', in Nixon and Honey (eds.), pp. 67–88

Fischer, Olga 1994. 'The development of quasi-auxiliaries in English and changes in word order', *Neophilologus* 78(1): 137–64

Fischer, Olga 2000. 'Grammaticalization: Unidirectional, non-reversable? The case of *to* before the infinitive in English', in Fischer, Rosenbach and Stein (eds.), pp. 149–70

Fischer, Olga 2007. *Morphosyntactic change: Functional and formal perspectives*. Oxford: Oxford University Press

Fischer, Olga 2011. 'Grammaticalization as analogically driven change?', in Narrog and Heine (eds.), pp. 31–42

Fischer, Olga 2015. 'The influence of the grammatical system and analogy in processes of language change: The case of the auxiliation of HAVE-TO once again', in Toupin and Lowrey (eds.), pp. 120–50

Fischer, Olga, and Olbertz, Hella forthcoming. 'The role played by analogy in processes of language change: The case of English *have to* compared to Spanish *tener que*', in Yáñez-Bouza, Moore, Hollmann and van Bergen (eds.)

Fischer, Olga, Rosenbach, Annette, and Stein, Dieter (eds.) 2000. *Pathways of change: Grammaticalization in English*. Amsterdam and Philadelphia: Benjamins

Fischer, Olga, and van der Wurff, Wim 2006. 'Syntax', in Hogg and Denison (eds.), pp. 109–98

Fischer, Olga, van Kemenade, Ans, Koopman, Willem, and van der Wurff, Wim 2000. *The syntax of early English*. Cambridge: Cambridge University Press

Fisher, Cynthia 1996. 'Structural limits on verb mapping: The role of analogy in children's interpretations of sentences', *Cognitive Psychology* 31(1): 41–81

Fisiak, Jacek (ed.) 1978. *Recent developments in historical phonology*. Berlin and New York: Mouton de Gruyter

Fisiak, Jacek (ed.) 1980. *Historical morphology*. The Hague, Paris and New York: Mouton

Fisiak, Jacek (ed.) 1985. *Historical semantics. Historical word-formation*. Berlin, New York and Amsterdam: Mouton de Gruyter

Fleischman, Suzanne 1982. *The future in thought and language: Diachronic evidence from Romance*. Cambridge: Cambridge University Press

Fletcher, Paul, and Garman, Michael (eds.) 1986. *Language acquisition. Studies in first language development*. Cambridge: Cambridge University Press

Fletcher, Paul, and MacWhinney, Brian (eds.) 1994. *The handbook of child language*. Oxford: Blackwell

Fodor, Janet D., and Inoue, Atsu 1994. 'The diagnosis and cure of garden-paths', *Journal of Psycholinguistic Research* 23(5): 407–34

Fodor, Janet D., and Inoue, Atsu 2000. 'Garden path reanalysis: Attach (anyway) and revision as last resort', in de Vincenzi and Lombardo (eds.), pp. 21–62

Forster, Kenneth I. 1976. 'Accessing the mental lexicon', in Wales and Walker (eds.), pp. 231–56

Fought, Carmen (ed.) 2004. *Sociolinguistic variation: Critical reflections*. Oxford: Oxford University Press

Francis, Elaine J., and Yuasa, Etsuyo 2008. 'A multi-modular approach to gradual change in grammaticalization', *Journal of Linguistics* 44(1): 45–86

Francis, W. Nelson, and Kučera, Henry 1979. *Brown corpus manual*. Brown University: Department of Linguistics

Frazier, Lyn 1979. On comprehending sentences: Syntactic parsing strategies. Doctoral dissertation. University of Connecticut.

Frazier, Lyn 1987. 'Sentence processing: A tutorial review', in Coltheart (ed.), pp. 559–86

Frazier, Lyn, and Clifton, Charles 1996. *Construal*. Cambridge, MA: The MIT Press

Frazier, Lyn, and Rayner, Keith 1982. 'Making and correcting errors during sentence comprehension: Eye movements in the analysis of structurally ambiguous sentences', *Cognitive Psychology* 14(2): 178–210

Frenck-Mestre, Cheryl, and Pynte, Joël 1997. 'Syntactic ambiguity resolution while reading in second and native languages', *Quarterly Journal of Experimental Psychology* 50(1): 119–48

Freudenthal, Daniel, Pine, Julian M., Aguado-Orea, Javier, and Gobet, Fernand 2007. 'Modelling the developmental patterning of finiteness marking in English, Dutch, German and Spanish using MOSAIC', *Cognitive Science* 31(2): 311–41

Freudenthal, Daniel, Pine, Julian M., and Gobet, Fernand 2009. 'Simulating the referential properties of Dutch, German, and English root infinitives in MOSAIC', *Language Learning and Development* 5(1): 1–29

Freudenthal, Daniel, Pine, Julian M., and Gobet, Fernand 2010. 'Explaining quantitative variation in the rate of optional infinitive errors across languages: A comparison of MOSAIC and the Variational Learning Model', *Journal of Child Language* 37(3): 643–69

Friederici, Angela 2002. 'Towards a neural basis of auditory sentence processing', *Trends in Cognitive Sciences* 6(2): 78–84

Frisch, Stefan F., Large, Nathan R., Zawaydeh, Bushra, and Pisoni, David B. 2001. 'Emergent phonotactic generalizations in English and Arabic', in Bybee and Hopper (eds.), pp. 159–80

Fuchs, Susanne, Grice, Martine, Hermes, Anne, Lancia, Leonardo, and Mücke, Doris (eds.) 2014. *Proceedings of the 10th International Seminar on Speech Production (ISSP), 5–8 May 2014*. Cologne, Germany. Köln: Universität Köln

Gaeta, Livio, and Ricca, Davide 2006. 'Productivity in Italian word formation: A variable-corpus approach', *Linguistics* 44(1): 57–89

Gahl, Susanne 2008. 'Time and thyme are not homophones: The effect of lemma frequency on word durations in spontaneous speech', *Language* 84(3): 474–96

Gahl, Susanne, and Baayen, R. Harald in preparation. 'Vowel space expands over the lifespan'.

Gahl, Susanne, Cibelli, Emily, Hall, Kathleen, and Sprouse, Ronald 2014. 'The "UP" corpus: A corpus of speech samples across adulthood', *Corpus Linguistics and Lingustic Theory* 10(2): 315–28

Gahl, Susanne, Yao, Yao, and Johnson, Keith 2012. 'Why reduce? Phonological neighborhood density and phonetic reduction in spontaneous speech', *Journal of Memory and Language* 66(4): 789–806

Galaburda, Albert M. (ed.) 1989. *From reading to neurons. Issues in the Biology of Language and Cognition.* Cambridge, MA: The MIT Press

Galbi, Douglas A. 2002. 'Long-term trends in personal given name frequencies in England and Wales', *A Journal of Onomastic* 51(4): 105–32

García Mayo, María d. P., Gutiérrez Mangado, María J., and Martínez Adrián, María (eds.) 2013. *Contemporary approaches to second language acquisition.* Amsterdam: John Benjamins

Gardner, Anne 2014. *Derivation in Middle English: Regional and text type variation.* Mémoires de la Société Néophilologique de Helsinki 92. Helsinki: Société Néophilologique

Gardner, Michael K., Rothkopf, Ernst Z., Lapan, Richard, and Lafferty, Toby 1987. 'The word frequency effect in lexical decision: Finding a frequency-based component', *Memory and Cognition* 15(1): 24–28

Garnsey, Susan M., Pearlmutter, Neal J., Myers, Elizabeth, and Lotocky, Melanie A. 1997. 'The contributions of verb bias and plausibility to the comprehension of temporarily ambiguous sentences', *Journal of Memory and Language* 37(1): 58–93

Garrett, Andrew 2011. 'The historical syntax problem: Reanalysis and directionality', in Jonas, Whitman and Garrett (eds.), pp. 52–72

Garrod, Simon, and Anderson, Anthony 1987. 'Saying what you mean in dialogue: A study in conceptual and semantic co-ordination', *Cognition* 27(2): 181–218

Garrod, Simon, and Clark, Aileen 1993. 'The development of dialogue co-ordination skills in schoolchildren', *Language and Cognitive Processes* 8(1): 101–26

Garrod, Simon, and Doherty, Gwyneth 1994. 'Conversation, co-ordination and convention: An empirical investigation of how groups establish linguistic conventions', *Cognition* 53(3): 181–215

Gass, Susan M., and Mackey, Alison (eds.) 2012. *The Routledge handbook of second language acquisition.* London and New York: Routledge

Geeraerts, Dirk, and Cuyckens, Hubert (eds.) 2007. *The Oxford handbook of cognitive linguistics.* Oxford and New York: Oxford University Press

Gentner, Dedre 1983. 'Structure-mapping: A theoretical framework for analogy', *Cognitive Science* 7(2): 155–70

Gentner, Dedre 1988. 'Metaphor as structure mapping: The relational shift', *Child Development* 59(1): 47–59

Gentner, Dedre 2003. 'Why we're so smart', in Gentner and Goldin-Meadow (eds.), pp. 195–235

Gentner, Dedre 2010. 'Bootstrapping the mind: Analogical processes and symbol systems', *Cognitive Science* 34(5): 752–75

Gentner, Dedre, Anggoro, Florencia K., and Klibanoff, Raquel S. 2011. 'Structure mapping and relational language support children's learning of relational categories', *Child Development* 82(4): 1173–88

Gentner, Dedre, and Colhoun, Julie 2010. 'Analogical processes in human thinking and learning', in Glatzeder, Goel and Müller (eds.), pp. 35–48

Gentner, Dedre, and Goldin-Meadow, Susan (eds.) 2003. *Language in mind: Advances in the study of language and cognition.* Cambridge, MA: The MIT Press

Gentner, Dedre, Holyoak, Keith J., and Kokinov, Boicho K. (eds.) 2001. *The analogical mind. Perspectives from cognitive science.* Cambridge, MA: The MIT Press

Gentner, Dedre, Levine, Susan C., Ping, Raedy, Isaia, Ashley, Dhillon, Sonica, Bradley, Claire, and Honke, Garrett 2016. 'Rapid learning in a children's museum via analogical comparison', *Cognitive Science* 40(1): 224–40

Gentner, Dedre, and Markman, Arthur B. 1997. 'Structure mapping in analogy and similarity', *American Psychologist* 52(1): 45–56

Gentner, Dedre, and Medina, Jose 1998. 'Similarity and the development of rules' *Cognition* 65(2): 263–97

Gentner, Dedre, and Namy, Laura L. 2006. 'Analogical processes in language learning', *Current Directions in Psychological Science* 15(6): 297–301

Gentner, Dedre, Rattermann, Mary J., and Forbus, Kenneth D. 1993. 'The roles of similarity in transfer: Separating retrieval from inferential soundness', *Cognitive Psychology* 25(4): 524–75

Gentner, Dedre, and Smith, Linsey 2012. 'Analogical reasoning', in Ramachandran (ed.), pp. 130–36

Gernsbacher, Morton A. (ed.) 1994. *Handbook of psycholinguistics.* San Diego, CA: Academic Press

Gescheider, George A. 2013. *Psychophysics: The fundamentals.* New York and London: Psychology Press

Giacalone Ramat, Anna, Carruba, Onofrio, and Bernini, Giuliano (eds.) 1987. *Papers from the 7th International Conference on Historical Linguistics.* Amsterdam: John Benjamins

Giacalone Ramat, Anna, Mauri, Caterina, and Molinelli, Piera (eds.) 2013. *Synchrony and diachrony: A dynamic interface.* Amsterdam: Benjamins

Gibson, Edward 1991. A computational theory of human linguistic processing: Memory limitations and processing breakdown. Unpublished doctoral dissertation. Carnegie Mellon.

Gibson, Edward 1998. 'Syntactic complexity: Locality of syntactic dependencies', *Cognition* 68(1): 1–75

Gibson, Edward, and Pearlmutter, Neal 1998. 'Constraints on sentence comprehension', *Trends in Cognitive Sciences* 2(7): 262–68

Gibson, James J. 1977. *The theory of affordances*. Hillsdale, NJ: Lawrence Erlbaum

Gick, Bryan 2002. 'The use of ultrasound for linguistic phonetic fieldwork', *Journal of the International Phonetic Association* 32(2): 113–21

Gick, Mary L., and Holyoak, Keith J. 1980. 'Analogical problem solving', *Cognitive Psychology* 12(3): 306–55

Gilhooly, Ken J., and Logie, Robert H. 1980. 'Age-of-acquisition, imagery, concreteness, familiarity, and ambiguity measures for 1,944 words', *Behavior Research Methods and Instrumentation* 12(4): 395–427

Giora, Rachel 1997. 'Understanding figurative and literal language: The graded salience hypothesis', *Cognitive Linguistics* 8(3): 183–206

Giora, Rachel 2003. *On our mind: Salience, context, and figurative language*. New York: Oxford University Press

Giora, Rachel 2012. 'The psychology of utterance processing', in Allan and Jaszczolt (eds.), pp. 151–67

Givón, Talmy 1971. 'Historical syntax and synchronic morphology: An archeologist's field trip', *Chicago Linguistic Society* 7(1): 394–415

Givón, Talmy 1979. *On understanding grammar*. New York: Academic Press

Givón, Talmy 1998. 'On the co-evolution of language, mind and brain', *Evolution of Communication* 2(1): 45–116

Givón, Talmy 2002. 'The visual information-processing system as an evolutionary precursor of human language', in Givón and Malle (eds.), pp. 3–50

Givón, Talmy 2009. *The genesis of syntactic complexity: Diachrony, ontogeny, neurocognition, evolution*. Amsterdam: John Benjamins

Givón, Talmy, and Malle, Bertram (eds.) 2002. *The evolution of language out of pre-language*. Amsterdam: Benjamins

Glatzeder, Britt, Goel, Vinod, and Müller, Albrecht (eds.) 2010. *On thinking, vol. 2: Towards a theory of thinking*. Berlin: Springer

Gleitman, Lila R. 1990. 'The structural sources of verb meaning', *Language Acquisition* 1(1): 3–55

Gluck, Mark A., Meeter, Martijn, and Myers, Catherine E. 2003. 'Computational models of the hippocampal region: Linking incremental learning and episodic memory', *Trends in Cognitive Science* 7(6): 269–76

Glushko, Robert J. 1979. 'The organization and activation of orthographic knowledge in reading aloud', *Journal of Experimental Psychology: Human Perception and Performance* 5(4): 674–91

Glynn, Dylan, and Fischer, Kerstin (eds.) 2010. *Quantitative methods in cognitive semantics: Corpus-driven approaches*. Berlin and New York: Mouton de Gruyter

Gnutzmann, Claus 1975. 'Some aspects of grading', *English Studies* 56(5): 421–33

Godden, Duncan R., and Baddeley, Alan D. 1975. 'Context-dependent memory in two natural environments: On land and underwater', *British Journal of Psychology* 66(3): 325–31

Goebel, Rainer, and Indefrey, Peter 2000. 'A recurrent network with short-term memory capacity learning the German-s plural', in Broeder and Murre (eds.), pp. 177–200

Goldberg, Adele E. 1995. *Constructions: A construction grammar approach to argument structure*. Chicago: University of Chicago Press

Goldberg, Adele E. 2003. 'Constructions: A new theoretical approach to language', *Trends in Cognitive Science* 7(5): 219–24

Goldberg, Adele E. 2006. *Constructions at work. The nature of generalization in language*. Oxford: Oxford University Press

Goldrick, Matthew, Ferreira, Victor S., and Miozzo, Michele (eds.) 2014. *The Oxford handbook of language production*. Oxford: Oxford University Press

Goldschneider, Jennifer M., and DeKeyser, Robert 2001. 'Explaining the "natural order of L2 morpheme acquisition" in English: A meta-analysis of multiple determinants', *Language Learning* 51(1): 1–50

Goldwater, Micah B., Tomlinson, Marc T., Echols, Catharina H., and Love, Bradley C. 2011. 'Structural priming as structure-mapping: Children use analogies from previous utterances to guide sentence production', *Cognitive Science* 35(1): 156–70

Goodman, Judith C., Nusbaum, Howard C., Lee, Lisa, and Broihier, Kevin 1990. 'The effects of syntactic and discourse variables on the segmental intelligibility of speech'. The First International Conference on Spoken Language Processing, ICSLP 1990, Kobe, Japan, November 18–22.

Goosens, Louis 1982. 'On the development of the modals and of the epistemic function in English', in Ahlqvist (ed.), pp. 74–84

Gould, Stephen Jay 1977. *Ontogeny and phylogeny*. Cambridge, MA: Harvard University Press

Graddol, David 2000. *The future of English*. London: The British Council

Greene, Robert L. 1986. 'Sources of recency effects in free recall', *Psychological Bulletin* 99(2): 221–28

Gries, Stefan Th. 2003. 'Towards a corpus-based identification of prototypical instances of constructions', *Annual Review of Cognitive Linguistics* 1(1): 1–27

Gries, Stefan Th. 2005. 'Syntactic priming: A corpus-based approach', *Journal of Psycholinguistic Research* 34(4): 365–99

Gries, Stefan Th. 2008. 'Dispersions and adjusted frequencies in corpora', *International Journal of Corpus Linguistics* 13(4): 403–37

Gries, Stefan Th. 2010. 'Dispersions and adjusted frequencies in corpora: Further explorations', in Gries, Wulff and Davies (eds.), pp. 197–212

Gries, Stefan Th. 2013. 'Sources of variability relevant to the (cognitive) sociolinguist, and quantitative corpus methods to handle them', *Journal of Pragmatics* 52(6): 5–16

Gries, Stefan Th. 2015. 'The most underused statistical method in corpus linguistics: Multi-level (and mixed-effects) models', *Corpora* 10(1): 95–125

Gries, Stefan Th., and David, Caroline 2007. 'This is *kind of/sort of* interesting: Variation in hedging in English', *VARIENG e-Series* 2: *Towards Multimedia in Corpus Studies*. Helsinki: Research Unit for Variation, Contacts and Change in

English (VARIENG). www.helsinki.fi/varieng/journal/volumes/02/gries _david/ [accessed August 23, 2010]

Gries, Stefan Th., and Divjak, Dagmar S. 2009. 'Behavioral profiles: A corpus-based approach towards cognitive semantic analysis', in Evans and Pourcel (eds.), pp. 57–75

Gries, Stefan Th., and Divjak, Dagmar S. (eds.) 2012. *Frequency effects in language learning and processing*. Berlin and New York: Mouton de Gruyter

Gries, Stefan Th., and Ellis, Nick C. 2015. 'Statistical measures for usage-based linguistics', *Currents in Language Learning* 65(s1): 228–55

Gries, Stefan Th., Hampe, Beate, and Schönefeld, Doris 2005. 'Converging evidence: Bringing together experimental and corpus data on the association of verbs and constructions', *Cognitive Linguistics* 16(4): 635–76

Gries, Stefan Th., and Stefanowitsch, Anatol 2004. 'Extending collostructional analysis: A corpus-based perspective on "alternations"', *International Journal of Corpus Linguistics* 9(1): 97–129

Gries, Stefan Th., Wulff, Stefanie, and Davies, Mark (eds.) 2010. *Corpus linguistic applications: Current studies, new directions*. Amsterdam: Rodopi

Griffin, Zenzi M. 2001. 'Gaze durations during speech reflect word selection and phonological encoding', *Cognition* 82(1): B1–B14

Guo, Jiansheng, Lieven, Elena V. M., Budwig, Nancy, Ervin-Tripp, Susan, Nakamura, Kei, and Özçalişkan, Seyda (eds.) 2008. *Cross-linguistic approaches to the psychology of language: Research in the tradition of Dan Isaac Slobin*. New York and London: Psychology Press

Hahn, Ulrike, and Nakisa, Ramin C. 2000. 'German inflection: Single route or dual route?', *Cognitive Psychology* 41(4): 313–60

Haiman, John 1983. 'Iconic and economic motivation', *Language* 59(4): 781–819

Haiman, John (ed.) 1985. *Iconicity in syntax*. Amsterdam: John Benjamins

Haiman, John 1994. 'Ritualization and the development of language', in Pagliuca (ed.), pp. 3–28

Hale, John T. 2004. *Grammar, uncertainty and sentence processing*. Doctoral dissertation. The Johns Hopkins University.

Hale, John T. 2011. 'What a rational parser would do', *Cognitive Science* 35(3): 399–443

Hall, Kira, Koenig, Jean-Pierre, Meacham, Michael, Reinman, Sondra, and Sutton, Laurel A. (eds.) 1990. *Proceedings of the Sixteenth Annual Meeting of the Berkeley Linguistics Society*. Berkeley, CA: Berkeley Linguistics Society

Halle, Michael 1962. 'Phonology in generative grammar', *Word* 18: 54–72

Hanks, Patrick 2013. *Lexical analysis: Norms and exploitations*. Cambridge, MA: The MIT Press

Hansen, Björn, and de Haan, Ferdinand 2009. *Modals in the languages of Europe*. Berlin: Mouton de Gruyter

Hansen Mosegaard, Maj-Britt, and Waltereit, Richard 2006. 'GCI theory and language change', *Acta Linguistica Hafniensia* 38(1): 235–68

Harm, Michael W., and Seidenberg, Mark S. 1999. 'Phonology, reading acquisition, and dyslexia: Insights from connectionist models', *Psychological Review* 106(3): 491–528

Harnad, Steven R., Steklis, Horst D., and Lancaster, Jane (eds.) 1976. *The origins and evolution of language and speech*. New York: New York Academy of Sciences

Harris, Alice C., and Campbell, Lyle 1995. *Historical syntax in cross-linguistic perspective*. Cambridge: Cambridge University Press

Hartsuiker, Robert J., Bernolet, Sarah, Schoonbaert, Sophie, Speybroeck, Sara, and Vanderelst, Dieter 2008. 'Syntactic priming persists while the lexical boost decays: Evidence from written and spoken dialogue', *Journal of Memory and Language* 58(2): 214–38

Hartsuiker, Robert J., and Kolk, Herman H. J. 1998. 'Syntactic persistence in Dutch', *Language and Speech* 41(2): 143–84

Haselow, Alexander 2011. 'Discourse marker and modal particle: The functions of utterance-final *then* in spoken English', *Journal of Pragmatics* 43(14): 3603–23

Haselow, Alexander 2012. 'Discourse organization and the rise of final *then* in the history of English', in Hegedüs and Fodor (eds.), pp. 153–75

Haspelmath, Martin 1998. 'Does grammaticalization need reanalysis?', *Studies in Language* 22(2): 315–51

Haspelmath, Martin 1999. 'Why is grammaticalization irreversible?', *Linguistics* 37(6): 1043–68

Hawkins, John A. (ed.) 1988. *Explaining language universals*. Oxford: Basil Blackwell

Hawkins, John A. 1994. *A performance theory of order and constituency*. Cambridge: Cambridge University Press

Hawkins, John A. 2004. *Efficiency and complexity in grammars*. Oxford: Oxford University Press

Hawkins, John A. 2012. 'The drift of English towards invariable word order from a typological and Germanic perspective', in Nevalainen and Traugott (eds.), pp. 622–32

Hawkins, John A. 2014. *Cross-linguistic variation and efficiency*. Oxford: Oxford University Press

Hay, Jennifer 2001. 'Lexical frequency in morphology: Is everything relative?', *Linguistics* 39(6): 1041–70

Hebb, Donald O. 1949. *The organization of behaviour*. New York: John Wiley and Sons

Hegedüs, Irén, and Fodor, Alexandra (eds.) 2012. *English historical linguistics 2010*. Amsterdam: Benjamins

Heine, Bernd 1993. *Auxiliaries: Cognitive forces and grammaticalization*. Oxford: Oxford University Press

Heine, Bernd 2002. 'On the role of context in grammaticalization', in Wischer and Diewald (eds.), pp. 83–101

Heine, Bernd 2014. 'Grammaticalization, metaphor, and explanation: What accounts for unidirectionality?'. Plenary paper presented at the Workshop de Gramaticalização II, Universidade Federal Fluminense, Niterói, May 7, 2014

Heine, Bernd, Claudi, Ulrike, and Hünnemeyer, Friederike 1991. *Grammaticalization: A conceptual framework*. Chicago: University of Chicago Press

Heine, Bernd, and Narrog, Heiko (eds.) 2011. *The Oxford handbook of grammaticalization*. Oxford: Oxford University Press

Hendriks, Petra, Englert, Christina, Wubs, Ellis, and Hoeks, John 2008. 'Age differences in adults' use of referring expressions', *Journal of Logic, Language and Information* 17(4): 443–66

Hendrix, Peter 2015. Experimental explorations of a discrimination learning approach to language processing. Doctoral dissertation. University of Tübingen

Herron, Daniel, and Bates, Elizabeth 1997. 'Sentential and acoustic factors in the recognition of open- and closed-class words', *Journal of Memory and Language* 37(2): 217–39

Hickey, Raymond (ed.) 2003. *Motives for language change*. Cambridge: Cambridge University Press

Hickey, Raymond 2013. 'English as a contact language in Ireland and Scotland', in Schreier and Hundt (eds.), pp. 206–46

Hill, Robin L., and Murray, Wayne S. 2000. 'Commas and spaces: Effects of punctuation on eye movements and sentence parsing', in Kennedy, Radach, Heller and Pynte (eds.), pp. 565–89

Hilpert, Martin 2008. *Germanic future constructions: A usage-based approach to language change*. Amsterdam: John Benjamins

Hilpert, Martin 2011. 'Dynamic visualizations of language change: Motion charts on the basis of bivariate and multivariate data from diachronic corpora', *International Journal of Corpus Linguistics* 16(4): 435–61

Hilpert, Martin 2013. *Constructional change in English: Developments in allomorphy, word formation, and syntax*. Cambridge: Cambridge University Press

Hilpert, Martin, and Gries, Stefan Th. 2009. 'Assessing frequency changes in multi-stage diachronic corpora: Applications for historical corpus linguistics and the study of language acquisition', *Literary and Linguistic Computing* 34(4): 385–401

Himmelmann, Nikolaus P. 2004. 'Lexicalization and grammaticization: Opposite or orthogonal?', in Bisang, Himmelmann and Wiemer (eds.), pp. 21–42

Hinskens, Frans, Auer, Peter, and Kerswill, Paul 2005. 'The study of dialect convergence and divergence. Conceptual and methodological considerations', in Auer, Hinskens and Kerswill (eds.), pp. 1–50

Hock, Hans Heinrich 1991. *Principles of historical linguistics*. Berlin and New York: Mouton de Gruyter.

Hodge, Carleton 1970. 'The linguistic cycle', *Linguistic Sciences* 13(7): 1–7

Hoffmann, Sebastian 2005. *Grammaticalization and English complex prepositions: A corpus-based study*. London and New York: Routledge

Hoffmann, Thomas, and Trousdale, Graeme (eds.) 2013. *Oxford handbook of construction grammar*. Oxford: Oxford University Press

Hofstadter, Douglas 1995. *Fluid concepts and creative analogies. Computer models of the fundamental mechanisms of thought*. New York: Basic Books

Hofstadter, Douglas, and Sander, Emmanuel 2013. *Surfaces and essences: Analogy as the fuel and fire of thinking.* New York: Basic Books

Hogg, Richard M. 1988. 'Snuck: The development of irregular preterite forms', in Nixon and Honey (eds.), pp. 31–40

Hogg, Richard M., and Denison, David (eds.) 2006. *A history of the English language.* Cambridge: Cambridge University Press

Hollmann, Willem B. 2003. Synchrony and diachrony of English periphrastic causatives: A cognitive perspective. Doctoral dissertation. University of Manchester.

Hollmann, Willem, and Siewierska, Anna 2006. 'Corpora and (the need for) other methods in a study of a Lancashire dialect to require independent factors', *Zeitschrift für Anglistik und Amerikanistik* 53: 203–16.

Holmes, Virginia, Stowe, Laurie, and Cupples, Linda 1989. 'Lexical expectations in parsing complement-verb sentences', *Journal of Memory and Language* 28(6): 668–89

Holyoak, Keith J., and Thagard, Paul 1995. *Mental leaps: Analogy in creative thought.* Cambridge, MA: The MIT Press

Hooper, Celia R., and Cralidis, Ann 2009. 'Normal changes in the speech of older adults: You've still got what it takes; it just takes a little longer!', *SIG 15 Perspectives on Gerontology* 14(2): 47–56

Hooper, Joan B. 1976. 'Word frequency in lexical diffusion and the source of morphophonological change', in Christie (ed.), pp. 96–105

Hooper, Joan B. 1980. 'Child morphology and morphophonemic change', in Fisiak (ed.), pp. 157–87

Hopkins, Gerald M. 1918. *'Pied Beauty': Poems of Gerald Manley Hopkins.* London: Humphrey Milford

Hopper, Paul J. (ed.) 1982. *Tense-aspect: Between semantics and pragmatics.* Amsterdam and Philadelphia: John Benjamins

Hopper, Paul J. 1998. 'Emergent grammar', in Tomasello (ed.), pp. 155–75

Hopper, Paul J., and Thompson, Sandra A. 1980. 'Transitivity in grammar and discourse', *Language* 56(2): 251–99

Hopper, Paul J., and Traugott, Elizabeth C. 2003. *Grammaticalization.* 2nd edition. Cambridge: Cambridge University Press

Horn, Laurence R. 1984. 'Toward a new taxonomy for pragmatic inference: Q-based and R-based implicature', in Schiffrin (ed.), pp. 11–42

Huang, Yi Ting, and Pinker, Steven 2010. 'Lexical semantics and irregular inflection', *Language and Cognitive Processes* 25(10): 1411–61

Huddleston, Rodney D., and Pullum, Geoffrey K. 2002. *The Cambridge grammar of the English language.* Cambridge: Cambridge University Press

Hume, Elizabeth, Johnson, Keith, Seo, Misun, and Tserdanelis, Georgios 1999. 'A cross-linguistic study of stop place perception', in Ohala, Hasegawa, Ohala, Granville and Bailey (eds.), pp. 2069–72

Hundt, Marianne (ed.) 2014a. *Late Modern English syntax.* Cambridge: Cambridge University Press

Hundt, Marianne 2014b. 'The demise of the *being to V* construction', *Transactions of the Philological Society* 112(2): 167–87

Hundt, Marianne, and Leech, Geoffrey 2012. '"Small is beautiful": On the value of standard reference corpora for observing recent grammatical change', in Nevalainen and Traugott (eds.), pp. 175–88

Huttenlocher, Janellen, Vasilyeva, Marina, Cymerman, Elina, and Levine, Susan 2002. 'Language input and child syntax', *Cognitive Psychology* 45(3): 337–74

Huttenlocher, Janellen, Vasilyeva, Marina, and Shimpi, Priya 2004. 'Syntactic priming in young children', *Journal of Memory and Language* 50(2): 182–95

Ibbotson, Paul 2013. 'The scope of usage-based theory', *Frontiers in Psychology* 4: 255

Ibbotson, Paul, and Tomasello, Michael 2009. 'Prototype constructions in early language acquisition', *Language and Cognition* 1(1): 59–85

Itkonen, Esa 2005. *Analogy as structure and process*. Amsterdam: Benjamins

Ivanova, Iva, Pickering, Martin J., Branigan, Holly P., McLean, Janet F., and Costa, Albert 2012. 'The comprehension of anomalous sentences: Evidence from structural priming', *Cognition* 122(2): 193–209

Jackendoff, Ray 2002. *Foundations of language*. Oxford: Oxford University Press

Jacob, Gunnar, and Felser, Claudia 2015. 'Reanalysis and semantic persistence in native and non-native garden-path recovery', *Quarterly Journal of Experimental Psychology* 69(5): 1–19

Jaeger, T. Florian, and Snider, Neal E. 2013. 'Alignment as a consequence of expectation adaptation: Syntactic priming is affected by the prime's prediction error given both prior and recent experience', *Cognition* 127(1): 57–83

Jäger, Gerhard, and Rosenbach, Anette 2008. 'Priming and unidirectional language change', *Theoretical Linguistics* 34(2): 85–113

James, William 1890a. *The principles of psychology*, vol. 1. New York: Dover

James, William 1890b. *The principles of psychology*, vol. 2. New York: Holt

Jankowski, Bridget 2004. 'A transatlantic perspective of variation and change in English deontic modality', *Toronto Working Papers in Linguistics* 23: 85–113

Jared, Debra, McRae, Ken, and Seidenberg, Mark S. 1990. 'The basis of consistency effects in word naming', *Journal of Memory and Language* 29(6): 687–715

Jescheniak, Jörg D., and Levelt, Willem J. M. 1994. 'Word frequency effects in speech production: Retrieval of syntactic information and of phonological form', *Journal of Experimental Psychology: Learning, Memory, and Cognition* 20(4): 824–43

Jespersen, Otto 1909–49. *A Modern English grammar on historical principles*. 7 vols. Heidelberg: Winter

Jespersen, Otto 1922. *Language: Its nature, development and origin*. London: Allen and Unwin

Jiang, Nan, and Nekrasova, Tatiana M. 2007. 'The processing of formulaic sequences by second language speakers', *The Modern Language Journal* 91(3): 433–45

Johnson, Christopher R. 1999. *Constructional grounding: The role of interpretational overlap in lexical and constructional acquisition.* Doctoral dissertation. University of California, Berkeley

Johnson, Christopher R. 2001. 'Constructional grounding: On the relation between deictic and existential *there* constructions in acquisition', in Cienki, Luka and Smith (eds.), pp. 123–36

Johnson, Christopher R. 2005. 'Developmental reinterpretation in first language acquisition'. Paper presented at the Symposium 'Exemplar-based models in linguistics, 79th meeting of the Linguistic Society of America', Oakland, January 9

Jonas, Dianne, Whitman, John, and Garrett, Andrew (eds.) 2011. *Grammatical change: Origins, nature, outcomes.* Oxford: Oxford University Press

Jones, Benjamin F. 2005. 'The burden of knowledge and the "death of the Renaissance man": Is innovation getting harder?' Working Paper 11360.

Jones, Gregory V. 1985. 'Deep dyslexia, imageability, and ease of predication', *Brain and Language* 24(1): 1–19

Jones, Mari C., and Esch, Edith (eds.) 2002. *Language change: The interplay of internal, external, and extra-linguistic factors.* Berlin and New York: Mouton de Gruyter

Joseph, Brian D., and Janda, Richard D. (eds.) 2003. *The handbook of historical linguistics.* Oxford: Blackwell

Jucker, Andreas H. 1995. *Historical pragmatics: Pragmatic developments in the history of English.* Amsterdam: Benjamins

Jurafsky, Daniel 2002. 'Probabilistic modeling in psycholinguistics: Linguistic comprehension and production', in Bod, Hay and Jannedy (eds.), pp. 39–96

Jurafsky, Daniel, Bell, Alan, Gregory, Michelle, and Raymond, William D. 2001. 'Probabilistic relations between words: Evidence from reduction in lexical production', in Bybee and Hopper (eds.), pp. 229–54

Kamide, Yuki, and Mitchell, Don 1999. 'Incremental pre-head attachment in Japanese parsing', *Language and Cognitive Processes* 14(5–6): 631–32

Kamin, Leon J. 1969. 'Predictability, surprise, attention, and conditioning', in Campbell and Church (eds.), pp. 279–96

Kantola, Leila, and van Gompel, Roger P. G. 2011. 'Between- and within-language priming is the same: Evidence for shared bilingual syntactic representations', *Memory and Cognition* 39(2): 276–90

Kaschak, Michael P. 2006. 'What this construction needs is generalized', *Memory and Cognition* 34(2): 368–79

Kaschak, Michael P., and Borreggine, Kristin L. 2008. 'Is long-term structural priming affected by patterns of experience with individual verbs?', *Journal of Memory and Language* 58(3): 862–78

Kaschak, Michael P., and Glenberg, Arthur M. 2004. 'This construction needs learned', *Journal of Experimental Psychology: General* 133(3): 450–67

Kaschak, Michael P., Kutta, Timothy J., and Coyle, Jacqueline M. 2014. 'Long and short term cumulative structural priming effects', *Language, Cognition and Neuroscience* 29(6): 728–43

Kaschak, Michael P., Kutta, Timothy J., and Schatschneider, Chris 2011. 'Long-term cumulative structural priming persists for (at least) one week', *Memory and Cognition* 39(3): 381–88

Kastovsky, Dieter (ed.) 1994. *Studies in Modern English*. Berlin: Mouton de Gruyter

Kay, Paul 1997a. 'The *kind of/sort of* construction', in Kay (ed.), pp. 145–58

Kay, Paul (ed.) 1997b. *Words and the grammar of context*. Stanford, CA: CSLI Publications

Ke, Jinyun 2006. 'A cross-linguistic quantitative study of homophony', *Journal of Quantitative Linguistics* 13(1): 129–59

Kecskes, Istvan 2012. 'Sociopragmatics and cross-cultural and intercultural studies', in Allan and Jaszczolt (eds.), pp. 599–616

Kecskes, Istvan 2013. *Intercultural pragmatics*. Oxford: Oxford University Press

Keizer, Evelien 2007. *The English noun phrase: The nature of linguistic categorization*. Cambridge: Cambridge University Press

Keller, Rudi 1994. *On language change: The invisible hand in language*. London: Routledge [Trans. Brigitte Nerlich; first published 1990 in German]

Kello, Christopher T., Brown, Gordon D. A., Ferrer-i-Cancho, Ramon, Holden, John G., Linkenkaer-Hansen, Klaus, Rhodes, Theo, and van Orden, Guy C. 2010. 'Scaling laws in cognitive sciences', *Trends in Cognitive Science* 14(5): 223–32

Kemps, Rachel, Ernestus, Mirjam, Schreuder, Robert, and Baayen, R. Harald 2005a. 'Prosodic cues for morphological complexity: The case of Dutch noun plurals', *Memory and Cognition* 33(3): 430–46

Kemps, Rachel, Wurm, Lee H., Ernestus, Mirjam, Schreuder, Robert, and Baayen, R. Harald 2005b. 'Prosodic cues for morphological complexity in Dutch and English', *Language and Cognitive Processes* 20(1–2): 43–73

Kennedy, Alan, Radach, Ralph, Heller, Dieter, and Pynte, Joël (eds.) 2000. *Reading as a perceptual process*. Amsterdam: North-Holland/Elsevier Science Publishers

Kepser, Stephan, and Reis, Marga (eds.) 2005. *Linguistic evidence. Empirical, theoretical, and computational perspectives*. Berlin and New York: Mouton de Gruyter

Kerswill, Paul 1996. 'Children, adolescents and language change', *Language Variation and Change* 8(2): 177–202

Kerswill, Paul, and Williams, Ann 2002. '"Salience" as an explanatory factor in language change: Evidence from dialect levelling in urban England', in Jones and Esch (eds.), pp. 81–110

Keuleers, Emmanuel, Stevens, Michaël, Mandera, Pawel, and Brysbaert, Marc 2015. 'Word knowledge in the crowd: Measuring vocabulary size and word prevalence in a massive online experiment', *The Quarterly Journal of Experimental Psychology* 66(8): 1665–92

Kiparsky, Paul 1968. 'Linguistic universals and linguistic change', in Bach and Harms (eds.), pp. 170–202

Kiparsky, Paul 2014. 'New perspectives in historical linguistics', in Bowern and Evans (eds.), pp. 64–102

Kirby, Simon 1999. *Function, selection and innateness*. Oxford: Oxford University Press

Kirjavainen, Minna, Lieven, Elena V. M., and Theakston, Anna L. 2016. 'Can infinitival *to* omissions and provisions be primed? An experimental investigation into the role of constructional competition in infinitival *to* omission errors', *Cognitive Science*: 1–32 [DOI: 10.1111/cogs.12407]

Kirjavainen, Minna, and Theakston, Anna L. 2011. 'Are infinitival *to* omission errors primed by prior discourse? The case of WANT constructions', *Cognitive Linguistics* 22(4): 629–57

Kirjavainen, Minna, Theakston, Anna L., and Lieven, Elena V. M. 2009. 'Can input explain children's *me-for-I* errors?', *Journal of Child Language* 36(5): 1091–114

Kirjavainen, Minna, Theakston, Anna L., Lieven, Elena V. M., and Tomasello, Michael 2009. '"I want hold Postman Pat": An investigation into the acquisition of infinitival marker *to*', *First Language* 29(3): 313–39

Klein, Wolfgang 1998. 'The contribution of second language acquisition research', *Language Learning* 48(4): 527–50

Köhler, Reinhard 1986. *Zur linguistischen Synergetik: Struktur und Dynamik der Lexik*. Bochum: Brockmeyer

Köhler, Reinhard, Altmann, Gabriel, and Piotrowski, Rajmund G. (eds.) 2005. *Quantitative linguistics. An international handbook*. Berlin and New York: Mouton de Gruyter

Kohnen, Thomas, and Mair, Christian 2012. 'Technologies of communication', in Nevalainen and Traugott (eds.), pp. 261–84

Konopka, Agnieszka E., and Bock, J. Kathryn 2005. 'Helping syntax out: What do words do?' Paper presented at the CUNY Sentence Processing Conference, Tucson, Arizona

Konopka, Agnieszka E., and Bock, J. Kathryn 2009. 'Lexical or syntactic control of sentence formulation? Structural generalizations from idiom production', *Cognitive Psychology* 58(1): 68–101

Köpcke, Klaus-Michael 1993. *Schemata bei der Pluralbildung des Deutschen: Versuch einer kognitiven Morphologie*. Tübingen: Narr

Köpcke, Klaus-Michael 1998. 'The acquisition of plural marking in English and German revisited: Schemata vs. rules', *Journal of Child Language* 25(2): 293–319

Kortmann, Bernd, and Lunkenheimer, Kerstin (eds.) 2013. *The Mouton world atlas of variation in English*. Berlin and New York: Mouton de Gruyter

Krasnegor, Norman A., Rumbaugh, Duane M., Schiefelbusch, Richard L., and Studdert-Kennedy, Michael (eds.) 1991. *Biological and behavioral determinants of language development*. Mahwah, NJ: Erlbaum

Krause, Anne 2017. *Frequency effects on entrenchment: converging evidence from ongoing language change*. Doctoral dissertation, University of Freiburg

Kroch, Anthony 2001. 'Syntactic change', in Baltin and Collins (eds.), pp. 699–729

Krug, Manfred G. 1998. 'String frequency. A cognitive motivating factor in coalescence, language processing, and linguistic change', *Journal of English Linguistics* 26(4): 286–320

Krug, Manfred G. 2000. *Emerging English modals: A corpus-based study of grammaticalization*. Berlin: Mouton de Gruyter

Kruschke, John K. 2006. 'Learned attention'. Fifth International Conference on Development and Learning, June 2006. Indiana University

Kruschke, John K., and Blair, Nathaniel J. 2000. 'Blocking and backward blocking involve learned inattention', *Psychonomic Bulletin and Review* 7(4): 636–45

Kuiper, Koenraad 1996. *Smooth talkers: The linguistic performance of auctioneers and sportscasters*. Mahwah, NJ: Erlbaum

Küntay, Aylin C., and Slobin, Dan I. 2002. 'Putting interaction back into child language: Examples from Turkish', *Psychology of Language and Communication* 6(1): 5–14

Kuperman, Victor, Pluymaekers, Mark, Ernestus, Mirjam, and Baayen, R. Harald 2007. 'Morphological predictability and acoustic duration of interfixes in Dutch compounds', *Journal of the Acoustical Society of America* 121(4): 2261–71

Kuryłowicz, Jerzy 1949. 'La nature des procès dits "analogiques"', *Acta Linguistica* 5(1): 15–37

Kytö, Merja 1991. *Manual to the diachronic part of the Helsinki Corpus of English Texts: Coding conventions and lists of source texts*. 3rd edition. Helsinki: Department of English, University of Helsinki

Kytö, Merja (ed.) 2012. *English corpus linguistics: Crossing paths*. Amsterdam: Rodopi

Kytö, Merja, and Pahta, Päivi (eds.) 2016. *The Cambridge handbook of English historical linguistics*. Cambridge: Cambridge University Press

Labov, William 1982. 'Building on empirical foundations', in Lehmann and Malkiel (eds.), pp. 17–92

Laird, John E., Newell, Allen, and Rosenbloom, Paul S. 1987. 'Soar: An architecture for general intelligence', *Artificial intelligence* 33(1): 1–64

Laird, John E., Rosenbloom, Paul S., and Newell, Allen 1986. 'Chunking in Soar: The anatomy of a general learning mechanism', *Machine learning* 1(1): 11–46

Lakoff, George 1987. *Women, fire, and dangerous things: What categories reveal about the mind*. Chicago: University of Chicago Press

Lamb, Michael E., and Brown, Ann L. (eds.) 1982. *Advances in developmental psychology*, vol. 2. Hillsdale, NJ: Lawrence Erlbaum

Lamendella, John T. 1976. 'Relations between the ontogeny and phylogeny of language: A neo-recapitulationist view', in Harnad, Steklis and Lancaster (eds.), pp. 396–412

Landauer, Thomas K., and Dumais, Susan T. 1997. 'A solution to Plato's problem: The latent semantic analysis theory of acquisition, induction, and representation of knowledge', *Psychological Review* 104.2: 211–40.

Lang, Jürgen, and Neumann-Holzschuh, Ingrid (eds.) 1999. *Reanalyse und Grammatikalisierung in den Romanischen Sprachen*. Tübingen: Max Niemeyer Verlag

Langacker, Ronald W. 1977. 'Syntactic reanalysis', in Li (ed.), pp. 57–139

Langacker, Ronald W. 1987. *Foundations of cognitive grammar, vol. 1: Theoretical prerequisites*. Stanford, CA: Stanford University Press

Langacker, Ronald W. 1991. *Foundations of cognitive grammar, vol. 2: Descriptive application*. Stanford, CA: Stanford University Press

Langacker, Ronald W. 2000. 'A dynamic usage-based model', in Barlow and Kemmer (eds.), pp. 1–63

Langacker, Ronald W. 2008. *Cognitive grammar: A basic introduction*. Oxford: Oxford University Press

Langer, Jonas 2000. 'The descent of cognitive development', *Developmental Science* 3(4): 361–78

Larsen-Freeman, Diane 1997. 'Chaos/complexity science and second language acquisition', *Applied Linguistics* 18(2): 141–65

Lass, Roger (ed.) 1999. *The Cambridge history of the English language, vol. 3: 1476–1776*. Cambridge: Cambridge University Press

Laxon, Veronica, Masterson, Jacqueline, and Coltheart, Veronika 1991. 'Some bodies are easier to read: The effect of consistency and regularity on children's reading', *Quarterly Journal of Experimental Psychology: Human Experimental Psychology* 43(4): 793–824

Łęcki, Andrzej M. 2010. *Grammaticalisation paths of* have *in English*. Bern: Peter Lang

Leech, Geoffrey 1981. *Semantics: The study of meaning*. 2nd edition. Harmondsworth: Penguin

Leech, Geoffrey, Hundt, Marianne, Mair, Christian, and Smith, Nicholas 2009. *Change in contemporary English: A grammatical study*. Cambridge: Cambridge University Press

Leech, Geoffrey, Rayson, Paul, and Wilson, Andrew 2001. *Word frequencies in written and spoken English: Based on the British National Corpus*. London: Longman

Legate, Julie A., and Yang, Charles 2007. 'Morphosyntactic learning and the development of tense', *Language Acquisition* 14(3): 315–44

Lehmann, Christian 2002. *Thoughts on grammaticalization*. 2nd edition. Seminar für Sprachwissenschaft der Universität Erfurt (ASSidUE, 9) [under Schriftenverzeichnis, 2002] www.christianlehmann.eu/ [accessed April 19, 2016]

Lehmann, Winfred P., and Malkiel, Yakov (eds.) 1968. *Directions for historical linguistics: A symposium*. Austin: University of Texas Press

Lehmann, Winfred P., and Malkiel, Yakov (eds.) 1982. *Perspectives on historical linguistics*. Amsterdam: Benjamins

Lenker, Ursula 2010. *Argument and rhetoric. Adverbial connectors in the history of English*. Berlin and New Work: Mouton de Gruyter

Levelt, Willem J. M., and Kelter, Stephanie 1982. 'Surface form and memory in question answering', *Cognitive Psychology* 14(1): 78–106

Levelt, Willem J. M., Roelofs, Ardi, and Meyer, Antje S. 1999. 'A theory of lexical access in speech production', *Behavioral and Brain Sciences* 22(1): 1–38

Levinson, Stephen C. 1995. 'Three levels of meaning', in Palmer (ed.), pp. 90–115

Li, Charles N. (ed.) 1977. *Mechanisms of syntactic change*. Austin, TX and London: University of Texas Press

Liberman, Mark 2010. '"Begging the question": We have answers'. http://langua gelog.ldc.upenn.edu/nll/?p=2290 [accessed April 19, 2016]

Lieberman, Erez, Michel, Jean-Baptiste, Jackson, Joe, Tang, Tina, and Nowak, Martin A. 2007. 'Quantifying the evolutionary dynamics of language', *Nature* 449(7163): 713–16

Lieven, Elena V. M. 2008. 'Learning the English auxiliary: A usage-based approach', in Behrens (ed.), pp. 61–98

Lieven, Elena V. M. 2010. 'Input and first language acquisition: Evaluating the role of frequency', *Lingua* 120(11): 2546–56

Lieven, Elena V. M., Behrens, Heike, Speares, Jennifer, and Tomasello, Michael 2003. 'Early syntactic creativity: A usage-based approach', *Journal of Child Language* 30(1): 333–70

Lieven, Elena V. M., Pine, Julian M., and Dresner Barnes, Helen 1992. 'Individual differences in early vocabulary development: Redefining the referential expressive dimension', *Journal of Child Language* 19(2): 287–310

Lieven, Elena V. M., and Tomasello, Michael 2008. 'Children's first language acquisition from a usage-based perspective', in Robinson and Ellis (eds.), pp. 168–96

Lightbown, Patsy M., and Spada, Nina 1999. *How languages are learned*. Oxford: Oxford University Press

Lightfoot, David 1979. *Principles of diachronic syntax*. Cambridge: Cambridge University Press

Lightfoot, David 1991. *How to set parameters: Arguments from language change*. Cambridge, MA: The MIT Press

Lightfoot, David 1997. 'Catastrophic change and learning theory', *Lingua* 100(1): 171–92

Lightfoot, David 1999. *The development of language: Acquisition, change, and evolution*. Malden, MA and Oxford: Blackwell

Lightfoot, David 2006. *How new languages emerge*. Cambridge: Cambridge University Press

Lightfoot, David 2010. 'Language acquisition and language change', *Wiley Interdisciplinary Reviews: Cognitive Science* 1(5): 677–84

Lima, Susan D., Corrigan, Roberta L., and Iverson, Gregory K. (eds.) 1994. *The reality of linguistic rules*. Amsterdam: John Benjamins

Lindquist, Hans, and Mair, Christian (eds.) 2004. *Corpus approaches to grammaticalization in English*. Amsterdam: Benjamins

Lipka, Leonhard 1985. 'Inferential features in historical semantics', in Fisiak (ed.), pp. 339–54

Lively, Scott E., Pisoni, David B., and Goldinger, Stephen D. 1994. 'Spoken word recognition: Research and theory', in Gernsbacher (ed.), pp. 265–301

Loebell, Helga, and Bock, J. Kathryn 2003. 'Structural priming across languages', *Linguistics* 41(5): 791–824

López-Couso, María José 2007. 'Frequency effects: Middle English *nis* as a case in point', in Mazzon (ed.), pp. 165–78

López-Couso, María José 2011. 'Developmental parallels in diachronic and onto-genetic grammaticalization: Existential *there* as a test case', *Folia Linguistica* 45(1): 81–102

Lorenz, David 2013. *Contractions of English semi-modals: The emancipating effect of frequency*. Freiburg: Rombach

Los, Bettelou 2005. *The rise of the* to-*infinitive*. Oxford: Oxford University Press

Loudermilk, Brandon C. 2013. 'Psycholinguistic approaches', in Bayley, Cameron and Lucas (eds.), pp. 132–52

Luce, Paul A. 1986. 'A computational analysis of uniqueness points in auditory word recognition', *Perception and Psychophysics* 39(3): 155–58

Lüdeling, Anke and Evert, Stefan 2005. 'The emergence of non-medical -*itis*. Corpus evidence and qualitative analysis', in Kepser and Reis (eds.), pp. 315–33

Luka, Barbara J., and Barsalou, Lawrence W. 2005. 'Structural facilitation: Mere exposure effects for grammatical acceptability as evidence for syntactic priming in comprehension', *Journal of Memory and Language* 52(3): 436–59

Luka, Barbara J., and Choi, Heidi 2012. 'Dynamic grammar in adults: Incidental learning of natural syntactic structures extends over 48 h', *Journal of Memory and Language* 66(2): 345–60

Lyons, John 1995. *Linguistic semantics: An introduction*. Cambridge: Cambridge University Press

MacDonald, Maryellen C. 1994. 'Probabilistic constraints and syntactic ambiguity resolution', *Language and Cognitive Processes* 9(2): 157–201

MacDonald, Maryellen C., Pearlmutter, Neal J., and Seidenberg, Mark S. 1994. 'The lexical nature of syntactic ambiguity resolution', *Psychological Review* 101(4): 676–703

MacDonald, Maryellen C., and Seidenberg, Mark S. 2006. 'Constraint satisfaction accounts of lexical and sentence comprehension', in Traxler and Gernsbacher (eds.), pp. 581–611

Mackintosh, Nicholas J. 1975. 'A theory of attention: Variations in the associability of stimuli with reinforcement', *Psychological Review* 82(4): 276–98

MacWhinney, Brian 1987a. 'The competition model', in MacWhinney (ed.), pp. 249–308

MacWhinney, Brian (ed.) 1987b. *Mechanisms of language acquisition*. Hillsdale, NJ: Lawrence Erlbaum

MacWhinney, Brian 2000. *The CHILDES-Project: Tools for analyzing talk*. 2 vols. 3rd edition. Mahwah, NJ: Erlbaum.

MacWhinney, Brian 2004. 'New directions in the competition model', in Tomasello and Slobin (eds.), pp. 81–110

MacWhinney, Brian 2012. 'The logic of the unified model', in Gass and Mackey (eds.), pp. 211–27

MacWhinney, Brian, and O'Grady, William (eds.) 2015. *The handbook of language emergence*. Oxford: Wiley-Blackwell

Mair, Christian 2004. 'Corpus linguistics and grammaticalisation theory: Statistics, frequencies, and beyond', in Lindquist and Mair (eds.), pp. 121–50

Mair, Christian 2012. 'From opportunistic to systematic use of the web as corpus: *Do*-Support with *got (to)* in contemporary American English', in Nevalainen and Traugott (eds.), pp. 245–55

Mair, Christian 2014. '*Do we got a difference?* – Divergent developments of semi-auxiliary *(have) got (to)* in BrE and AmE', in Hundt (ed.), pp. 56–76

Majid, Asifa, Bowerman, Melissa, Kita, Sotaro, Haun, Daniel B. M., and Levinson, Stephen C. 2004. 'Can language restructure cognition? The case for space', *Trends in Cognitive Sciences* 8(3): 108–14

Malchukov, Andrej, and Siewierska, Anna (eds.) 2011. *Impersonal constructions. A cross-linguistic perspective*. Amsterdam: Benjamins

Manabe, Kazumi 1989. *The syntactic and stylistic development of the infinitive in Middle English*. Fukuoka: Kyushu University Press

Mańczak, Witold 1958. 'Tendences générales des changements analogiques', *Lingua* 7: 298–325

Mandler, Jean M. 2008. 'On the birth and growth of concepts', *Philosophical Psychology* 21(2): 207–30

Marcus, Gary F., Brinkmann, Ursula, Clahsen, Harald, Wiese, Richard, and Pinker, Steven 1995. 'German inflection: The exception that proves the rule', *Cognitive Psychology* 29(3): 189–256

Marcus, Gary F., Pinker, Steven, Ullman, Michael, Hollander, Michelle, Rosen, T. John, Xu, Fei, and Clahsen, Harald 1992. 'Overregularization in language acquisition', *Monographs of the Society for Research in Child Development* 57(4): 1–178

Marcus, Gary F., Vijayan, S., Bandi Rao, Shoba, and Vishton, Peter M. 1999. 'Rule learning by seven-month-old infants', *Science* 283(5398): 77–80

Markman, Arthur B., and Gentner, Dedre 1993. 'Structural alignment during similarity comparisons', *Cognitive Psychology* 25(4): 431–67

Marslen-Wilson, William 1973. 'Linguistic structure and speech shadowing at very short latencies', *Nature* 244: 522–33

Marslen-Wilson, William 1990. 'Activation, competition, and frequency in lexical access', in Altmann (ed.), pp. 148–72

Marsolek, Chad J. 2008. 'What antipriming reveals about priming', *Trends in Cognitive Science* 12(5): 176–81

Maslen, Robert J. C., Theakston, Anna L., Lieven, Elena V. M., and Tomasello, Michael 2004. 'A dense corpus study of past tense and plural overregularization in English', *Journal of Speech, Language and Hearing Research* 47(6): 1319–33

Matthews, Peter H. 2014. *The positions of adjectives in English*. Oxford: Oxford University Press

Matthey, Marinette 2001. 'Le changement linguistique: Évolution, variation, hétérogénéité. Actes du colloque de Neuchâtel Université, Neuchâtel, Suisse

2–4 Octobre 2000 [Linguistic change: Evolution, variation, heterogeneity. *Proceedings of the University of Neuchâtel colloquium*, Neuchâtel, Switzerland, October 2–4, 2000]', *Travaux Neuchâtelois de Linguistique* 34: 273–303

Mayerthaler, Willi 1981. *Morphologische Natürlichkeit*. Wiesbaden: Athenaion

Mazzon, Gabriella (ed.) 2007. *Studies in Middle English forms and meanings*. Frankfurt am Main, etc.: Peter Lang

Menn, Lise, and Stoel-Gammon, Carol 1994. 'Phonological development', in Fletcher and MacWhinney (eds.), pp. 335–59

McCauley, Stewart M., and Christiansen, Morten H. 2014. 'Acquiring formulaic language: A computational model', *Mental Lexicon* 9(3): 419–36

McClelland, James L., and Elman, Jeffrey L. 1986. 'The TRACE model of speech perception', *Cognitive Psychology* 18(1): 1–86

McCullough, Gretchen 2012. 'Because reasons', *All Things Linguistic*, July 4, 2012. http://allthingslinguistic.com/post/26522214342/because-reasons [accessed December 27, 2014]

McCullough, Gretchen 2013. 'Where "because noun" probably came from', *All Things Linguistic*, 19 November 2013. http://allthingslinguistic.com/post/675073 11833/where-because-noun-probably-came-from [accessed December 27, 2014]

McDaniel, Dana, McKee, Cecile, Cowart, Wayne, and Garrett, Merrill F. 2015. 'The role of the language production system in shaping grammars', *Language* 91(2): 415–41

McDonald, Scott A., and Shillcock, Richard C. 2003a. 'Eye-movements reveal the on-line computation of lexical probabilities during reading', *Psychological Science* 14(6): 648–52

McDonald, Scott A., and Shillcock, Richard C. 2003b. 'Low-level predictive inference in reading: The influence of transitional probabilities on eye movements', *Vision Research* 43(16): 1735–51

McDonough, Kim, and Trofimovich, Pavel 2008. *Using priming methods in second language research*. London: Routledge

McRae, Ken, and Matsuki, Kazunaga 2013. 'Constraint-based models of sentence processing', in van Gompel (ed.), pp. 51–77

McRae, Ken, Spivey-Knowlton, Michael J., and Tanenhaus, Michael K. 1998. 'Modeling the influence of thematic fit (and other constraints) in on-line sentence comprehension', *Journal of Memory and Language* 38(3): 283–312

McWhorter, John 2001. 'The world's simplest grammars are creole grammars', *Language Typology* 5(2–3): 125–66

McWhorter, John 2002. *The power of Babel: A natural history of language*. San Franciso, CA: W. H. Freeman and Co.

McWhorter, John 2004. The story of human language. Lecture 24: Language interrupted. The Great Courses. The Teaching Company Limited Partnership

Meibauer, Jörg, Guttropf, Anja, and Scherer, Carmen 2004. 'Dynamic aspects of German -*er*-nominals: A probe into the interrelation of language change and language acquisition', *Linguistics* 42(1): 155–93

Meillet, Antoine (ed.) 1951/1958. *Linguistique historique et linguistique générale*. 2 vols. Paris: Klincksieck/Champion

Meillet, Antoine 1958. 'L'évolution des formes grammaticales', in Meillet (ed.), pp. 130–48 [First published 1912 in *Scientia [Rivista di Scienza]*: 12]

Meisel, Jürgen 2011. 'Bilingual language acquisition and theories of diachronic change: Bilingualism as cause and effect of grammatical change', *Bilingualism: Language and Cognition* 14(2): 121–45

Meisel, Jürgen, Elsig, Martin, and Rinke, Esther 2013. *Language acquisition and change: A morphosyntactic perspective*. Edinburgh: Edinburgh University Press

Meurman-Solin, Anneli, López-Couso, María José, and Los, Bettelou (eds.) 2012. *Information structure and syntactic change in the history of English*. Oxford: Oxford University Press

Meyerhoff, Miriam 1992. '"A sort of something" – Hedging strategies on nouns', *Working Papers on Language, Gender and Sexism* 2(1): 59–73

Meylan, Stephan C., and Gahl, Susanne 2014. 'The divergent lexicon: Lexical overlap decreases with age in a large corpus of conversational speech', in Bello, Guarini, McShane and Scassellati (eds.), pp. 1006–11

Michel, Jean-Baptiste, Shen, Yuan Kui, Presser Aiden, Aviva, Veres, Adrian, Gray, Matthew K., The Google Books Team, Pickett, Joseph P., Hoiberg, Dale, Clancy, Dan, Norvig, Peter, Orwant, Jon, Pinker, Steven, Nowak, Martin A., and Lieberman Aiden, Erez 2011. 'Quantitative analysis of culture using millions of digitized books', *Science* 331(6014): 176–82

Milin, Petar, Feldman, Laurie B., Ramscar, Michael, Hendrix, P., Baayen, R. Harald (2017). 'Discrimination in lexical decision.' *PLoS ONE*, 12(2), e0171935

Miller, George A. 1956. 'The magical number seven, plus or minus two: Some limits on our capacity for processing information', *Psychological Review* 63(2): 81–97

Miller, George A. 1958. 'Free recall of redundant strings of letters', *Journal of Experimental Psychology* 56(6): 485

Miller, George A. 1990. 'Linguists, psychologists and the cognitive sciences', *Language* 66(2): 317–22

Miller, George A., Bruner, Jerome S., and Postman, Leo 1954. 'Familiarity of letter sequences and tachistoscopic identification', *Journal of General Psychology* 50(1): 129–39

Miller, George A., and Selfridge, Jennifer A. 1950. 'Verbal context and the recall of meaningful material', *The American Journal of Psychology* 63(2): 176–85

Milroy, James 1992. *Linguistic variation and change: On the historical sociolinguistics of English*. Oxford: Blackwell

Mintz, Toben H. 2003. 'Frequent frames as a cue for grammatical categories in child directed speech', *Cognition* 90(1): 91–117

Mitchell, Tom M., Shinkareva, Svetlana V., Carlson, Andrew, Chang, Kai-Min, Malave, Vicente L., Mason, Robert A., and Just, Marcel A. 2008. 'Predicting human brain activity associated with the meanings of nouns', *Science* 320(5880): 1191–95

Molnar, Monika, and Sabastián-Galles, Núria (eds.) 2014. *The roots of language learning: Infant language acquisition.* Hoboken: Wiley

Montermini, Fabio, Boyé, Gilles, and Hathout, Nabil 2007. *Selected proceedings of the 5th Décembrettes: Morphology in Toulouse.* Somerville, MA: Cascadilla Proceedings Project

Montgomery, Chris 2012. 'Perceptions of dialects: Changing attitudes and ideologies', in Nevalainen and Traugott (eds.), pp. 457–69

Morton, John 1969. 'Interaction of information in word recognition', *Psychological Review* 76(2): 165–78

Mufwene, Salikoko S. 2001. *The ecology of language evolution.* Cambridge: Cambridge University Press

Mufwene, Salikoko S. 2008. *Language evolution: Contact, competition and change.* London: Continuum International Publishing Group

Mugdan, Joachim 1977. *Flexionsmorphologie und Psycholinguistik.* Tübingen: Narr

Müller, Max 1890. *The science of language.* New York: Charles Scribner

Naigles, Letitia R., Hoff, Erika, Vear, Donna, Tomasello, Michael, Brandt, Silke, Waxman, Sandra R., Childers, Jane B., and Collins, W. Andrew 2009. 'Flexibility in early verb use: Evidence from a multiple-N diary study', *Monographs for the Society for Research in Child Development* 74(2): 1–144

Narrog, Heiko 2005. 'Modality, mood, and change of modal meanings: A new perspective', *Cognitive Linguistics* 16(4): 677–731

Narrog, Heiko, and Heine, Bernd (eds.) 2011. *The Oxford handbook of grammaticalization.* Oxford: Oxford University Press

Nesselhauf, Nadja 2010. 'The development of future time expressions in Late Modern English: Redistribution of forms or change in discourse?', *English Language and Linguistics* 14(2): 163–86

Nevala, Minna 2016. 'Processes of sociolinguistic and sociopragmatic change', in Kytö and Pahta (eds.), pp. 286–300

Nevalainen, Terttu, and Raumolin-Brunberg, Helena 2003. *Historical sociolinguistics.* London: Longman

Nevalainen, Terttu, and Traugott, Elizabeth C. (eds.) 2012. *The Oxford handbook of the history of English.* Oxford: Oxford University Press

Newell, Allen 1990. *Unified theories of cognition.* Cambridge, MA: The MIT Press

Ninio, Anat 2006. *Language and the learning curve. A new theory of syntactic development.* Oxford: Oxford University Press

Ninio, Anat 2011. *Syntactic development, its input and output.* Oxford: Oxford University Press

Nixon, Graham, and Honey, John (eds.) 1988. *An historic tongue: Studies in English linguistics in memory of Barbara Strang.* London and New York: Routledge

Noël, Dirk 2012. 'Grammaticalization in diachronic construction grammar'. Lecture held at the Universidade Federal do Rio Grande do Norte, Natal, Brasil, November 27, 2012

Nowak, Martin A., Komaraova, Natalia L., and Niyogi, Partha 2002. 'Computational and evolutionary aspects of language', *Nature* 417(6889): 611–17

Nunberg, Geoffrey, Sag, Ivan A., and Wasow, Thomas 1994. 'Idioms', *Language* 70(3): 491–538

O'Donnell, Matthew B., Römer, Ute, and Ellis, Nick C. 2013. 'The development of formulaic sequences in first and second language writing: Investigating effects of frequency, association, and native norm', *International Journal of Corpus Linguistics* 18(1): 83–108

Ohala, John J., Hasegawa, Yoko, Ohala, Manjari, Granville, Daniel, and Bailey, Ashlee C. (eds.) 1999. 14th International Congress of Phonetic Sciences (ICPhS-14), San Francisco, CA, USA, August 1–7, 1999

Oldfield, Richard C., and Wingfield, Arthur 1965. 'Response latencies in naming objects', *Quarterly Journal of Experimental Psychology* 17(4): 273–81

Osgood, Charles E. 1957. *The measurement of meaning*. Illinois: University of Illinois Press

Pagliuca, William (ed.) 1994. *Perspectives on grammaticalization*. Amsterdam: Benjamins

Paivio, Allan 1971. *Imagery and verbal processes*. New York: Holt, Rinehart and Winston

Paivio, Allan 1986. *Mental representations: A dual coding approach*. Oxford: Oxford University Press

Paivio, Allan, Yuille, John C., and Madigan, Stephen A. 1968. 'Concreteness, imagery, and meaningfulness values for 925 nouns', *Journal of Experimental Psychology* 76(1): Suppl.: 1–25

Palmer, Frank R. (ed.) 1995. *Grammar and meaning. Essays in honour of Sir John Lyons*. Cambridge: Cambridge University Press

Palmore, Erdman B., and Manton, Kenneth 1973. 'Ageism compared to racism and sexism', *Journal of Gerontology* 28(3): 363–69

Papadopoulou, Despina, and Clahsen, Harald 2003. 'Parsing strategies in L1 and L2 sentence processing: A study of relative clause attachment in Greek', *Studies in Second Language Acquisition* 25: 501–28

Papafragou, Anna 2001. 'Linking early linguistic and conceptual capacities: The role of Theory of Mind', in Cienki, Luka and Smith (eds.), pp. 169–84

Parker, Frank 1976. 'Language change and the passive voice', *Language* 52(4): 449–60

Partington, Alan 2011. 'Phrasal irony: Its form, function and exploitation', *Journal of Pragmatics* 43(6): 1786–800

Paul, Hermann 1880/1960. *Prinzipien der Sprachgeschichte*. 6th edition. Halle: Niemeyer

Payne, Doris L. 2011. 'The Maa (Eastern Nilotic) impersonal construction', in Malchukov and Siewierska (eds.), pp. 257–84

Perdue, Clive (ed.) 1993. *Adult language acquisition: Crosslinguistic perspectives*. Cambridge: Cambridge University Press

Pérez, Aveline 1990. 'Time in motion: Grammaticalization of the *be going to* construction in English', *La Trobe Working Papers in Linguistics* 3: 49–64

Perruchet, Pierre, and Pacton, Sebastien 2006. 'Implicit learning and statistical learning: One phenomenon, two approaches', *Trends in Cognitive Sciences* 10(5): 233–38

Peter, Michelle, Chang, Franklin, Pine, Julian M., Blything, Ryan, and Rowland, Caroline F. 2015. 'When and how do children develop knowledge of verb argument structure? Evidence from verb bias effects in a structural priming task', *Journal of Memory and Language* 81: 1–15

Peters, Ann M. 1983. *The units of language acquisition*. Cambridge: Cambridge University Press

Peterson, Robert R., Burgess, Curt, Dell, Gary S., and Eberhard, Kathleen M. 2001. 'Disassociation between syntactic and semantic processing during idiom comprehension', *Journal of Experimental Psychology: Learning, Memory, and Cognition* 27(5): 1223–37

Petré, Peter 2009. 'Leuven English Old to New (LEON): Some ideas on a new corpus for longitudinal diachronic studies'. Paper presented at the Middle and Modern English Corpus Linguistics (MMECL) Conference, University of Innsbruck, July 5–9, 2009

Petré, Peter, and Cuyckens, H. 2008. 'Bedusted, yet not beheaded: The role of *be-*'s constructional properties in its conservation', in Bergs and Diewald (eds.), pp. 133–69

Pexman, Penny M., Siakaluk, Paul D., and Yap, Melvin J. 2013. 'Introduction to the research topic meaning in mind: Semantic richness effects in language processing', *Frontiers in Human Neuroscience* 7: 723

Pexman, Penny M., Siakaluk, Paul D., and Yap, Melvin J. 2014. *Meaning in mind: Semantic richness effects in language processing*. Frontiers E-Books

Phillips, Colin 2013. 'Some arguments and non-arguments for reductionist accounts of syntactic phenomena', *Language and Cognitive Processes* 28(1–2): 156–87

Piaget, Jean 1969. 'Genetic epistemology', *Columbia Forum* 12: 4–11

Piantadosi, Steven T., Tily, Harry, and Gibson, Edward 2011. 'Word lengths are optimized for efficient communication'. *Proceedings of the National Academy of Sciences* 108(9): 3526–9

Piantadosi, Steven T., Tily, Harry, and Gibson, Edward 2012. 'The communicative function of ambiguity in language', *Cognition* 122(3): 280–91

Pica, Teresa 1983. 'Adult acquisition of English as a second language under different conditions of exposure', *Language Learning* 33(4): 465–97

Pickering, Martin J. 2006. 'The dance of dialogue', *The Psychologist* 19(12): 734–37

Pickering, Martin J., and Branigan, Holly P. 1998. 'The representation of verbs: Evidence from syntactic priming in language production', *Journal of Memory and Language* 39(4): 633–51

Pickering, Martin J., and Ferreira, Victor S. 2008. 'Structural priming: A critical review', *Psychological Bulletin* 134(3): 427–59

Pickering, Martin J., and Garrod, Simon C. 2004. 'Toward a mechanistic psychology of dialogue', *Behavioral and Brain Sciences* 27(2): 169–225

Pickering, Martin J., and Garrod, Simon C. 2006. 'Alignment as the basis for successful communication', *Research on Language and Computation* 4(2–3): 203–28

Pickering, Martin J., and Garrod, Simon C. 2013. 'An integrated theory of language production and comprehension', *Behavioral and Brain Sciences* 36(4): 329–47

Pickering, Martin J., McElree, Brian, Frisson, Steven, Chen, Lillian, and Traxler, Matthew 2006. 'Underspecification and aspectual coercion', *Discourse Processes* 42(2): 131–55

Pickering, Martin J., and Traxler, Matthew 1998. 'Plausibility and recovery from garden paths: An eye-tracking study', *Journal of Experimental Psychology: Learning, Memory and Cognition* 24(4): 940–61

Pierrehumbert, Janet B. 2001. 'Exemplar dynamics: Word frequency, lenition, and contrast', in Bybee and Hopper (eds.), pp. 137–57

Pierrehumbert, Janet B. 2012. 'Burstiness of verbs and derived nouns', in Santos, Linden and Ng'ang'a (eds.), pp. 99–116

Pinker, Steven 1989. *Learnability and cognition: The Acquisition of argument structure*. Cambridge: The MIT Press

Pinker, Steven 1999. *Words and rules: The ingredients of language*. New York: Basic Books

Pinker, Steven, and Prince, Alan 1988. 'On language and connectionism: Analysis of a parallel distributed processing model of language acquisition', *Cognition* 28(1): 59–102

Pinker, Steven, and Ullman, Michael T. 2002. 'The past and future of the past tense', *Trends in Cognitive Sciences* 6(11): 456–63

Pintzuk, Susan, Tsoulas, George, and Warner, Anthony (eds.) 2001. *Diachronic syntax: Models and mechanisms*. Oxford: Oxford University Press

Plag, Ingo, Homann, Julia, and Kunter, Gero 2014. 'Homophony and morphology: The acoustics of word-final *s* in English'. Manuscript. University of Düsseldorf.

Podesva, Robert J., and Sharma, Devyani (eds.) 2014. *Research methods in linguistics*. Cambridge: Cambridge University Press

Polikarpov, Anatoliy A. 2006. *Cognitive model of lexical system evolution and its verification*. www.philol.msu.ru/~lex/articles/cogn_ev.htm [accessed April 19, 2016]

Preston, Dennis R. 2004. 'Three kinds of sociolinguistics: A psycholinguistic perspective', in Fought (ed.), pp. 140–58

Pritchett, Bradley 1992. *Grammatical competence and parsing performance*. Chicago: University of Chicago Press

Pullum, Geoffrey K. 1997. 'The morpholexical nature of English *to*-contraction', *Language* 73: 79–102

Pulvermüller, Friedemann 1999. 'Words in the brain's language', *Behavioral and Brain Sciences* 22: 253–336

Pye, Clifton 1980. 'The acquisition of person markers in Quich Mayan', *Papers and Reports on Child Language Development* 19: 53–9

Quirk, Randolph 1965. 'Descriptive statement and serial relationship', *Language* 41(2): 205–17

Quirk, Randolph, Greenbaum, Sidney, Leech, Geoffrey, and Svartvik, Jan 1985. *A comprehensive grammar of the English language*. London and New York: Longman

Rács, Péter 2013. *Salience in sociolinguistics: A quantitative approach*. Berlin and New York: Mouton de Gruyter

Radford, Andrew, Felser, Claudia, and Boxell, Oliver 2012. 'Preposition copying and pruning in present-day English', *English Language and Linguistics* 16(3): 403–26

Ramachandran, Vilayanur S. (ed.) 2012. *Encyclopedia of human behavior*. Oxford: Elsevier

Ramat, Paolo, and Ricca, Davide 1994. 'Prototypical adverbs: On the scalarity/radiality of the notion ADVERB', *Rivista di Linguistica* 6.2: 289–326.

Ramscar, Michael, and Baayen, R. Harald 2013. 'Production, comprehension, and synthesis: A communicative perspective on language', *Frontiers in Psychology* 4: 233

Ramscar, Michael, Dye, Melody, and McCauley, Stewart M. 2013a. 'Error and expectation in language learning: The curious absence of *mouses* in adult speech', *Language* 89(4): 760–93

Ramscar, Michael, Hendrix, Peter, Love, Bradley, and Baayen, R. Harald 2013b. 'Learning is not decline: The mental lexicon as a window into cognition across the lifespan', *The Mental Lexicon* 8: 450–81

Ramscar, Michael, Hendrix, Peter, Shaoul, Cyrus, Milin, Petar, and Baayen, R. Harald 2014. 'The myth of cognitive decline: Non-linear dynamics of lifelong learning', *Topics in Cognitive Science* 6(1): 5–42

Ramscar, Michael, Smith, Asha Halima, Dye, Melody, Futrell, Richard, Hendrix, Peter, Baayen, R. Harald, and Starr, Rebecca 2013c. 'The "universal" structure of name grammars and the impact of social engineering on the evolution of natural information systems'. *Proceedings of the 35th Meeting of the Cognitive Science Society*, Berlin, Germany, July 31–August 3, 2013.

Ramscar, Michael, Yarlett, Daniel, Dye, Melody, Denny, Katie, and Thorpe, Kirsten 2010. 'The effects of feature-label order and their implications for symbolic learning', *Cognitive Science* 34(6): 909–57

Rasmussen, Nicolas 1991. 'The decline of recapitulationism in early twentieth-century biology: Disciplinary conflict and consensus on the battle-ground of theory', *Journal of the History of Biology* 24(1): 51–89

Ravid, Dorit 1995. *Language change in child and adult Hebrew: A psycholinguistic perspective*. Oxford: Oxford University Press

Ravid, Dorit, Dressler, Wolfgang U., Nir-Sagiv, Bracha, Korecky-Kröll, Katharina, Souman, Agnita, Rehfeldt, Katja, Laaha, Sabine, Bertl, Johannes, Basbøll, Hans, and Gillis, Steven 2008. 'Core morphology in child directed speech: Crosslinguistic corpus analyses of noun plurals', in Behrens (ed.), pp. 25–60

Reali, Florencia, and Christiansen, Morten H. 2007. 'Processing of relative clauses is made easier by frequency of occurrence', *Journal of Memory and Language* 57(1): 1–23

Reber, Arthur S. 1993. *Implicit learning and tacit knowledge: An essay on the cognitive unconscious*. Oxford: Oxford University Press

Reber, Arthur S., Kassin, Saul M., Lewis, Selma, and Cantor, Gary W. 1980. 'On the relationship between implicit and explicit modes in the learning of a complex rule structure', *Journal of Experimental Psychology: Human Learning and Memory* 6(5): 492–502

Reber, Paul J., and Squire, Larry R. 1998. 'Encapsulation of implicit and explicit memory in sequence learning', *Journal of Cognitive Neuroscience* 10(2): 248–63

Rebuschat, Patrick (ed.) 2015. *Implicit and explicit learning of language.* Amsterdam: John Benjamins

Rebuschat, Patrick, and Williams, John N. (eds.) 2012. *Statistical learning and language acquisition.* Berlin: Mouton de Gruyter

Redington, Martin, and Chater, Nick 1998. 'Connectionist and statistical approaches to language acquisition: A distributional perspective', *Language and Cognitive Processes* 13(2–3): 129–92

Reitter, David, and Moore, Johanna D. 2014. 'Alignment and task success in spoken dialogue', *Journal of Memory and Language* 76: 29–46

Rescorla, Robert A. 1968. 'Probability of shock in the presence and absence of CS in fear conditioning', *Journal of Comparative and Physiological Psychology* 66(1): 1–5

Rescorla, Robert A. 1988. 'Pavlovian conditioning. It's not what you think it is', *American Psychologist* 43(3): 151–60

Rescorla, Robert A., and Wagner, Allan R. 1972. 'A theory of Pavlovian conditioning: variations in the effectiveness of reinforcement and nonreinforcement', in Black and Prokasy (eds.), pp. 64–99

Richards, Brian J. 1990. *Language development and individual differences: A study of auxiliary verb learning.* Cambridge: Cambridge University Press

Rissanen, Matti 1999. 'Syntax', in Lass (ed.), pp. 187–331

Robenalt, Clarice, and Goldberg, Adele E. 2015. 'Judgment evidence for statistical preemption: It is relatively better to *vanish* than to *disappear* a rabbit, but a lifeguard can equally well *backstroke* or *swim* children to shore', *Cognitive Linguistics* 26(3): 467–503

Roberts, Ian 1993. *Verbs and diachronic syntax: A comparative history of English and French.* Dordrecht: Kluwer

Roberts, Ian 2015. 'Formal and functional explanations: New perspective on an old debate'. Paper presented at the 48th Annual Meeting of the Societas Linguistica Europaea, Leiden, September 2–5

Roberts, Ian, and Roussou, Anna 2003. *Syntactic change: A minimalist approach to grammaticalization.* Cambridge: Cambridge University Press

Roberts, Leah, and Felser, Claudia 2011. 'Plausibility and recovery from garden-paths in second-language sentence processing', *Applied Psycholinguistics* 32(2): 299–331

Robinson, Peter (ed.) 2001. *Cognition and second language instruction.* Cambridge: Cambridge University Press

Robinson, Peter, and Ellis, Nick C. (eds.) 2008. *Handbook of cognitive linguistics and second language acquisition.* New York and London: Routledge

Rohdenburg, Günter, and Schlüter, Julia (eds.) 2009. *One language, two grammars? Differences between British and American English.* Cambridge: Cambridge University Press

Romaine, Suzanne (ed.) 1998. *The Cambridge history of the English language, vol. 4: 1776 to the present day.* Cambridge: Cambridge University Press

Rosemeyer, Malte 2016. 'Modeling frequency effects in language change', in Behrens and Pfänder (eds.), pp. 179–207

Rowland, Caroline F. 2007. 'Explaining errors in children's questions', *Cognition* 104(1): 106–34

Rowland, Caroline F., Chang, Franklin, Ambridge, Ben, Pine, Julian M., and Lieven, Elena V. M. 2012. 'The development of abstract syntax: Evidence from structural priming and the lexical boost', *Cognition* 125(1): 49–63

Rowland, Caroline F., and Pine, Julian M. 2000. 'Subject-auxiliary inversion errors and *wh*-question acquisition: What children do know?', *Journal of Child Language* 27(1): 157–81

Rowland, Caroline F., Pine, Julian M., Lieven, Elena V. M., and Theakston, Anna L. 2003. 'Determinants of the order of acquisition of *wh*-questions: Re-evaluating the role of caregiver speech', *Journal of Child Language* 30(3): 609–35

Rumelhart, David E., Hinton, Geoffrey E., and Williams, Ronald J. 1986. 'Learning representations by back-propagating errors', *Nature Reviews Neuroscience* 323(9): 533–36

Rumelhart, David E., and McClelland, James L. (eds.) 1986. *Parallel distributed processing: Explorations in the microstructure of cognition.* Cambridge, MA: The MIT Press

Saffran, Eleanor M., and Martin, Nadine 1997. 'Effects of structural priming on sentence production in aphasics', *Language and Cognitive Processes* 12(5–6): 877–82

Saffran, Jenny R., Aslin, Richard N., and Newport, Elissa L. 1996. 'Statistical learning by 8-month-old infants', *Science* 274(5294): 1926–28

Saffran, Jenny R., Johnson, Elizabeth K., Aslin, Richard N., and Newport, Elissa L. 1999. 'Statistical learning of tone sequences by human infants and adults', *Cognition* 70(1): 27–52

Säily, Tanja 2014. *Sociolinguistic variation in English derivational productivity: Studies and methods in diachronic corpus linguistics.* Helsinki: Société Néophilologique

Sampson, Geoffrey 1997. *Educating Eve: The 'Language Instinct' debate.* London: Continuum

Santelmann, Lynn, Berk, Stephanie, Austin, Jennifer, Somashekar, Shamitha, and Lust, Barbara 2002. 'Continuity and development in the acquisition of inversion in *yes/no* questions: Dissociating movement and inflection', *Journal of Child Language* 29(4): 813–42

Santos, Diana, Linden, Krister, and Ng'ang'a, Wanjiju (eds.) 2012. *Shall we play the Festschrift game? Essays on the occasion of Lauri Carlson's 60th birthday.* Berlin: Springer de Saussure, Ferdinand de 1916/1983. *Cours de linguistique générale [Course in general linguistics]*. *Translated and annotated by Roy Harris*. London: Duckworth

Savage, Ceri, Lieven, Elena V. M., Theakston, Anna, and Tomasello, Michael 2003. 'Testing the abstractness of children's linguistic representation: Lexical and structural priming of syntactic constructions in young children', *Developmental Science* 6(5): 557–67

Savage, Ceri, Lieven, Elena V. M., Theakston, Anna, and Tomasello, Michael 2006. 'Structural priming as implicit learning in language acquisition: The persistence of lexical and structural priming in 4-year-olds', *Language Learning and Development* 2(1): 27–50

Savin, Harris B. 1963. 'Word-frequency effects and errors in the perception of speech', *Journal of the Acoustic Society of America* 35(2): 200–6

Scalise, Sergio, and Vogel, Irene (eds.) 2010. *Cross-disciplinary issues in compounding*. Amsterdam: John Benjamins

Schaner-Wolles, Chris, Rennison, John R., and Neubarth, Friedrich (eds.) 2001. *Naturally! Linguistic studies in honour of Wolfgang Ulrich Dressler*. Torino: Rosenberg and Sellier

Scheibman, Joanne 2000. '*I dunno*: A usage-based account of the phonological reduction of *don't* in American English conversation', *Journal of Pragmatics* 32(1): 105–24

Scherer, Carmen 2005. *Wortbildungswandel und Produktivität: Eine empirische Studie zur nominalen '-er'-Derivation im Deutschen*. Berlin and New York: Mouton de Gruyter

Schiffrin, Deborah (ed.) 1984. *Meaning, form, and use in context: Linguistic applications; Georgetown University Round Table '84*. Washington, DC: Georgetown University Press

Schleicher, August 1861. 'Einige Beobachtungen an Kindern', *Beiträge zur vergleichenden Sprachforschung* 2: 497–98

Schlüter, Julia 2005. *Rhythmic grammar: The influence of rhythm on grammatical variation and change in English*. Berlin and New York: Mouton de Gruyter

Schmid, Hans-Jörg 2007. 'Entrenchment, salience, and basic levels', in Geeraerts and Cuyckens (eds.), pp. 117–38

Schmid, Hans-Jörg 2010. 'Does frequency in text really instantiate entrenchment in the cognitive system?', in Glynn and Fischer (eds.), pp. 101–33

Schmid, Hans-Jörg (ed.). to appear. *Entrenchment, memory and automaticity. The psychology of linguistic knowledge and language learning*. Berlin and New York: Mouton de Gruyter

Schmid, Hans-Jörg, and Küchenhoff, Helmut 2013. 'Collostructional analysis and other ways of measuring lexicogrammatical attraction: Theoretical premises, practical problems and cognitive underpinnings', *Cognitive Linguistics* 24(3): 531–77

Schmidt, Richard 1984. 'The strengths and limitations of acquisition: A case study of an untutored language learner', *Language, Learning, and Communication* 3: 1–16

Schmidtke-Bode, Karsten 2009. '*Going-to-V* and *gonna-V* in child language: A quantitative approach to constructional development', *Cognitive Linguistics* 20(3): 509–38

Schneider, Edgar W. 2011. *English around the world: An introduction.* Cambridge: Cambridge University Press

Schoenemann, P. Thomas 2005. 'Conceptual complexity and the brain: Understanding language origins', in Wang and Minett (eds.), pp. 47–83

Schönle, Paul W., Gräbe, Klaus, Wenig, Peter, Höhne, Jörg, Schrader, Jörg, and Conrad, Bastian 1987. 'Electromagnetic articulography: Use of alternating magnetic fields for tracking movements of multiple points inside and outside the vocal tract', *Brain and Language* 31(1): 26–35

Schooler, Lael J. 1993. *Memory and the statistical structure of the environment.* Doctoral dissertation. Carnegie Mellon University

Schoonbaert, Sofie, Hartsuiker, Robert J., and Pickering, Martin J. 2007. 'The representation of lexical and syntactic information in bilinguals: Evidence from syntactic priming', *Journal of Memory and Language* 56(2): 153–71

Schreier, Daniel, and Hundt, Marianne (eds.) 2013. *English as a contact language.* Cambridge: Cambridge University Press

Schumann, John H. 1978. *The pidginisation process: A model for second language acquisition.* Rowley, MA: Newbury House

Schumann, John H. 1987. 'The expression of temporality in Basilang speech', *Studies in Second Language Acquisition* 9(1): 21–41

Schütze, Carson 1996. *The empirical base of linguistics: Grammaticality judgments and linguistic methodology.* Chicago: University of Chicago Press

Segalowitz, Norman 2010. *The cognitive bases of second language fluency.* New York: Routledge

Seidenberg, Mark S. 1997. 'Language acquisition and use: Learning and applying probabilistic constraints', *Science* 275(5306): 1599–603

Seidenberg, Mark S., and Bruck, Maggie 1990. 'Consistency effects in the generation of past tense morphology', *Bulletin of the Psychonomic Society* 28(6): 522

Seidenberg, Mark S., and MacDonald, Maryellen C. 1999. 'A probabilistic constraints approach to language acquisition and processing', *Cognitive Science* 23(4): 569–88

Seidenberg, Mark S., and McClelland, J. L. 1989. 'Visual word recognition and pronunciation: A computational model of acquisition, skilled performance, and dyslexia', in Galaburda (ed.), pp. 255–303

Seidenberg, Mark S., Waters, Gloria S., Barnes, Marcia A., and Tanenhaus, Michael K. 1984. 'When does irregular spelling or pronunciation influence word recognition?', *Journal of Verbal Learning and Verbal Behavior* 23(3): 383–404

Seidlhofer, Barbara 2004. 'Research perspectives on teaching English as a Lingua Franca', *Annual Review of Applied Linguistics* 24: 209–39

Shanks, David R. 1995. *The psychology of associative learning.* New York: Cambridge University Press

Shannon, Claude E. 1949. *The mathematical theory of communication*. Champaign, IL: University of Illinois Press

Shaoul, Cyrus 2013. 'The consequences of accumulating experience for lexical processing'. Paper presented at the 8th International Morphology Meeting

Shaoul, Cyrus, Schilling, Natalie A., Bitschnau, S., Arppe, Antti, Hendrix, Peter, and Baayen, R. Harald 2014. *NDL2: Naive Discriminative Learning*. R package version 1.901 [Development version available upon request]

Shaoul, Cyrus, Willits, Jon, Ramscar, Michael, Milin, Petar, and Baayen, R. Harald under revision. 'A discrimination-driven model for the acquisition of lexical knowledge in auditory comprehension' [Under revision]

Shepherd, Susan C. 1982. 'From deontic to epistemic: An analysis of modals in the history of English, creoles, and language acquisition', in Ahlqvist (ed.), pp. 316–23

Shiffrin, Richard M., and Schneider, Walter 1977. 'Controlled and automatic human information processing: II. Perceptual learning, automatic attending and a general theory', *Psychological Review* 84(2): 127–90

Shimpi, Priya M., Gámez, Perla B., Huttenlocher, Janellen, and Vasilyeva, Marina 2007. 'Syntactic priming in 3- and 4-year-old children: Evidence for abstract representations of transitive and dative forms', *Developmental Psychology* 43(6): 1334–46

Simon, Herbert A. 1962. *The sciences of the artificial*. Cambridge, MA: The MIT Press

Simpson-Vlach, Rita, and Ellis, Nick C. 2010. 'An Academic Formulas List: New methods in phraseology research', *Applied Linguistics* 31(4): 487–512

Sinclair, John M. 1996. 'The search for units of meaning', *Textus* 9: 75–106

Singh-Manoux, Archana, Kivimaki, Mika, Glymour, M. Maria, Elbaz, Alexis, Berr, Claudine, Ebmeier, Klaus P., Ferrie, Jane E., and Dugravot, Aline 2012. 'Timing of onset of cognitive decline: Results from Whitehall II prospective cohort study', *British Medical Journal* 344: d7622

Skarabela, Barbora, Fish, Sarah, and Do, Anna H.-J. (eds.) 2002. *Proceedings of the 26th Annual Boston University Conference on Language Development (BUCLD 26)*. Somerville, MA: Cascadilla Press

Skousen, Royal 1989. *Analogical modeling of language*. Boston, MA: Kluwer

Skousen, Royal 2002. 'Introduction', in Skousen, Lonsdale and Parkinson (eds.), pp. 1–8

Skousen, Royal, Lonsdale, Deryle, and Parkinson, Dilworth B. (eds.) 2002. *Analogical modeling: An exemplar-based approach to language*. Amsterdam: Benjamins

Slattery, Timothy J., Sturt, Patrick, Christianson, Kiel, Yoshida, Masaya, and Ferreira, Fernanda 2013. 'Lingering misinterpretations of garden path sentences arise from competing syntactic representations', *Journal of Memory and Language* 69(2): 104–20

Slobin, Dan I. 1973. 'Cognitive prerequisites for the development of grammar', in Ferguson and Slobin (eds.), pp. 175–208

Slobin, Dan I. 1985a. 'Crosslinguistic evidence for the language-making capacity', in Slobin (ed.), pp. 1157–249

Slobin, Dan I. (ed.) 1985b. *The crosslinguistic study of language acquisition, vol. 2: Theoretical issues*. Mahwah, NJ: Erlbaum

Slobin, Dan I. 1992. *Psycholinguistics*. Glenview, IL: Scott, Foresman and Company

Slobin, Dan I. 1994. 'Talking perfectly. Discourse origins of the present perfect', in Pagliuca (ed.), pp. 119–33

Slobin, Dan I. 1997a. 'The universal, the typological, and the particular in language acquisition', in Slobin (ed.), pp. 1–39

Slobin, Dan I. (ed.) 1997b. *The crosslinguistic study of language acquisition, vol. 5: Expanding the contexts*. Mahwah, NJ: Erlbaum

Slobin, Dan I. 2002. 'Language evolution, acquisition and diachrony: Probing the parallels', in Givón and Malle (eds.), pp. 375–92

Slobin, Dan I., and Aksu, Ayhan A. 1982. 'Tense, aspect and modality in the use of the Turkish evidential', in Hopper (ed.), pp. 185–200

Smith, Jeremy J. 2012. 'History of English historical linguistics: The historiography of the English language', in Bergs and Brinton (eds.), pp. 1295–312

Smith, Nathaniel J., and Levy, Roger 2013. 'The effect of word predictability on reading time is logarithmic', *Cognition* 128(3): 302–19

Sommerer, Lotte 2012. 'Investigating the emergence of the definite article in Old English: About categorization, gradualness and constructions', *Folia Linguistica Historica* 33: 175–213

Spufford, Margaret 1981. *Small books and pleasant histories: Popular fiction and its readership in seventeenth-century England*. Athens, GA: University of Georgia Press

Stadler, Michael A., and Frensch, Peter A. (eds.) 1998. *Implicit learning handbook*. Thousand Oaks, CA: Sage Publications

Stampe, David 1969. 'The acquisition of phonetic representation', *Chicago Linguistics Society* 5: 443–54

Stanford, James N. 2014. 'Language acquisition and language change', in Bowern and Evans (eds.), pp. 466–83

Stede, Manfred, Chiarcos, Christian, Grabski, Michael, and Lagerwerf, Luuk (eds.) 2005. 'Salience in discourse: Multidisciplinary approaches to discourse 2005'. *Proceedings of the 6th Workshop on Multidisciplinary Approaches to Discourse (MAD-05)*, Chorin/Berlin, Oct. 2005. Münster: Nordus Publikationen

Stefanowitsch, Anatol, and Gries, Stefan Th. 2003. 'Collostructions: Investigating the interaction of words and constructions', *International Journal of Corpus Linguistics* 8(2): 209–43

Stemberger, Joseph P., and MacWhinney, Brian 1986. 'Frequency and the lexical storage of regularly inflected forms', *Memory and Cognition* 14(1): 17–26

Stephany, Ursula 1986. 'Modality', in Fletcher and Garman (eds.), pp. 375–400

Street, James A., and Dąbrowska, Ewa 2010. 'More individual differences in language attainment: How much do adult native speakers of English know about passives and quantifiers?', *Lingua* 120(8): 2080–94

Stromswold, Karin J. 1990. *Learnability and the acquisition of auxiliaries*. Doctoral dissertation. Massachusetts Institute of Technology [Distributed by MIT Working Papers in Linguistics]

Studdert-Kennedy, M. 1991. 'Language development from an evolutionary perspective', in Krasnegor, Rumbaugh, Schiefelbusch and Studdert-Kennedy (eds.), pp. 5–28

Stumper, Barbara, and Lieven, Elena V. M. 2011. 'Pronoun case errors in the acquisition of German are not rare, but systematic'. Poster presented at the 12th Triennial Conference of the International Association for the Study of Child Language (UQAM, Montreal)

Sturt, Patrick 2007. 'Semantic re-interpretation and garden path recovery', *Cognition* 105(2): 477–88

Sturt, Patrick, Pickering, Martin J. and Crocker, Matthew W. 1999. 'Structural change and reanalysis difficulty in language comprehension', *Journal of Memory and Language* 40(1): 136–50

Sturt, Patrick, Pickering, Martin J., Scheepers, Christoph, and Crocker, Matthew W. 2001. 'The preservation of structure in language comprehension: Is reanalysis the last resort?', *Journal of Memory and Language* 45(2): 283–307

Suttle, Laura, and Goldberg, Adele E. 2011. 'The partial productivity of constructions as induction', *Linguistics* 49(6): 1237–69

Swan, Toril, and Westvik, Olaf Jansen (eds.) 1996. *Modality in Germanic languages: Historical and comparative perspectives*. Berlin and New York: Mouton de Gruyter

Sweet, Henry 1888. *A history of English sounds*. Oxford: Clarendon Press

Sweetser, Eve E. 1988. 'Grammaticalization and semantic bleaching', in Axmaker, Jaisser and Singmaster (eds.), pp. 389–405

Swets, Benjamin, Desmet, Timothy, Clifton, Charles, and Ferreira, Fernanda 2008. 'Underspecification of syntactic ambiguities: Evidence from self-paced reading', *Memory and Cognition* 36(1): 201–16

Szagun, Gisela 2001. 'Learning different regularities: The acquisition of noun plurals by German-speaking children', *First Language* 21(62): 109–41

Szagun, Gisela 2006. *Sprachentwicklung beim Kind: Ein Lehrbuch*. 3rd edition. Weinheim and Basel: Beltz

Szagun, Gisela, Stumper, Barbara, Sondag, Nina, and Franik, Melanie 2007. 'The acquisition of gender marking by young German-speaking children: Evidence for learning guided by phonological regularities', *Journal of Child Language* 34(3): 445–71

Szmrecsanyi, Benedikt 2006. *Morphosyntactic persistence in spoken English. A corpus study at the intersection of variationist sociolinguistics, psycholinguistics, and discourse analysis*. Berlin and New York: Mouton de Gruyter

Szmrecsanyi, Benedikt 2013. 'Diachronic probabilistic grammar', *English Language and Linguistics [Journal of the English Linguistics Society of Korea]* 19(3): 41–68

Tabak, Wieke, Schreuder, Robert, and Baayen, R. Harald 2010. 'Producing inflected verbs: A picture naming study', *The Mental Lexicon* 5(1): 22–46

Tabor, Whitney 1993. 'The gradual development of degree modifier *sort of* and *kind of*: A corpus proximity model', in Beals (ed.), pp. 451–65

Tagliamonte, Sali A., and D'Arcy, Alexandra 2007. 'The modals of obligation/ necessity in Canadian perspective', *English World-Wide* 28(1): 47–87

Tagliamonte, Sali A., D'Arcy, Alexandra, and Jankowski, Bridget 2010. 'Social work and linguistic systems: Marking possession in Canadian English', *Language Variation and Change* 22(1): 149–73

Tannen, Deborah 1989. *Talking voices: Repetition, dialogue, and imagery in conversational discourse.* New York: Cambridge University Press

Taraban, Roman, and McClelland, James L. 1987. 'Conspiracy effects in word pronunciation', *Journal of Memory and Language* 26(6): 608–31

Terkourafi, Marina 2011. 'The pragmatic variable: Toward a procedural interpretation', *Language in Society* 40(3): 343–72

Terrell, Tracy 1991. 'The role of grammar instruction in a communicative approach', *The Modern Language Journal* 75(1): 52–63

Theakston, Anna L. 2004. 'The role of entrenchment in constraining children's verb argument structure overgeneralisations: A grammaticality judgment study', *Cognitive Development* 19(1): 15–34

Theakston, Anna L., Lieven, Elena V. M., and Tomasello, Michael 2003. 'The role of input in the acquisition of third-person singular verbs in English', *Journal of Speech, Language, and Hearing Research* 46(4): 863–77

Thomason, Sarah G. 2013. 'Innovation and contact: The role of adults (and children)', in Schreier and Hundt (eds.), pp. 283–97

Thompson, Sandra A., and Mulac, Anthony J. 1991. 'A quantitative perspective on the grammaticalization of epistemic parentheticals in English', in Traugott and Heine (eds.), pp. 213–329

Thurner, Stefan, Hanel, Rudolf, Liu, Bo, and Corominas-Murtra, Bernat 2015. 'Understanding Zipf's law of word frequencies through sample-space collapse in sentence formation', *Journal of The Royal Society Interface* 12(108): 20150330

Timberlake, Alan 1977. 'Reanalysis and actualization in syntactic change', in Li (ed.), pp. 141–77

Tomaschek, Fabian, Tucker, Benjamin V., Wieling, Martijn, and Baayen, R. Harald 2014. 'Vowel articulation affected by word frequency', in Fuchs, Grice, Hermes, Lancia and Mücke (eds.), pp. 429–32

Tomasello, Michael 1992. *First verbs: A case study of early grammatical development.* Cambridge: Cambridge University Press

Tomasello, Michael (ed.) 1998. *The new psychology of language: Cognitive and functional approaches to language structure.* Mahwah, NJ: Lawrence Erlbaum

Tomasello, Michael 1999. *The cultural origins of human cognition.* Cambridge, MA: Harvard University Press

Tomasello, Michael 2003. *Constructing a language: A usage-based theory of language acquisition.* Boston, MA: Harvard University Press

Tomasello, Michael 2008. *Origins of human communication.* Cambridge, MA: The MIT Press

Tomasello, Michael, and Call, Josep 1997. *Primate cognition*. Oxford: Oxford University Press

Tomasello, Michael, and Slobin, Dan I. (eds.) 2004. *Beyond nature-nurture: Essays in honor of Elizabeth Bates*. Mahwah, NJ: Lawrence Erlbaum

Tooley, Kirsten, and Bock, J. Kathryn 2014. 'On the parity of structural persistence in language production and comprehension', *Cognition* 132(2): 101–36

Toupin, Fabienne, and Lowrey, Brian (eds.) 2015. *Studies in linguistic variation and change: From Old to Middle English*. Newcastle: Cambridge Scholars Publishing

Townsend, David, and Bever, Thomas 2001. *Sentence comprehension: The integration of habits and rules*. Cambridge, MA: The MIT Press

Traugott, Elizabeth C. 1989. 'On the rise of epistemic meaning in English: An example of subjectification in semantic change', *Language* 65(1): 31–55

Traugott, Elizabeth C. 1995. 'The role of the development of discourse markers in a theory of grammaticalization'. Paper presented at the 12th International Conference on Historical Linguistics (ICHL 12), Manchester, UK, August 13–18, 1995. www.stanford.edu/~traugott/papers/discourse.pdf [accessed April 19, 2016]

Traugott, Elizabeth C. 1999. 'The role of pragmatics in semantic change', in Verschueren (ed.), pp. 93–102

Traugott, Elizabeth C. 2008a. 'Testing the hypothesis that priming is a motivation for change', *Theoretical Linguistics* 34: 135–42

Traugott, Elizabeth C. 2008b. 'The grammaticalization of NP of NP patterns', in Bergs and Diewald (eds.), pp. 23–45

Traugott, Elizabeth C. 2011. 'Grammaticalization and mechanisms of change', in Narrog and Heine (eds.), pp. 19–30

Traugott, Elizabeth C. 2012a. 'Pragmatics and language change', in Allan and Jaszczolt (eds.), pp. 549–65

Traugott, Elizabeth C. 2012b. 'The status of onset contexts in analysis of micro-changes', in Kytö (ed.), pp. 221–55

Traugott, Elizabeth C., and Dasher, Richard B. 2002. *Regularity in semantic change*. Cambridge: Cambridge University Press

Traugott, Elizabeth C., and Heine, Bernd (eds.) 1991. *Approaches to grammaticalization*. 2 vols. Amsterdam: Benjamins

Traugott, Elizabeth C., and König, Ekkehard 1991. 'The semantics-pragmatics of grammaticalization revisited', in Traugott and Heine (eds.), pp. 189–218

Traugott, Elizabeth C., Labrum, Rebecca, and Shepherd, Susan (eds.) 1980. *Papers from the Fourth International Conference on Historical Linguistics*. Amsterdam and Philadelphia: John Benjamins

Traugott, Elizabeth C., and Trousdale, Graeme 2010a. 'Gradience, gradualness and grammaticalization: How do they intersect?', in Traugott and Trousdale (eds.), pp. 19–44

Traugott, Elizabeth C., and Trousdale, Graeme (eds.) 2010b. *Gradience, gradualness and grammaticalization*. Amsterdam: Benjamins

Traugott, Elizabeth C., and Trousdale, Graeme 2013. *Constructionalization and constructional changes*. Oxford: Oxford University Press

Traxler, Matthew 2002. 'Plausibility and subcategorization preference in children's processing of temporarily ambiguous sentences: Evidence from self-paced reading', *The Quarterly Journal of Experimental Psychology* 55(1): 75–96

Traxler, Matthew J., and Gernsbacher, Morton A. (eds.) 2006. *Handbook of Psycholinguistics*. 2nd edition. London: Elsevier

Treisman, Anne M., and Gelade, Garry 1980. 'A feature-integration theory of attention', *Cognitive Psychology* 12: 97–136

Tremblay, Antoine, Derwing, Bruce, Libben, Gary, and Westbury, Chris 2011. 'Processing advantages of lexical bundles: Evidence from self-paced reading and sentence recall tasks', *Language Learning* 61(2): 569–613

Trimmer, Pete C., McNamara, John M., Houston, Alasdair I., and Marshall, James A. R. 2012. 'Does natural selection favour the Rescorla–Wagner rule?', *Journal of Theoretical Biology* 302: 39–52

Trousdale, Graeme 2013. 'Gradualness in language change: A constructional perspective', in Giacalone Ramat, Mauri, and Molinelli (eds.), pp. 27–42

Trudgill, Peter 1983. *On dialect: Social and geographical perspectives*. Oxford: Blackwell

Trudgill, Peter 2002a. 'Linguistic and social typology', in Chambers, Trudgill and Schilling-Estes (eds.), pp. 707–28

Trudgill, Peter 2002b. *Sociolinguistic variation and change*. Edinburgh: Edinburgh University Press and Washington, DC: Georgetown University Press

Trueswell, John, Sekerina, Irina, Hill, Nicole, and Logrip, Marian 1999. 'The kindergarden-path effect: Studying on-line sentence processing in children', *Cognition* 73(2): 89–134

Trueswell, John, Tanenhaus, Michael, and Garnsey, Susan 1994. 'Semantic influences on parsing: Use of thematic role information in syntactic ambiguity resolution', *Journal of Memory and Language* 33(3): 285–18

Trueswell, John, Tanenhaus, Michael, and Kello, Christopher 1993. 'Verb-specific constraints in sentence processing: Separating effects of lexical preference from garden-paths', *Journal of Experimental Psychology: Learning, Memory, and Cognition* 19(3): 528–53

Tulving, Endel, and Thomson, Donald M. 1973. 'Encoding specificity and retrieval processes in episodic memory', *Psychological Review* 80(5): 352–73

Underwood, Geoffrey (ed.) 1978. *Strategies of information processing*. San Diego, CA: Academic Press

van Bergen, Linda 2013. 'Early progressive passives', *Folia Linguistica Historica* 34(1): 173–207

van der Auwera, Johan, and Plungian, Vladimir A. 1998. 'Modality's semantic map', *Linguistic Typology* 2(1): 79–124

van der Horst, Joop 2008. *Geschiedenis van de Nederlandse syntaxis*. Leuven: Leuven University Press

van de Velde, Freek 2015. 'Schijnbare syntactische feniksen', *Nederlandse Taalkunde* 20: 69–107 van Geert, Paul, and Steenbeek, Henderien 2005. 'Explaining after by before: Basic aspects of a dynamic systems approach to the study of development', *Developmental Review* 25(3–4): 408–42

van Gelderen, Elly 2004. *Grammaticalization as economy*. Amsterdam: Benjamins

van Gelderen, Elly 2011. *The linguistic cycle: Language change and the language faculty*. Oxford: Oxford University Press

van Gompel, Roger (ed.) 2013. *Sentence processing*. New York: Psychology Press

van Halteren, Hans, Baayen, R. Harald, Tweedie, Fiona, Haverkort, Marco, and Neijt, Anneke 2005. 'New machine learning methods demonstrate the existence of a human stylome', *Journal of Quantitative Linguistics* 12(1): 65–77

van Kemenade, Ans, and de Haas, Nynke (eds.) 2012. *Historical linguistics 2009: Selected papers from the 19th international conference on historical linguistics, Nijmegen, 10–14 August 2009*. Amsterdam and Philadelphia: Benjamins

van Kemenade, Ans, and Los, Bettelou (eds.) 2006. *The handbook of the history of English*. Oxford: Blackwell

van Kemenade, Ans, and Westergaard, Marit 2012. 'Syntax and information structure: V2 variation in Middle English', in Meurman-Solin, López-Couso and Los (eds.), pp. 87–118

van Marle, Jaap 1985. *On the paradigmatic dimension of morphological creativity*. Dordrecht: Foris

van Petten, Cyma, and Luka, Barbara J. 2012. 'Prediction during language comprehension: Benefits, costs, and ERP components', *International Journal of Psychophysiology* 83(2): 176–90

van Steenis, Lindsey 2013. The grammaticalization of *have to* and *hebben te*: A comparative study between English and Dutch. MA thesis. University of Amsterdam: Faculty of Humanities

Vasilyeva, Marina, Waterfall, Heidi, Gámez, Perla B., Gómez, Ligia E., Bowers, Edmond, and Shimpi, Priya 2010. 'Cross-linguistic syntactic priming in bilingual children', *Journal of Child Language* 37(5): 1047–64

Vennemann, Theo 1972. 'Phonetic detail in assimilation: Problems in Germanic phonology', *Language* 48(4): 863–92

Veronique, Daniel 1999. 'L'émergence de catégories grammaticales dans les langues créoles: Grammaticalisation et réanalyse', in Lang and Neumann-Holzschuh (eds.), pp. 181–203

Veronique, Daniel 2001. 'Genèse(s) et changement(s) grammaticaux: Quelques modestes leçons tirés de l'émergence des créoles et de l'acquisition des langues étrangères', in Matthey (ed.), pp. 273–303

Verschueren, Jef (ed.) 1999. *Pragmatics in 1998: Selected papers from the 6th international pragmatics conference*, vol. 2. Antwerp and Amsterdam: International Pragmatics Association

Vihman, Marilyn May 1980. 'Sound change and child language', in Traugott, Labrum and Shepherd (eds.), pp. 303–20

Vincent, David 1993. *Literacy and popular culture: England 1750–1914*. Cambridge: Cambridge University Press

Visser, Frederikus Th. 1963–1973. *An historical syntax of the English language.* 3 vols. Leiden: Brill

Visser, Frederikus Th. 1984. *An historical syntax of the English language, vol. 2: Syntactical units with one verb (continued).* Leiden: Brill [First edition 1966]

von Eye, Alexander 1990. *Introduction to configurational frequency analysis.* Cambridge: Cambridge University Press

Wagner, Michael, Breen, Mara, Flemming, Edward, Shattuck-Hufnagel, Stefanie, and Gibson, Edward 2010. 'Prosodic effects of discourse salience and association with focus'. *Proceedings of the Fifth International Conference on Speech Prosody,* Chicago, May 11–14, 2010. http://prosodylab.org/~chael/www/papers/wagneretal10only.pdf [accessed April 19, 2016]

Wales, Roger J., and Walker, Edward (eds.) 1976. *New approaches to language mechanisms: A collection of psycholinguistics studies.* Amsterdam: North Holland

Walling, Anne D., and Dickson, Gretchen M. 2012. 'Hearing loss in older adults', *American Family Physician* 85(12): 1150–56

Waltereit, Richard 2006. 'The rise of discourse markers in Italian: A specific type of language change', in Fischer (ed.), pp. 61–76

Wang, William S.-Y., and Minett, James W. (eds.) 2005. *Language acquisition, change and emergence: Essays in evolutionary linguistics.* Hong Kong: City University of Hong Kong Press

Warner, Anthony A. 1993. *English auxiliaries: Structure and history.* Cambridge: Cambridge University Press

Warrington, Elizabeth K. 1975. 'The selective impairment of semantic memory', *The Quarterly Journal of Experimental Psychology* 27(4): 635–57

Waterfall, Heidi R. 2006. *A little change is a good thing: Feature theory, language acquisition and variation sets.* Doctoral dissertation. University of Chicago: Department of Linguistics

Wegener, Heide 1999. 'Die Pluralbildung im Deutschen – ein Versuch im Rahmen der Optimalitätstheorie', *Linguistik online* 4.3/1999

Weinreich, Uriel, Labov, William, and Herzog, Marvin 1968. 'Empirical foundations for a theory of language change', in Lehmann and Malkiel (eds.), pp. 95–198

Wexler, Ken 1998. 'Very early parameter setting and the unique checking constraint: A new explanation of the optional infinitive stage', *Lingua* 106(1): 23–79

White, Katherine S., Yee, Eiling, Blumstein, Sheila E., and Morgan, James L. 2013. 'Adults show less sensitivity to phonetic detail in unfamiliar words, too', *Journal of Memory and Language* 68(4): 362–78

Whitman, John 2001. 'Relabelling', in Pintzuk, Tsoulas and Warner (eds.), pp. 220–38

Whitman, John 2012. 'Misparsing and syntactic reanalysis', in van Kemenade and de Haas (eds.), pp. 69–87

Wiechmann, Daniel 2015. *Understanding relative clauses – A usage-based view on the processing of complex constructions*. Berlin and New York: Mouton de Gruyter

Wiechmann, Daniel, Kerz, Elma, Snider, Neal, and Jaeger, T. Florian 2013. 'Introduction to the Special Issue: Parsimony and redundancy in models of language', *Language and Speech* 0(0): 1–8

Wiemer, Björn 2015. '*Quo vadis* grammaticalization theory? Why complex language change is like words', *Folia Linguistica* 48(2): 425–67

Wiese, Richard 1996. *The phonology of German*. Oxford: Oxford University Press

Wijnen, Frank, Kempen, Masja, and Gillis, Steven 2001. 'Root infinitives in Dutch early child language', *Journal of Child Language* 28(3): 629–60

Williams, Jake R., Lessard, Paul R., Desu, Suma, Clark, Eric M., Bagrow, James P., Danforth, Christopher M., and Dodds, Peter S. 2014. 'Zipf's law holds for phrases, not words', *Scientific Reports* 5: 12209

Wills, Andy J. 2005. *New directions in human associative learning*. Mahwah, NJ: Lawrence Erlbaum

Wills, Andy J. 2009. 'Prediction errors and attention in the presence and absence of feedback', *Current Directions in Psychological Science* 18(2): 95–100

Winters, Margaret E. 2010. 'Introduction: On the emergence of diachronic cognitive linguistics', in Winters, Tissari and Allan (eds.), pp. 3–27

Winters, Margaret E., Tissari, Heli, and Allan, Kathryn (eds.) 2010. *Historical cognitive linguistics*. Cognitive Linguistics Research 47. Berlin: Mouton de Gruyter

Wischer, Ilse, and Diewald, Gabriele (eds.) 2002. *New reflections on grammaticalization*. Amsterdam: John Benjamins

Wolk, Christoph, Bresnan, Joan, Rosenbach, Anette, and Szmrecsanyi, Benedikt 2013. 'Dative and genitive variability in Late Modern English: Exploring cross-constructional variation and change', *Diachronica* 30(3): 382–419

Wood, Frederick T. 1955–6. 'Verb-adverb combinations: The position of the adverb', *English Language Teaching* 10(1): 18–27

Wood, Simon N. 2006. *Generalized Additive Models: An introduction with R*. CRC Texts in Statistical Science. New York: Chapman and Hall/CRC

Xu, Fei, and Tennenbaum, Joshua B. 2007. 'Word learning as Bayesian inference', *Psychological Review* 114(2): 245–72

Yáñez-Bouza, Nuria, Moore, Emma, Hollmann, Willem, and van Bergen, Linda (eds.) forthcoming. *Analysing English syntax*. Cambridge: Cambridge University Press

Yanovich, Igor 2013. Four pieces for modality, context and usage. Doctoral dissertation. Massachusetts Institute of Technology.

Ziegeler, Debra 1997. 'Retention in ontogentic and diachronic grammaticalization', *Cognitive Linguistics* 8(3): 207–41

Zipf, George K. 1935. *The psycho-biology of language: An introduction to dynamic philology*. Cambridge, MA: The MIT Press

Zipf, George K. 1949. *Human behaviour and the principle of least effort: An introduction to human ecology.* Cambridge, MA: Addison-Wesley and New York: Hafner

Zuraw, Kie 2003. 'Probability in language change', in Bod, Hay and Jannedy (eds.), pp. 139–76

Zwaan, Rolf A., and Radvansky, Gabriel A. 1998. 'Situation models in language comprehension and memory', *Psychological Bulletin* 123(2): 162–85

Index

Printed by Printforce, United Kingdom